THE TRAGEDY OF AFRICA

Mike Walsh

MINERVA PRESS
ATLANTA LONDON SYDNEY

THE TRAGEDY OF AFRICA

ISBN 0 75410 388 9

First Published 1998 by
MINERVA PRESS
195 Knightsbridge
London SW7 1RE

Printed in Great Britain for Minerva Press

THE TRAGEDY OF AFRICA

In memory of John Seaman, Maun, Botswana
A good friend from Livingstone,
Northern Rhodesia, in the 1960s

To all those, black and white, especially those in
HM's colonial service whose 'Pax Britannica' made possible
my early magical years in Africa, before the Cold War
and the United Nations destroyed Africa

About the Author

Mike Walsh served in 2/10 GR in 43rd Gurkha Lorried Brigade in Italy, alongside our 2nd Battalion. After the war he played many parts, from farming to trading crocodile skins, in East, Central and South Africa. As described under 'Charities' in this Journal. He is now the Honorary Secretary of the Dominions and Ex-Services Literary Society. His Book, based on his 35 years in Africa makes grim reading. It charts the progress of what he believes to be the catastrophic consequences of Western actions and attitudes in the Continent. Many people with the background of Association members will have more or less the vaguely comprehended the unhappy situation. Few will know much of the dreadful detail given in this book: detail which is underlined by the author's patent sincerity and his burning sense of disgust for the West's record in Africa since World War II. It should be required reading in Universities and the House of Parliament, bringing out, as it does, the absolute necessity for a new approach to Africa's problems – a continent where 27 million people were reported to be starving in 1991.

Acknowledgements

To the three who made the publication of my book possible: authors Ron Jeffery and Vere Harvey-Brain (both now in New Zealand) and Tad Filipowicz-Phillips, director of the printing firm Caldra House Ltd, Hove, Sussex.

To my wife Joyce, who helped during my heart troubles of 1984–85 by giving up smoking herself, thus helping my withdrawal symptoms, and for her encouragement during the writing of my book.

To my brother Paul, and his wife Barbara, who also helped so much over this difficult time.

To the various Gurkha associations (and the Liaison Officer, Brigade of Gurkhas, at the MOD); to Lieutenant Colonel Gregory, Hon. Sec. 10th Gurkha Regimental Association; to J. B. Wilson, 2/8 GR Hon. Sec. 43 Gurkha Brigade Association, for address list; to Bob Wilson, 2/10 GR, for picture of 2/10 Gurkha officers in Italy; to TAAL's ex-service supporters who, with the various pro-South African organisations, have helped me with valuable information and advice. Thanks also to Hon. Pres. Desmond Wilson, MBE MC, 2/10 GR and Hon. V. Pres. Peter Tidman, MBE, 2/8 GR, for all their help with DELS (The Dominions & Ex-Services Literary Society). Finally, very many thanks to Roger Neath, OBE, Editor of 6th GR Journal, whose write-up helped greatly with my ex-service book sales.

With a special word of thanks to the late Colonel Smail, MC, of the *New Zealand News*, who published my first letter in his newspaper (he also served in Italy with New Zealand forces in World War II); and the Royal British Legion, whose publication of my two-column letter in their *Legion* magazine in early 1986 helped so much to start TAAL.

To the headmasters of Yardley Court, Tonbridge, and The King's School, Canterbury, and to the housemaster of School House, Mr Dobbin. Also to Paul Pollak, school archivist, a contemporary at Carlyon Bay, Cornwall (to where we were evacuated in 1940), for the brochures and pictures that brought back so many happy memories.

To Inkatha's London representative, Ben Skosana, for sending me Inkatha's many policy publications.

In Africa

To the mayor of Durban, 1989, Councillor Watterson, who sent details and pictures of Durban's famous 'Lady in White'.

To the national president, South African Legion, the late Major General I.S. Guilford, whose information and advice was invaluable to TAAL's early days.

To Edward Cain of *Signposts*, who regularly sends their 'Digest for Concerned Christians' in South Africa.

To Ray Rose, MOTH, of Johannesburg, who sends *The Aida Parker Newsletter* and other publications from South Africa.

To Dorothy and Dennis Lown of Port Elizabeth, World War II ex-services and Victory Services Club members, who traced my South African relatives in PE.

To Mary and Jack White, DFC: many thanks for the family pictures especially those of my grandfather, Captain Greenwood White, at the siege of Kimberley during the Boer War.

To Peter Becker, MD of Botswana Game Industries in Francistown, Botswana, for permission to reproduce the first two pages of BGI's catalogue.

To Bishop Paul Ruzoka of Kigoma, Tanzania, whose father, a sub-chief, gave me a lot of help while I was farming in the Kakonko area, and to Father LaForest of the Catholic Mission in Kakonko, for news of those I knew there in the 1950s.

In Canada

To Peter Worthington, journalist and author, for his permission to reproduce *The ANC Method – Violence*, especially the 'Slovo Dossier' on Moscow's man in the ANC.

Also to Geoff Hinson of Nancoose Bay, and other ex-servicemen, for their support and information.

In America

To Don McAlvany, a knowledgeable and true friend of South Africa, whose newsletter *The McAlvany Intelligence Advisor* gave a true picture of the dangers facing South Africa.

To the many Americans who supported TAAL.

To the publishers Messrs Harcourt Brace Jovanovich, a special word of thanks for allowing me to quote from *The Destruction of a Continent*, one of the best and most informative books about Africa ever published.

In New Zealand

To the Wilkinsons of Christchurch, whose organisation, Truth about Southern Africa, did so much to counter communist and socialist propaganda.

In Australia

To the IPA Bureau, and other organisations like them, who have done so much to counter the insidious communist and socialist propaganda against South Africa.

A special word of thanks to Bruce Ruxton, the state president of Victoria's Returned Services League, and to the many other ex-servicemen who have supported TAAL.

Inevitably there will be many TAAL (Truth About Africa League) supporters who it is impossible to mention by name. To them I say: please accept my heartfelt thanks for the generous support that I have received over the past six years while I have been running TAAL.

A final word of thanks to Ms Carol Sykes, who did such an excellent job of editing and typing my book (although our views did not always coincide). I strongly recommend her to others who have an interesting story to tell and want a first-class job done. I was lucky enough to see her advertisement in our local Bayswater magazine, *The Hill*. She can be contacted on 0171-262-7480.

How Suez changed it all for Britain

The crisis of 1956 ended an era, says John Charmley

THE Suez Crisis of 1956 changed Britain for ever — not only did it bring the country to the edge of an abyss and diminish irrevocably our stature as a world power, it also marked the dawn of a new age.

In that one year, every aspect of our lives changed. From the cinema to the coffee bar, from atomic power to the decline of open fires in homes, from the supermarket to the supersonic bang, our world would never be the same again.

When he came to No 10 in the aftermath of the Suez Crisis, Harold Macmillan assured us that Britain was still a "great power". But his actions as Prime Minister showed that he had drawn another conclusion from the crisis.

Eden, having shadowed Churchill for so long, shared his view that, when Britain was in a crisis, America could be relied upon to help. But this had only ever been true up to a point — it had taken the US three years to join the Great War and 18 months to get into World War Two. Suez showed that America would no longer back Britain if it meant alienating the Third World nationalist movements. That was the first lesson. In a world order dominated by the Cold War, Britain, as part of the US sphere, could no longer resist American anti-imperialism. Macmillan decided to yield with good grace what British arms could no longer sustain. Plans for a slow decolonisation over 50 years were speeded up so that, after five years, most of the African colonies had gone.

This meant there was no time to establish a stable social structure to support independence — but Macmillan was more concerned with liquidating the Empire than with its future fate. Lesson number two.

The third lesson followed the first two. If Britain was no longer able to be a truly independent imperial power, what was her future role? Macmillan had been an early advocate of the Common Market. The Americans had always been keen on the idea of a United States of Europe: it would make their lives easier on an economic and military level. Attlee, Churchill and Eden had all resisted pressure to join "Europe". Macmillan did not.

If Britain had been great as leader of the Empire, then perhaps she could continue to be so by joining another large entity. But Macmillan had reckoned without De Gaulle. The General believed there could be only one cock in the farmyard — his answer was: "Non."

So, Suez changed the foreign policy priorities of this country for ever.

In following long-standing American desires so closely, Macmillan went a long way to restoring good Anglo-American relations. But behind the rhetoric about "special relationships", the true nature of the relationship was, as Macmillan had put it years ago: "We are the Greeks in the new Roman Empire."

EVEN this contained an element of self-delusion. America had come of age as a world power and did not need Britain's advice. It would be easy to underrate the effect of Suez on the national psyche; after all, it was not even an issue in the 1959 election. But the effect was profound. In 1945, we were one of the "Big Three"; 11 years on, we couldn't defeat Egypt, albeit because our friends would not let us. It was a shock and a humiliation.

Not until Mrs Thatcher and the Falklands were we to find a means of exorcising the demon of Suez — and by then it was too late.

● *John Charmley is a senior lecturer in history at the University of East Anglia and is the author of Churchill: The End Of Glory and Churchill's Grand Alliance.*

THE WAY IT WAS – next page

Foreword

Few people can be as well qualified as the author to write about the tragic events that have taken place in Africa since the end of World War II. He spent thirty-five years (from 1948 to 1983) living and travelling extensively in East, central and South Africa.

His farming experience in East Africa enabled him to compare, with an expert eye, the farce of the Tanganyika Groundnuts Scheme with the highly successful agricultural project at Luso – in what was then the Portuguese Angola. The horrifying figure of 27 million starving Africans provides powerful backing for the view that there has to be a new approach to Africa's agricultural problems. The author points out how miserably all the grandiose schemes have failed and advocates small self-help projects.

The debacle at Suez in 1956 decided the fate of colonial Africa when, under communist and American pressure, Britain and France decided to abandon their responsibilities by granting almost immediate independence to their colonies, with disastrous results. The tragedy was that the colonial era had marked the high point of Africa's development: independence brought famine, civil wars, genocide, corruption, misrule and economic disaster.

Even wealthy African countries, like oil-rich Nigeria, were not immune to the madness that swept over Africa in the next three decades: in colonial times Nigeria exported its agricultural surplus; today it spends billions of dollars on imported food. Its oil wealth has been squandered and misappropriated.

The United Nations (UN) has failed miserably in its duty by not taking action to curb the disastrous population explosion in Africa: for over thirty years it has been clear that the time would come when Africa would no longer be able to feed its own people.

Since the South African government was obliging enough to pass new apartheid laws at a time (the early 1950s) when world opinion was hardening against racial segregation, the country has become the scapegoat for everything that is wrong in Africa. When Kurt Waldheim took over as UN Secretary

General in 1972, South Africa's fate was sealed and a whole chapter is devoted to the part he played during his ten years in office – and to his Nazi past.

If starvation is not to spread through the whole continent, a new approach to Africa's problems is an absolute necessity and the book has several suggestions to make.

Preface to the Second Edition

Africa's endless crises continue unabated and the suffering of the ordinary African caught up in ghastly civil wars shows no sign of improvement.

Some of the reasons for this are shown in the *Daily Express* article: 'How Suez changed it all for Britain'. There is a welcome understanding of why decolonisation should have been a slow process. America, Russia and the socialists in Europe made sure that Africa was never given enough time to build up a stable social structure.

The results were brutal military dictators in Uganda, Zaire, Nigeria and so on, and civil wars in countries such as Rwanda and Burundi. However, the biggest question mark of all now is South Africa and how long it will take to become another Nigeria or worse.

The outlook for the future is not good with Johannesburg already the murder and crime centre of the world. The most testing time for South Africa will come shortly when President Mandela retires. The economic situation is bad enough now with the rand at over R8 to £1. When we moved to Umkomaas on Natal's south coast at the end of 1969 after twenty-one years in the black North the rand was R2 something to the £1.

15th November, 1997

What inspired the great British Empire is very aptly summed up on page 150 of Vere Harvey-Brain's book *My Seychelles Years* in a poem by an unknown author.

To laugh, is to risk appearing a fool
To weep, is to risk appearing sentimental,
To reach out to another, is to risk involvement,
To expose one's feelings, risks exposing one's true self,
To place your ideas, your dreams, before the crowd, is to risk their loss.
To love, is to risk not being loved in return,
To live is to risk dying.
To hope is to risk despair.
To try is to risk failure.
But risks must be taken, because the greatest hazard
in Life is to risk nothing.
The person who risks nothing, does nothing, has nothing and is nothing.
He may avoid suffering and sorrow, but he simply cannot learn, feel, change, grow, love and live.
Chained by his certitudes, he is a slave, he has forfeited his freedom.
Only the person who risks... *is free*.

Contents

Part One

The Prelude to Africa: World War II

Part Two

East Africa: 1948–1959

Part Three

Central Africa: 1959–1969

Part Four

South Africa: 1970–1983

Part One

The Prelude to Africa: World War II

The events and factors I consider most important about my thirty-five years in Africa (from 1948 to 1983) are the colonial and dominion links of my family and the fact that, over this period, I witnessed the turbulent and tragic history of East Africa and the Rhodesias at first hand.

My mother's family went out to South Africa in the 1870s. They could just as easily have gone to one of the other great dominions of the British Empire – Australia, Canada or New Zealand – but gold and diamonds had been found in South Africa in the 1870s and they anticipated that it would develop dramatically. They chose well, and still run the family business in Port Elizabeth that was founded by my mother's father.

It is well worth remembering that it was ordinary British people, like my own grandparents, settling all over the world, who helped to build the greatest empire that the world has ever seen. I am proud of the part played by my family. My father was in HM's colonial administration in Nigeria from 1919 to 19-3, having survived World War I despite being wounded four times. I am also proud of my brother's MC in Korea and my South African cousin's DFC in Italy in World War II.

It is this family background, together with my wartime service in the Indian Army, my thirty-five years in Africa and a mixed marriage, that gives me the right and experience to challenge the multiracial nonsense that has been deliberately fostered and exploited in certain quarters in Britain today, and which is making a mockery of democratic life in Britain.

By manipulating the system in London, with the aid of the now defunct GLC and other left-wing organisations, approximately ten per cent of the population, mainly immigrants, were able to dictate to the long-suffering majority of the British population. The same happened in most of Britain's other large cities and anyone who complained was immediately branded a racist

To enforce this farcical situation, and at huge annual expense, the CRE (Commission for Racial Equality) came into existence and took on the task of hounding any who disagreed with its policies.

One glaring example of how the CRE operates concerns former Bradford headmaster, Mr Honeyford, who was sacked by the council for criticising its race policies in education. The CRE, in a 1988 leaflet, branded him a racist. In

May 1991 Mr Honeyford accepted £20,000 libel damages from the CRE! To me this sums up the madness and tragedy of Britain today, and no one had the guts to insist that Mr Honeyford should have been reinstated and the Bradford council severely censured. This is by no means an isolated case.

My book will show how the same attitudes and ignorance are fostered by the UN and such organisations as NIEO (New International Economic Order) to obscure the truth about what has happened in Africa since the end of World War II. South Africa and apartheid have been used as propaganda to conceal the tragedy of the rest of Africa. The 1991 figure of 27 million starving Africans is a damning indictment of the UN's failure in Africa.

★

You could say my education in life really started when I volunteered for the army straight from public school – The King's School, Canterbury – and joined my home county regiment, the Suffolk Regiment. At the end of 1941, after initial training at the regimental depot in Bury St Edmunds, I was sent to the 70th Battalion in my home town, Felixstowe, on coastal defence. Funnily enough we were billeted in one of the beachfront hotels that I used to visit in the holidays before the war: it was owned by the mother of a pre-war friend, John Richmond. I heard later that he had survived the war and gone to Canada.

Being colonial service children, my brother, my sister and I spent most of our holidays in Felixstowe with our grandparents, who had retired there. My father was in the colonial administration in Nigeria and we saw our parents only when they were on home leave – for six months every eighteen months. In those days life was more leisurely and it was thought proper to give the civil servants a decent break in 'civilisation' after a year and a half enduring the tough conditions in West Africa. No children were allowed in Nigeria for health reasons, although my brother was born there by mistake and, in consequence, has had a lot of passport problems ever since.

Before conscription was introduced, young recruits were put into a '70th Battalion', to protect them from the bad habits of the old 'army sweats' until they had learnt to look after themselves. This was amusing as there were quite a few Borstal boys in the 70th – I believe their sentences were squashed if they volunteered. In fact, most of them made very good soldiers due, I think, to the Borstal discipline. I, too, found it easy to adapt, as army discipline was not much different from public school and the OTC (Officer Training Corps) training at The King's School, in particular, gave me a head start over most of the others and I was promoted to (unpaid) lance corporal after a month or so.

What really shook me at the time was the number of Suffolk farm boys who had difficulty reading and writing. I made my beer money writing their love letters for them and found it difficult to believe that the greatest empire in the world had failed to educate them.

Looking back now, I realise how happy and carefree these early army days were. At weekends I was still able to play tennis with the local bank manager's daughters, Mary and Jane Bicknell. However, the CO chose three or four of us who could read and write for Octu (Officer Cadet Training Unit) and I could not wait to get away t o the pre-Octu camp at Wrotham in Kent.

There I saw another side of the class system. There were some scions of our top nobility there and even the NCO instructors found it hard to believe just how thick they were. Clearly they had not been required to pass the rigorous entrance tests and had been admitted purely because of who they were. They had been raised to be leaders, however, and, in the end, usually made excellent officers.

Looking back, I think it was this early example of class distinction that started me subconsciously questioning what I was to see overseas, at first courtesy of HM forces and then during my civilian life in East, central and South Africa. I came to realise just how unnecessary the awful tragedy of Africa has been and how stupidity and ignorance have played a large part in this post-war tragedy.

*

Wrotham's noticeboard asking for volunteers to go to Octu in India decided my future life. I still remember our troopship leaving Liverpool on a miserably wet and foggy day and running into heavy seas almost straight away, which did not help our departure from Britain. As officer cadets, just about the lowest form of life in the army, we received pretty appalling treatment and our accommodation was about the worst. It was in the bowels of the troopship and being packed in like sardines did not help. If we had been hit by U-boats, as others were in the convoy, we would never have had a chance to get out.

Zigzagging across the Atlantic to avoid the U-boats did not help us make good time and we were all heartily glad to arrive at Durban. Our first sight of South Africa, eight weeks after leaving Liverpool, was on a gloriously sunny day, and we were sung into our berth by the famous Lady in White (see Appendix). I remember she was wearing a large-brimmed hat of the type my mother was very fond of wearing in the summer. My mother was, like the Lady in White, born and bred in South Africa, near another beautiful east coast port – Port Elizabeth.

The hospitality of South Africans, especially those from Natal, is legendary and, although most of my memories of that visit to Durban are a beautiful haze in a very alcoholic background, I can still remember my very first breakfast ashore, at the Cumberland Hotel on the beachfront. Each of us ate about six fried eggs, a pleasant change from the ghastly wartime egg powder in Britain, while the Indian waiters looked on in absolute amazement. Most early mornings we were marched past the Cumberland Hotel to the nearby beach, for PT followed by a welcome swim in the Indian Ocean. We never thought about sharks and, after being marched back to the ship, we were free for the rest of the day.

Sadly it all had to end and, all too soon, we were on our way again for Bombay. Leaning on the troopship's rails as Durban and the coast of Africa disappeared, I promised myself that, should I be lucky enough to survive, I would return to Africa and to the country of my mother's birth – South Africa. I still realise how fortunate I was to emerge largely unscathed by the war, and how lucky to be able to fulfil my youthful wartime dreams.

★

There is an almost physical pull about Africa, especially in the rural, unspoilt and un-Westernised areas, that is difficult to describe. Only those who have lived, worked and hunted in bush areas will know of the joy of waking up on the ground beside a wood fire – a very necessary precaution to keep lions and other predators away in the night – as dawn came and the noises of the big game could be heard all around and you knew that you had a week or two of hunting to look forward to.

Never has it been more necessary than now to remind those high-minded, ignorant animal conservationists in the West that they are largely responsible for the present ghastly plight of Africa's elephants and other big game animals. In colonial times all hunting was very strictly controlled and some animals, including elephants, had to be culled in many areas, as they were increasing too quickly. Today this is true only in some of Southern Africa's game reserves, such as Kruger National Park.

The corruption of black Africa's rulers is well known in Africa. The Kenyatta family was deeply involved in Kenya's illicit ivory trade, and highly placed 'aid cheats' swindle the British and other Western countries out of millions of pounds.

Until recently the West seemed too frightened to do anything, but a recent book by Kathleen Corbett and Dr Karl Borgin (*The Destruction of a Continent*) marks an important change in some Western attitudes. How refreshing it is to know that both authors spent over twenty-five years in Africa: normally Western authors consider a visit of two to three weeks sufficient to write their books, especially the ones on South Africa.

★

However, back on the troopship, we had to endure another four weeks of great discomfort before we were to reach Bombay. Nothing in our comfortable middle-class lives in Britain prepared us for the ghastly realities of India. Most of us expected Bombay to be a very much hotter version of Durban.

Our first taste of the noise, confusion, flies and filth of the Bombay docks, and the congestion caused by masses of brown bodies milling around everywhere, had a staggering effect, never to be forgotten.

I particularly noticed the emaciated dock workers, so different from the burly, smiling Zulu dock workers in Durban. There were such seething masses of Indians everywhere in Bombay that we had to step over bodies lying on the pavements and were besieged by mutilated beggars wherever we went. From what I have heard, conditions for the poor are the same today, if not worse, in all the big Indian cities.

There are some very beautiful parts of India, of course. I particularly like Kashmir, the Punjab, the Nilgiri Hills and Bangalore. But the hard fact is that there are just too many Indians to feed. Unless something is done about Africa's population explosion, by much stricter birth control, then Africa will get just as bad as India, which would not benefit anybody – black, brown or white.

★

What puzzles those of us who have spent most of our working lives abroad is why the West's media have always been so keen to play Russia's game. What motivates their obsession with apartheid and the continual hounding of South Africa?

The critical situation in most of black Africa is almost completely ignored by the media in the West, although starvation gets worse the whole time. The ever-growing threat of disintegration was barely reported until *The Destruction of a Continent* started questions being asked and it is my hope that my book will also help to explain why the West has to wake up before it is too late.

Why did we have to wait so long before the colonial era got some praise for the good that was done in Africa? Why was there so much colonial guilt in the West? Do communism's fellow-travellers in the West wield more power than the public suspects?

Doesn't television in the West have a lot to answer for, especially Channel 4, with its communist producers such as Tariq Ali? Is it jealousy of South Africa because it has been so successful under white rule and much of black-ruled Africa is in such a mess?

Whatever the reasons, the Russians have now reached their final goal – South Africa. Should they succeed and their Marxist ANC (African National Congress) puppets take over South Africa, then there will be a fatal balance of power swing to the Russians and the world will be that much nearer to World War III.

The tragic irony of all this communist success is that the anti-Christian forces of communism have been aided and abetted by the Churches in the West. Money from the West has poured into South Africa for the use of the South African Council of Churches and to finance the demagogic activities overseas of Archbishop Tutu, Boesak, Chikane, and other black leaders, demanding sanctions against South Africa.

It seems to those of us who know Africa's real problems that Archbishop Tutu, in his palatial mansion, does not seem to care how many of his fellow Africans starve provided he and his ANC friends eventually get control of South Africa.

As early as 1973 President Leonid Brezhnev made Russia's long-term goals clear: 'Our aim is to gain control of the two great treasure houses on which the West depends: the energy treasure house of the Persian Gulf and the minerals treasure house of Central and South Africa.'

★

All these events were in the future, and few of us realised then how soon we were going to see the decline and demise of the British Empire, or that we would witness, personally, the beginning of the end of the British Raj in India.

Soon we were being marched to Victoria Station, the main railway station in Bombay, for the final part of our journey to Octu at Mhow, in the Central Province, near Indore state. We had expected a comfortable journey on the

Indian railways, in a requisitioned second or third class train. What we got was a filthy fourth class train with narrow wooden benches. Some of us slept on these the others on the equally filthy floor.

We were fed along the railway line by army cooks out in the open, our train being shunted off to nearby railway sidings. Before the journey we were warned of the dangers of eating any Indian food on offer near the railway sidings; especially dangerous were cut fruit and sweetmeats. Some ignored the warning and paid the penalty later. Two died of amoebic dysentery in Mhow's military hospital and four had to be sent back to South Africa to convalesce.

During the three-day journey we had to perform our ablutions at the railway stations, as there was little water on the trains and the outlets were unusable for health reasons. In any case, we were not used yet to squatting – the practice in the East.

Trains passing the stations were packed and overflowing with Indians, and those who could not get in the carriages travelled on the roof. Most of them seemed to be travelling with all their possessions and carried huge bundles on their heads, and in their arms as well. We could hardly believe what we saw but no one else seemed to find things in any way abnormal. This was life in the raw for the poor of India.

★

Mhow couldn't come soon enough and, for India, turned out to be quite an attractive place. After a few days to get over the trip, we got back to a well-ordered military life in a typical British military cantonment in India, of which our Octu bungalows took up a large part. Mhow Octu was a mixed Indian and British affair which provided a very competent officer training course. We had, also, to spend at least two hours a day learning Urdu (usually called Hindustani at that time) from a local teacher.

I don't think I am being unfair when I say that few of us would have been happy serving under the Indians we came in contact with there, especially under wartime conditions. This feeling had nothing to do with colour, or any of that nonsense, but was simply a matter of military competence.

I was commissioned in due course, then disaster struck me personally. I had never been ill in my life, except for the usual childhood ailments like chicken pox, and had always been extremely fit. We were on night manoeuvres shortly before being commissioned, and spent most of the night lying in muddy water near an Indian village. Obviously the local Indians used the area, which was near a river, for their daily ablutions. Within two days of this manoeuvre I became completely paralysed and was taken to the military hospital.

The IMS (Indian Medical Service) doctors were completely baffled and, if my military record had not shown that I had volunteered for the army, I think they would have liked to have accused me of malingering. They fed me M & B tablets constantly and gave me daily heat treatment, which eventually gave me back some movement in my legs, but improvement was very painful and slow.

Some months later I went before a medical board, which downgraded me as much as possible and sent me on temporary posting to an Indian Pioneer battalion in Iraq. They intimated that if my movements did not improve I would be discharged from the army on medical grounds. To this day I do not know what caused the paralysis but, at a recent medical examination for a war disability pension, the specialist said it was some kind of massive muscular seize-up which, due to lack of the proper treatment, took much longer to clear up than it should have done. I still believe it was some kind of polio, or some tropical bug!

The IMS doctors had warned me that I should not expect to be able to run or take any strenuous exercise for at least five years. I intended to prove them wrong. Indian friends during this period told me my only hope was to do yoga exercises and swim. Maybe the hot, dry weather of Iraq helped, because I began to make dramatic progress. When I went before another medical board they couldn't understand why I had been downgraded medically. They passed me as fit again for active service and I was sent back to India for further training, at the 10th Gurkha Rifles depot at Alilal, near Pathankot.

*

I was then posted to the special Gurkha jungle training camp at Saharanpur for the 7th and 10th Gurkha Rifle Bns in Burma. These camps were based on General Wingate's ideas of long-range patrols going into Burma to hit and harass the Japanese lines of communication. We were trained to believe in General Wingate's dictum: 'If you believe in yourselves, anything is possible.'

What the Chindits achieved in Burma proved him right, as well as lifting the morale of everybody concerned in the operations. We had to undergo ten to fourteen-day training patrols in the jungles near to Saharanpur and I naturally wondered how my legs would react to the damp and wet conditions. Everything went fine, even if it was tiring and uncomfortable, and that reinforced my view that the paralysis had been some kind of polio, or a tropical bug I had picked up at Octu.

The instructors were all of the highest calibre. I remember particularly Colonel Jim Corbett, known all over India for his tiger hunting exploits, even before his books about his hunting experiences were published – *The Maneaters of Kumaon* was one. He taught us many ways of using bamboo for military purposes, including making lethal booby traps for the Japanese, but, aside from the military aspects of jungle warfare, he taught us to appreciate and enjoy the jungle and to lose our fear of surviving there for long periods. Later, during my hunting days in Africa, I made use of a lot of what he had taught us during the jungle training.

In the early part of 1944 we had nearly finished our training prior to being posted to Burma, and my luck really started changing when ten replacement officers were required for casualties suffered in the 43rd Gurkha Lorried Brigade. The Gurkha Brigade in Italy was made up of three battalions of Gurkhas (Gurkha Rifles): 2/6 GR, 2/8 GR and 2/10 GR. I was one of the lucky ten chosen to go.

Looking back, it was probably this posting to Italy, together with my time out with my paralysis, painful though it was at the time, that enabled me to survive. The Burma jungles, apart from being extremely dangerous, took a very heavy toll of even the fittest person's health. If one were wounded or became sick while on patrol, the chances of survival were very small. To add to this, the Japanese, angry at the success of our patrols, had issued orders that any officer captured was to be beheaded on the spot.

*

Soon the ten of us were on our way to Bombay, with other reinforcements for the three Gurkha battalions in the 43rd Gurkha Lorried Brigade in Italy, together with our own transport, including Bren gun carriers. Ironically we were to go overland, via the port of Basra in Iraq, Damascus in Syria, Beirut in Lebanon and Port Said in Egypt, from where we were to go by landing craft to either Brindisi or Bari in Italy: quite a Cook's tour, even though it was hellishly hot.

In Basra I had quite a bad bout of dysentery, but nothing was going to keep me in Iraq again and I lived mainly on tea, with chocolate and cheese to bind me up, for the next few weeks. We had to travel mainly at night, as it was hot enough to fry an egg on the metal of a Bren gun carrier by day.

*

We got to Italy in the latter part of 1944 and joined our Gurkha Brigade in the Florence area. It soon became apparent that there was plenty of fighting to come, and rivers to cross, before the Germans surrendered near Trieste, in May 1945.

The winter of 1944 was a pretty bad one, with plenty of snow, and we took over trenches on the Senio river, which meant frequent night patrols across the water. By day we could see the Germans on the other side of the river. They were adept at rigging up very unpleasant booby traps and, if you were wise, you soon learnt to leave everything alone and touched nothing without checking it carefully first, not even dead bodies.

It was the policy to send young officers out on patrol with an experienced Gurkha officer. Most of these were old enough to be my father and without their help I doubt if I would have survived long. Shortly after my arrival, for example, I was detailed to lead a patrol over the river to gauge the strength of the Germans. I think it was at the time we were opposite one of their parachute battalions and they had been more active than usual. There were dead and stinking cattle, both in and out of the river, but there was one relatively clear stretch near the water, opposite a small path on the other side of the river, and I wanted to go that way. Fortunately the Gurkha officer persuaded me to approach from behind the stinking cattle instead. As we got near to the river we could hear the faint sounds of German movements on either side of the path I had wanted to follow. Obviously they were expecting us to use that route and, if we had done so, they would have cut us all to bits.

I soon discovered that a week in action is worth years of training, and you learn the art of survival quickly or you do not last very long. My main memory of this time is the complete exhaustion caused by getting nothing but broken sleep. One night, however, I must have fallen into a pretty heavy sleep, because I woke to find a rat scratching on my chest. He had nibbled through my battledress pocket to get at some chocolate in my shirt pocket, and it was his teeth biting on my chest that had woken me up. I was most annoyed at the time because he had already eaten a lot of my chocolate.

On another occasion we had taken over forward positions from the Poles, who had a most disconcerting habit of not always marking accurately the landmines they had laid. We had our Company HQ in a bombed-out Italian farmhouse at the top of a small hill. The cellars were about all that was usable but we were glad to sleep there – it was much better than being outside in the trenches. There were plenty of iron beds all over Italy, as Mussolini had given one to each child, to try and build up the birth rate. The drawback was that the Germans knew the Poles had been using the farmhouse as a forward observation post, so they shelled the area every morning.

One day I was delayed returning from HQ and entered the communication trenches at the back of the farmhouse, which we had to use by day, just as the shelling started. I ran whenever there was a break and I was near to the farmhouse when two shells fell just behind me as I was running. The next landed right beside me, on the wall of the communication trench, and I thought I would be buried there. But it didn't go off and I said a prayer for whoever had sabotaged it in the factory.

On top of all the 'normal' war risks, accidents were a continual hazard and many died or were wounded through a moment's carelessness, not always their own. I was asleep on a bed in the farm cellars when the company commander and Gurkha officer came back from patrol. One of them threw his Thomson or Sten gun on the bed. It fell off and started firing the rest of the magazine over my head. When I woke up I saw the neat line of bullet holes just above me on the bed. If I had woken earlier and sat up I would have been full of bullets.

An actual tragedy happened shortly after this. We had been halted in convoy on the road, as there was firing at the head of the convoy, and one of the officers, who had joined the battalion shortly after me, grabbed his Sten gun as he was getting out of the jeep. It went off, wounding him badly in the head.

Nothing illustrates better the terrible ironies of war than what happened to Ted Harrison, who had survived the Gothic Line battles and had then been transferred to a staff job. Shortly after the transfer he was travelling well away from the front line when, out of the blue, he was strafed by a single German plane. He was very badly wounded in the legs and never fully recovered.

Priming the hand grenades was another potentially hazardous operation, from which I kept as far away as possible. It was all too easy to get careless and there were plenty of near misses and some casualties. I still remember one officer in our battalion, who wore a BLAV (British Latin American Volunteer) badge on his arm. I think his name was von Andrap, and he always walked around with at least half a dozen primed hand grenades on his belt.

*

Those of us who survived always remembered the army lessons in careful handling of all firearms and Jim Corbett's lectures on survival in the wild. I frequently used what I learnt then during the days when I was hunting elephants in Africa.

A South African friend, who worked for Tanganyika's Agricultural Department, was a very experienced and careful elephant hunter. He would very rarely, if ever, agree to take out another hunter on his elephant hunting trips, as he reckoned another hunter, unless you knew him well, doubled your risks of an accident. His name was Chummy Lockwood and there were plenty of occasions during my hunting days in Tanganyika when I was glad I had listened to his advice.

★

Delousing was a way of life when we came out of the line, and our clothes were either burnt or thoroughly fumigated and cleaned. Then, if we were lucky, we had a few days' leave in Rome before starting training again.

I had managed to wangle a few more trips than most, as I was now with the support company that handled transport and the Bren gun carriers which were used to bring ammunition and other supplies to the various companies in the front line. This could only be done at night as it was generally impossible to move around by day. The Germans, with their multiple mortars and self-propelled 88s, made sure of that.

We had had a spate of new battalion commanders and this, of course, made it easier for us to get away with a few extra trips to Rome, and our excuses for arriving back late were always accepted. I think Brigade HQ must have realised something was going on, because they brought in Colonel Bill Ingall, DSO, of the 2/6 GR, to tighten up discipline and to crack down in general.

I tried it once too often, as I thought I could still get away with it with Colonel Ingall, especially as we were short of officers then. I soon learnt how wrong I was when I got back late from Rome one night and my excuse was not accepted. He gave me the option of accepting his punishment or going for court martial. Naturally I took his punishment and for two weeks I had to get up every two hours during the night, put on full kit, then go to the battalion's main guardhouse to turn out the guard and inspect them. This meant I got virtually no sleep but by day I was still expected to carry out the normal training duties, starting with PT every morning.

Before Colonel Ingall's arrival (incidentally, I think he was the best CO that we ever had), we got some real gung-ho specimens. One in particular I have never forgotten. He had just come out of Burma, where they used Bren gun carriers offensively to support battalion attacks, and he wanted to do the same in Italy. I was unfortunate enough to be in charge of the Bren gun carriers at the time and I was called into the battalion briefing by the CO and ordered to take up a position forward, to cover the battalion attack the next morning. I pointed out that, by day, we would never get up the dirt road to take our position among the trees without being spotted by the Germans, with their self-propelled 88s. He wouldn't listen, and repeated his orders, so all I could do was to ask my Gurkha officer to work out the best plan possible.

Although we were meant to go up in close formation, the Gurkha thought our best chance of survival would be to spread out as far as possible. Fortunately the trees were thick, so the CO couldn't see our progress, but the Germans saw our dust pretty soon and it was the one day I was glad to be in the front Bren gun carrier, as they zeroed in on our dust. They must have thought it was a tank build-up prior to a big attack, for they shelled us all day and night.

I think two or three carriers were hit before they could get off the road into the trees. The rest of us dug in under the carriers for twenty-four hours of almost non-stop shelling, but we only lost two more carriers and suffered no further casualties, as we were pretty well-protected, dug in underneath. A week or so after this the CO was transferred. Nothing was said, but the Bren gun carriers were never used in this way again.

It was obvious that the top brass were planning to speed up the rate of advance as soon as the weather improved, in the early spring of 1945.

We started special training in cut-away tanks; this meant that the top was cut off a tank, for easy entry and quick exit, and we, the poor bloody infantry, were carried inside. This was fine in theory, but I couldn't help thinking how easy it would be for the Germans to drop one of their stick grenades inside before we ever had a chance of getting out.

We were attached to, and trained with, the New Zealand Armoured Division. The New Zealand Armoured was used to pound the Germans in the villages, or wherever they were holed up, and the New Zealanders were a marvellous bunch, who kept our casualties to the minimum. By now, most of the Germans had realised that once the Po river was crossed it was the beginning of the end for them in Italy. In consequence, our job was made a lot easier and we moved on quickly most of the time. It was only occasionally that we came across some fanatical diehard Germans who caused us a lot of unnecessary casualties. However, by previous standards our advance was pretty quick and soon we had taken Padua.

I still remember Padua very well, as we were billeted for a short time in an egg-nog factory. The New Zealanders had an incredible knack of sniffing out any booze that was available and they were soon around with their water trucks, queuing up to fill the trucks with egg-nog. In the few days that we were in Padua I got heartily sick of the stuff. We had it with our tea, coffee and tinned fruit, along with some brandy we had also liberated.

Soon it was on to Mestre and over to Venice, to liberate some beautiful cut glass, then swiftly on, with very few stops, to Trieste – and the end of the war in Europe.

We moved into an almost permanent camp near Trieste, as there had been a certain amount of trouble with the Yugoslav partisans under Marshal Tito. I think they wanted to annex Trieste, or some such nonsense. So, to relieve the tension and show some of our army strength, a visit from a Yugoslav army general was organised. We were all drawn up for inspection and expected to see the usual smart staff car with escort appear. What we eventually got was a very dirty motorcycle and sidecar, from which stepped a very dusty Yugoslav general.

I thought this made a very fitting finale to our Italian campaign.

*

Once we had taken Mestre and Venice, the prisoners of war started streaming in and on occasion we were hard pressed to deal with the numbers involved. After the war in Europe had ended, in May 1945, we started to get some of the real Nazis surrendering. Some were still very arrogant, especially a few of the young officers from parachute battalions, who had been brought in to stiffen the German resistance in the winter of 1944. We had had trouble with them when we were opposite them in the line and, on more than one occasion, they had refused to respect our white flags and had shot and wounded our Gurkha stretcher-bearers.

One Para officer who spoke English had the nerve to complain about the treatment they were getting. I told him, pretty forcefully, that we hadn't forgotten or forgiven the way his comrades had treated our Gurkha wounded, and I couldn't resist the temptation to teach him and the other Germans a lesson they would not forget. I could see that they were already scared of the Gurkhas. In those days few of our Gurkhas spoke English, except the Gurkha officers and some of the NCOs, so I told them in Ghurkhali to draw their kukris and look fierce. Then I told the English-speaking German that Gurkhas never drew their kukris without drawing blood and that they were for the chop, as the Gurkhas believed they were personally responsible for shooting down the Gurkha stretcher-bearers.

As I turned to leave, all the Germans really panicked, and their interpreter was on his knees like the others, begging me not to leave them to their fate. I must admit I loved it, and strung it out as much as possible. The Gurkhas were looking on in absolute amazement and I told them to feel the sharpness of the edges of their kukris. By now things were getting a bit out of control, with the Germans flat on the ground around my feet, so I felt I had better tell the Gurkhas what had been going on. It appealed to their sense of humour and they started falling around laughing. We were near the main assembly camp, where we were to hand them over. The guards there couldn't understand why the Germans were running into the camp to get away from us, while we were standing outside, still laughing.

Years later, when I was at Usumbura, Ruanda-Urundi (part of the Belgian Congo in those days) I met a German ex-officer who had been in Italy during World War II, and he was boasting to me about the hammering Germans had given the Gurkhas who were trying to take Monte Cassino. When I told him the above story, suitably embellished (it was a much ruder version of what had happened), it soon took the smile off his face. He kept well away from me in the hotel bar for the day or two that I was there.

Although none of us had the same kind of hatred for the Germans that we had for the Japanese, there is no doubt in my mind that the majority of Germans love giving you a kick if you are down, but that they hate having the same kind of treatment dished out to them.

*

Soon we were on our way back to the Middle East and landed at Haifa, in Palestine. Then we moved into the Tripoli area, via Beirut, and later we went on to Latakia, now renamed Al Ladhiqiyah, in Syria. Most of our time was spent on convoy duty and other law and order duties, as the troubles between Jews and Arabs in Palestine started escalating. We began escorting convoys right through to Cairo, which gave us the chance to see some of the sights in Egypt. The pyramids outside Cairo were popular, because we could swim at the nearby Mena House Hotel after our sightseeing.

I had thought that, having survived the war in Italy, my troubles in the army were over, but I had reckoned without the Indian Army Medical Service. We had lost our wartime medical officer shortly after we left Italy and his replacement was some failed Bombay medical student. Shortly after a party in Latakia, at which we had drunk quantities of the local arak, I became violently ill and the next day I could not eat anything without being sick.

At first I put it down to the local drink, which had affected some of the other officers as well. But they all recovered after a day or two and I did not. Our failed Bombay medic put my illness down to a touch of colic.

Fortunately for me our adjutant had had a year or so as a medical student before joining the army, and he reckoned it was my appendix and I must get to hospital without any further delay. By this time I had been without food for five days and if my appendix had not already burst then it did so on the two hundred-mile journey to the nearest military hospital, in Beirut. The only ambulance we had in the battalion was a jeep with a stretcher and, although my Gurkha driver was as careful as possible, the trip was absolute agony. The roads were either dirt or badly rutted (or both) and the bumps were unavoidable.

We arrived at the Beirut military hospital at about two in the morning and, as luck would have it, the chief surgeon had just arrived on a call. After examination, he told me that he would have to operate straight away, otherwise I would be dead by morning. I learnt later that he had been the chief surgeon at Vienna's largest hospital and that he had to leave as Hitler marched in, in 1938. He was, of course, a Jew and a very good and experienced surgeon. Even with his skills I still had to have a tube in my stomach to drain off the poisons for the next two months.

When I told him the full story later, he could hardly believe what had happened. He reckoned it was only my age and fitness that had enabled me to survive.

Up until then I had the average British views and mild dislike of the Jews, due mainly to the anti-Jewish propaganda in Europe that was spread by the Germans. Some of the newspapers in Britain certainly encouraged this propaganda.

During my convalescence I decided to see more of Palestine – I had already seen something of Haifa and Tel Aviv, and I had been impressed by what I had seen. The difference between Arab and Jewish areas was incredible and, after seeing a kibbutz and how the Jews had transformed a barren waste into a green paradise, it was impossible not to change my conventional views on Jews.

★

Every Christian should visit Jerusalem, and the other holy places, to get a historical background to Israel's importance. Israel's magnificent military victories against the Arabs, in the face of seemingly impossible odds, were still in the future and again proved the value of the individual who believes in himself and his cause.

What a complete contrast to the shame of Suez for Britain. Any hope for a true multiracial Christian solution to Britain's colonial problems in Africa ended at Suez. In the Falklands War Britain regained some of its national pride, and it may just be possible to save the remnants of Christianity in South Africa, if the West and the 'old' Commonwealth face up to the threat of communism and the ANC before it is too late.

There are important comparisons to be drawn between Israel and South Africa and the way the Israelis defeated their Arab enemies. South Africa, if it keeps faith, can also defeat all her enemies – the anti-Christian communist forces that surround it in the same way as the Arabs surround Israel. This is why it is so important that the message of true Christians like Father Arthur Lewis MA, with his forty years as a missionary in Africa, should be listened to. For too long Britain and the rest of the Western world have been misled by a bunch of trendy clergymen who are, for various reasons, promoting the aims of communism.

Even at this late hour, those of us from Britain, Australia, Canada, New Zealand, South Africa and the USA who volunteered to fight and, where necessary, to die in the cause of freedom against Nazi Germany, can do much more to influence our governments, when more understand that most of what happened in Africa after World War II was completely unnecessary.

What few realise and even fewer, who know the truth, will admit is that India's problems, based mainly on religion and the ever-increasing tension between Hindu and Muslim, were totally different to the problems in Africa. There was very little economic value to Britain in its African colonies, and there was not the slightest need for the indecent haste with which they were given independence. Owing mainly to a few of Labour's left-wing activists in Britain, power was handed over prematurely to a bunch of Marxist or military dictators far more grasping, greedy and incompetent than even their East European communist counterparts.

As ex-servicemen who fought for Britain in its hour of need, we have kept quiet for far too long about this disgraceful betrayal of the majority of rural Africans, who relied on Britain to protect them from these Marxist and military murderers who now rule, or rather misrule, these bankrupt and in many cases now starving African countries. Please do not be misled into thinking that things have now improved. Marxist Mugabe, supported by Britain, massacred thousands of Matabele (some reports have indicated that it was as many as forty thousand) because they were opposed to his rule. Can you imagine the outcry if this had happened in South Africa?

It has become increasingly obvious to those who have lived in Africa since the end of World War II that black-on-black violence, mayhem and murder is quite acceptable to the West, Britain in particular, and to the UN.

Have there been any protests about the current black genocide in Sudan, where the Muslim north has been allowed to murder thousands of black Christians in the south? Church and other protests about Africa have, as usual, been restricted to protests about apartheid in South Africa. These incredible double standards, masterminded by the communists and their Western fellow-travellers, brought to an end the well-organised administrations of the colonial era, and were replaced by civil wars, chaos, starvation and corruption.

Since Rhodesia fell to the communists in 1979, all the above forces of evil have been turned against South Africa. The media, and others in the West, are quite happy to ignore the above, and to see that the public in the West never get the true facts about Africa, and the five million Africans who died due mainly to premature independence being granted so irresponsibly by Britain and other countries in the West. Until the publication of *The Destruction of a Continent* none of these facts was ever admitted. Yet the West still seems to think it has the right to sit in judgement on South Africa.

Beirut is another example of this madness. For most servicemen, the writer included, Beirut was the favourite place for local leave and weekends. It was then a beautiful and well-ordered place with a strong French flavour, and rightly deserved to be known as the 'Paris of the Middle East'. Today it is a ruin, a mass of rubble, with murder and mayhem a daily occurrence and Muslim fighting Christian. The Lebanon has been wrecked, and I suspect South Africa's enemies would like to see the same thing happen there.

Britain, of all countries, should have learnt something from the last four hundred years in Ireland, and the obsessive religious war that still goes on there today. Yet our political masters are so blinded by their own ignorance that they allowed Hindu and Muslim Indians to flood into this country, to be followed by thousands more Muslims from Iran and Kurdistan. The stage has been set for future racial and religious violence and the Salman Rushdie affair, with Muslim violence on our streets, is only a mild forerunner of the blood that will flow in the future. Yet when a senior government minister tried to warn the public of the folly of mass immigration, he was branded a racist and dismissed from the government.

Need I add that, in World War II, Mr Enoch Powell went from private to brigadier? Many will still remember how Winston Churchill was treated in the 1930s. He was called a warmonger, and worse, by the media and our rulers then, who refused to listen to his continual warnings regarding the threat to peace if we went on appeasing Adolf Hitler and Nazi Germany. Later the whole world, and the Jews in particular, were to pay a terrible price for ignoring his warnings.

How many times has history got to repeat itself before anyone will listen? Surely the callous and brutal murder of a London policeman, PC Blakelock, by a black mob is sufficient warning that we must listen to Mr Enoch Powell before it is too late?

The government is now, annually, spending millions of pounds of taxpayers' money on the Commission for Racial Equality, to try to rectify the racial tensions it itself created by its immigration policies. The Commission recommends increasingly authoritarian laws and we now have a ridiculous situation, where a minority of under ten per cent (mainly Muslims) try to dictate how the majority (mainly Protestant British) shall behave.

Why was a referendum not held? Surely when the whole structure of the British way of life was going to be changed the people should have been consulted about whether millions of immigrants, largely of other religions, should be allowed into Britain, especially when there was the unsolved, bloody Irish problem there for all to see. In the early 1960s Britain's non-white population figure was given as only fifty to sixty thousand (in Harold Macmillan's memoirs).

Did we really volunteer to fight the tyranny of Hitler's Nazi Germany, only to allow a more insidious tyranny to take over?

*

Britain was still the same old Britain, although badly battered in the war and still with food rationing, when I eventually got away on leave after four years' overseas service.

Everything at home seemed so much smaller than I remembered and what was embarrassing was the continual questioning about the war. I found I didn't want to discuss any part of it, from my complete paralysis in India to my experiences in Italy, and this probably explains why, later, I didn't bother to collect my free issue of war medals until after I returned to Britain in 1983.

To be quite honest, I was glad when the time came for me to return to the Middle East. I had to go to GHQ Cairo to report to AG Indian for posting, as the 43rd Gurkha Lorried Brigade had been recalled to India while I was on leave.

I knew staff officers were required to help wind up the affairs of the three Indian divisions in the Middle East (the 4th, 8th and 10th Indian Divisions) and I was glad when they gave me a staff job, otherwise I would have had to go back to India. However, I can't say I was very impressed with how GHQ worked – it did explain why it takes at least ten soldiers in the rear to get one soldier to the front line!

Life in Cairo was extremely pleasant. I shared a flat at Gezira, not far from the Gezira Sporting Club, where we used to go to swim and lunch almost every day. Groppi's Restaurant and the famous bar at Shepheard's Hotel also became part of the daily round. It was said that you couldn't drink there without meeting someone you knew in the army.

All too soon AG Indian had completed its work and was going to close down, so I had to start looking for another job, or I would still be posted back to India. One night a drinking buddy suggested I try a friend of his, who had been a sergeant in London's metropolitan police and was now a captain in the SIB (Special Investigation Branch of the military police).

We got on well and he sent me on a short course at the military police depot in Cairo. All I can remember now is learning Judges' Rules by heart, and how to caution a suspect, then I was temporarily attached to the SIB in Cairo and given a job that every soldier must dream about. All I had to do was to patrol around the Cairo nightclubs every evening, in a jeep with an NCO and driver, to places like the famous Madame Bardia, that every soldier who served in the Middle East will remember, and pick up any drunks, making sure they weren't robbed at closing time.

Egypt being the land of baksheesh, none of the SIB officers or NCOs were ever expected to pay for a drink, as the owners knew we had the power to close their premises to HM forces.

Some of the girls who worked in the nightclubs were surprisingly beautiful. One, a White Russian, I took out during the day for most of the time that I was in Cairo. I still remember how the fat Egyptian officials and businessmen sat mesmerised when the girls did their belly dances.

We came in contact with the Egyptian police on our occasional trips to save British troops who had got into trouble, bailing them out of the hell-holes that the Egyptians called prisons. During this time I got quite friendly with one of the younger police officers. I knew that, like most of them, he smoked hashish, using a hookah or hubble-bubble, as I had been invited to some of his house parties where they smoked. I had tried the odd puff, but wasn't impressed.

Then a half-French local girl I had met at Groppi's said she was keen have a go, but her block of flats was far too public, as it was still officially against the law to smoke hashish. I lived in a very secluded house, rented from a retired Egyptian general. It was split into two flats, but I had to invite my friend in the other flat as the smell of hashish is pretty strong.

So my Egyptian police chum and his girlfriend agreed to bring along the necessary paraphernalia, in other words, hookahs, separate mouthpieces and the hashish. It was extremely fortunate that we chose a Friday because, by the end of the night, I had collapsed on the bed – and I was unable to move for the next three days. Most of that time I was having the vivid dreams that hashish brings on, and I needed my girlfriend to bring me water and look after me while I recovered. The Egyptian chum thought it a huge joke, but he had told me one evening, when he was drunk, that he had to have his hashish every night and he knew it would kill him eventually. I never touched the stuff again, but our place stank for the next week. We had given our Sudanese servant two weeks' leave, and we sprayed the house every day to try and clear the smell of the hashish before he returned.

All good things have to come to an end, especially in the army, and the SIB captain who had given me the job in Cairo went back to Britain for demobilisation. His successor did not take kindly to having an ex-Gurkha from the Indian Army doing a job in the SIB, a British army unit as well, and he wanted me out of Cairo, so he arranged to transfer me to Fayid, a large military settlement in the Suez Canal area.

As I only had a few months left before my own demobilisation was due, I was actually quite glad to go. Cairo nightlife was beginning to get me down, as it was very difficult to refuse the free drinks on offer every night and, in consequence, I was finding that alcohol was affecting my health and I looked a real wreck.

At Fayid I ran the SIB section responsible for patrolling the perimeter fence surrounding the military camp. Even this wire fence could not keep out the very determined Egyptian thieves, and we had to use patrol vehicles with spotlights to check, every night, that they had not cut the wire.

I had a very good sergeant from one of the Scottish regiments, who had also been in Italy during the war. He would cover for me whenever I wanted to go to Cairo at weekends to visit some of my old girlfriends there.

All too soon my demobilisation date came up and I was on my way home from the Middle East for the last time, by ship from Port Said to Toulon, then by train across France and finally a channel ferry home to Britain in early 1947, after over six years in the army.

*

War souvenirs and weapons that we had all acquired in Italy were a bit of a problem now. Most of us had Luger pistols and Nazi ornamental daggers, as well as German caps, badges, Iron Crosses, and anything else we had taken from dead or captured German officers. I had given away a Luger or two in the Middle East and I carried one most of the time I was there. I knew, from a previous leave, that very few of us were searched and I carried everything through customs without any trouble.

Later, after the amnesty for handing in German weapons had expired and I was due to go to Tanganyika, I decided it was too risky to travel there with my Luger pistol. But to get rid of it in London wasn't easy and, in the end, I wrapped it up in brown paper, sealed it, went to Westminster Bridge late one night and dropped it into the Thames.

Army friends had told me about the Rubens Hotel in Victoria, not far from Buckingham Palace, which was run by the WVS as an officers' hostel at 5/-d per night. Meals were also incredibly cheap. The snag was that if you had a home in the UK you could stay only a maximum of ten days. My father had now retired from the colonial service in Nigeria but had just taken up another job in Africa, with the War Graves Commission, so I had no UK base and was able to use the Rubens Hotel for the next few months, throughout my demobilisation leave.

This turned out to be extremely convenient as, in those days, the Royal British Legion had an office in Victoria, where I eventually got my job in Africa. There were quite a few ex-Gurkhas and others from the Indian Army who, like me, were using the Rubens as a base. A few of their names still come to mind: Jimmy Brodie of the 5th Gurkhas, now in Iraq; Doug Cumming, also of the 5th Gurkhas; Denis Nolan, a man with strong feelings about his native Ireland; ex-2/10 GR Bob Wilson, who lost some of his fingers through grenade wounds; Des Wilson, MC, joined the Nigerian colonial service (like my father); John Newbery, MBE, later with the battalion in Hong Kong; finally, Colonel Gregory, OBE, who runs the 10th GR Regimental Association's annual lunch at Chelsea Barracks, and invited me as a guest. It was there I met, among others, Nick Carter, Denis Rawlins and Ian Mayman.

Back in Britain in 1947 I believed I could soon put my wartime experiences in Italy behind me. However, I found the repercussions took far longer to recede than expected. When I cut down on my alcoholic intake the dreams of dead bodies in Italy recurred. So the old cycle started again – more alcohol meant no dreams. The whole thing didn't finish until a year later, when I was in Africa. Ironically it ended just after my first hunting trip, near the Serengeti National Park – perhaps the headshrinks can make something of that! It was only when I at last got out of uniform and into civilian clothes, after my demobilisation leave, that I really began to accept the fact that I had survived more or less intact and, although I now felt middle-aged, I was still not quite twenty-four years old.

Money wasn't a problem, as I had accumulated quite a lot in India, where Indian Army officers were much better paid than British Army officers, although money didn't mean much when you didn't know if you were going to be alive to spend it.

Living expenses at the Rubens Hotel were so low that there was no urgency in finding a job, but soon the urge to start a new life in Africa became stronger, as I began to see just how restrictive life in Britain would be.

I had no intention of sitting in some London office for the rest of my working life.

Most survivors of the war, including myself, felt that the British Empire owed them quite a lot. Additionally, I had got used to the sun and heat in the Middle East and I found post-war Britain pretty drab after the colourful life I had lived out there. I knew that I could use my father's connections in the colonial service, and I had always admired the work he did in the Nigerian administration, but this string-pulling would be a last resort, used only if I had difficulty getting a job in commerce overseas. I had no desire to be any part of a dying colonial service.

In any case, I was just beginning to realise how regimented my whole life had been – first at prep school at Yardley Court, Tonbridge, Kent, then at The King's School, Canterbury, and then straight into the British Army before going out to India. I had also picked up some pretty low, but amusing, habits and enjoyed associating with all the wrong, but exotic, women that I had met during my overseas service.

*

It had all started with a standard lecture (at the 10th Gurkha Rifles Regimental Centre in India), which the commanding officer gave to all young officers, on the dangers of associating with the local Eurasian women. Indian women were absolutely out, and not even mentioned, but I still remember the first Indian woman I danced with in Bombay, and how surprised I was at the amount of bare flesh under her sari.

As ECOs (Emergency Commissioned Officers), we did not suffer from quite the same restraints as the regular officers and it was a fact of life in India that there were few attractive British women, while a great many of the Eurasian women were absolutely beautiful.

★

It is the hypocrisy that exists in Britain, even today, that I dislike the most. My present wife is an Indian, a Christian and a South African. Ironically, she has never been to India or worn a sari in her life. During the recent Pamella Bordes affair, when the media were having their fun daily, it was almost impossible for my wife to go out alone without the locals shouting across the street, asking 'How's Pamella today?' Big joke! And this in a so-called multi-racial area of central London! It didn't stop even when she was taking our daughter of five and a half to school.

It is a fact that since we returned from South Africa to get married in 1983 (I wanted my daughter to be born in Britain so she will automatically get a British passport), my wife has suffered far more racial insults on the streets of London than she ever had to put up with on the streets of Durban.

Of course the Kinnocks and their hard-left buddies have never admitted how racist most Labour and trade union members were. I learnt this when listening to NCOs and other ranks airing their views on Egyptians, Indians and the like in both Cairo and Fayid.

Kinnock, of course, has had no military service, but he was still very foolish to provoke the armed drunken African NCO on a trip to Zimbabwe, and lucky not to have been shot. Many people have been shot in similar circumstances and being head of the Labour Party then would not necessarily have saved him. Africans in such circumstances are notoriously unpredictable.

War taught all of us some very important lessons in life and clearly showed us just how thin a veneer our civilisation has. Money had no value in Italy: everything was bartered, from cigarettes to soap. I was lucky, as some of our Gurkhas did not smoke and I was regularly able to exchange their cigarettes for chocolates. So when I went on leave to Rome I always had plenty of cigarettes, and they were all I needed to cover my expenses while I was on leave.

I have never met so many countesses as I did in Rome, in fact it seemed to me that every other woman in Rome called herself a countess. I often wondered what the Germans thought of it, and whether they were just as impressed as we were at the start. In the end it just meant exchanging more cigarettes than was usual.

Although I am making no excuses for my two failed marriages, there is no doubt that my wartime experiences made a stable relationship much more difficult, especially as I had found that many of the girls who were frowned upon socially were far more generous-spirited than their so-called 'respectable' sisters.

What came out of it all in the end, linked together with my thirty-five years in Africa, is a very deep feeling that God is far more welcoming to sinners who truly repent than to those who like to call themselves Christians but preach hatred and seem to delight in stirring up racial tension between black and white.

Although I had a religious background at The King's School – I was confirmed there by the then Archbishop of Canterbury, Dr Cosmo Lang – and I was brought up at home by very religious grandparents, I could not say I was a very good Christian. In fact it was only when I was in great danger in Italy that I really prayed properly, and the same applied in Africa later, in similarly dangerous circumstances. But this has never changed my view that we all have a part to play in God's plans, although we may not recognise it at the time. It may well be only a small part, but everything is important in God's eyes and I don't think it is a coincidence that I was spared, while others who were much better Christians than I died in Africa. I believe my task is to write of my multiracial experiences in Africa and to follow the lead given by Kathleen Corbett and Karl Borgin in their excellent book: *The Destruction of a Continent*.

I believe that more and more of us will come forward to write a more balanced and true account of what really went on in Africa after the end of World War II, about how tragic and unnecessary most of the bloodshed was, and how stupidity and ignorance about the real issue in Africa, namely the unrelenting drive of the communists to take over the whole of Southern Africa, including South Africa, have contributed so much to the present disastrous situation, with South Africa surrounded by Marxist African states.

At some stage the present double standards adopted towards South Africa will have to change, and more appreciation be given to the reforms that are already taking place there. How can countries like India be so sanctimonious towards South Africa when it is completely unable to solve its own, far worse, problems? These are caused largely by the Hindu caste system, which affects the lives of millions of untouchables, as it has done for centuries.

What is also conveniently forgotten in Europe is that South Africa is more devoutly Christian than most of Europe or America. They would be well advised to attend to their ever-growing Aids and drugs problems, as well as the breakdown in law and order which seems to be increasing the whole time in the West, and leave South Africa to solve its own problems.

★

I had now started to make more frequent visits to the Royal British Legion's jobs section and I was soon taken on as a trainee manager by the British firm Booth & Co. Ltd, an offshoot of the Booth's South American Shipping Line, with tanneries in the UK and the USA. After about a year's training I would be going out to Tanganyika to open up their new hides and skins branch at Mwanza, on the shores of Lake Victoria. My training entailed working in their tanneries in Nottingham and Abingdon and then returning to London to work in the head office.

Just before leaving London I had a brush with the past. I used to go fairly regularly to the Overseas League, near Green Park, as it was full of women members wanting to meet people from overseas, and the weekly dances were cheap and quite amusing. Near the League one morning I met one of the Bicknell girls, with whom I used to play tennis in Felixstowe. I think it was the younger one, Mary. She was now working in London, but the childhood days seemed to me to be from a different life and I never followed things up – nor went back to Felixstowe – as my grandmother had moved away.

★

Soon I was off to Nottingham to learn all about the leather trade, and very fascinating I found it to work right through the factory, from the raw goatskins to the glacé kid finish of the leather in a variety of colours for men's and women's shoes.

In the raw skin department I learnt about some of the dangers of handling goatskins from Africa, notably anthrax – which can lie dormant in a skin for months and be absolutely deadly. One of the factory graders had an unbandaged cut hand which came into contact with an anthrax-infected skin and he died in hospital within forty-eight hours. Strict precautions were brought into the factory and no one with a cut hand was, thereafter, allowed to work with raw skins. Before we ate lunch, and before we left work in the evenings, we all had to wash our hands in a strong solution of Dettol.

Later, in Tanganyika, I always kept to these precautions if I had been handling raw skins. Outbreaks of anthrax were a fairly frequent occurrence in most parts of Africa, including Tanganyika. However, in colonial times every efficient government department made sure that any animals with anthrax were burnt, including the skins. Very few got out of Africa in those days but, with the shambles in Africa today, it is a very different story.

A large proportion of the goatskins handled by the tannery came from Nigeria, and were named after the places they came from. This evoked memories of old letters I had received from my father from places whose names I still remember to this day: Maiduguri, Sokoto, Kaduna, Kano and Bauchi among them.

Like the army, there were unpleasant jobs to be done in the tannery and we knew that we, as trainee managers, would be detailed to do the dirty jobs sooner rather than later. The workmen delighted in telling us about the worst job in the tannery, which was to clean a large outside tank which gave off a pretty strong smell, and how, if you were careless enough to slip or fall, you wouldn't get rid of the smell for days. The job entailed cleaning out the tank after loading into a lorry all the pieces that had been trimmed off the goatskins once all the hair had been soaked off. These included bits of hooves and gristle – everything unwanted was thrown into the outside tank.

Sure enough, the next time one of the lorries came from the clear gum manufacturers we were put on the job and, although everything was cleaned and boiled, I could never eat a clear gum again. The stench when cleaning the tank afterwards was pretty awful. It was quite amusing when going home in the evening: nobody would come near us on the bus and it took a really good scrub in the bath to get rid of the smell.

We were soon to have our first experience of the 'English Disease' in industry when one of the union representatives in the tannery somehow found out that none of the trainee managers were union members, and immediately called the whole tannery out on strike. After two or three days of talks with the management they agreed to go back to work, when a time limit of three or four months was put on our stay at the tannery.

Soon I was on the move again, to Abingdon near Oxford, where the tannery handled mainly sheepskins for gloves and coats. It was just as interesting, and a lot cleaner than the Nottingham tannery. I can't remember handling any cattle hides in the UK but on my way to Tanganyika I got off the boat in Mombasa and went up to Nairobi by train. Our East African head office was based in Nairobi and about thirty miles away, at Thika, the company had bought a tannery that handled predominantly hides. I spent some time there before returning to Mombasa and catching another boat to Dar es Salaam.

From Abingdon I was sent to the firm's head office, in the Strand, London, where I learnt all about the bookwork involved in the business. I also attended London's School of Oriental and African Studies, where I learnt Swahili, the lingua franca of most of East Africa and the Belgian Congo.

★

Once I knew I was going to Africa, and Tanganyika appealed to me particularly as an ex-German colony, I knew I would have to get married before I left for Africa, although my wife would not be able to come until I had fixed up accommodation in Mwanza.

I knew, from friends in the Indian Army who had been to Africa and from my father, that the style of life in Africa was much the same as in India except, of course, it was much rougher since there wasn't the same kind of money in Africa, except in South Africa.

Everything in the colonies revolved around married life and it was not much fun in most parts of Africa being a bachelor, as opportunities to meet women were few. So, all in all, it was much more sensible to be married, and much safer. There was no Aids problem in Africa then but the VD rate, especially in East Africa, was absolutely astronomical.

It was common for the ex-Gurkhas I knew on leave in London to swap girlfriends' addresses, and it certainly made it safer. I had been taking out one of the more attractive ones, Betty, who had come from Wales, Swansea in fact, and now worked in a central London hotel as private secretary to the manager. Shortly before leaving for Tanganyika we got married, holding our reception in the hotel where she worked. It was called the Mapleton Hotel, just off Leicester Square, and it has long since closed. We spent our honeymoon in Dublin.

Life in London in those days, from 1947 to 1948, was pretty cheap by today's standards. We had a very pleasant flat in South Kensington and, with both of us working, we lived very well.

★

In India I had met a sub-collector in the Indian Civil Service. There they made no bones about it and collectors did just that – collected taxes. I think he was a friend of a fellow Gurkha or a school chum. Anyway, he was going away on short leave and offered me his house for ten days or so, for free. I had been absolutely amazed at how grandly he lived. There were at least five or six servants and quite a few polo ponies that had to be exercised. Indoors everything seemed to be made of marble, including a huge indoor swimming pool.

I didn't expect East African standards to be as high, but I was still a bit shocked at the way most district officers and district commissioners lived. In comparison to India, it was abject poverty, except for the buildings that the Germans had built during their days in Tanganyika before World War I.

The Kaiserhof in Kigoma had been built for a visit by the German Kaiser before World War I. There were also quite a few castles and forts scattered over the countryside, which were very much more impressive than those built later by the PWD (Public Works Department).

But, of course, it must be remembered that, even by African standards, Tanganyika was a very poor country and must, even then, have cost the British taxpayer quite a lot of money. Since Tanganyika joined with Zanzibar to become Tanzania, and got its independence, I suspect it costs the British taxpayer even more.

Appendix One

A Business Times Survey January 28, 1990

JOHN WHITE ... great-grandfather the founder

Still in the family 100 years on

ONE of SA's oldest owner-owned freight forwarding companies celebrates its centenary this year.

Lockhead, White & Womersley still serves one of its original clients, Cape Town leather importer J Woodhead & Sons.

Present manager John White recalls another owner-owned freight forwarding concern, AJ Keeler, which celebrated its 100th anniversary some years ago before being taken into Union Corporation and subsequently the Grindrod fold.

Mr White's great-grandfather Greenwood White came to Cape Town from England in 1878 and trekked to Kimberley in 1889.

In 1905 Greenwood White moved offices to Port Elizabeth where he could more conveniently tackle the customs clearing and transport arrangements required by his clients.

In 1971 G White & Sons amalgamated with two other Port Elizabeth shipping and forwarding agents set up in the 1890s, Lockhead Limited and Palmer Womersley.

John White is chairman of the Transvaal Association of Freight Forwarders.

Foreign &
Commonwealth
Office

London SW1A 2AH

Telephone: 071-

NIGERIAN ADMINISTRATIVE SERVICE. POLITICAL

Edgar Stanley Walsh: Nigeria 1919 - 1941
(As recorded in Nigeria Staff lists)

Edgar Stanley Walsh, Captain (Honorary)

Date of Birth:	26 December 1893
Educated:	Bradford Grammar School & Downing College, Cambridge
Military Service:	12 September 1914-24 July 1919 Mentioned in Despatches, November 1918

1919	Listed as Assistant District Officer, Northern Province. Appointed 27/8/1919 (Probationer £500 per annum) Class IV.
1927	Listed as Administrative officer Class III
1932	Recorded as having passed intermediate standard language exam: in Hausa.*
1936	Listed as Acting Resident. Posted to Kabba.**
1937	Listed as Administrative officer Class II. Posted to Bauchi.**
1940	Listed as posted to Zaria.** Last recorded posting before retirement.

Notes. * Hamitic language of the Hausa from Northern Nigeria.
** All towns in the Nothern Province of Nigeria.

Further correspondence on this subject should quote ODO (AWARDS)

THE WAR OFFICE,
STANMORE,
MIDDX.

5 July, 1951.

Sir,

1. I am directed to inform you that His Majesty the King has been graciously pleased to approve the following award to you :-

The Military Cross.

Authority, London Gazette dated 29th June, 1951.

2. In order that the award may be entered on your Record of Service you should show this letter to your Commanding Officer for publication of the occurrence in Part II/III Orders.

3. A further communication will be addressed to you shortly regarding the presentation of the award.

I am, Sir,
Your obedient Servant,

[signature] Col

for Director of Personnel Administration.

Lieut. E.P. Walsh, MC, (360738) RA,
c/o HQ, No.1 Independent Field Records,
British Army Post Office 5.

MILITARY CROSS

Lieutenant Edward Paul WALSH

45 Fd. Regt. R.A.

On the night of 22nd and 23rd April 1951, Lieutenant WALSH was an Artillery Forward Observer with the Belgian Battalion attached to 29 Infantry Brigade. His Observation Post was on a hill occupied by C. Company and some little distance from the remainder of the unit. During the night the enemy put in a heavy attack all along the line and more especially on this hill, which they managed to surround. All that night and the following day Lieutenant WALSH remained in wireless touch with the guns and though wounded in the head, called down accurate Artillery fire on the enemy, who were at times only a few yards from the Belgian positions. Without this support it is doubtful if the Company could have held out. Lieutenant WALSH's coolness and devotion to duty not only saved a dangerous situation but proved a magnificent example to his comrades.

Place and date	)	River Imjin, Korea
of deeds	)	22nd and 23rd April 1951

P.O. BOX-POSBUS 1014
DURBAN 4000
TELEPHONE-TELEFOON
300-6015

DURBAN

MAYOR'S PARLOUR
KANTOOR VAN DIE BURGEMEESTER

3rd July, 1989

REF: M P 18/15/ 1

Mr. M. Walsh
Victory Services Club
63/79 Seymour Street
LONDON W2 2HF
England

Dear Mr. Walsh,

Thank you for your very interesting letter dated 20 June, 1989.

At the outset let me say how pleased I am to hear of your fine efforts in promoting South Africa. With the terrible publicity we get in the outside world we certainly could do with the support organisations such as yours lend our country.

Any book by an ex-serviceman who passed through Durban during the war years must, of course, contain something about that magnificent "Lady in White", Perla Siedle Gibson.

I have been able to acquire two suitable photographs for you and some notes from our Local History Museum which I am enclosing herewith.

As a matter of interest the Administrator of Natal, Mr. Radclyffe Cadman, recently opened a new wing at the Highway Hospice in Durban which was named "The Perla Siedle Gibson Wing", in honour of this very special lady.

Yours sincerely,

D W Watterson

COUNCILLOR D. W. WATTERSON, J. P.
MAYOR

ENCLS.

PERLA SIDDLE GIBSON - "THE LADY IN WHITE"

Perla was born in 1888, the daughter of pioneer Natal shipping magnate Otto Siedle. She married Air Sergeant Jack Gibson in 1917 and they had three children, Roy, Barrie and Joy. Lt. Roy Gibson was killed in action in Italy during the Second World War; Mr Barrie Gibson resides in Durban (at 250 Chelmsford Road, where his parents had lived and died) and her daughter, Mrs H.F. Liddiard has settled in England. Perla was widowed some time in the 'fifties. She died on the 6th March, 1971 and a memorial plaque, presented by the officers and men of the Royal Navy, was erected on the North Pier and unveiled on the 22nd February 1973.

Internationally known as "The Lady in White", Perla's wharfside work started on the 16th April, 1940 when, as she put it, one morning dressed in her tea-stained canteen uniform she was washing cups at the back of a dockside canteen, when an Irish lad whom the family had entertained, coo-eed across the water, "Please sing something Irish", and, cupping her hands to her mouth, she sang "When Irish Eyes are Smiling". The reaction was amazing. The boys cheered and clapped and would not let her stop. Later she was given a special permit and sang across the water to the convoys, (over 1 000 troopships and 300 hospital ships) during the war years, singing at any time and in all weathers. She became a legendary figure to the troops, an essential part of arrival and departure at the Durban quay, in her white canteen uniform, red hat and red scarf. She sang through a megaphone, a gift from the survivors of the torpedoed "Llandaff Castle".

After the war she continued to sing to naval vessels and indeed was preparing to welcome the British submarine (H.M.S. Anchorite) in 1968 when she met with an accident that caused her to lose an eye. She was then 79.

Mrs Gibson had a distinguished career as a singer and in addition was an excellent artist and had studied both subjects in England and in Germany and also in New York. She was an excellent pianist too - in fact art and music were her main interests.

Perla Siedle Gibson was an Honorary Moth and a member of the Contemptible Shellhole, in recognition of her war work, and her name is included in Durban's Civil Honours List. On visits to Europe she was presented to the late King, the Queen Mother and twice to the present Queen.

16/8/98

To MR. M. WALSH,
16, QUEENSBOROUGH TERRACE.
LONDON, W2 3SS.

6 December 1985

Ministry of Defence,
Army Medal Office,
Government Office Buildings,
DROITWICH, Worcs.
WR9 8AU.

Issue Voucher Number 7102

Authority D/MEDALS/2/59

The under-mentioned Awards have been issued to you this day.

You are requested to acknowledge receipt hereon, **in ink**, and to return this paper in the enclosed pre-paid envelope.

If any Award cannot be delivered to the person for whom it is intended, it is requested that it may be returned by registered post.

OLD — RECEIVED — FOLD

Awards and Ribbons		For
No.	Description	
1	ITALY STAR	EC 8252
		LT.
1	DEFENCE MEDAL	MICHAEL
		WALSH
1	WAR MEDAL 1939-45	
		INDIAN ARMY
	WITH COVERING LETTER.	

TO BE SIGNED AND RETURNED WITHOUT DELAY

Signature .... Address ....

Date ....

WAP 15133—201 665743/M704367 4,000 bks. 9/69 Grp. 712

Mystery . . . Jane has medical experts baffled

Disease is named after me

Exclusive by MICHAEL O'FLAHERTY

JANE Boorman shines with courage. Vivacious and sporting, she was stricken with a mystery disease so rare that doctors are naming it after her.

Dark-haired Jane, 29, sat in her country cottage yesterday and spoke of the terrible illness which has changed her life.

From a keen skier, swimmer, horse riding enthusiast and tennis player, as well as taking part in amateur dramatics, she became suddenly paralysed.

Yet still, with smiles and depths of bravery which make her parents and doctors eye her with wonder, she fights back.

"They now call it Boorman's Disease, because nobody really knows what it is or what has caused it," says Jane.

The illness first struck after the October hurricane of 1987. Jane thought she had a virus. Then she had terrible pains in the joints and couldn't walk.

"I was like that for seven months and because of it I lost my job as a marketing manager for Ford," says Jane from her home in Wadhurst, Sussex.

"A year later, they decided I had Lupus — then there was a deviation and my eyes did not synchronise properly.

"This was very frightening. I was put on steroids and the pains went away and I was able to go back to work."

The disease struck again last year. "I suddenly had this stroke, for want of a better word," she says.

"The doctors say it was strictly not a stroke, but all the symptoms were there.

"They had absolutely no idea why I had it. All their tests showed nothing wrong, but I was paralysed down my right side.

"I began to get better, then in December I had another one.

"I am still paralysed to a certain extent. I have little or no use of my hands and have difficulty walking, but I go to the gym regularly and have chemotherapy.

"The specialist in London told my parents that he could only call it Boorman's Disease because there was no real name for it.

"I have been called many things in my life, but never a disease," laughs the brave young woman.

Overseas Development Administration,
Pensions Department, att: Mrs S.M.Irvine,
Abercrombie Hse, Eaglesham Road,
East Kilbride, Glasgow. G75 8EA.

M.Walsh,
16 Queensborough Terrace,
London W2 3SS.
30 September 1989.

Re: My Claim for WWII War Disablement Pension.

Dear Mrs Irvine,

Your letter of the 29 August 1989 enclosing my WWII War disablement gratuity of £2426.00 is acknowledged with thanks.

I am sure you will appreciate, from the correspondence that started with the ODA in 1986, that the amount of the gratuity is not so important as the fact that all these years later, over 45 years to be precise, I have received some compensation & acknowledgement for the lack of proper medical treatment at Lucknow, India in 1943 when I was " completely paralysed ".

Nothing of course can compensate for the veiled insinuations of certain IMS doctors that I was malingering and I still believe it was only the fact that I had volunteered for the army before conscription was brought in in UK that stopped these insinuations going any further.

In fact the above explains why I did not bother to collect the medals I had earned later , the hard way, in Italy with the 2/10 Gurkha Rifles, part of the 43 Indpt. Gurkha Lorried Brigade, until after I returned to Britain from Africa in 1983.

Once again many thanks for your department's help in this matter.

Yours sincerely,

M.Walsh.

Please read the notes overleaf and detach this counterfoil before presenting voucher below.
Please keep this counterfoil.

Issued by
The Overseas Development Administration
Abercrombie House
Eaglesham Road
East Kilbride GLASGOW G75 8EA

ODA

24 AUG 89 T

Tax Code NT

When writing to Overseas Development, please quote 303568/001

M WALSH

Pension or Deduction Description	Taxable Amounts	Non-Taxable Amounts	Totals
IND DISABILITY PENS		£2426.00	£2426.00
TOTALS:	£0.00	£2426.00	£2426.00

Part Two

East Africa: 1948–1959

Chapter One

The Early Days in Tanganyika

In 1948 it was a very different departure from Britain: no troopship this time but a small, very comfortable BI Line boat going to East Africa via the Suez Canal. As we made our leisurely way through the canal, I could see part of the huge British military camp at Fayid, which brought back quite a few wartime memories.

The other passengers were mainly colonial civil servants, returning either from home leave in Britain or from wartime service. Few of them had any interest in talking about anything except postings, promotions or whether I had come across 'old so-and-so', who had also served in the Indian Army. There were a few missionaries and businessmen, but we were a small minority.

This mix of passengers was indicative of one of the reasons for the tragedy that was to befall colonial Africa. Few of the colonial civil servants I met on board, or later in Africa, had any knowledge of, or interest in, commercial life. Their attitude seemed to be: 'Let's leave trade to the Indians. They know so much more than we do about the sordid process of making money.'

British colonial policy towards commerce was to encourage a very few multinational firms to control trade, almost on a monopoly basis: 'Much less trouble for us this way, old boy!' These huge firms' main interest in Africa was to make money, and they did not seem to care much about the damage they might cause to the lifestyle of the local people.

But nothing could spoil the euphoria of my mood as I began to study the maps of East Africa. Even the names – Dar es Salaam, Nairobi, Kampala, Kigoma, Bukoba and Mwanza – had a romantic ring. I was amazed at the size of Lake Victoria, where I would be living. Mwanza was an important port on the lake, and the rail link connected it with Dar es Salaam.

The biggest excitement of all was knowing that, very shortly, I would be able to see Africa's fabulous herds of big game. When I actually saw some of these herds, however, I was staggered by the vast numbers of animals – a sight for which I was totally unprepared, and one I would never forget.

*

I got off the ship at Mombasa and went by train to Nairobi, to report my arrival to our East African head office there. Visits to the company's tannery at Thika, about thirty miles from Nairobi, gave me a chance to see some of Kenya's countryside. Some of the areas were strikingly beautiful: I particularly liked the Ngong Hills and Muthaiga Club areas around Nairobi.

Although I much admired what I saw and heard of the Masai, and their reluctance to have anything to do with European ways, it was obvious even then that they were going to lose out to the Kikuyu, who knew the value of learning from the Europeans, so that they could take over when the country gained its independence.

Although my first visit to Nairobi was, of necessity, fairly short, it was impossible not to notice the snobbery of certain sections of the white community and their obsession with the goings-on of Kenya's Happy Valley set. I certainly hadn't come to Africa to be any part of a transported British class system.

Even during this first short trip to Nairobi I think I knew that I had chosen the right place when I opted to go to Mwanza in Tanganyika. Few in the firm could understand my choice since the supposedly more desirable Nairobi, Kampala and Kisumu branches were all available at the time. But to me the big advantage of Mwanza was its distance from head office in Nairobi. The remoteness meant that I would be my own boss in most things and this autonomy later influenced my decision to open up my own business.

Those days were still far in the future but I suspected, even then, that the fewer Europeans there were in the rural parts of Africa the better for everybody – and so it proved in Tanganyika. With only some five thousand Europeans, there was never any trouble, but it didn't take Julius Nyerere long to wreck the economy with his African socialism, after independence.

*

I returned to Mombasa to board another BI Line boat for the last stage of my journey to Tanganyika, and a short stop at Tanga only whetted my appetite for my first sight of Dar es Salaam. I wasn't disappointed.

The deserted beaches, palm trees and many dhows showed the Arab influence, all the way from Mombasa down the east coast to Dar.

Soon we were in the harbour, but in those days there were no berths and no quays. The area around the boat was a mass of small craft and soon my tin boxes, retained from my Indian Army days, were being lowered down into the shipping company's small wooden boat. Fate was smiling on me that day, as I followed my luggage down the side of the ship, for the sea was fairly calm and the weather good. I couldn't help wondering how different it would have been in bad weather.

As the Africans rowed me ashore, I began to feel some of the excitement that Livingstone, Speke and Stanley must have felt at their first sight of Dar es Salaam, and I didn't think things had changed much since their time. They probably went ashore in exactly the same kind of small boat. But conditions would have been a lot more dangerous as, in their day, Arabs still controlled the port (from Zanzibar) and, having landed, those early explorers had to walk as they made their way across Africa.

Dar es Salaam did not have much to recommend it, and the climate was very hot and sticky. It was much too like Bombay for comfort and, in fact, I was soon suffering from prickly heat again. I was glad to get on the first train going to Mwanza, on the shores of Lake Victoria – the biggest lake in Africa.

The train from Dar to Mwanza took between two and a half and three days at that time. It was a very slow, wood-burning train and, which surprised me, had a European train driver. In India most of the train drivers, and other key railway staff, were Eurasians.

The journey was an ideal introduction to Africa. The slow pace seemed to sum up life as it should be lived there: slow and sure and unlike the frenetic pace of the West. Slowly we passed through places I remember to this day: Morogoro, Dodoma and Tabora. There the railway line branches, one fork leading to Kigoma on Lake Tanganyika (near Ujiji, where Stanley found Livingstone sick with fever in an African hut), the other going on via Shinyanga to Mwanza.

My lasting impression was of vast empty space, so unlike the terrible overcrowding in India. But now the warning signs are there. As Dr Borgin points out, in *The Destruction of a Continent*, Africa's population will double in the next twenty years: from 450 million to 900 million! As it is, Tanzania and other African countries cannot feed their existing populations without massive annual aid from the West. Dr Borgin also warns of the dangers of this aid dependence.

★

All too soon the train was pulling into Mwanza station, not a very impressive place. When I asked one of the old Africa hands on the train about a taxi, he laughed and pointed to a line of Africans outside the station. Eventually all my belongings were balanced on African heads (I agreed to pay extra for the heavy tin trunks) and we set off, in Livingstone style, down the dusty road leading to the only hotel in town.

Mwanza Hotel was a shock, a really appalling place run by a genial Greek, George Mavrikous, who just shrugged off any complaints. I remember tackling him later that first night, when I was in the bar. I complained about my bed having no sheets. He merely shrugged and said most of his customers were miners, who slept with their boots on, and he had therefore ceased to supply sheets. I can't say I fancied his blankets much either and I ended up using my own bedroll (essential when travelling in India) until I left the hotel.

Finding temporary office and storage space for the company's hides and skins business was easy, but finding accommodation for myself, so I could get out of the Mwanza Hotel, was much more difficult. Nothing had been built since before World War II and, like most places in East Africa, private housing was now in short supply.

I took my problems to Mwanza's DC (District Commissioner), Gordon Russell. When he heard of my father's colonial connections, Gordon was most helpful and arranged for me to rent a government building on the outskirts of Mwanza: at Mwanza South, near to the industrial area. It had been used in the war as an officers' transit mess. It consisted of four large rondavels, round buildings with thatched roofs and cement floors, at each corner of a large open cement veranda. It was situated about halfway up a very steep hill and enjoyed spectacular views of Lake Victoria. The mosquitoes were a bit of a problem, but I got around this later by closing in the whole veranda with mosquito gauze.

I loved it from the first moment I saw it, and looked at the view of the lake from the veranda. Even the primitive plumbing, outside lavatory and mosquitoes did not spoil the charm of the surroundings. There were tin baths still there and I fitted a Tanganyika boiler, in other words, a forty-four gallon drum cemented outside the bathroom with a pipe running through the wall. A good wood fire under the drum heated the bath water.

Somehow I don't think Betty was quite so enthusiastic when she arrived from Britain. She knew we would eventually move into a more conventional company house in Mwanza, but this was still a few years away as no building plots for houses were available.

Being colonial Africa, everything had to be done by the book, and in Dar at that! First plots had to be surveyed, then put up for commercial tender in the government gazette, and final permission to build was years away. The delay didn't worry me, however, as I loved the rondavel and was in no hurry to leave it.

Not long after we moved in, I was to learn an important lesson about Africa, and the reason why the verandas were left open. The rainy season soon started and we had our first heavy tropical storm. I had just finished closing in the whole front veranda with mosquito gauze, as the mosquitoes were a real problem and I had already had malaria quite badly twice.

I woke early in the morning after the storm and found all our carpets and other furnishings floating in a mixture of mud and water. We had built a small wall for the mosquito gauze frames and the water and mud were flowing over this. Most of our stuff was ruined and had to be thrown away, and it didn't help that it rained heavily for two more days, which delayed our enlarging and deepening the drainage furrows at the back of the house. This and a small wall on top stopped any flooding in the future.

Mwanza, in those early post-war years, was a small and friendly place, with a few retail firms from Dar starting to open branches there. In our line of business, hides and skins, our main competition was from the United Africa Company, part of Unilever, but the Indians had the place tied up commercially. They owned most of the retail shops, and their cotton and sisal factories handled most of the local produce. UAC bought the produce for export and did not have a factory in Mwanza.

Mwanza was also the business centre of the Lake Province, which was probably the most prosperous in Tanganyika. The PC (Provincial Commissioner) had a very impressive hillside residence, German-built, like most of the local government buildings. Another reminder of German days was Bismarck Rock, a well-known local feature.

The social life of the place centred around the Mwanza Club, with its tennis courts, golf course and other recreational facilities – but no swimming pool. Anyone wanting a dip in those early days had to go some miles away from Mwanza, as the area around the port was badly infected with bilharzia. In a safe part of the lake, therefore, the club had arranged a specially protected pool. It was a stretch of water surrounded by a steel frame that was firmly fixed in the water. This kept out all the crocodiles and hippos, but I believe that one day someone carelessly left the club entrance gate open and a crocodile entered the pool. Fortunately it was spotted, and removed, before anyone was hurt.

★

For some time I had to make do with hiring transport in Mwanza until Nairobi head office purchased new vehicles for all the branches and I was to fly to Nairobi on the next flight in the small weekly plane, a six-seater, to collect the new pick-up, a Chevrolet, and then drive it down to Mwanza

I was looking forward to the trip, as it would be my first chance to visit the Serengeti. It also gave me a chance to see more of the Kenyan countryside, especially some of the White Highlands with their well-run farms. Unfortunately it was raining for most of the trip through Kenya and I got stuck in the mud more than once around Kisii.

It was also my first experience of catching the Musoma ferry, a wartime landing craft which ran regularly across the Mara river and carried vehicles between Kenya and Tanganyika. Officially it was meant to run at least four times a day, but the actual schedule depended on the weather and the whims of the owner – and whether he was sober.

If such a thing were possible, the Musoma Hotel was even more appalling than the Mwanza Hotel, and about the only safe thing to drink was the bottled Tusker beer. I remember once being told to get my beer from the fridge in the dining room, and I was horrified to see that there were literally dozens of dead cockroaches in the bottom of the fridge.

The road from Musoma to Mwanza runs by the fabulous Serengeti National Park and I could scarcely believe the sight of thousands and thousands of animals, as far as the eye could see: lion, buffalo, zebra, wildebeest, impala and gazelle were seemingly everywhere. In the dry season it was possible to drive among them for hours.

The surroundings then were completely unspoilt and unexploited, with no commercial safari trucks racing each other and frightening the animals. In fact I only saw one bus on that magical first day – as well as a burnt-out car which had run into a herd of buffalo the previous night, killing the Indian driver and his wife. It was extremely dangerous to travel on this stretch of road at night in those days, as there were always animals on the road, or crossing it, but only those living in Musoma seemed to be aware of the dangers.

★

By the time I left Tanganyika, in 1959, all this was changing, and ever-increasing numbers of vehicles were using the road between Musoma and Mwanza.

Even so, as this was still before both the communists and the West had provided machine-guns and automatic rifles that were used to massacre elephants and other game in huge numbers all over Africa, there were still large herds of animals left in the Serengeti area. You cannot blame the Africans in this instance. The West and the communists are still training the drunken, undisciplined local African soldiery and guerrilla fighters, many of whom later become poachers, and they wonder in the West why all the elephants and other big game animals are being exterminated!

At least President Moi of Kenya recently had the courage to burn millions of pounds' worth of poached ivory. What a refreshing change from the days of the late President Kenyatta, whose family grew even wealthier with their ill-gotten gains from the proceeds of illegally-hunted ivory.

*

I have never regretted the hunting trips we organised to the area adjacent to the Serengeti National Park. Everything was shot on a licence and we killed only enough for meat for our own use or for a few friends.

Every now and again we were asked to entertain visitors from overseas; people on business, or friends or relatives of the Booths, who owned the company. Once, a cousin of theirs wanted me to take him hunting near the Serengeti. I think his name was Nick Wollaston and he was about my age. I lent him my rifle and, to speed things up as it was a working day and I couldn't stay away from the office too long, I had him ride outside the Chevrolet on the footplate, with the rifle in his hands. He was meant to jump off in the middle of the herd when I slowed down, as it was illegal to shoot from a vehicle. Anyway, he got so excited at the huge numbers of game animals we were passing through that he jumped off too soon and snapped the wooden butt of the rifle in two.

I had Mohamed, the son of my Arab hides and skins grader, with me and we stripped some of the canvas cover and tacks off the wooden frame on the back of the pick-up. Cutting up canvas strips, we tacked and patched up the wooden butt of the rifle so Nick could shoot. Even though the rifle buckled after each shot, he managed to get a kill or two before we returned to Mwanza.

*

At this stage, my main effort was devoted to finishing a new hides and skins godown in Mwanza South, next to the United Africa Company and almost opposite where we lived. I had taken on Mohamed's father, Abdul Kader, as head grader of hides and skins. The Arabs controlled this side of the business and Abdul had a very good reputation among the local Arab community. We all have our little quirks and Abdul was fond of telling me that he was of proper Arab stock, and that he and his family came from Aden. Being born in Zanzibar or Africa was not as good as coming from Arabia.

Abdul ran the godown when I went off in the lorry with Mohamed, to buy hides and skins in Shinyanga and other districts of the Lake Province. Some of the district traders refused to leave their businesses and insisted we came to collect. Considerable sums of money were involved, and quite a few men insisted on being paid in cash, so I had to go along to make the pay-out.

The Lake Province was a great area for hides and skins, but we and the provincial veterinary department wanted to improve the quality as soon as possible and, with the help of the chief provincial veterinary officer, Sandy Milne, we launched a campaign to change the local drying methods, from sun-dried on the ground to shade-dried in a frame.

Tragically, Sandy Milne was later killed in a plane crash on his honeymoon. The aircraft hit Mount Kilimanjaro, near the top, during a heavy tropical storm.

Basically the main problem with a sun-dried hide or skin is that the inside never dries properly, and causes trouble later in the tanning, whereas the shade-dried hide or skin dries slowly and properly in the wind and produces a high-class durable leather in the tannery. To put over the message properly, we had to pay a high price differential for all shade-dried hides and skins and this, of course, was to the benefit of everybody in the hides and skins business.

A great deal of reliance had to be placed on our Arab graders, and there was a balance to be maintained between the suppliers and what the company demanded in quality. Bribes were a way of life in the business, and it was a matter of letting your grader know, very tactfully, that you were fully aware of what was going on but you expected him to see that nothing was done to the detriment of the company.

I was extremely pleased with the work of both the Kaders and we were, in fact, the first branch to make a profit. Later, Nairobi head office took Abdul Kader and put him in charge of the Nairobi godown. Although it was a compliment to my choice of staff, I was still annoyed at losing him.

*

Improvements and other developments were encouraged in all areas of life in Tanganyika, but it was the first trip of a UN delegation, in the early fifties, that really brought home to me just how damaging the UN could be to real progress in Tanganyika.

It was compulsory for all African peasant farmers to grow a certain amount of cassava annually, as a precaution against famine. Julius Nyerere's African socialist party (Tanu) wanted to undermine the British administration as much as possible, and used the UN to insist that the growing of cassava should not be compulsory.

It was obvious to all of us that the Africans preferred to grow maize and to eat posho (Swahili for mealie-meal) and that, left to themselves, they would not grow cassava. This was understandable, since few people would consider that cassava had a gourmet taste, but it is a very nutritious root that can be stored for many years before it begins to deteriorate. It is, therefore, an ideal crop in places where the rainfall is unreliable. The world has seen the disasters that have followed the cessation of cassava cultivation. Today, despite vast sums of Western aid, Nyerere's Tanzania cannot feed itself. In colonial days famine was non-existent.

It was also accepted practice in rural Tanganyika for all Africans to work on their district roads for two or three weeks a year, to keep the minor roads open for buses, lorries and private transport. The workers' only payment was in salt, but this was more valuable to them than money. The UN madmen reckoned it was slavery and wanted the practice to stop. When Julius Nyerere forced millions of rural Africans to leave their homes in order to populate his 'model villages', rich farming lands were abandoned and the local roads deteriorated, with the result that many potentially fertile areas are now inaccessible and massive expenditure will be required if they are to be restored to their previous productivity.

For how long are we going to allow the madmen to wreck Africa? Do we want to see Africa disintegrate and starvation take over? Why do we allow them to waste our hard-earned money? How many in the West realise that African countries who contribute virtually nothing have been given a third, I repeat a third, of the UN voting power? When will the people of the West wake up and tell the politicians they have had more than enough? Will the West ever have the guts to say to Russia that part of the price for supporting glasnost and perestroika is that they get out of Africa and stop sending arms and the rest of their hardware to stir up trouble in Africa? Only then will Africa start to sort out its problems. The horrific 1991 figure of Africa's starving people – 27 million – speaks for itself.

*

I will always be grateful to Booth's, the firm that employed me, for insisting I studied Swahili in London before I went to Tanganyika, even though the high-flown variety taught at the School of Oriental and African Studies is not much used by African villagers. It did, however, provide me with a basic knowledge that was invaluable and within a few months of arrival I was able to converse quite easily with ordinary Africans.

No UN, or other so-called Western expert, should be allowed in Africa unless he can speak the language of the area. Nothing could better the colonial system in which a DO (District Officer) spent at least fifteen days a month on foot visiting, and staying in, African villages in his district.

This book is intended as a tribute not only to my father and mother, who upheld the highest traditions of the British colonial service in the Nigerian administration (Nigeria was not exactly healthy for either of them in those days: 1919–1943), but also to all those brave men and women who ventured to the remotest corners of the mighty British Empire while carrying out their duties as HM's British colonial servants.

Chapter Two

Crocodiles and their Importance

Little did I realise, in my early days in Tanganyika, the important part that crocodiles, or rather their skins, would play in my future life in Africa. It is not an exaggeration to say that I owed most of my financial success to them, and that they enabled me to travel all over East and central Africa, and to see a variety of places and people: Angola, Mozambique, the Belgian Congo, the Rhodesias and Nyasaland, before the end of the colonial era.

I was also privileged to see the awful and unnecessary stupidity of the West, as it abandoned its own kind as well as the poor peasant Africans, who never understood what Marx and Lenin and the communists had to do with their struggle for survival under the harsh conditions of rural Africa.

I saw such rivers as the Zambezi, Mara, Rufiji, Lualaba, Luapula, Luangwa, Kafue and others too numerous to mention, and such lakes as Victoria, Tanganyika, Nyasa (now Malawi), Bangweulu and Kariba, as well as the Okavango swamps.

I visited towns such as Nairobi, Kampala, Entebbe, Élisabethville, Kolwezi, Usumbura, Lourenço Marques, Beira, Bulawayo and Salisbury – their names mostly changed since colonial days and their once-prosperous economies wrecked in the name of African socialism, or rather communism. Now they are kept going only with massive annual aid, not from the communists but from the West. The stupidity of what was allowed to happen is mind-boggling!

⋆

At the beginning few of us had much idea of the value of crocodile skins, or how they were hunted. Then, in Mwanza, I met a German called Dekker who had hunted crocodiles on Lake Victoria before the war, and he and others, like Eric Nawotny, taught me the most economical way of killing the creatures.

This was to use a hook about the size and shape of a shark hook. This was wrapped in (mainly) crocodile meat, as bait – a little carbide inside the meat helped to keep the crocodile floating. The hook was attached to a flexible steel cable, to stop the crocodile biting through the sisal rope that was attached to it as well, and a light piece of the local balsa wood was used as a float to mark the position of the hook.

Then all that was necessary was to go around checking the hooks. Most of the smaller crocodiles could be killed with an axe blow to the head; only the larger ones needed to be shot.

I went out hunting with Dekker and others, and saw for myself the great number of crocodiles that were around by day in Smith's Sound and on the other side of the lake. So I informed my head office in Nairobi that there would be a large supply of crocodile skins as soon as a regular overseas market had been fixed up. Skins could be obtained regularly from hunters like Dekker and Nawotny, and I could add to the supply by encouraging the local African fishermen to put out hooks near their camps.

★

To give the reader some idea of the number of crocodiles around Mwanza in those days, at least one hundred and fifty people were killed each year in the Tanganyikan part of Lake Victoria, and probably as many again were killed in the Ugandan and Kenyan parts of the lake.

We moved into our new hides and skins godown at Mwanza South, which was near to the lake, and I was called out on numerous occasions to try and save African women who had been taken by crocodiles while washing their clothes in the lake. Although I fired a shot or two into the water as a gesture, I never saw anything more than a few bubbles as the unfortunate victim was dragged under the water and drowned.

I had my first close encounter with a crocodile while I was collecting crocodile eggs for hatching out at home. I used to keep them in one of the spare tin baths before my wife came out from England. Betty objected to having them in the next bath and I had to move them to the godown.

The nests with the crocodile eggs were normally on a bank in fairly thick cover and I used the runway to the lake to guide me to the eggs. This particular runway had a bend and I could not see the nest, so I started crawling along it. Then I heard a noise in front and suddenly saw the crocodile coming towards me, at speed. I just had time to turn and dive for the boat, which had drifted out a bit, when the crocodile hit the water not far from me. Adrenalin aided, I was in the boat before Dekker had even fired! My swinging into the boat upset his aim and he missed the creature.

Later, after Gerald Chopra (his father, the Hon. I.C. Chopra, QC, was Williamson's diamond mine legal adviser) and my wife had formed a company to handle all the crocodile business in Mwanza, we (Gerald and his wife, Betty and myself) used to go sailing quite often. One evening, fairly late, we were on our way back to the Mwanza Yacht Club when we hit a sudden squall which turned the boat over. Fortunately it was quite close to shore, but it still took us two to three hours of pushing and paddling, with the help of the wind, to get to water shallow enough to push the boat the rest of the way to shore.

I don't think the others were aware of just how many crocodiles there were in the area, but I told them to splash and make as much noise as possible. We were also extremely fortunate that we eventually came ashore at one of the very few sandy beaches between my godown at Mwanza South and Mwanza itself. Most of the rest of the shoreline was covered in thick reeds, which provided a favourite place for the crocodiles to lurk while waiting for their prey.

*

Dekker had told me about a pile of crocodile skins that he had stored at the start of World War II, having been unable to export them in time. This made the skins about ten years old, and I told him it was unlikely that they would still be in good enough condition to sell. However, he said he had used a German preservative called Merpin and, when he had examined them from time to time, they had seemed all right except for a few at the top of the pile. Eventually he persuaded me to go to Ukerewe Island, not far from Mwanza, where he had the skins stored. I certainly never believed they would be of any commercial value after all those years, and I was amazed to see their condition. The top few had scale-slip, a sure sign they were going rotten, but the Merpin, mixed with the damp salt, had kept the rest in almost perfect condition. They were in a well-ventilated thatched hut with a cement floor, which must also have helped in preserving them.

In the end we worked out a deal together, but I told him it would be unwise to include more than ten per cent in my consignments at the start until we found out if any complaints were going to come back. In the event there were none. The overseas tanner was, in fact, very satisfied with the quality of the crocodile skins from Booth's Mwanza branch.

With my initial profits from the Dekker skins, I started to get hundreds of crocodile hooks made, together with all the other materials needed. By the time head office in Nairobi had arranged overseas contracts, the crocodile skins were beginning to roll in and many of our hides and skins customers by the lake were given hooks (and other equipment), so that, with my own African camps that I had set up near the fishermen's camps, we were really in business. I know Nairobi were surprised at the number of crocodile skins I was sending them monthly.

Soon I was earning more in a week than I was paid monthly by the company, and the same applied to the Africans, as they had only to catch one large crocodile to earn more than they got in a month for their fish. The only snag I found was that, once they had been paid for one or two skins, the Africans would go off and spend the proceeds, so when I came back the following week I found no skins.

The company wanted monthly estimates of the approximate number of crocodile skins they could expect. This I found easy to assess with the European hunters, but my African estimates used to vary alarmingly although I was organising more and more African camps the whole time. In the end I had to refuse to supply any of the African camps which did not produce a certain number of crocodile skins every month. Most of the camps had to be supplied with everything on credit, which meant I had an ever-increasing outlay. They now expected food as well as salt for the skins, and I had the cost of delivering the supplies as well as collecting the skins.

*

Gerald Chopra was a lawyer, like his father. His mother was English and he had been educated at public school and university in England. He qualified as a lawyer and returned to Mwanza not long after I had arrived, and we got on well from the start.

I found I had very little in common with the majority of the colonial civil servants, most of whom were middle-aged and had spent the war years in Tanganyika. There were, of course, some notable exceptions. Gordon Russell, Mwanza's DC, was one: he was far too independent to please his superiors, so he had little chance of promotion and took early retirement. Peter Haynes, the DC in Kibondo, was another.

Later I met John Gaunt, our MP in Lusaka (in what was then Northern Rhodesia). He had been a DC in Northern Rhodesia before his retirement and he later became Ian Smith's UDI Minister of Mines. I had hunted crocodiles with his son, Denis, and he went out of his way to help me when I had trouble with the Angolan authorities, as well as with the immigration authorities in Northern Rhodesia.

When I left Tanganyika, I just moved down to Northern Rhodesia without completing any official formalities. Like most World War II ex-servicemen, I held the view that I had earned the right, the hard way, to move anywhere I wanted to in British Africa. Some petty little Northern Rhodesian immigration officer did not agree and tried to make things awkward. I needed John Gaunt's help to sort things out.

Chapter Three

Tanganyika Groundnuts Scheme

With all the talk and post-mortems about the failure of the Groundnuts Scheme in Tanganyika, there has never been a satisfactory explanation of why pilot schemes were not carried out in the three areas chosen: Kongwa, Tabora and Nachingwea, before large-scale planting was attempted.

Although there were plenty of scurrilous tales circulating locally about the part the United Africa Company (part of the multinational firm Unilever) had played in the scheme, I don't think the experts who chose the areas for planting the groundnuts can be blamed for the failure. I believe it was more a matter of the blind leading the blind.

What cannot be denied is that there were, at the time, literally mountains of groundnuts in northern Nigeria that could not be moved, because the Nigerian railways hadn't sufficient rolling stock to transport them. It is also a fact that UAC, or whatever it was called in Nigeria, knew the exact amounts there – it was its business to know such things.

Surely, in view of the world shortage after World War II, it was in everybody's interest to move the existing mountains of groundnuts before starting to produce more with the Tanganyika Groundnuts Scheme? It is hard to believe that even a British Labour government, if it had all the facts, would have been too stupid to work this out. But it is a fact that there has never been a satisfactory explanation as to why the Nigerian groundnuts were ignored.

Local farmers, and certain friends I had in the Agricultural Department, were at a complete loss as to why they were not asked to clear and plant just enough ground for a small pilot scheme in each of the chosen areas, using the type of machinery that was to be used for the scheme. Yet again, no satisfactory explanation has ever been given as to why there was no small-scale trial of the proposed methods before the scheme was put into full operation, nor has it been explained why the proponents of the scheme were not asked to produce rainfall figures for previous years. Anyone living in the vicinity could have told the authorities that both Kongwa and Tabora fell into a notoriously bad rainfall area, where drought conditions were not unusual.

But the whole crux of the matter, for most of us in Tanganyika, was why it was considered necessary to bring in large numbers of Europeans to grow a crop that the African farmers were already growing successfully in many areas of Tanganyika.

All we considered necessary to increase the yield of groundnuts was to ask district commissioners in all the growing areas how much extra land could be used if machinery and staff were sent to clear the land and plough, ready for planting by the African farmer. This preparatory work could have been done free and the machinery moved from district to district. Doing it this way was too easy for the politicians and, of course, it lacked the grandiose madness of losing billions of pounds of the British taxpayers' money.

Some of this madness comes to light when one studies the figures of the Europeans employed on the staff of the Groundnuts Scheme, mostly in a non-productive capacity. At one time there were 1,283 people in administration and only 384 staff employed by the construction company who were doing the actual clearing and levelling of the ground! To add to the idiocy, few of the European supervisors had any experience of African conditions and few spoke Swahili.

During this period I met quite a few of the staff employed on the Groundnuts Scheme. A lot of them were ex-servicemen with no real interest in Africa. Their only motive was to make as much money as possible before the inevitable end of the scheme.

It certainly didn't help, either, when trade union practices were brought in by the socialist bosses in the UK, who had no idea of labour conditions in Tanganyika. As a result, African wages soared in the areas surrounding the Groundnuts Scheme, which brought disastrous inflation for those of the local population who were not employed on the scheme. These included the local chiefs, who found themselves in an impossible position, with their authority completely undermined.

★

The recipe for disaster was complete, and duly followed, aided by other factors that could have been avoided to a great extent if pilot schemes had been carried out in the three areas chosen.

Clearing the bush cost ten times the original estimate, as the very long roots encountered were much tougher and far harder to clear than had originally been anticipated. This delayed the whole scheme and everything took four or five times longer than planned which, of course, slowed down and delayed ploughing and planting of the groundnuts.

More delays occurred during the ploughing, as the hard surface blunted the ploughs until they became useless. Also, groundnuts like a light soil and the machinery used compacted and made worse the already hard soil, making it completely unsuitable for the crop.

As if this wasn't bad enough, there were further setbacks when it came to harvesting the groundnuts, because a large proportion broke off during mechanical harvesting and stayed in the hard soil. The only solution was to revert to the traditional method of gathering the nuts by hand, while the expensive modern machinery stood idle. This increased harvesting costs to many times that of the original estimate.

Worse was to follow, with wild pigs and insect pests destroying much of the crop and diseases such as black spot destroying the rest of the groundnuts in many places.

All this was aggravated further by unusually dry years from the start of the scheme, but this is not unusual in the Tropics and provision should have been made for the weather. The Tanganyikan Agricultural Department would have been fully aware of all the potential problems, and why its advice was so rarely sought will never be known.

One especial irony of the whole situation was that the third place chosen for growing groundnuts, Nachingwea, might have proved successful if all the effort had been concentrated there. Unlike Kongwa and Tabora, the whole Nachingwea area is fairly well watered and, with the port of Mtwara nearby, the transport and shipping costs would have been cut to the minimum.

One rather pathetic aftermath of the Groundnuts Scheme, when it finally finished and large numbers of staff had been paid off, was that some of the Europeans elected to stay on in Tanganyika. They tried to set up their own businesses with their savings, but soon found that life in the commercial world was a very different business to the Groundnuts Scheme. Most lost all their savings very quickly and I believe a special camp had to be set up in Dar es Salaam to handle them until they could be repatriated to Britain – at the British taxpayers' expense, of course.

★

The most important thing about the Groundnuts Scheme is not that it failed, however, but that it paved the way for the monstrous aid hoax that the UN perpetuated when it and the politicians in the West, especially the socialists in Britain, realised just how easy it was to get money from the taxpayer. When one lot has been frittered away the authorities have no penalties to pay and all that has to be done is to extract yet more billions from the Western taxpayers.

To anyone except the political morons, the obvious area for development in Tanzania is the Rufiji lowland, because of the proximity to Dar es Salaam and the fact that it is the only part of the country where there is too much water. The whole area is flooded for much of the year and European technology is needed to install an efficient flood control system for an area of over four million acres. Now unusable because of flooding, this could be turned into one of the best food producing areas in Africa – and for a fraction of the money that was wasted on the Groundnuts Scheme.

The tsetse fly problem is bad in the lowlands but, with aerial spraying and ground clearance and spraying, the problem could be solved, as it has been in other parts of Africa.

*

Fortunately for the West, the communists are sometimes even more stupid than them when dealing with Africa. In this instance I refer to Tanzania's other white elephant, so beloved of Julius Nyerere: the Tanzam railway. This was financed and constructed by the Chinese, after the World Bank and others in the West had turned it down as being uneconomic.

The railway was built to bring Zambia's copper from Kapiri Mposhi to Dar for shipment, to avoid Zambia's dependence on Rhodesia and South Africa.

But when, if ever, the railway will become an economic proposition is another matter entirely.

*

It is only right, and in stark contrast to the Tanganyika Groundnuts Scheme, that a tribute should be paid to the remarkable role that was played by white farmers in East Africa and the Rhodesias who, by their vision, courage and endless toll, brought prosperity and modern agriculture to these regions. Africa's black politicians, and socialist colleagues in the West, like to ignore the fact, but these pioneers from Britain and South Africa should always be remembered with pride, and we should all feel shame for the shabby way that they were treated.

What a contrast to those of their fellow countrymen who came after the end of World War II, with much publicity and bombastic statements to the press. They failed miserably, due to the incompetence of their British socialist government masters and their multitude of advisers – all of whom lacked real practical knowledge of Africa.

These new settlers arrived in 1947, boasting that they would clear 3,200,000 acres of African bush by 1953, to grow their groundnuts in Tanganyika. When they departed in failure, no figures were given about the tonnage of groundnuts produced, nor what it had all cost the British taxpayer.

So it is appropriate, here, that some figures be given to show what the original white farmers in the highlands of Kenya achieved on only five per cent of Kenya's land mass. These pioneers produced over eighty per cent of Kenya's gross income, and most of its exports. They were also responsible for most of the commercial crops that Kenya now exports: coffee, tea, wheat, pyrethrum, sugar, sisal, wattle, and so on. It was the same story in the Rhodesias.

In Southern Rhodesia the main export crop was tobacco and eventually it accounted for more than one third of Southern Rhodesia's exports. Once again the pioneer farmers, mainly from Britain and South Africa, built up the export markets, with citrus fruit and juices, tea, sugar, cotton, sunflowers and, ironically, groundnuts featuring prominently. How many people in Britain know, or care, that these same pioneers from South Africa are now held in economic bondage by Mugabe's Marxist government since, if they return to South Africa, they are allowed to take only $1,000 (Zimbabwean) with them. The fact that their farms are mainly either freehold or on 999-year government leases means nothing, nor does the fact that previous British governments actively encouraged them to settle and farm in East Africa and the Rhodesias.

In Northern Rhodesia the story was much the same, but on a smaller scale. Most of the agriculture was geared to supply the demands of the Copperbelt, which it did so successfully in the colonial era that it was able to export maize, as well as building up export markets for tobacco and cotton.

Today, in Kaunda's Zambia as with Nyerere's Tanzania, maize and other food stuffs have to be imported, using massive aid from the West to pay for it. Ironically, a lot of the maize is supplied by the only efficient farming country left – South Africa.

Zimbabwe is another aid recipient which has to turn a blind eye to maize imports from South Africa. On more than one occasion, when television has been showing some banquet for visiting British politicians in Lusaka or

Harare, the camera has inadvertently focused on South African wine being served.

To those of us who have spent most of our adult lives in Africa, it is the hypocrisy and the mealy-mouthed double standards that are the most annoying.

Even discounting South Africa's loyal service to Britain in two world wars, and the fact that there are over two million South Africans of British descent, no one except a politician or a complete fool would deny that South Africa's sins pale into insignificance compared to what is happening in the rest of black Africa. It is only the fact that black African politicians command more than a third of the voting power at the UN that stops the West from criticising them.

★

Late in 1964 Zambia became independent. I lived in Livingstone during the early years of independence, in fact until the end of September 1969 (by which time I had had enough and emigrated with the family to South Africa), so I can speak from personal experience of how quickly Zambia's prosperous colonial economy was wrecked by the wailing and weeping leader of UNIP (United National Independence Party) and Zambia, Kenneth Kaunda. If anything, he made an even greater mess of things than Tanzania's Julius Nyerere, as Zambia had been left with a thriving copper industry and a healthy credit balance from colonial days.

It was incredible how quickly everything disintegrated! The credit balance was squandered, even the main roads fell into disrepair – with huge holes where the surface had broken up – hospitals and other public services deteriorated and food shortages became a way of life, as in most communist countries.

The brutal truth, which the do-gooders in the West will never admit, is that no African state was ready to govern itself efficiently. What was required was a gradual Africanisation of the whole colonial system over a period of fifteen to twenty years. To show good faith, a UN peace force could have been sent to each country as required.

But slow progress would not have suited the plans of the handful of educated Africans. Radicalised on Lenin and Marx, they wanted power immediately, regardless of what it cost their fellow Africans. All they were interested in was furthering their own political ambitions. The tragedy for Africa was that the West was short-sighted enough to support them and give them virtually instant independence.

During this early period of independence, I travelled fairly frequently by road between Livingstone and Lusaka, and also to the Copperbelt, and it was depressing to see the ever-increasing number of abandoned white farms along the roadside.

As law and order broke down, it became dangerous to travel, even on the main roads, especially at night. Acquaintances of mine from Livingstone were killed and robbed by bandits, and Zambia soon became like all the other newly-independent states in East and central Africa.

Very soon Livingstone, like all the other towns in Zambia, began to experience acute food shortages and soon we were forced to travel to Bulawayo every month to buy our food requirements. In Ian Smith's booming UDI Rhodesia, food prices were at least a third lower than in Livingstone, and there were certainly no shortages at all in Bulawayo.

This insane policy of destroying prosperous countries like Rhodesia showed the stupidity of the West, and illustrated how easily Western leaders were influenced by the communists, who were also manipulating the UN through Kurt Waldheim.

The Russians supported Waldheim's appointment as UN Secretary-General in 1972, and it should not surprise anybody that it was only when he was of no further use to them, after 1982, that the news was leaked of his war crimes under the Nazis.

★

Although the war in Angola has probably destroyed the Portuguese farming scheme on the outskirts of Luso, it is only fitting that there should be some record and appreciation of what can be achieved with very little money using intelligent irrigation and good farming methods.

Typical of the media coverage of Africa is the fact that the excellent Portuguese farming scheme at Luso (in Angola) received no publicity in the West, while the abortive Tanganyika Groundnuts Scheme was highly publicised until it became obvious it was failing.

What is important is that the Luso farming scheme could be repeated in many parts of Africa, if only the West would realise that Africa does not need grandiose schemes, but is crying out for small, low-cost schemes in which the Africans themselves can be involved from the start.

Luso is not an easy place to reach at the best of times and I doubt if many English-speaking people actually visited the scheme. It is ironic that, in my case, it was probably a letter of introduction from Ian Smith's Minister of

Mines, John Gaunt, that indirectly got me an invitation. At that time, British passports were not exactly popular in Angola and it was only the letter from John Gaunt that enabled me to enter the country at all. I was also lucky that the provincial veterinary officer who showed me around so enthusiastically spoke excellent English, and he explained the scheme from start to finish.

What the Portuguese authorities in Angola had done so cleverly, and at only a fraction of the cost of the Tanganyika Groundnuts Scheme, was to bring selected Portuguese peasant farmers and their families from Portugal to reproduce an African village from scratch on the outskirts of Luso. They were allowed to use only the raw materials and simple hand tools that were available to the ordinary African villagers in Angola.

So the Portuguese farmers constructed an entire African village without using any modern technology; only grass, poles of local timber, sisal rope and so forth – materials that would be available to any rural African. Their huts were completely traditional, with the usual mud floors and thatched roofs, and their few simple bits of furniture were also made entirely from local materials.

Nor, when the village was finished, were they allowed any modern machinery to help them with the actual farming. Once again, they had to manage on the same level as the Africans.

The farmers had, of course, brought from Portugal tin and wooden trunks containing their personal effects but, other than those, there was absolutely nothing manufactured outside the scheme.

The only thing I found a bit disturbing, while watching the work going on in the irrigation channels, was that all the Portuguese were working barefoot. I knew, from my Tanganyika years, just how dangerous it was to walk anywhere barefoot. I had discovered this to my own cost when I managed to collect a very nasty infestation of 'jiggers'. To quote the Oxford Dictionary: '*chigoe* – a small tropical flea, *Tunga penetrans*, the impregnated female of which burrows under the skin' and, before you know anything about it, they have multiplied alarmingly under the skin of your toes. Fortunately the Africans are experts at pulling them out with a needle when they are near the surface of the skin, but it is still a very unpleasant, and sometimes painful, experience.

It was, of course, Luso's highly efficient irrigation system that was at the heart of the scheme's success. I have never seen, elsewhere in Africa, such healthy crops of maize, sunflowers and groundnuts. Such fruits as papaws and bananas were superb, and so were the vegetables. The farmers gave us a huge basketful of fruit for our journey back to Rhodesia and I have never tasted better anywhere in Africa.

It should be mentioned that my visit was completely impromptu and no prior notice was given to anybody on the scheme. I had been talking to the provincial veterinary officer, and had casually mentioned my eleven years in Tanganyika and the Groundnuts Scheme, when he asked me if I would like to visit the scheme on the outskirts of Luso. When I had given him the letter of introduction I had played up my connections with John Gaunt (and his position as Minister of Mines in Salisbury), because I knew the Portuguese were impressed by that kind of thing, but my visit to Luso was in no way official, and the smiling faces there were completely natural.

I have often wondered what happened to those Portuguese farmers and their families. I only hope that they got out of Angola in time, and that they were suitably recompensed by the Portuguese-Angolan authorities They certainly deserved it. I have never forgotten my visit to that oasis of progress and sanity in war-torn Angola. It would be tragic if the lessons learnt there are not used in other areas of Africa, where good farming methods are so desperately needed.

★

To give readers further understanding of the madness of the West, and the UN in particular, it is strongly recommended that the book by Dr Karl Borgin and Kathleen Corbett, *The Destruction of a Continent*, should be read. It explains why the real problems have not been tackled, in other words, the population explosion, bad farming methods and wasting huge amounts of money on producing manufactured goods that can be obtained much more cheaply in the West, while ignoring rural agricultural needs. These problems create a vicious circle, with more and more aid food needing to be imported.

To stress the seriousness of the situation, I quote from their chapter 'Aid Fanatics and Superbureaucrats':

> The aid fanatics, the superbureaucrats, and the experts may be different from one another, but they have one thing in common: they write articles and reports, pamphlets and books. The most alarming discovery is that among eighty-seven contributors to the sample books on international aid and the conditions in Africa we have chosen, there is only one technologist and not a single agriculturist. 40.2% were politicians, 19.5% economists, 16.1% sociologists, 5.7% journalists, 1.2% technologists… 0% agriculturists – the group needed most…

> Some of them have spent some time in Africa, but mainly as visiting scientists at universities and research establishments there. We have met them all over Africa as they continue with their learned but futile discussions, in these instances with African colleagues, at the universities in Nairobi, Dar es Salaam, Lusaka, Makarere, Cairo, and Maputo. In the field, out in the bush, in the plantation, or in the factories, they are never seen.

Finally, to sum up the futility of international aid (in their chapter entitled 'The Aid Syndrome'):

> International bureaucracy, especially the UN and all its organisations, long ago reached such proportions that it is completely uncontrollable, and nobody knows what really goes on in the numerous committees, meetings, conferences, congresses and commissions all over the world.
>
> International organisations have degenerated into institutions where men and women talk, discuss, and argue how to save the world from disaster. When little or nothing is accomplished, new committees and new meetings are called, and additional organisations are established to give the bureaucracy and the rest of the world the impression or illusion that they are still working on the problems.

Those few Portuguese peasant farmers near Luso did more with a few thousand pounds of expenditure than has been achieved by all the billions of pounds the UN and the West have wasted on impractical schemes elsewhere in Africa.

Chapter Four

Williamson Diamond and Geita Gold Mines

Without the two mines in the area, with their large European staff, social life in Mwanza would have been very restricted. Williamson Diamond Mine was the more interesting of the two, because its Canadian owner and discoverer, Dr Williamson, spent most of his time there, whereas Geita Gold Mine was part of a large gold-mining group – South African, I believe – in those days.

There were endless stories in Mwanza of how Dr Williamson had found his diamond mine in the Mwadui diamond field near Shinyanga, in Tanganyika's Lake Province, in the early years of World War II. I believe it was in 1940. One popular version was that Dr Williamson's cook had brought him some stones to look at one day and among them was the first diamond from the now famous Mwadui diamond field.

What is known for a fact is that Dr Williamson had been employed for some years by a big South African mining company (De Beers, I think) as a geologist in Tanganyika's Lake Province, but he had had no luck in finding commercial quantities of diamonds and eventually the South African mining company terminated his appointment. He refused to leave the area and return to South Africa, however, because he was firmly convinced, from what the local Africans had told him of previous finds in German days, that there were diamonds somewhere in the Shinyanga district of the Lake Province. He was sure it was only a matter of time and effort before he would discover where the diamonds were.

He stayed on in the Shinyanga district and financed his own work until his money ran out. Luckily for him he had friends in Mwanza, who also believed that he would eventually find diamonds and were prepared to lend him money so that he could carry on his work. In the end they were rewarded beyond their wildest dreams, as Dr Williamson gave each of the four who had helped him financially a quarter share in the diamond mine next to his. It was appropriately named Alamasi (Swahili for diamond).

I can't remember their names now (it's over forty years ago), but I do remember that one had been the manager at Mwanza's Standard Bank and another had owned a local garage – he repaired Williamson's vehicle and gave him petrol on credit to keep him going. The Hon. I.C. Chopra, QC, was also given one share in Williamson's mine, and became the mine's legal adviser as well. It was in this capacity that he gave Queen Elizabeth the famous Pink Diamond.

At one stage Williamson's was one of the world's leading diamond mines and diamonds were one of Tanganyika's chief sources of income, forming fifteen to twenty per cent of the country's total exports. So Dr Williamson's personal contribution to the Tanganyikan economy was immense.

*

To see both these mines, and to take part in the social activities that went with them, the obvious answer was to join the Mwanza cricket team, because regular trips were made on weekends to play cricket against either the Williamson Diamond Mine or the Geita Gold Mine. Shinyanga was south of Mwanza, while Geita was west of Mwanza – along the lake towards Bukoba.

I had played cricket at The King's School and I always remember how pleased my father was when the school cricket coach, Frank Woolley (a famous England left-hander in the 1920s and 1930s), told my father I was capable of fifty plus at good club level. I think that impressed him more than my academic results.

David Gower (who went on to captain England) was at The King's School. So was Brian Fern, who was in charge of the Tanganyikan police at Mwanza. Brian's father had also been in the colonial police and his family had a farm at Smarden in Kent. I had spent one school holiday there and was amazed to run into Brian again, playing cricket at Mwanza. He had been a flying officer in the RAF and returned to it after doing one or two tours in Tanganyika with the police. I heard later that he had been killed while flying in Britain.

*

Anyway, I duly joined the Mwanza cricket team and we soon went to play the Williamson Diamond Mine team at Mwadui. It was on either my first or second trip that I first met Dr Williamson – late at night in the Mine Club.

He came in just as the Saturday-night dance was finishing, at about 3 a.m. He had obviously been drinking pretty heavily. This was not unusual but on this occasion he had got it into his head that he wanted to hold a board meeting. The general manager and other senior staff tried to get him to change his mind, but in vain, and he became even more insistent. The fact that so many strangers were at the bar, or sitting around finishing their drinks, didn't worry him at all. As the board members were getting seated, he told the general manager to take off his dinner jacket as he wanted to write the minutes of the meeting on his dress shirt.

It all began to get very embarrassing and we left the club as soon as we could finish our drinks. I couldn't help noticing that Dr Williamson had already begun writing on his general manager's dress shirt, so presumably at the end of the meeting the man had to take his shirt off for his boss to have the minutes.

I believe it was at around this time that Dr Williamson's drink problem began to get out of hand and, in the later stages, he was very rarely seen in public. It wasn't many years after this that he died.

Africa can be a pretty hard place to live, and most of the old timers had some kind of drink problem, which was not surprising as health conditions were still pretty bad and malaria was prevalent everywhere. Alcohol seemed to make life easier and heavy drinkers like Dr Williamson were not uncommon. Nothing, of course, could detract from his amazing achievements against all the odds and, if anything, the drinking problem made his success even more remarkable. All of us who met him in those days admired Dr Williamson tremendously, especially the way he refused to let the big diamond-mining companies buy him out. They tried for years, but it wasn't until after his death that they finally succeeded.

*

I had seen my first diamonds shortly before I went to the Williamson Diamond Mine to play cricket. In my early days in Mwanza I wasn't exactly overpaid by my firm, and my salary didn't stretch to the frequent bottles of whisky that I had got used to in my Indian Army days. So I cultivated some of the local Indian merchants, who liked to hear about my days in their country and were very liberal with the whisky bottle while they listened.

One, in particular, had a large house not far from the Mwanza Hotel and, to get out of the ghastly place, I used to visit him quite frequently. He had business connections with the mine at Mwadui and one evening he asked me if I wanted to see some diamonds. I could hardly believe my eyes when he opened up the back of his cocktail cabinet and, on specially fitted shelves, there were rows and rows of diamonds. Most of them, even to my inexperienced eye, looked pretty large and valuable.

In those days I had never had the slightest desire to deal in diamonds, but I must say that, after my army days, I found the so-called rogues I met in Africa much more amusing and helpful than the more respectable types. The rogues were also far more generous when I had to borrow some money, and I don't think they really expected it back. When I made a lot of money out of the crocodiles later on, I remembered these men's helpfulness towards me and was much more ready to lend money in my turn.

Some time later the police, at the insistence of Dr Williamson, brought to Mwanza an expert in illicit diamond dealing called Inspector Joti. He turned out to be one of those very rare Indians who are completely incorruptible, and he certainly caused plenty of alarm and despondency among the local Indians involved in the diamond trade.

Inspector Joti successfully jailed some of the smaller dealers, but the larger ones seemed unaffected for the most part, although they had to be more careful. Some took off for India while the going was good. So some results were achieved by Joti, but nothing could ever stop the illicit diamond business, even though Dr Williamson later brought in experts from London's Scotland Yard.

I suffered some personal inconvenience due to all this increased activity as, on one of my trips to Nairobi, I was searched by police at Mwanza's airport – an unheard of thing to happen on an internal East African flight. On my return, I asked a police chum, over a drink at the club, why I had been searched. He laughed and told me I should be more careful about the people I mixed with, especially as some of my Indian friends were known to be illicit diamond dealers. I got mad and told him what he could do with the Tanganyikan police.

Later he warned me that I was on the police list as a suspected diamond dealer and repeated that I should be more choosy about my choice of friends. Innocent as I was, I knew I still had to be careful. There were plenty of people who were jealous of the money I was earning from crocodiles and some of them were only too happy to spread stories that this was not the only way I was making money, in the hope that the police would suspect me of diamond dealing as well. One of them even had the bloody cheek to write an anonymous letter to the income tax department in Dar, suggesting it would be well worth their while to investigate my business affairs!

It was incredible to me that, even in a small place like Mwanza, there were people petty-minded enough to start completely unsubstantiated rumours, mainly out of spite. In the end I narrowed down the suspects to one or two of the lower echelon government servants, whose wives I had badly upset over some remarks made in the Mwanza Club bar about how the women dressed. I had not made the remarks, but I had laughed when they were made and I came to the conclusion that they had been harbouring a grudge against me.

From my days with the SIB, the Special Investigation Branch of the military police in Cairo, I had learnt never to trust a policeman too much With my Tanganyikan police chum, I sometimes had the feeling that he didn't entirely believe that I was completely innocent of dealing in diamonds. I knew, also from my SIB days in Cairo – and later at Fayid – how often people were proved guilty by association.

In time the whole thing blew over, but my friend would never tell me whether the police had kept my file open.

*

The Geita Gold Mine was a bit more difficult to get to than the Williamson Diamond Mine at Mwadui, as it entailed using the ferry from Mwanza across Smith's Sound – and any ferry in Tanganyika always seemed to involve delays.

The surroundings at Geita were much more attractive. Being near to Lake Victoria, it was green for most of the year, with plenty of trees around and enough water for gardens. Also, it had been established much longer than the mine at Mwadui, which remained very hot, dry and sandy, however much the actual living conditions were improved.

Geita's gold production came nowhere near the value of the diamonds from Mwadui but I always enjoyed going to Geita much more. At Mwadui there always seemed to be an air of tension and undercurrents were noticeable between the staff. At Geita the atmosphere was much more pleasant.

On our first trip to play cricket at Geita, Betty and I learnt more of the local health hazards that awaited the unwary. There is a particularly unpleasant mango fly, known also as the putzi fly, which at certain times of the year lays its eggs on anything it can find. The wife of the couple we were staying with over the weekend used to dry her washing under a mango tree and a putzi fly used one of her bras as its nest. The eggs made an awful mess of her breasts, as they burrow under the skin in the same way as a jigger burrows under your toes, and deep pit marks were left in the woman's breasts when the eggs were taken out.

*

My main memories of Geita involve one of the most colourful characters in the area, who had helped me in the early days of the crocodile business. Eric Nawotny had a small gold mine near to Geita, and some of the locals were unkind enough to say that it only existed to take the unofficial overflow of gold from Geita which somehow, they reckoned, found its way into Eric's small mine. He, of course, laughed off these rumours and I must say, in all fairness, that nothing was ever proved against him. Our attitude was, of course good luck to him if he could get away with it. Somehow the mealy-mouthed standards of the West, with its bogus civilisation, had very little meaning in Africa.

Eric, like Dekker, had spent many years in Tanganyika, and he had travelled and hunted over most of the country. Years later I used one of his old maps and information to get into a certain little-known area where it was still possible to kill at least fifty crocodiles a night. Hunting there was highly irregular at that time, and could only be done from Northern Rhodesia. I had left Tanganyika in 1959 and I needed his map and directions to get me back on my feet financially. I owe him a great debt for this, and for the many ways he helped me during my early years in Tanganyika.

I first met Eric Nawotny in 1948 and, even then, he must have been well into his forties, but he always looked ten years younger than his age. Some time later I asked one of the Africans who went hunting with him how Eric kept his youthful looks. The man firmly believed it was because Eric used to drink the blood of the animals he had just killed, in the same way as the Masai.

Certainly he believed in a lot of the African customs. One of the local witch doctors had told him about a local beetle which was said to improve one's sexual powers no end, in much the same way as the Spanish fly. The snag was it only swarmed once a year, somewhere in the Tabora-Kigoma area, so Eric dropped everything when this happened and took off to get enough to supply him until the following year. I had often seem him grinding it up into an evil-looking powder and, although it certainly seemed to work wonders for him, I always turned down his offers to try some.

It was soon after I met him that Eric became involved in a scandal that eventually spread further than the communities in the Lake Province. Eric had a lot of friends working at Geita Gold Mine and in those days he often visited the Mine Club on social occasions. It was at one of these social events that he first met Gertie Brown. She had been on the London stage before coming out to Africa and her husband was the general manager of the mine. Before long Gertie moved in with Eric Nawotny, at his place near the Geita Gold Mine.

Over the years Eric had reared many animals here, but his pride and joy were his pet cheetahs and, unfortunately, Brown decided that the best way for him to get back at Eric was to poison them. While Eric and Gertie were away in Mwanza for the weekend this was just what he did – evidently he went over to Eric's place and fed them poisoned meat. In the circumstances, Eric did the only possible thing – took Brown to court in Mwanza (in an earlier age I suspect Eric would have killed him!), and won his case, getting damages from Brown. This didn't bring back Eric's cheetahs, of course, but the case was reported in the *Tanganyika Standard* and, soon after, Brown lost his job at Geita Gold Mine.

★

Shortly after this Geita was once again in the news, following a gruesome murder and robbery on the road from Geita to Mwanza.

It was the practice for the mine to send in the gold about once a month with a Land Rover and an African driver, so the gold could be deposited at a Mwanza bank. Normally the driver was on his own but on this occasion, at the very last minute, one of the mine's European wives needed a lift to go to Mwanza with a bad toothache. On the road to Mwanza the vehicle was stopped and both the driver and the woman were shot dead and buried nearby. The gold was stolen, and never recovered.

The Tanganyikan police were not really up to handling murders of this kind, as violent crimes were extremely rare in those days. Months of extensive inquiries at Geita eventually narrowed down to one main suspect, a one-armed German miner, and just about everybody knew the police were coming over from Mwanza to arrest him. The German miner had, of course, received plenty of warning and, as the police arrived to arrest him, he shot himself.

It was widely suspected locally that this was the outcome the police wanted, as they had no other suspects and certainly didn't want any awkward questions asked in court as to how a one-armed man could bury two bodies unaided. There was absolutely no sign of any of the gold at the German's house, and the evidence connecting him to the murders was pretty thin. It was known locally that there had been continual pressure from Dar for the Mwanza police to make an arrest, as there had been a considerable local outcry about the amount of time that had gone by without any results. So the Mwanza police were quite happy to close the murder and robbery inquiry with the death of the one-armed German miner.

What the police never considered, or perhaps never knew, was that it was quite possible, in the dry season, to travel from Mwanza to Geita without taking the ferry from Mwanza. Via the bottom part of Smith's Sound, which was waterless during the dry season, it was only a rough bush track, but any four-wheel drive vehicle could manage it in about twelve hours without undue trouble.

The Mwanza police had investigated only those people who had used the ferry over the period of the murders. As the murders had not been discovered for over twenty-four hours, this meant anybody from Mwanza would have had plenty of time to return home. What made this line of inquiry so interesting was that it did tend to throw suspicion on our circle of crocodile hunters and a few other hunters with four-wheel drive vehicles and, even though it never went any further than idle speculation, I knew there were at least four or five hunters in the area who could have been involved without anybody suspecting.

What surprised us most of all was the fact that there were never any rumours of what did happen to the gold.

*

I was to have one more connection with Geita that was going to cost me dear.

Gerald Chopra had been approached about the possibility of our company taking over a small gold mine in the Geita area. The company, which we had formed to handle the crocodile business, was growing the whole time and producing excellent profits, with the minimum amount of financial risk. The only losses we made in those early days were a few pounds when workers at some of our African camps did not produce any skins but did make off with the food and other supplies that we had advanced to them.

I wasn't keen to take over a gold mine as Betty and I were off to Europe on leave, to spend some of the money we had made out of crocodiles. But Gerald was keen, and said he would help run it. I didn't know then he would depend on unreliable people and, to be fair, I must admit I liked the idea of saying that I owned a gold mine. So the deal went ahead.

Gerald also had his legal work to attend to, and made the mistake of thinking everything at the mine would go well, just as the crocodiles had done, without constant supervision.

By the time I came back from Europe we had already lost thousands; I was still too inexperienced to know that we should cut our losses then and get out of the mine immediately.

Instead we poured in good money after bad, which only increased our losses. Only then did Gerald Chopra agree to close the mine and write the whole thing off as a complete loss. Fortunately for us, the crocodiles were still very profitable and we were well able to cover our losses at the mine without the crocodile business being affected.

Chapter Five

Some Characters in Tanganyika

I had met Norman Waugh first at the Williamson Diamond Mine, when he was Dr Williamson's personal pilot. Communications were so bad in those early days that the mine had to run its own small airline to transport mine equipment and food supplies for the European staff. Being Williamson's personal pilot was a plum job.

Norman was a very useful cricketer and, from the early days, we became very friendly, an added factor being that we both came from the same county in Britain – Suffolk. I believe he started his flying career there, with Cobham's Air Circus in the 1930s, and he was a very experienced pilot.

Eventually Norman found the mine, and the atmosphere there, too much to take, so he resigned and took over the Bukoba Hotel.

Bukoba was a very attractive little port on the west side of Lake Victoria, with the usual single hotel. The owner, whose son had committed suicide there, wanted to leave Bukoba as soon as possible, so Norman had to decide quickly. In his hands the Bukoba Hotel improved immensely, and we were pleased when he invited us there for Christmas.

He used to stay with us in Mwanza when he came on business trips, usually flying his own aircraft, which was an ancient biplane (from the 1930s) that somehow, miraculously, he managed to keep airworthy. As we couldn't afford to be away from Mwanza for too long, he offered to fly us there and back.

His biplane could just take three at a pinch, although it was a pretty tight fit and there was very little room for luggage.

The outward journey wasn't too bad. Although the engine spluttered alarmingly every now and again, Norman seemed quite unperturbed. All I could think of was the distance to shore if the single engine did cut out and the number of crocodiles lurking about below us – so I was heartily glad to see Bukoba's little airport. We landed safely, however, with only a few bumps.

We thoroughly enjoyed Christmas and had some very pleasant trips on the lake but, as one of the locals had recently been savaged by a hippo, we were not at all keen to get into the water. Evidently the man had been swimming near the mouth of the river and had got between the hippo and the lake. The hippo had picked him up with such force that it had bitten off one side of the unfortunate man's bottom. After a few drinks in the bar he was fond of showing off his scars! There can't be many people around who have survived a hippo attack like that, and he was extremely lucky to get out of the water before the crocodiles came, attracted by the blood.

For some reason there were hundreds of hippos around Bukoba in those days, and they were often to be found at night grazing on the golf course – or in people's gardens near the lake. It was almost impossible to grow any vegetables without the hippos eating them. But if you ran into the creatures, even at night, it was almost unheard of for them to attack you. Probably the one in the water had a baby hippo to protect.

Getting back to Mwanza after the holiday proved extremely difficult. It had been raining there heavily on and off ever since we had left, and Norman was told that the airport at Mwanza had been closed for the past two days as it was waterlogged. It was expected that it would be closed for at least a further two days. As we were enjoying ourselves, we weren't particularly put out at having to stay a little longer. When the airport closure stretched to a further three days, however, we began to get anxious about returning to Mwanza, so we were relieved that when Norman phoned the airport he was given the all-clear.

Everything went fine until we got close to Mwanza, when we saw that another heavy storm had just set in. In those days Norman had no radio but we could just make out some of the airport staff waving us away when we approached to land. Not long afterwards, while we were still over Mwanza and Norman was deciding what to do next, the rain slackened off a bit and, as none of us wanted to divert to Geita or Shinyanga, he decided to attempt a landing. It certainly was a bit dicey but, with a lot of splashing about and water seeming to come in everywhere, soaking all of us thoroughly, we skidded around the verges of the airstrip very alarmingly. Finally we skidded right around and came to a stop, very thankful to have made it in one piece.

I believe the airport authorities later made a bit of a fuss about Norman landing in such conditions and there was some talk of a fine for landing without permission, but it all died down in the end and nothing more was said. I don't know what else Norman could have done in the circumstances, as there was no guarantee that Geita would have been clear had he gone there.

Some time later Norman offered to fly me on a business trip that I had to make and he seemed quite surprised when I turned down his offer and went by car!

Years later, in South Africa, I saw an article about Norman Waugh in some business magazine in Johannesburg. He looked very opulent in his smart city suit, and the picture brought back memories of forty years before, our Christmas in Bukoba and the nightmare landing in the storm at Mwanza.

★

Tanganyika seemed to be a country full of good ideas that never got off the ground. BOAC's idea of using the great lakes of Africa for a flying boat service across the whole continent was typical. But, despite all the time and money spent on trial runs and setting up staff all along the route, only one flying boat ever landed at Mwanza. The BOAC representative there seemed to be around for years, just waiting for another flying boat to land. He was ex-RAF aircrew and he had been badly wounded over Berlin during World War II.

Why he was left in Mwanza no one knew, but when I arrived (in 1948) he was already an alcoholic. He was staying at the Mwanza Hotel, with a room just across the way from me, and he often invited me in for a drink in the morning. He never seemed to be able to get up until he had knocked off most, if not all, of a bottle of brandy. He used to stagger down most days at about noon and make his daily trip to see if there was a flying boat coming in. Of course none ever came. Perhaps BOAC had forgotten all about him.

Eventually friends in Mwanza arranged for him to go away to try a drying-out cure for his alcoholism, and I left the hotel before he returned. I heard later that he had come back much improved and, shortly afterwards, he had been transferred.

Actually the whole idea of the flying boats was an excellent one because, if you have to fly, what better way of doing it than in this leisurely and picturesque way? Far better than being herded like cattle into huge, impersonal modern aircraft.

I believe the idea was for the flying boats to end up in Durban, using the Vaal Dam outside Johannesburg for the last leg of the journey. Entebbe, at the top end of Lake Victoria, was to be used, with the next stop at the bottom of the lake at Mwanza, then on to Lake Tanganyika and then to Lake Nyasa.

It would have been a fascinating trip over some of the most beautiful parts of East, central and South Africa and, as the flying boat is so much slower, it can fly much lower. So all the glory of the African lakes could have been admired at leisure, instead of the boredom of modern jets, with mile after mile of nothing to see except sky.

There was a TV programme about some flying boat enthusiasts who tried using the old BOAC route, even landing at an island off the Mozambique coast. It proved too hazardous flying over war-torn African countries, however, and the venture did not last long.

More recently, some other enthusiasts fitted up an old Catalina flying boat with an observation room and took small groups of rich tourists from Cairo to Harare, with stops between each leg of the journey. During these stops, the tourists visited game reserves and historic sites, but the main object of the trip was to follow the old BOAC mail route and try to recreate the atmosphere of the old days.

*

During my first months in Africa, at the Mwanza Hotel, I made two other friends who caused more gossip and outrage in local colonial government circles than anybody else except, maybe, Eric Nawotny and Gertie Brown.

Philip Sackville-Scott had been the general manager at the Williamson Diamond Mine, and he had lost his wife to Dr Williamson. His friend, Colin McCloud, had been a senior superintendent in the Tanganyika police and had been seconded to Williamson's as the chief security officer. This was in the early days, before it was found necessary to bring in at least four experts from Scotland Yard to try to curb the diamond thefts that were increasing the whole time.

Philip Sackville-Scott had received an undisclosed amount of damages when he left the mine, and Colin McCloud had taken early retirement so that they could start a papaw plantation on the shores of Lake Victoria, between Geita and Mwanza.

These events provided the local gossips with endless possibilities and speculation about what had really happened at the mine. There were countless rumours circulating, about bags of diamonds and various other pay-offs. In fact, every type of skulduggery was considered possible. Even after forty years, it is probably wiser to say no more about what really happened, as there must be relatives still alive who would be upset if they heard the stories that were circulated at the time. But it did provide an endless topic of conversation.

I found Philip Sackville-Scott especially interesting as he was the first South African in Tanganyika that I got to know well. My brief time in Durban, on the troopship on my way to Octu during the war, had not been long enough for me to get to know any South Africans well, but I had never forgotten their hospitality.

Philip had spent all his working life in the mining industry, and knew just about everything there was to know about the industry in South Africa, including some pretty scurrilous stories about what really went on in the higher echelons of the diamond business. Perhaps fortunately, most of his reminiscences came pretty late at night, and I could rarely remember them in detail the next day, except that much was unprintable.

The only times he became a bit embarrassing were when, occasionally, he got very bitter about his wife and Dr Williamson. I sometimes wondered whether it was because of this that he took such a delight in openly flaunting his African mistress. He never made any effort to conceal their affair, which infuriated the British colonial civil servants. He used to drive around Mwanza with her quite openly whenever they visited the town and, on occasion, sent her into Mwanza from their papaw plantation, to collect supplies and mail. Eventually he even bought her a house in town.

One night, when I had been drinking with Philip and Colin at the Mwanza Hotel, Philip asked me to take a note down to her house and collect something or other that was needed at the hotel. I agreed to go, as I had never been in an African house and I was curious to see how she lived. What took me completely by surprise was the mass of people in the house. In Africa, one is expected to share good fortune with one's family, and all her relatives were there, tucking into a huge pot of posho. The noise, smell and smoke were quite indescribable and as, in those early days in Africa, my nose was not yet attuned to all the local smells, I was very glad to beat a hasty retreat.

Later, while on my way to hunt elephants, I often slept in African village guest houses, used mostly by visiting district officers, or in ordinary African huts, but these were small grass huts and there were always separate cooking facilities – normally out in the open. It is part of the way of life for the African to sit, eat and sleep near his cooking pot, and there is no doubt that the smoke helps keep the mosquitoes away.

⋆

It was accepted practice, in those days, for bachelors to have some contact with local females, but only in a very discreet manner, and, on reflection now, I find it extremely ironic that it should have been a South African who ignored the rules set by the British colonial service and flaunted his African girlfriend in public.

There was one fairly senior government official who annoyed us particularly at the Mwanza Club, as he was continually sounding off on the subject, and stating how disgraceful Philip Sackville-Scott's behaviour was. What he didn't know was that a friend of mine had a house overlooking his, and he had been seen groping his children's African nanny on the nights his wife was out at some meeting.

So some of us started making pointed remarks about certain government officials notorious for this kind of weakness and, although it did not stop our hypocritical friend, we noticed he kept a low profile when we were in the club, and avoided us as much as possible.

Looking back now, I wonder if I was wrong to leave him off my list of those mean enough to have written anonymously to the income tax department in Dar, asking them to investigate my crocodile business, as that would certainly have been in character.

Fortune seemed to be smiling on Philip Sackville-Scott and Colin McCloud in those days as, shortly after they started their papaw plantation, there was an overseas boom in the juice of papaws, which had been found to be an ideal meat tenderiser. Whether they survived Julius Nyerere's disastrous agricultural policies is another matter.

★

Solitude played a big part in life in Africa, especially for bachelors, and bouts of malaria being thrown in could produce a recipe for disaster, as in the case of an antipodean journalist who was writing regular articles for the *Tanganyika Standard* in Dar, under the pen-name of Rufiji. He was hunting crocodiles for me in the Musoma district when we first met. I know, from my own experiences of malaria, how easy it is to have vivid hallucinations, and to suffer bouts of illogical behaviour when the malarial fever is at its worst. Nor do I believe that the early cure – using large quantities of quinine – helped, because it frequently produced side effects that were just as unpleasant as the malaria.

I learnt from the local grapevine that Rufiji had had some government job with the Tanganyikan authorities before World War II. He had been on tour when he came down with a bad attack of malaria and, while he was sick, he had threatened his African cook that if he served hash again he would shoot him. The cook was ill-advised enough to ignore these warnings and to produce hash once again while Rufiji was still very sick with fever, and Rufiji did shoot him dead. His friends begged him to plead ill health and temporary insanity, but he refused. He was duly convicted of manslaughter and spent about six years (I forget the precise number) in Pentonville Prison in Britain, as there were no facilities for long-term European prisoners in Tanganyika at that time. When he was released, he returned to Africa.

Rufiji's articles in the *Tanganyika Standard* were extremely popular and I found his immense knowledge of life in the African bush very useful in my early days in Tanganyika. I always made a point of inviting him out for a drink whenever we met in Musoma, or when I was buying his crocodile skins. He had a very disconcerting habit of falling asleep in the middle of a conversation, regardless of the time of day, but he would normally wake up again in twenty to thirty minutes and continue the conversation where he had left off.

People who did not know him would get up and leave, but his friends just carried on talking and drinking until he woke up again and continued with his reminiscences. He would never discuss his days in Pentonville Prison, however, nor how he had landed up there.

I never saw him without his Aussie slouch hat, in fact no one had ever seen him without it, his theory being that it was vital for a European to protect his head against the African sun at all times.

*

Another character I am not likely to forget was called 'Walkie-Talkie' Cooper. The nickname was richly deserved, as I never knew him to stop talking.

I had met him on several occasions during my years in Mwanza, but I never sought out his company, as he could be very trying at times. However, after we left Mwanza and went farming in the Kakonko-Kibondo district, he invited us, on more than one occasion, to visit him at his Game Department camp in the nearby Biharamulo district, from where he was carrying out a game count of all the elephants in the area during the dry season. Out in the African bush there aren't many Europeans, and one soon comes to appreciate any social contact, so after a while we accepted his invitation and found that, in his own surroundings, Cooper was a totally different person.

Walkie-Talkie had told me, also more than once, that he and his game guards slapped whitewash on all the elephants' rear ends, so that they could be easily identified and, with this method, there was less likelihood of the numbers of elephants being duplicated. I had thought it was just one of his tales but, when we did eventually visit him, he insisted on taking us along to see how they applied the whitewash. Sure enough, that was just what Walkie-Talkie Cooper and his game guards did that day to all the elephants we came across.

I asked him what would happen if the wind changed direction while they were doing it. Evidently this had happened only once, and they were lucky it had involved a small herd of just four or five elephants, since they had all turned around in surprise and made one or two mock charges. But it hadn't been necessary to fire more than a few warning shots. The game guards always had some empty four-gallon kerosene tins ready and, when these were beaten by hand, the noise was normally enough to frighten the elephants away.

Later in the evening we went back to Walkie-Talkie's house for drinks and dinner. He kept his revolver beside him all the time, both on the open veranda and in the dining room, and we soon found out why. Every bat that came in he shot, and one of his servants swept up the mess. I think he killed ten that night. We were just glad that none of them fell into our food or drinks. Nothing was said and it was obviously a nightly ritual.

Solitude affects everybody differently, and it certainly made me more tolerant of other people's foibles. I ended up with a few myself before I left Tanganyika. I have now stopped inspecting my toes daily for jiggers, but I still shake out my shoes every morning in case of scorpions!

There was a great amount of game around in those days and, on our way home later that night, we came across about ten giraffe feeding by the roadside. They seemed quite unconcerned to see us.

It is when I am reminiscing about those early years in Africa that my anger towards the superpowers returns; they have a lot to answer for in the mass murder of most of the African elephants, and other big game, due to the automatic AK-47 rifles and other hardware that they supplied so indiscriminately all over Africa.

*

Few of us were unaffected by life in Africa, and few could resist the free and easy lifestyle, so different to life in the West. Little did we know then how quickly this way of life would be destroyed by the communists and UN, together with the colonial powers turning against their own kind.

In the success story of the British Empire, public schools like The King's School, Canterbury, played a big part, by producing considerable numbers of the type of people needed to ensure the smooth and efficient running of the widespread British Empire. It is no exaggeration to say that the high ideals of justice and fair play taught at public schools were a very significant factor in the success of the British Empire.

In *The Destruction of a Continent*, the authors make a point of mentioning that it was the colonial powers themselves who, by turning against their own kind, played such a significant part in the destruction of the British and other European empires, to the detriment of the very people they pretended to support – the subsistence farmers of Africa. I can do no better than to quote from the last paragraph of *The New American*'s review, 'How the West destroyed black Africa':

> The authors' discussion of colonialism is refreshingly realistic; they aren't afraid to say that Africa was infinitely better off under colonialism. The settlers brought much good in the form of law and order, modern agriculture, technology and economic progress. In short, the colonials made Africa's high point of development possible by devoting their lives to the continent with vision, courage, and endless toil. This is quite the opposite from the new aid elite, who are incomparably more high-handed and imperious than the colonials ever were. In one of their most telling passages, the authors assert that the colonies were not destroyed by any of the usual causes of the decline and fall of empires, nor by Africans seeking independence, as is commonly thought. Rather the colonial powers themselves turned against their own kind. At their peak of development, the colonies were destroyed by a new breed, different from any the world has ever seen before. Radicalised in the twentieth century, these Westerners preached Marx and Lenin and taught African students to hate capitalism and whites, and to take up arms and destroy the great civilisation the colonials had created.
>
> The well-organised colonial administrations disintegrated into chaos, peace was replaced by revolutions, plenty gave way to poverty.

The above facts have been very cleverly concealed from the general public in the West, and it is only a few Europeans, those who have travelled over most of East, central and West Africa, who have any idea of the ghastly and unnecessary tragedy that took place in most of black-ruled Africa after independence. This is why *The Destruction of a Continent* is so important, as is the fact that both the authors spent over twenty-five years in Africa, rather than the two or three weeks which appear to be the norm for most so-called 'African experts'. It is to be hoped that others who have spent all (or most) of their working lives in Africa, especially ex-servicemen, will add their voices and pens to stop the present madness, which, if unchecked, will end in chaos and poverty in South Africa, just about the last prosperous country left there.

*

I have already mentioned meeting again in Mwanza a former school-friend, Brian Fern. Ivor Butcher was another man who had been at The King's School at the same time as I, and whom I met (and stayed with) when visiting Salisbury. Like Brian, Ivor's parents were in the colonial police.

It was only in the tranquillity of Africa, and seeing the importance placed on public schools by most people in the colonial service, that I realised why my parents had ensured that I, my brother and my sister should get a good education. At the time I had taken everything, including all the cricket, tennis, squash, fives gear, bicycles, and so on, for granted. In Africa, for the first time, I began to appreciate the financial sacrifices my parents had made for us, including sweating it out in Nigeria: the actual school fees alone came to over £600 a year, which was more than the annual average wage in Britain before the war!

Over the years I met many other OKS (Old Boys of The King's School) in Salisbury, Nairobi, Kampala, Lusaka and Bulawayo, but none were at King's during my time except Hanna (or Hannah – I can't remember the spelling), who was a senior magistrate (later he became a judge) when we met in a Lusaka court. How lucky that meeting was for me!

The Game Department had (justifiably, I must admit) taken me to court on a poaching charge and one of my accusers had gloated that I would lose my trophy dealer's licence if I were found guilty. My lawyer had warned me it was a fifty-fifty case that depended largely on the magistrate's attitude.

To my relief I was acquitted and, after the case, Hanna called me into his chambers and told me he had recognised me from schooldays.

I hadn't known him in all his legal regalia but, after the lecture he gave me then, I followed his advice and kept a very low profile, and out of trouble, for the rest of my years in the Rhodesias.

Chapter Six

A Drop in the Crocodile Market

Our crocodile business continued to flourish and we had to buy one of the largest privately owned boats on the lake to cope with the ever-increasing numbers of crocodile skins. This expansion had meant, also, that we had ever-increasing supplies of salt, food and other basics to be delivered to the crocodile camps. Using our boat for the deliveries saved us both time and money.

Soon all this was to change, and we were to learn the first lessons of supply and demand caused by fluctuating overseas markets for crocodile skins, due to the huge number that were now being exported from Africa.

Others had taken note of our success and similar crocodile hunting organisations were growing in the Rhodesias, covering the Congo, Mozambique, Angola and Malawi. I had, in fact, started to travel to these areas myself, to collect consignments of crocodile skins and to make arrangements for our hunters to go there.

⋆

Gerald Chopra, since he was a lawyer, had very wisely insisted that our crocodile skins were covered by forward contracts with Booth's and, as Booth's branch manager in Mwanza, I had helped organise the contracts with head office in Nairobi. As far as I remember, these were based on an annual contract price and Booth's had been very happy with the results that I had achieved while the overseas crocodile market was booming. In fact, Mwanza was the only branch making a profit at that time, due mainly to the crocodile skins, as the hides and skins business in the other branches (at Nairobi, Kampala, Kisumu and Mombasa) was not progressing as well as had been expected.

I had been told by London that I would be getting a share of the Mwanza profits but, with all the other branches making losses, it was now decided that I would only get a share of the overall profits when all the branches made a profit. Peter (later Sir Peter) Meinertzhagen, the local general manager, with whom I got on very well, tried to get this changed, but to no avail. This change of policy annoyed me intensely at the time, and I was not slow in letting head office in Nairobi know my feelings. At this stage they had no idea that my wife was in the crocodile business with Gerald Chopra.

Then came the bombshell: head office in Nairobi panicked at the sudden drop in overseas prices and wanted to renegotiate our crocodile contracts. This placed me in an extremely awkward situation, and I knew it meant I had to decide whether I wanted to stay with Booth's indefinitely and eventually, if I was lucky, draw a pension from them, or resign and go it alone.

I had seen some of the managers of Unilever's UAC, and of other large British firms in East Africa, reach retirement age, and knew that a combination of drink and malaria made it unusual for them to survive very long to enjoy their pensions – many didn't live long enough to draw their pensions at all. From my army days, and the fact that I had already had some bad doses of malaria, I knew I would have to move to the more temperate Rhodesias or South Africa before middle age if I was myself to stand a chance of surviving long enough to draw my pension – at sixty. Colonial civil servants like my father were much better treated and could retire at any time after they had put in twenty years of service.

So, after long discussions with Gerald Chopra, it was decided that we would fight the case in court, which meant the High Court in Nairobi. We won a considerable sum of money, so Booth's and their lawyers were not best pleased. During their investigations, they had discovered that my wife had fifty per cent of the shares in the crocodile business. So along came the inevitable ultimatum: I had to accept immediate transfer to another branch in East Africa or resign from the company.

As I was earning, at a conservative estimate, twenty to thirty times more from the crocodile business than from my job with Booth's, it did not take me long to make up my mind. I never regretted the decision to go it alone, although I had some hard times later.

*

We decided to start our own hides and skins business, to be run in conjunction with our thriving crocodile business.

This was to prove a big mistake: we should have stuck to crocodiles only. The bulk of the hides and skins meant that we had to build a large store at Mwanza South, while more than a thousand crocodile skins could be stored in a large garage.

Also, we had worked out a very effective way of air-drying the crocodile skins after a thorough salting, which cut down air-freight charges to Europe considerably. Nor did we have to wait for payment, since we received a letter of credit when we made delivery to the aircraft. So the crocodile business gave us the maximum profit for the minimum outlay.

The real trouble with the hides and skins business, however, was the unreliability of local staff. Most of my time was now being spent on the lucrative crocodile side of the business and I was unable to keep a close eye on what was going on elsewhere.

The inevitable happened and I found out, at an annual stocktake, that there were huge losses of hides and skins. By the time these losses were discovered, it was impossible to track down where and how the thefts had occurred. I spent some days travelling around, checking with our suppliers, but it soon became obvious that there had been collusion all round and I realised we would never get enough evidence to take to court.

Although at the time I didn't appreciate it, I was learning valuable lessons for the future and never again would I run a business that I could not control completely myself.

As a sideline, we had negotiated a local agency deal with Shell, which should have been very profitable but, incredible as it now seems, we also had a bad setback there – when a five-ton truckload of four-gallon tins of kerosene (known in the UK as paraffin) disappeared without trace. We did eventually find out how it was done but, again, getting proof to take to court was impossible.

These, and other setbacks, were spread over quite a considerable period. The end result was that, in order to pay off our losses, we had to sell the hides and skins store, as well as the double-storey house we had eventually built in Mwanza – after we had to move out of Booth's company house when I left their employ.

*

Fortunately, Northern Rhodesia, the Congo and other areas were now building up very profitably, as I was beginning to feel that my wife and I had had enough of Mwanza. While on my travels, I had passed through a very attractive area close to the Rwanda-Burundi border. The DC of this district (Kibondo-Kakonko), Peter Haynes, was Kenya-born and a very fine DC who knew what Africa was all about. His father was a farmer in Kenya, who was tragically killed by a rhino on his farm not long after we had moved to Kakonko.

Peter Haynes was keen to encourage white farmers to his district and when he took me to see some of the land available near Kakonko I knew it was exactly what I had been looking for. There was an all-year stream running through the property and a hill where I could build a house that would overlook the whole area. Although I had already decided this was what I wanted, I told Peter Haynes that my final decision depended on my getting a Tanganyikan bank loan and, with his help, this was granted pretty quickly.

I also bought a five-ton Ford diesel lorry with the loan, which came in very useful from the start, as Peter Haynes gave me a transport contract to carry some of the salt needed in his district. The local Africans were paid in salt for their annual work on the district roads. The salt came from the Uvinza mine, not far from Kigoma. At the start, when we were pushed for money for wages, I drove the lorry to Uvinza myself.

Peter Haynes was very helpful and friendly, but he was HM's representative in the area and I don't think he would have approved of my using the lorry to smuggle in the odd load or two of coffee at night from nearby Ruanda-Urundi. Prices for coffee in Tanganyika were much higher than in the Belgian Congo. Later we grew local tobacco, which sold in coils, and that came in very useful to barter for the coffee. To cover ourselves, even though we were right out in real bush country, I had planted some coffee trees on the farm. No one ever checked, however.

*

At the start of the war, I had still been at The King's School when it was evacuated from Canterbury to St Austell, in Cornwall, and I had obtained my parents' permission to work on a local farm during the school holidays. I had enjoyed the farm work very much and had got on well with the couple who owned the farm: they had no children, and wanted me to stay. Their foreman had been an ex-regular soldier from India and his tales of life there, often very earthy, had enthralled me.

Later, when I was at pre-Octu at Wrotham and had the chance to volunteer to go to India, I took the opportunity. I'm quite sure this decision had a lot to do with the foreman's stories, and it was what started me on my travels in India, the Middle East, Italy, back to the Middle East and then on to Africa.

It was only after we had moved to the farm at Kakonko that I came to realise fully just how little the average European knew about the life of rural Africans or, indeed, about any Africans. Most Europeans met the locals only as servants, and you cannot get to know anyone properly in a master-servant situation.

I had begun to learn about the Africans during my dealings with Booth's labour force, who handled the hides and skins in the company store. Invaluable in helping me understand something of the African mentality were my two Arab hides and skins selectors, Mohamed and Abdul Kader.

At the start, for example, I could never understand why a request for urgent leave of absence was always phrased the same: *Ngombe yangu ngongwa sana* – this translates from the Swahili as 'My cattle are very sick.'

Never was there a request for urgent leave for a sick wife or child, and Mohamed explained to me that cattle are symbolic of the rural African's position and power in his tribal life, so they were cited in any emergency, including all family disasters. So when cattle are mentioned nothing will stop an African going home. Contracts mean nothing to the rural African and it has to be accepted that, if needed, he will return to his village regardless of the consequences.

In my early days in Mwanza I did not always have enough sense to listen to Abdul Kader's advice and, quite often, an African labourer left despite the fact that he was owed two or three weeks' wages, and he never returned to collect his money. The workers were also fond of using another Swahili expression, *Shauri ya Mongu*, which it is difficult to translate into English. The nearest I can get is: 'It's in God's hands,' and it covered most of the misfortunes that occurred in their lives.

When I left Mwanza to farm in the Kibondo-Kakonko district, I did not know that I was to be given the opportunity of really getting to know the rural African in his true village life, a chance that is given to very few Europeans.

There were only a handful of Westerners in the district, mostly dedicated colonial civil servants and missionaries. In fact I was the only European 'commercial' (the local term for anyone engaged in business who was not a civil servant) in the whole district. That suited me fine, but did not please my wife Betty very much, as she missed Mwanza's social life.

As my farming and elephant hunting developed, and I got to know the rural Africans well, I was filled with admiration for their fortitude, courage, courtesy and kindness, from the local chief down to the lowest tribesman.

In fact, as I will explain later, I owed my life to some of these tribesmen when things went wrong on one of my hunting trips.

★

My admiration for the ordinary African was one of the reasons why I promised myself that some day I would write a book about what really happened in East and central Africa in those vital post-war years, and why the African tragedy that I saw unfolding in front of my eyes was completely unnecessary. It was a betrayal of the trust that the ordinary rural African had for our colonial service.

Julius Nyerere and his socialist and Marxist advisers from Europe should never have been allowed to wreck the traditional tribal way of life when, after Tanganyika's independence in 1961, he was allowed (even encouraged) by the UN and Britain to uproot millions of tribal Africans and forcibly herd them into his so-called 'model villages'. The madness of his African-socialist dream inevitably ended in miserable failure, with human suffering and a catastrophic drop in Tanzania's food production, which had been so carefully built up during the colonial days.

The UN and Britain shrugged off this completely unnecessary catastrophe as 'developmental' and poured millions of pounds' worth of aid into emergency food supplies, a familiar pattern that was to repeat itself tragically over most newly independent states of Africa. It must again be stressed that in colonial days in West, East and central Africa, famine was unknown. The well-run agricultural departments insisted that precautions be taken against famine and a minimum amount of cassava had to be planted. It was, in fact, a legacy of the colonial era that, well into the 1960s, Africa was self-sufficient in food.

★

Another inspiration in writing my book was the publication in 1988 of *The Destruction of a Continent*, which exposes the UN in Africa. The two authors have worked in universities in black Africa, as well as South Africa, so know both well. Their book is a real eye-opener, especially regarding the role played by Austria's Kurt Waldheim, who had taken over as the UN's Secretary-General in 1972.

It didn't take Waldheim and the communists long to realise how best to exploit Western weakness. So, at a special session of the UN in 1974, the New International Economic Order (NIEO) came into being. It draws together an international body of extortioners, communists, Western socialists, fellow-travellers in the West and Commonwealth countries who work for communism. They continually demand more and more money from the West, money which is then redistributed to Third World countries. Repayment or compensation to the West is never even considered.

NIEO is the most potent weapon for propaganda and blackmail that the world has ever known. The African (and other Third World) extortioners are named in the book, as are their allies in Europe: social democrats, trade unions, radical intellectuals and aid fanatics of all kinds, with the communists in the background pulling the strings while the puppets in the West happily dance to their tune.

★

The British Empire's excellent system, which benefited countless millions of poor peasant farmers in both India and Africa was, unfortunately, marred by some grave faults, mostly at the very top (where it mattered most) as independence loomed. The viceroys and governors were mainly distinguished figureheads, who had little knowledge about the national characteristics and traditions of the locals and, in any case, it was in Whitehall that the major decisions were made.

Twining of Twining's Tea, for example, was Tanganyika's last governor. He was, no doubt, a very worthy city of London business gentleman, but his knowledge of Africa was minimal and Whitehall's pinstriped specimens at the Colonial Office had little more knowledge than he did of Tanganyika's tribal Africans. These authorities dealt with the local demagogue, Julius Nyerere. He, in turn, was told what to do by left-wing elements and advisers, who were intent on helping the communists destroy the British Empire as soon as possible. In carrying out their plans, the Russian Communists, having killed well over one hundred million of their own people since their 1917 Revolution, were not at all worried by the millions of Africans who were going to die in the process. Nor were they deterred by the resultant famine and starvation of millions more Africans, which continues up to this day and shows signs of getting even worse.

★

I want to refer once again to the book *The Destruction of a Continent*, as the authors are among the few who are prepared to concede that the British

Empire, and the brave colonials who made it all possible, were the high point in Africa's development, and to say that Africa was better off under colonialism.

The colonial settlers brought much good, in the form of law and order, modern agriculture, technology and economic progress, with the minimum of interference in African tribal life. In short, the colonials made Africa's high point of development possible by devoting their lives to the continent with vision, courage and endless toil.

I endorse their views entirely, as do others who have spent most of their working lives in Africa since the end of World War II and who know Africa well.

But unfortunately the socialists, working with the communists, were able to undermine all the colonial achievements by vicious and untrue anti-colonial propaganda. It continues unabated to this day and has brought in its wake famine, civil war, corruption, misrule and economic disaster.

What happened in Tanganyika was repeated all over Africa, with demagogues pretending to be working for the good of all Africans until they came to power. In Tanganyika, Tanu (Tanganyika African National Union) was formed and quickly spread its message all over the country, even to insignificant little places like Kibondo and Kakonko. The message to local chiefs was brutally clear – support Tanu or lose your job after independence.

The world, via the Labour and communist parties, was led to believe that these African organisations were spontaneously formed to reflect the desire of the majority of Africans for independence. Nothing could be further from the truth, and it is very doubtful if more than one per cent of the population voluntarily supported Tanu. This was borne out in my conversations with chiefs and headmen right down as far as Kigoma.

In India it had been exactly the same story, except that there were a lot more town dwellers there who supported the Congress Party. This myth has, of course, been carefully fostered by the communists, but the truth is that the millions of near-starving peasant farmers in India and Africa had one interest only, and that was to survive the harsh conditions of their lives. They had no interest in politics.

When one looks at the leaders that were foisted on the unfortunate African countries, it is easy to understand why so many millions are now starving. It cannot be repeated often enough how unnecessary the tragedy in Africa was, and how easily it could have been avoided.

India was completely different to Africa, and had to have independence quickly due to religious pressures from Hindus and Muslims. Africa had none of these pressures and was of very little economic importance to the West, so there should have been a slow and gradual Africanisation of the existing colonial system, which was working very well. To have any chance of success, a twenty-year period of Africanisation was needed.

This could have been supervised by the UN, backed up by UN troops if necessary. Approximately five thousand UN troops were sent to Namibia, and others have been used in various trouble spots in Africa and around the world.

It might not have been possible to continue the East Africa Federation, but it was certainly possible to continue the Central African Federation (made up of the two Rhodesias and Nyasaland), and far more important, since it was the only hope of building up a strong multiracial and economic force to counter the overwhelming strength of South Africa.

Opposition to the Federation was really very small, but so well organised, with Labour and communist backing, that the Colonial Office in London caved in almost immediately and the last chance to stabilise Southern Africa was lost.

In Tanganyika, the people on the spot who should have been consulted, like district commissioners with years of experience of African rural tribal life and the local chiefs, who knew exactly what was needed and what would improve the existing colonial system during the period of Africanisation, were never consulted. London heard only the strident voices of Nyerere and Tanu.

Tanu was, of course, based in Dar es Salaam, where the Legislative Council and the colonial administration had their headquarters, so Whitehall, in effect, heard only the views of Tanu.

The colonial service is very much like the army in some respects. Orders and policies are decided at the top and independent thought is not encouraged. Local settlers' views were also ignored, even by the Conservatives, as they waffled on about the 'wind of change'. So nothing was done to protect the large majority of the population, the African peasant farmers, from future exploitation, civil war, starvation and death at the hands of their tyrannical leaders.

In the future someone had to be blamed for this misrule, and the disasters that followed, and who better than the colonial settlers, who were now abandoned by their own kind in Europe and were an easy target to take the blame for all Africa's ills after independence? Just as South Africa is now the convenient villain for the Commonwealth and the front-line states who have already extorted billions of pounds in aid and can see no reason why they cannot extort further billions from gullible Britain and the rest of the West.

Only those in the Federation of Rhodesia and Nyasaland (also known as CAF – Central African Federation) who, like me, lived in Africa during the ten years of CAF's existence (1953–1963), will understand how events in East Africa helped influence the tragic course of events in the Rhodesias.

If Whitehall had stood firm, and honoured its promise to Sir Roy Welensky to allow the Federation to continue, there would have been no need for Ian Smith's UDI. But Whitehall seemed to have forgotten that appeasement didn't work with Hitler, and the communists were able to complete their takeover of all South Africa's neighbours.

This is why *The Destruction of a Continent* is so important. It is the start of a vital reassessment of what really went on in Africa in colonial times and after independence. With the present political climate in Russia, and the end of the Cold War, it should be possible to repair a great deal of the damage, but only if the West faces up to the fact that the UN has failed miserably in Africa (see 'An Indictment' at the end of this book).

Then, perhaps, every sane person will begin to understand why South Africa cannot be handed over to the ANC and the Communists. There is already enough untold misery and starvation in most of black-ruled Africa, and only a madman or a communist would want to extend this misery and starvation to South Africa as well. Yet it is this for which many black members of the Commonwealth are working, with a great deal of encouragement from the World Council of Churches (WCC). If they succeed, the destruction of Africa will be complete.

That is why Mrs Thatcher's opposition to sanctions against South Africa was so important. The world must be allowed to see the real situation and conditions in black-ruled Africa, and told how its leaders use deceit and hypocrisy to disguise their own countries' failings, by continually using South Africa's apartheid as a convenient diversion to cover their own faults. Some of them were mentioned in Amnesty International's 1989 report (published in October 1989), which lists twenty-two Commonwealth countries that are abusing human rights by using repression, torture, brutality and intolerance of any opposition.

These are only some of the crimes cited in the report and among the main offenders are two countries who continually criticise South Africa at Commonwealth meetings – namely Zimbabwe and Zambia.

The death of one African (Biko), while in South African police custody, is certainly regrettable, but it is typical of the arrogance and deception of Mugabe that he had the effrontery to help finance Richard Attenborough's blatantly misleading propaganda film on the subject, *Cry Freedom*. Mugabe provided financial backing to the tune of five million US dollars, as well as all the necessary facilities for the film to be made in Zimbabwe. What appalling hypocrisy when you consider that Mugabe has been responsible for the massacre of tens of thousands of Matabele – reports reaching the respected Rhodesia Christian Group in London have indicated that the figure could be as high as forty thousand!

Full details of the Zimbabwean 5th Brigade, who were specially trained for internal security control and murder by North Korea's military mission in Zimbabwe, are available to the West. In fact, a British military mission was sent to Zimbabwe especially to retrain the notoriously brutal 5th Brigade. Yet, protected by his communist friends and as one of Africa's most accomplished extortioners of aid from the West, there was absolutely no world outcry or condemnation of Mugabe.

It is not necessary to spell out the double standards here. It's easy to imagine what the world reaction would have been if these brutal mass murders had occurred in South Africa. Worse massacres than Sharpeville occur regularly all over Africa, but are seldom reported by the Western media.

The African leaders and their brutal henchmen, who exploit their own people and use a considerable part of the aid money extorted from the West for their own personal use (or for armaments to slaughter their people), have been very aptly named 'Wa-Benzis' – the Africans who drive around in opulent Mercedes-Benz cars while the rest of the Africans live in abject poverty.

To refer again to that excellent book *The Destruction of a Continent*, the authors make another very valid point when they detail all the good that the white settlers brought to Africa, and stress that the new 'aid elite' African rulers are incomparably more high-handed and imperious than the colonial rulers ever were.

To give an example of this: in a lot of tinpot African countries, like Malawi, drivers must get off the road before someone like President-for-life Kamuzu Banda comes along. Anyone failing to do so, especially if he is white, is arrested for insulting the president by not showing enough respect, and invariably given a good beating-up as a lesson on how he must behave in the new Africa.

★

Neil Kinnock, who seems to champion every black demagogue – including those in the church like Tutu and Boesak – should always remember his first lesson on the realities of Africa. Brutality far worse than he received when he was manhandled and locked up in a small room for some hours by drunken Zimbabwe troops (when he, with his wife and party, landed at the wrong airport), is the normal way of life in Africa. He was extremely lucky that his Welsh temper did not get him shot.

It is, I know, a lot to ask, but I suggest that, before Neil Kinnock and his wife sign the anti-South Africa petitions that appear with such monotony before any Commonwealth or UN meeting on South Africa, they spend some time reflecting on the realities of Africa. They were very lucky to come out unscathed from their Zimbabwe ordeal, but appear to have learnt nothing from this experience.

I can only assume that Kinnock did not read Amnesty International's report, which listed so many of his Marxist friends' Commonwealth countries, including Zimbabwe and Zambia, among the twenty-two that featured so prominently.

If he had read the report, perhaps he and his wife might not have been quite so keen to sign the so-called Southern African Coalition petition – a collection of signatures that made up a full-page advertisement in *The Times* on 18th October, 1989. It was timed to coincide with a meeting of the Commonwealth heads of government in Kuala Lumpur.

Chapter Seven

Some Colonial Stories

I can't think of a better place than Mwanza to have spent my first years in East Africa, with the added bonus of Lake Victoria and the Serengeti National Park within easy reach. I count myself very lucky to have had those eleven happy years before independence and Nyerere wrecked the country.

In those early post-war years Mwanza's European population was composed mainly of civil servants, as Mwanza was the administrative headquarters for the Lake Province, then one of the most prosperous provinces of Tanganyika. Although there were, without doubt, some very able colonial civil servants – such as Mwanza's district commissioner, Gordon Russell – there were also some very pompous specimens, who seemed to be unable to understand that the world had changed since the end of the war, and that India and Pakistan's independence in 1947 spelt the inevitable end of the British Empire in Africa, as well as elsewhere in the world.

There were very few 'commercials' in Mwanza at that time, and most had, like myself, seen active service in World War II. Some names still come to mind: Ken Lee, DFC, manager of UAC; Gerry Dashwood of Barclays Bank, who was often, even in those early days, immobilised by gout; George Irving of Lehmann's, a firm from Dar es Salaam; and John Miles, also of UAC.

Our social life centred on the Mwanza Club, with its weekly dances, tennis courts, golf course, billiard room and other facilities, including a very good library. Before we all came along, after the end of the war, the place had been dominated by some of the most pompous colonial civil servants and I, with a colonial service family background, was ideally placed to debunk them which, I must admit, I enjoyed doing – especially after a few beers. It always amused me how the 'commercials' used to drink at one end of the bar while the colonial servants kept to the other end.

Looking back now, after all these years, I can see I was far more soured by my experiences in India than I was prepared to admit. I never told anyone in the family, nor for that matter anyone outside the family, about my paralysis. Although I greatly admired my father, and his career with HM's administrative service in Nigeria, I drew on it for ammunition to mock the local civil servants with, and I told them I had no desire to be any part of the decline and fall of the British Empire.

While in India, I had seen something of the beginning of the end of British rule there but I had no idea just how quickly and disastrously independence was to come to East Africa. The fact that most of the civil servants had sat out the war in comfort in Tanganyika, and the biggest inconvenience caused to them by the conflict had been the fact that they had been unable to get back to the UK on leave, made it more of a pleasure for us to rub in our various wartime experiences.

*

One of my stories about India, I knew, annoyed them all intensely, so it was always a particular pleasure for me to go into detail about the size and luxury of the sub-collector's house, where I had stayed while he was away on local leave, with its indoor marble swimming pool and the polo ponies in the adjacent stables. This story made the houses built by the Public Works Department look very squalid indeed. In fact, the only impressive houses in Tanganyika were those that had been built in German times.

I also knew that quite a few of the colonial service audience at the club bar had gone to very minor public schools, or grammar schools, so it always helped to mention that Brian Fern of the Tanganyika police and others I knew had been at The King's School at the same time as my brother and myself.

It often surprised me how long it took us all to forget our early backgrounds in Britain. In the war it had meant nothing, but in the hothouse colonial atmosphere in Mwanza it all came back to me.

To give the civil servants a little bit of their own medicine, as they preferred to have their administrative officers from Oxbridge, I would bring up the fact that my father had been to Downing College, Cambridge. It would have spoiled the story to mention that he had been educated at Bradford Grammar School, and that it was by sheer brains and merit, not privilege, that he had got to Cambridge University.

What infuriated them most was the fact that I was able to make comparisons between India, Nigeria and Tanganyika, and to give them some idea of how colonial civil servants were posted to these various areas. India, 'the jewel in the Imperial Crown' in more ways than one, was the plum colonial posting, with certain other Far East postings not far behind. Then came Nigeria, followed by some of the other west-coast postings. On the east coast, poor countries like Tanganyika and Malawi came right at the end of the list of desirable colonial postings.

'Commercials' came very low in the colonial system in those days, so it gave me a great deal of satisfaction to level the score somewhat.

*

Normally most of us used to stick to a few beers in the evenings at the club, but sometimes we made a night of it, switching to whisky or brandy and, on occasion, having an all-night game of poker.

One evening an accountant from one of the banks joined our regular poker school. I can't say that any of us found his behaviour in any way strange, except perhaps that he was drinking pretty heavily – but that was nothing unusual in those free and easy days. One thing I do remember is that he had not been in Mwanza long and none of us knew that he had been a prisoner of war of the Japanese and, like most of their captives, had had a very bad time while in captivity.

In the early morning some of us were having a last drink before going home when he decided to phone his wife and get her to pick him up from the club. Unfortunately her car broke down and she had to walk the rest of the way. Naturally she was not in the best of moods by the time she came into the bar. Someone gave them both a lift to his bank and the rest of us went our various ways, mostly home to bed.

None of us had found the morning's events very unusual, as it was not uncommon in those days to have irate wives coming to the club to drag their husbands home, but we were unaware of the man's history. Apparently, due to his wartime experiences in the hands of the Japanese, the accountant was prone to bouts of depression and had threatened suicide on several occasions. On this day he left the bank and drove to the bottom of a well-known local landmark called Bismarck's Rock. Then he climbed to the top and shot himself.

These facts only came out later, and we were all subpoenaed to appear in court for the inquest. The final irony was that a senior magistrate who had been playing poker with us that night was in charge of the inquiry into the circumstances of his death.

*

The Mwanza Club, and later the Mwanza Yacht Club, provided all the sports facilities we needed, but the standard of tennis at the club was pretty low, so playing there didn't interest me at first.

My father had played tennis for Nigeria and, when on leave in England, had taken part in the East of England Championships at Felixstowe, where we lived with our grandparents during the school holidays. We all played a lot there, as well as when we were at The King's School.

I had never been keen on mixed doubles unless there were some attractive women as partners and, at that time in Mwanza, there weren't any attractive ones playing tennis. Then along came a half-blue at tennis from either Oxford or Cambridge (Gavin Green, I think his name was). He was one of the bright boys in the administration.

I knew he would beat me at first, as I hadn't played since before the war, and my early defeats were much to the delight of some of the audience from the club bar, which overlooked the tennis courts. But I felt, from the very start, that I would be able to beat him once I was back to form. One weakness was that he had a slightly superior, languid approach to the game, especially when he was winning.

Sure enough, I began to beat him regularly and, although he concealed it well, I could see that he did not like it. He certainly lost most of his languid approach. He represented all that I disliked and, nearly forty years later, I still remember the satisfaction that beating him gave me. I think he was quite glad when I left Mwanza and he resumed his position as the undisputed club champion.

*

Without wishing to sound conceited, I should say that I was also very good at squash, and could beat most of the local opposition without really trying. Gerald Chopra had lived with his parents in their large house in the centre of town (near the sports field where we played cricket, hockey and football) until he got married and built his own house not far from the club. He built his own squash court next to the house, and we played there regularly until I left Mwanza.

So, although most of us drank pretty heavily, we were also very fit. I'd had back problems ever since my mysterious paralysis, but at this stage it gave me little trouble provided I did my yoga exercises regularly. So I did them meticulously except when I was down with malaria. I think the heat of the tropical sun also helped a lot. Since I returned to Britain I have felt only half alive and suffer from almost continual back trouble. More than anything else, I am aware of missing the feel of the strong tropical sun on my back.

★

While I was working for Booth's, I had a monthly allowance which was supposed to cover entertaining the local colonial officials. I didn't see why I should entertain people I did not particularly like, however, and, as my head office was hundreds of miles away, it was a long time before they realised that I had never bothered to entertain HM's chief representative in the Lake Province, the PC (Provincial Commissioner).

Although I can't remember his name, I do remember that he was married but had no children. I am a great believer in the theory that children stop parents becoming pompous. I don't believe that my own father, in similar circumstances, would ever have acted in the way that Mwanza PC did.

Many years later, after returning to Britain and remarrying, I was reminded of this when we had an unexpected addition to the family, a daughter (now seven years old). I learnt the art of changing a baby's nappy at first hand, as we couldn't afford a nanny as we had done in Africa, and there's no room for pomposity in that procedure!

I had finally given in to pressure from head office in Nairobi and invited our local provincial commissioner, together with some of his heads of department, to a party at my house. I also invited some of my commercial friends to enliven the evening somewhat. Little did I know then just how exciting it was going to become.

Parking was always a problem, because of the steep approach to our rondavel-style house, which was about three-quarters of the way up a hill. There was some level parking, both in front and at the rear of the house, but not nearly enough when we were giving a party, so the late arrivals had to park on the steep slope.

The provincial commissioner arrived late, so he was among those who had to park on the hill. What none of us knew was that one of our African servants had helpfully made sure the car would not roll away by putting quite a large rock in front of the rear wheel. Unfortunately, he forgot to tell anyone of this action. We used tilley lamps in those days, so there was no outside lighting: there was electricity in Mwanza itself, but we were a mile or two out of town, in the Mwanza South industrial area. Our refrigerator used kerosene, while the boiler for our bathwater and our stove were both heated by wood fires.

The party went well as, to cut down on the boring colonial gossip, we had organised a roulette table for some mild gambling. It was quite late before the provincial commissioner decided to leave, and we were all quite merry by then. The African servants had already gone home, and it didn't occur to any of us to look under the PC's car, which would not move when he started it. We began pushing, with the PC half in and half out of the car – it was not his large official car but his wife's small Volkswagen.

It had been raining earlier in the evening and we must have gradually pushed the rock down into the mud. Anyway the car shot forward suddenly, with the PC only half inside. He was a fairly large man and could not squeeze into the car fast enough as it began to move. He lost his footing on the wet ground and ended up lying on his back in the mud as the car gathered speed and disappeared down the hill. Soon we heard the sound of an almighty crash, as the car wrecked itself on the rocks below.

We were all pretty shocked by what had happened, until we realised the PC was unharmed, and we sobered up quickly when we saw the rock. I knew then there was going to be trouble, as I could see that the PC did not believe me when I told him that no one knew anything about how the rock had got under his car.

Everything was a bit chaotic and I believe his wife was jumping up and down, telling everybody who would listen that we had tried to kill her husband. In fact it was all quite funny, even at the time, and we carried on the party for some hours after the couple had left with most of their colonial service colleagues.

Offended dignity was quick to act and, the very next day, we received an official letter giving us one month's notice to vacate the government property at Mwanza South, in other words, our rondavel-type house that I had renovated extensively. There was no mention, of course, of the previous night's events. The letter merely stated that we had occupied the property longer than was originally agreed, and that the premises were now wanted.

It was true that, in my original agreement with Gordon Russell, I had given a date by which I expected the company house to be completed but, verbally with Gordon Russell, I had been given an extension. In fact he had told me I could stay there as long as necessary.

I had never pushed the builders to complete Booth's company house, and they were months behind the original completion date. This had never worried me, since I much preferred our rondavels to the suburbia of Mwanza and all the colonial civil servants.

At the time of the party completion was not more than three months away. But I was in no mood to be pushed around by any pompous PC, and I went around to see Gordon Russell. He advised me to allow a few days for the PC to cool off before I went to see him. Unofficially, Gordon told me he didn't think we would be thrown out, even if I insisted on staying the three months until the company house was completed.

I could see he was much more interested in knowing what had actually happened the previous night, as the others who had been there were refusing to talk about it. He fell around laughing when I gave him a slightly embellished version of events, and he made me repeat the bit where the PC fell on his back in the mud and ruined his nice, clean, white tropical suit, and how his wife had been jumping about in rage when she saw her car disappearing down the hill and had been screaming that we had tried to kill her husband.

By now I was beginning, again, to see the funny side of what had happened, and we went off to have a drink together before the PC came back to his office from some meeting or other. Gordon's office was near his and it wouldn't have been exactly tactful for him to find us laughing together. Gordon told me later that the PC had warned the others who had been at the party not to talk about what had happened.

When I did get to see the PC a few days later, I found him far worse than I expected, and still in no mood to listen to reason. It ended up with me telling him I had no intention of moving for three months, at which time the company house would be ready, and that, as an ex-serviceman who had fought to keep him in his job in comparative luxury in Tanganyika, I was appalled at his petty-minded attitude over an unfortunate accident.

He told me he didn't believe my story, as some of his informants at the club had told him that I often instigated jokes and stories about the colonial service that he did not find amusing and that, in view of my attitude, he would be writing to my managing director in Nairobi, insisting that we vacated our house in one month. This he duly did, but I also wrote to head office, saying I had no intention, whatever happened, of moving within a month. Nairobi found a very neat way around the problem.

I had recently had another bad attack of malaria, which had affected my spleen, and my doctor had recommended sick leave. The firm agreed to send me to the White Highlands of Kenya, provided that I was prepared to move out of the house in about six or seven weeks' time. They said we needn't return to Mwanza until the new company house there was ready for us to move into. So everything was settled reasonably amicably, and off we went for an extended holiday in Kenya.

Although my boss in Nairobi, Peter Meinertzhagen, wasn't best pleased at first at what had happened, he did appreciate the funny side when I told him the full story.

★

During my sick leave I was able to visit some of the farms in the area. I found it particularly interesting to learn how some of the farmers were crossing local sheep with imported Hampshire rams, with outstanding results. The local strain meant the offspring were more resistant to all the local diseases.

Speaking to some of the more senior farm workers on more than one occasion, I asked whether they preferred working for British or Afrikaner farmers, and I was quite surprised by how many of them preferred Afrikaners. They reckoned the latter took more interest in, and were more knowledgeable about, local farming methods, and that they handled their African labour force better. What a tragedy so many of their achievements were wasted after independence.

An ironical final twist to this colonial chapter of my life is that, while I was in Mwanza, I received a letter from the War Office in Whitehall, London. How they found me I can't remember now – it was probably through the Royal British Legion in London, through whom I had originally got my job with Booth & Co. in East Africa.

It warned me I was still on their list of officers on reserve, and would I advise them if I changed my address. I never answered, nor heard any more, but it was around the time of the Korean War (1950–1953), where my brother Paul was wounded and awarded the Military Cross.

★

Although I had enjoyed my years in Mwanza, and seeing how the provincial administration worked, the army had given me a taste for travel and I had had enough of Mwanza's colonial civil servants. I knew it was time for me to move on and start farming in the Kibondo-Kakonko district, which would give me much more freedom to go hunting.

There I would be able to see the colonial system at grass-roots level, with the district commissioner, district officers and other departmental officers of the Public Works, Agricultural, Game and Veterinary Departments – and all the others who did so much to make the colonial service such an outstanding success all over Africa.

I am very proud of my father's contribution to the colonial administration in Nigeria, from 1919 to 1942, and very privileged that I could spend twenty-one glorious years in East and central Africa before the evil forces of communism, with the help of the UN, succeeded in destroying the whole system, bringing in its wake famine, civil war, corruption, misrule and economic disaster.

It was not until I returned to Britain (in 1983) after thirty-five years in Africa, that I fully began to realise the extent of the conspiracy of silence imposed by the communists and their Western allies: the social democrats in Europe, the Labour Party in Britain, the trade unions and the radical intellectuals – with the active assistance of the Western media, especially television, and with the open connivance of the Commonwealth and UN. Not only had they stopped the truth being published about what had really happened in Africa since the end of the war, but they had effectively stopped almost all critical reports coming out of the newly independent African nations.

Starvation is put down as an act of God, although famine conditions were unknown in the well-organised days of the colonial era. Instead the Western media, in particular television, confine the news about Africa to almost daily stories of apartheid in South Africa. The wholesale massacres in Uganda, Nigeria, Zimbabwe, Ethiopia, Eritrea, Somalia and the Sudan are virtually ignored.

These massacres, civil wars and the almost universal breakdown of law and order, with the resultant starvation and general instability all over Africa, are the result of impetuous and ill-conceived plans for the independence of these unfortunate African states. Can any sane person, except a communist, really blame the South African authorities for trying to ensure that their gradual reforms do not affect the stability and prosperity of the country?

To illustrate the instability and violence brought about by premature independence, the changes of leadership are shown below for three Commonwealth countries, two in West Africa and one in East Africa.

Sixteen of the changes (more than half) in these three countries were the result of bloody *coups d'état* and six resulted in the violent death of the deposed leader – indicated below by **. It will be noted that three were from Ghana and three from Nigeria: a third of the total number of leaders in those two countries since independence!

Ghana – Independence 1957 – five coups

Leaders and Tenures

President Kwame Nkrumah (1957–1966)
General J. Ankrah (1966–1969)
**Brigadier A. Afrifa (1969–1970)
Prime Minister (Dr) Kofi Busia (1969–1972)]#
President E. Akufo-Addo (1970–1972)
**General I. Acheampong (1972–1978)
**General W. Akuffo (1978–1979)
Flight Lieutenant J. Rawlings (1979)
President H. Limann (1979–1981)
Flight Lieutenant J. Rawlings (1981–)

Nigeria – Independence 1960 – five coups

Leaders and Tenures

**Prime Minister A.T. Balewa (1960–1966)]#
President N. Azikiwe (1963–1966)
**General J. Aguiyi-Ironsi (1966)
General Y. Gowon (1966–1975)
**General M. Mohamed (1975–1976)
General O. Obasanjo (1976–1979)
President S. Shagari (1979–1983)
Major-General M. Buhari (1983–1985)
Major-General I. Babangida (1985–1993)
General Sani Abacha (1993–1998)

Uganda – Independence 1962 – six coups

Leaders and Tenures

Prime Minister Milton Obote (1962–1966)]#
King E. Mutesa (1963–1966)
President Milton Obote (1966–1971)
Field Marshal Idi Amin (1971–1979)
President Y. Lule (1979)
President G. Binaisa (1979–1980)
President P. Muwanga (1980–)
President Milton Obote (1980–1985)
Lieutenant-General T. Okello (1985–1986)
President Y. Museveni (1986–)

#The fact that these leaders overlap is due to a change in their countries' constitutions.

Assassinations and Executions

During the above period of independence in Africa, a total of twenty-one African heads of government were assassinated or executed.

Successful Bloody *Coups d'État*

Nothing illustrates the instability and violence of this period better than the number of successful bloody coups: an incredible sixty-eight!

There is, of course, no record of the number of unsuccessful coups during this time, nor of the total number of people who died violently, but the pattern all over black Africa is very much the same.

The chart below gives a general idea of the overall instability. During this period there were also eleven forced resignations and dismissals.

Successful *Coups d'État* since 1963

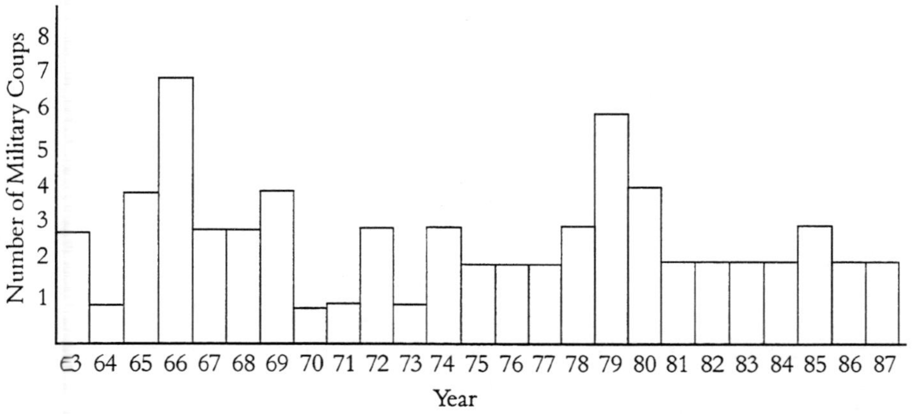

Before 1963: 4 Coups

1963 – 1987: 68 Coups

For all the details given above on African leaders, tenures in office, assassinations, executions and successful *coups d'état*, I am indebted to *African Insight*'s publication 'Africa at a Glance'.

That publication contains a wealth of interesting information, ideal for those interested in learning some of the basic statistics about Africa following independence after the end of World War II. No judgements are made: it just gives facts and figures, with plenty of easily understandable maps of Africa.

It shows that there is no such thing as democracy in Africa. Opposition parties are virtually non-existent except, ironically enough, in much-maligned South Africa. Commonwealth countries like Zimbabwe, Zambia and Tanzania, who lead the Commonwealth in demanding sanctions against South Africa, are among the worst offenders and ruthlessly dispose of opposition elements in their countries in the most brutal manner.

★

An interesting aspect of the bias against South Africa, which extends to British public libraries, was revealed at my local Westminster Library when I tried to get a copy of *The Destruction of a Continent*. It was not available. While looking round the African section, I happened to pick up a book by a distinguished black author, Dr W.E. Burghardt du Bois, *The World and Africa*, and I thought it would be interesting to see what an American black made of Africa today.

The main part of the book is concerned with Africa's role in world history, but it includes some of the doctor's new writings on Africa, covering the period from 1955 to 1961. These new writings are, in my view, a great mistake, but still of interest because they expose the astonishing ignorance of even learned historians like Dr Burghardt du Bois.

Even being as charitable as possible about his obvious desire to show the African, and his fascinating history on Africa, in the best light possible, I feel obliged to say that it is a great mistake for him to distort historical facts to such a degree that one begins to doubt his so-called inquiry into the part which Africa has played in world history. This is a very great pity, because I found his chapters on early Egyptian history absolutely fascinating: especially Chapter V ('Egypt') and Chapter VI ('The Land of the Burnt Faces'). But even here he lets his obsession with black Africa show, when he makes a point of mentioning that Queen Hatshepsut (whose granite head is in the British Museum) had distinct, to use his words, 'Negro features'.

There is, of course, no substitute for being on the spot when history is being made, and this is my main reason for believing that the truth about what really went on in Africa after the war has not yet been told. One of my main reasons for writing this book is the hope that it will help to set the record straight, even if it is forty years late.

That is why I wish to comment on the new writings of Dr Burghardt du Bois. The doctor's twelve-line reference to Tanganyika cannot escape criticism, and I quote in full his ludicrously inaccurate four-line reference to the Tanganyika Groundnuts Scheme:

> In Tanganyika after the war the British tried to herd the inhabitants on to plantations run by the greatest monopoly in the world on land seized from the natives. The scheme failed so completely that Britain now does not even mention it.

The whole idea of the Groundnuts Scheme was to use machinery (and British employees) to show what modern methods could achieve. It was only later, when these failed, that African labour had to be brought in, to dig out – by hand – any groundnuts that could be salvaged from the sun-baked earth.

He also writes about a representative of the UN Trusteeship Council who visited the country and received a petition from workers protesting discrimination in wages and housing.

Never in my eleven years in Tanganyika were we lucky enough to get just one UN representative. They came in droves, freeloading on the UN expenses and mainly from countries who had never heard of democracy. They assisted Nyerere and Tanu to draft petitions in Dar for the benefit of world opinion and the UN, giving a completely erroneous impression to the world that the country was ready for independence. No one locally dared speak against them.

The tragic consequences for African farmers herded into Marxist 'model villages' have been mentioned earlier in the book. It should be noted that there was never the slightest criticism from the Western world, nor the UN.

To hoodwink the West, this Marxist and socialist madness was described as 'developmental', to make it possible for Western aid fanatics to increase the millions in aid money necessary to feed Tanzania's starving millions, all of whom had enough to eat during my days in Tanganyika, before independence.

Can you wonder that the ordinary African hates and despises the UN and communists, who keep saying that they are helping him, when he knows he was far better off in colonial days? He was far less exploited then by the white settlers and colonial officials than he is today, governed by the new class of

African elite, the Wa-Benzis. They, with the help of the communists, outmanoeuvred his own tribal chiefs and seized power, with the help of the UN.

He sees his new leaders, in their smart Bond Street suits, taking part in eternal meetings with the Organisation of African Unity (whoever named the OAU must have had a sense of humour!), or with one of the multitudinous departments of the UN, which promise much but achieve very little. Politicians from all over the world love attending these meetings, which are mainly an excuse to travel at the Western taxpayers' expense, with wine and women lavishly provided. Only recently has the risk of Aids rather spoiled their fun in the sun.

Ironically, it is mainly those very earnest specimens from Europe, who profess to be able to cure all the ills of the world (but who have caused most of the misery in Africa), who love this junketing around the most.

The social democrats of Europe, with the communists, the Labour party in Britain, the trade unions and all their radical intellectual friends, make up the bulk of these experts and junketeers who so love to criticise prosperous South Africa. Rather than help with the reforms taking place there, they try to sabotage the efforts of people like Mrs Thatcher to stop sanctions against South Africa. Their main aim is to reduce South Africa to the same conditions that they have achieved in the rest of Africa: famine, civil war, corruption, misrule and economic disaster.

The ANC and the Communists realise what valuable allies these do-gooders are, with a great deal of support from the Churches, who, in the luxury of the West, have very little idea of the realities of the abject poverty of Africa.

Although, in the past, the Churches – or, rather, the missionaries – have done a lot of good in Africa, the present policy of the WCC (World Council of Churches), and other such Church organisations, of active political interference in the internal affairs of South Africa, is a great mistake and cannot be excused. Neither can the way the advice of churchmen with years of missionary experience in Africa is ignored when they retire to Britain.

The active Church support for various peace movements in Europe is naive, to say the least, especially when there is clear evidence that most of these organisations have been heavily penetrated by the communists at all levels. What is also unforgivable is the one-sided Church approach to Africa's problems, and the way it will only very rarely criticise the mass murders of Christians and others in black-ruled Africa, for fear of the consequences. Yet it knows it is safe to do this in South Africa, even to the extent of encouraging civil disobedience and financing other ways of undermining the government there. Such behaviour would never be tolerated in any black-ruled state in Africa.

Church demagogues like Tutu and Boesak are made fully aware of these facts by their Church mentors in Britain, and regular trips to Britain are organised so that they can get full coverage from the British media, most of who are only too happy to promote any anti-South Africa propaganda which will back their obsession with apartheid.

To illustrate the lengths to which the national newspapers and television news programmes will go to promote the frequent propaganda visits of South African demagogic priests like Tutu, Boesak and, to a lesser extent, other priests like Chikane, it is only necessary to mention the extensive national coverage given by the media, and the large amounts of money the Church of England is prepared to spend on advertising and other expenses involved in these trips.

It was only when the Bishop of Aston overestimated Tutu's appeal, on his 1989 trip to Birmingham, that the public became aware of the amounts involved. This Birmingham fiasco cost the Church of England over £250,000 and forced the resignation of the Bishop of Aston.

As in the case of Viraj Mendis, a bogus refugee from Sri Lanka who hoodwinked the Church for thirteen years before he was deported, and cost the Manchester ratepayers thousands of pounds, no public apologies were given by the bishops of Manchester or Birmingham for abusing British generosity.

Never is there any mention by the Church or the media that Tutu, Boesak and their ilk do not represent all South Africa's black Christians and, if it had not been for a letter in the *Daily Telegraph* on 24th March, 1988 by the Reverend Father Arthur Lewis, MA Oxon, forty years a missionary in Africa, I too would have been unaware of these facts.

In complete contrast to the propaganda trips of Tutu and Boesak, there was no mention in the national media of the March 1989 trip of two other black South African churchmen, Bishop Mokoena and Bishop Masiya, because I do *not* favour sanctions against South Africa. In fact their trip, sponsored by London's Freedom Association, was only reported in the *City of Westminster Post* on 20th April, 1989. I have reproduced that article (see Appendix) to show readers in Britain that there is always another side.

Father Arthur Lewis is also the honorary president of the recently formed Good Hope Christian Group (PO Box 430, Chingford, London E4 9SQ), which is funded entirely by voluntary donations. There must be many more in Britain, like myself, who do not want the money they give to their church to go to ANC, Swapo, or any other organisation that supports terrorism, nor to people like Tutu and Boesak, or Church organisations like WCC, who openly support and finance terrorist organisations.

There is another Christian organisation at the same address: the Rhodesia Christian Group, which helps all races in Zimbabwe who are being persecuted by the Marxist Mugabe's ruthless anti-Christian regime.

These two Christian groups offer a solution to all, like the writer, who want to continue paying their tithe to the Church, but who object very strongly to their money going to terrorist organisations. To see that your local church gets the message properly, write to your vicar, with a copy going to either the Good Hope or Rhodesia Christian Group, explaining exactly why you are, in future, going to send your donations to these Christian groups instead of continuing to give them to your church.

⋆

The Reverend Father Lewis's June 1989 'Letter to Friends' makes very interesting reading:

> For the Church of England the two bishops [author's note: from South Africa] were received on behalf of the Archbishop of Canterbury, by the Bishop of Coventry. Bishop Barrington-Ward, flanked by other churchmen, opened the meeting at 9.25 a.m. 19/4/89, taking off his watch and placing it in front of him. 'I have another meeting at ten o'clock,' he stated. 'Perhaps we might begin by giving the two bishops fifteen minutes to speak.' The black bishops spoke of the hunger of their people because of sanctions. They received short shrift [sic], scant courtesy and no sympathy. I met them later in the day. 'We won't be going through that again,' said Bishop Mokoena. One wonders if there is any limit to the arrogance and blindness of British churchmen.

Chapter Eight

Farming and Elephant Hunting

I first visited the Kakonko-Kibondo, Kasulu and Kigoma districts of Tanganyika while we were still living in Mwanza, and found the whole area very attractive, although I thought that both the Kakonko Catholic Mission and the DC in Kibondo were getting carried away when they talked of the amount of big game in the area. After moving there I was soon to find out that they hadn't exaggerated!

Shortly after moving, when we returned from a night out in Kibondo we regularly found a pride of lions parked on the farm's driveway, frequently passed elephants and giraffes at the roadside and had to put up with a leopard who carried off a goat from our herd every night. I began to realise that there was so much game around that it was like living in our own game reserve for free, and we did not have to pay a minimum of five hundred dollars a day to be herded around by some 'white hunter'.

★

Most people I spoke to in Mwanza before we left permanently for Kakonko reckoned we were quite mad to move to such an isolated place, but I have never stopped thanking my lucky stars that I followed my instincts and did not listen to sensible business advice to stay on in Mwanza where, no doubt, we would have made more money.

Had we not gone to Kakonko, I'm sure I would not be writing this book and I'm convinced that it must be written to help put the record straight. It is my most fervent hope that what I write will expose the crass stupidity of the West, particularly Britain, in dealing with the problems of Africa. The almost criminally stupid interference of British socialists, together with their communist friends and the UN, helped to create most of the unnecessary havoc and starvation that is now widespread in Africa.

The most important colonial powers, France and Britain, should have forgotten their petty differences and insisted on a sensible period of Africanisation so that the, on the whole, very successful colonial system could be gradually adapted for a minimum fifteen-year period before full independence was granted. Thus most of the terrible mistakes and excesses would have been avoided, including those in Tanzania.

Africa (with the exception of South Africa), unlike India, had very little commercial value to Britain but the Labour Party, with its short-sighted partisan policies, made sure that the British taxpayer would have to continue paying millions of pounds in aid money annually ad infinitum, and the Conservatives, without a Churchill to guide them, were too gutless after Suez to do anything about it.

The 'New World Order' at the UN developed (in 1974) into the 'New International Economic Order'. The basic aim of this organisation is the redistribution of ever-increasing amounts of Western money to the Third World, largely to pay for socialist-communist mischief in Africa. The aid payments will be compulsory, automatic and permanent. Further details can be obtained from *The Destruction of a Continent*.

Africa had some advantages over India: there were no pressing and intractable religious divisions, as with the Hindus and Muslims, and no overpopulation then. But this situation is changing with the advances in medical care in rural areas, especially in South Africa. If drastic steps are not taken to curb the increases, however, even that prosperous country will experience the same grinding poverty as India.

The unscrupulous African leaders and their followers represented only a very small proportion of the people – the urban educated Africans. The vast majority of the population, the rural Africans, were quite contented with their tribal systems, which had worked relatively well for centuries. But they were never represented in the West, nor at the UN, as the socialists and communists made sure that it was only their Marxist minions who were given a hearing in Europe and America. These minions were given lavish amounts of money and arms to ferment trouble all over colonial Africa, and gave the impression to the avid media in the West that they were the leaders of popular African uprisings.

Nothing could be further from the real truth, but the Western colonial powers were not interested in listening to the colonial civil servants or to the tribal chiefs, and readily caved in to UN and American pressure.

⋆

Although I did not realise it at the time (the mid-1950s), I was being given a chance, granted to very few Europeans, of getting to know the rural Africans on an equal footing, rather than the usual master-servant level. This was largely due to the fact that my financial resources were very limited and I knew my only chance of getting the farm going was to be on good terms with the local chief. It was essential that his men should work for me on a part-time basis until the farm began to make a profit.

I was lucky. Two or three large herds of elephants had been in the area recently and had caused considerable damage to all the crops, especially the maize, which had been trampled underfoot. So the chief and I came to an agreement whereby I would always be available to kill elephants who became troublesome in the future and I would keep the tusks. But the Africans could have all the meat and, in return, would work part-time on my farm when needed. Without this help it's unlikely that I could have kept the farm going in those early days.

Having Peter Haynes as our DC was another break. He had been born in Kenya and brought up on his father's farm there, so he understood the difficulties of farm life in Africa and was able to pass on a lot of invaluable advice. He also gave us a contract to transport the district salt, and that was an enormous help financially when we were getting started.

★

A third source of help was the Kakonko Catholic Mission (see Appendix for map) Apart from advice about the district, it gave us fresh fruit and vegetables, which were very welcome in our early days on the farm.

I often stayed the night at the mission, so that the brother and myself could make an early start the next morning to go hunting. We shared the meat and the farm's Ford lorry was very useful for transporting the African staff, who helped with the skinning and cutting up of the game as well as transporting the meat out of the bush at the end of the hunt.

I can't remember ever coming back empty-handed in those days, when game was plentiful everywhere, if not quite in the quantities found on the Serengeti Plains.

One of the brother's specialities was making very potent orange wine and liqueur, and rarely did we drink anything that was less than four years old. On my first visit, I drank the wine for most of the evening. I had misjudged its strength, as I discovered the next morning when I tried to get up early to go hunting. They found it very amusing at the mission and later told me that I was not the first person to have suffered through miscalculating the potency of the orange wine. I learnt to be more careful on future visits, although the missionaries were always very generous with their hospitality.

I came to admire their work tremendously. Being Church of England, I had always been slightly mistrustful of the Catholics working in Mwanza, and I never came to know any of them well. But here in the bush it was impossible to deny their tremendous work for the local Africans, and their efforts outshone all the other missions. They took their bush schools all over the district and I often saw the White Fathers chugging along bush tracks on small motorcycles when I was out hunting in the remoter districts – they stayed in the most primitive conditions. Their period of service in Africa far exceeded that of the other missionaries, too, and they got a break in Europe only after ten years. They were all remarkable men and I feel privileged that I got to know some of them.

The brother was also responsible for maintaining all the mission machinery but, busy as he was, he was always willing to come out to our farm when we had any serious mechanical problems.

Looking back thirty years later, I can appreciate more fully how much all this help did to make life easier and more successful for us.

★

A special mention has to be made of our Swiss/Italian farm manager, Rengli. He did a great deal to set things up for us before we actually moved from Mwanza to Kakonko. I had known him in Mwanza, when he was a crocodile hunter, and I knew he had once been a Catholic missionary, but I never found out whether he had been a White Father or a Brother, nor his reasons for leaving the missions. He was very good with the Africans and got a lot more work out of them than anyone else could. He was also an excellent builder and I know he shared my regret that we never finished the massive stone house that we were building on a hill on the farm.

Rengli never talked about his past, which was not unusual in Africa, but he was now a very keen Rosicrucian: he received their magazine regularly and often tried to get me interested. But I told him I was happy as an ordinary member of the Church of England and eventually he gave up.

He was invaluable to me, as I could leave the farm in his care when I went off hunting. The isolated life of the farm never seemed to worry him at all.

Kakonko was very well positioned from my point of view, being near the Ruanda-Urundi border and between two of the great lakes of East Africa: Victoria and Tanganyika.

*

In the planning stages, we had realised that it would be quite some time before we could expect the farm to show a profit, but we felt that we could get by with the help of a few little sidelines: ivory, transporting the salt, a little bit of bartering and some coffee smuggling. We had decided to concentrate on cash crops in the early days, such as the tobacco coils and chilli powder, because they were easy to barter both locally and over the nearby Ruanda-Urundi border. At first we sold our dried chillies in bags, but we soon found them too bulky to transport and concentrated on the tobacco.

Coffee prices were high and the demand good, so we had planned on that being our long-term bulk crop but, sensibly, we listened to local advice and, at first, planted only a small experimental area with coffee trees. This was extremely lucky because, in the second year, we were hit by locusts. Fortunately we had just gathered in the tobacco and chillies for drying, so our losses were restricted to most of the coffee trees, the fruit trees and the cape gooseberry bushes, together with all the vegetables except the onions and potatoes, which were still under the ground.

Thus we were given a very clear early warning of the unpredictable nature of tropical farming, and how necessary it was to keep the crocodile business going as well as the new ventures.

The crocodile business necessitated frequent trips to Ruanda-Urundi and to the Congo, via Kigoma and Albertville, which helped disguise the fact that I was indulging in a certain amount of coffee smuggling as well – the prices in Tanganyika were much higher than those paid in Ruanda-Urundi, so it was a profitable sideline.

Some Indian traders in Biharamulo and Bukoba were able to smuggle coffee on a large scale, but it was obvious that my own dealings in Kakonko would have to be kept low-key, to prevent them coming to the attention of the district commissioner, Peter Haynes. Since he was a friend of ours, that could have produced an awkward situation.

*

I didn't have to wait long for my first elephant and the chance to put my recent acquisition of an elephant gun – a second-hand 4.25 Westley-Richards – to good use. Although it was a bit ancient, I had tested it on the farm and it was accurate for about fifty yards.

The local elephant hunting expert was Chummy Lockwood, ex-South Africa and our local agricultural officer. He recommended shooting at close range, using a tripod-shaped branch of a tree, held by an African, on which the elephant gun could be rested for extra accuracy.

I still remember vividly the first time I was called out on an elephant hunt by a runner from the local sub-chief. Peter Haynes had asked me to take a local game guard for my first few trips as two European hunters had recently been trampled to death. Luckily the game guard was in the district and came with the runner, so we were able to set off almost immediately.

We knew the elephants had destroyed quite a lot of the maize fields and were nearby, but it was still a surprise how close they were. Another villager, who had been following them, took us down to the edge of a sandy area by a stream (the one that ran through my property) only about ten minutes' walk from the farm.

The wind was in the right direction, so we were able to crawl quite close and see the elephants playing in the water and in the sand. There was a small anthill nearby, from which I could see that we would get a clear shot at the largest bull elephant, which was lying down asleep in the middle of the herd. When we got on the anthill, I saw that I was at just the right angle to get in an ear shot, or rather a shot just behind the ear, that would go directly into his brain.

The elephants were still completely oblivious of our presence, so I took what seemed to me a long time setting up the tripod, with the African holding it steady. I knew it was extremely important that I made no mistake with my first shot. I was, however, still surprised when, after I fired, he just jerked once or twice before lying still. To be doubly sure, although the game guard said it was quite unnecessary, I pumped in another shot quickly. I could not quite believe that it had been so easy to kill my first elephant. Each tusk, we found later, weighed fifty-five to sixty pounds, which was a good size for this area, so the game guard told me, although I was still too elated to take in much of what he was saying.

*

Perhaps it was because of the ease with which I had killed my first tusker that I began to take unnecessary risks, and I became a bit careless. I cannot remember how many more elephants I shot without incident before I learnt a proper respect for them.

Another herd was reported to be destroying the villagers' food crop nearby and I think the game guard had been sent to the Kakonko district to do something about this. Anyway, he called in at the farm, as he had seen a big bull in the herd nearby, and asked me to come along. I should perhaps mention that I paid a bonus to anybody who came and brought me news of a good tusker that I subsequently shot. This meant I was pretty busy. The elephants had to be driven away from the area, as they were always raiding and destroying the villagers' crops, and I naturally shot the ones with the most ivory.

I soon realised this herd was not going to be as easy to approach as the first. They kept moving for most of the day, as we followed them, and in the early evening they began to lead us back to the area of my farm. I eventually got a shot at the largest one, but it was not fatal and he disappeared into the thick reeds on the opposite side of the stream from where I had shot my first elephant. Conditions there were not easy – in fact they were downright dangerous – and, as the light was beginning to fade, the game guard begged me to leave it until the morning. But I knew I had wounded the animal and I wanted to go into the reeds and finish him off (see map in Appendix for details of where the two elephants were shot close to my farm).

I have always regretted my decision to go after the wounded elephant, as it meant the game guard had to come as well, but I had no idea how things were going to turn out. The four or five local villagers who worked part-time on my farm insisted on coming too. They had seen only the easy kills and, for that matter, so had I, otherwise I would never have allowed them to come with us and risk their lives with nothing but a spear in their hands.

The light was deteriorating rapidly, as it does in the Tropics, and I knew I had to get into the tall reeds, over six feet high, as soon as possible. There were two or three well-defined elephant tracks going in that obviously led to the stream that ran through our farm, but there were disconcerting turns in the elephant pathway that made it impossible to get a clear field of fire. The light was getting really bad and I was just about to suggest that it might be wise to leave, and come back in the morning, when we came to another bend and heard movement ahead. The game guard was just ahead of me and turning the bend when the elephant, which had obviously been waiting for us to come, charged.

The next thing I knew the game guard had panicked, turning around in terror with the elephant only a yard or so behind him. As he passed me he threw down his rifle to get away quicker, and I had a wounded, trumpeting elephant, with his trunk raised, charging straight at me. To this day I believe it was my army training in the Gurkhas that saved me as, otherwise, I would probably have run, following the game guard. But there was no way we could have got away from the elephant and, without a shadow of doubt, both of us would have been trampled to death.

Everything that followed was purely instinctive. As I saw the charging elephant looming up in front of me, with its trunk up and mouth open, I aimed my elephant gun upwards, towards his open mouth – only a yard or so from me – and fired. The shock of the bullet knocked him back slightly and, as he started collapsing, I jumped back to avoid his falling trunk. But not quite far enough back, as the tip of his trunk knocked my elephant gun out of my hands. By then it was almost completely dark and I could hardly believe I was still alive as I moved his trunk to get my gun out of the mud.

It was only then that I became aware of the four or five Africans standing transfixed not many yards behind me. I think they still could not quite believe that the elephant was dead.

I remember all of us standing absolutely still, not speaking, in the sudden silence. I pretended to clean the mud off my elephant gun, to try to stop my hands shaking. Then, laughing and shouting, they began to cut up the elephant and I knew it wouldn't be long before the whole village was out to help. It was necessary for them to take what they wanted immediately, before vultures discovered the corpse, and by morning all the elephant meat would have been carried away to the village.

I asked one of my Africans to bring the game guard's rifle, as I was pretty sure we would find him on the road or at the farm, and I told the others to bring the elephant's tusks to the farm the next day.

Sure enough, I saw the game guard sitting with his head in his hands near the entrance to the farm. When I spoke to him I could see he was still in shock and looked very surprised to see me alive. I took the rifle from my African and told him to hurry back to get his share of the elephant meat.

The game guard just sat, saying nothing, and asked no questions as to how I had killed the elephant. I tried to do what I could to comfort him, by telling him how sorry I was about what had happened, that I would not say anything to the district commissioner when I saw him, that I had seen the same kind of thing happen to some of the bravest soldiers in Italy, and that the whole thing would be forgotten very quickly. But we both knew he would never come back to the Kakonko district or to my farm, and that the best thing for him was to apply to be transferred to another district, or even province.

When I visited the sub-chief the next day, he knew everything that had happened and, although I told him it was all my fault, he just shrugged and said it was *Shauri ya Mongu* (in God's hands), and that nothing could change the facts, so the game guard would have to leave the district.

In the early days of my elephant hunting, the game guard had been very fond of telling us all how he had shot over a hundred elephants for the Game Department and, of course, he could not resist mentioning that the district commissioner had sent him along to make sure I wasn't killed by elephants like the two European hunters who had been trampled to death not long before. This boasting had not gone down too well with one or two of the local Africans who went out with us, and were expert trackers themselves.

For those who have lived only in the West, it is difficult to understand just how much losing face means in the East and in Africa. The most familiar example is the behaviour of the fanatical Japanese officers in World War II. But the whole British Empire depended to a large degree on the 'face' it derived from the pomp and ceremony that helped to keep its colonial service going so successfully for so long.

So I knew what would have happened if I had run that night, and blessed the army training that had produced the instinct to stand and fire. My part-time labour force depended almost entirely on the local sub-chief's goodwill and that would certainly have vanished if I had run and thereby been responsible for the unnecessary death of some of his men.

He never again mentioned the matter, but I knew he was well aware that I had, through inexperience, put the lives of four or five of his villagers at extreme risk that night – a spear is not much protection against a charging elephant – but I had saved face in his eyes by holding my ground.

For the next few weeks I kept out of the way of the district commissioner, Peter Haynes. When we did meet again the game guard had gone on sick leave pending his transfer to another district. Peter asked me if I wanted the new game guard to come out with me on my next elephant hunt. I told him I could manage now, using local trackers, and nothing more was ever said about the matter.

★

I think it was that night of the charging elephant that I first began to admire the courage and fortitude of the rural Africans and, although I admire the courage have never been a do-gooder, it was the events of that night and subsequent elephant-hunting trips with them that shaped my final decision to help start the Truth About Africa League (TAAL) when I was back in Britain after thirty-five years in Africa. Despite my strong feelings about Africa, I doubt if, without this very personal incentive, I would have bothered to write this book.

It is probably too late to do much to help the Tanzanians, as they have already suffered grievously from years of Julius Nyerere's disastrous African socialism, but it may just be possible to stop the same thing happening in Namibia and South Africa, if we can get more ex-servicemen to face up to the truth about Africa. Maybe we can get the politicians in the West to realise the madness of forcing the pace of reform in South Africa, as the end result will be the same as it has been elsewhere. If ever the African National Congress takes control in South Africa, it will become just another disaster area with tribal war, starvation, corruption, misrule and economic disaster.

Enquiries have been coming in to TAAL regarding the possibility of forming a literary society of Africa, to encourage others to write about their African experiences. What is vital is that there should be a true record of events in East, West, central and South Africa in the post-war years. It is hoped, therefore, that this book, like *The Destruction of a Continent*, will encourage more books on Africa that set the record straight. The literary society of Africa would be able to give detailed information about books published on Africa by people, like the writer, who lived there for many years.

*

During the colonial era it was the job of the district game ranger, and his game guards, to cull elephant herds regularly, in order to preserve the balance of nature in the area, as well as to protect the crops of the rural Africans. As I have explained, the villagers were continually losing their food crops to roaming elephants and it was not unusual for the animals to be seen on the road between Kakonko and my farm.

That all the good work of game conservation in colonial times should have been wasted is absolutely tragic and was quite unnecessary – due solely to the completely unwarranted interference of the superpowers in African affairs. This was scandalous enough, but even worse is the way they now try to blame the Africans for the wholesale slaughter of elephants and other big game. It was the superpowers themselves who supplied automatic rifles completely indiscriminately to all and sundry, and it is really carrying their hypocritical behaviour to new extremes when they blame the Africans for using the guns.

It should be pointed out that in colonial days the authorities kept a very tight check on all big game hunting and it was virtually impossible to kill elephant, rhino, lion, buffalo (and many other species) without a licence. Any stranger in the district had to report his presence to the district commissioner on arrival and would have to produce a licence before he was allowed to shoot any of the game mentioned above.

As a resident farmer, I had certain perks. Apart from shooting elephants that were bothering the local chief, I was allowed to kill as necessary to protect the livestock on my own farm and nothing was said when I took out extra licences for ivory in a friend's name. It was also possible, sometimes, to use a licence twice, when the weights were not written on the licence. But the whole system was pretty effective on the whole, and the total number of elephants I shot annually was insignificant when compared with the numbers that were culled in the district by the Game Department.

In the early days I used the ivory money to keep my farm going, but most of it went back into the local economy in the form of wages to my workers. Since the local villagers also got all the elephant meat, I had no qualms at all about the extra elephants I was able to shoot unofficially. But there was no way anybody could have got away with large-scale elephant poaching in those well-run colonial days.

For some time I had been planning a longer, larger-scale elephant safari, going farther from the Kakonko district, where large herds of elephants were now on the decrease due to the very efficient elephant control that had been introduced to limit the damage the animals had been doing to the local food crops.

Chummy Lockwood, the local elephant expert, had told me that there were huge areas of the Kasulu district where large herds of elephants were regularly seen, and one of the best had a bush access road that led down to the Kagera river. There was one drawback to the area once the river was crossed, however – it was impossible to avoid the masses of river tsetse flies. Some land had been cleared right down to the river for scattered African villages and their small farms, which meant that it was possible to camp in a place relatively free of tsetse flies so long as we stayed on our side of the river.

We were all due to go to Kasulu for a cricket weekend, so I decided to get more information from the district commissioner and other government servants. The DC at the time was, I remember, a New Zealander and I gathered from him and the others that Chummy Lockwood had not been exaggerating the number of elephants in the area, but what they said about the tsetse flies made me fear they would be worse than I had previously imagined. But I was also told that hunters rarely had to go across the river, because there were plenty of elephants on both sides, so I hoped that it might not be necessary for me to cross into tsetse country.

Chummy had mentioned one special area by some salt pans that the elephants used regularly. He reckoned it was at least two days' hard march to get there, and it was not a place to stay long, as the only available water was from the salt pans and, no matter how long the water was boiled, it still tasted very salty, however much sugar was put in the tea. So I took a small drinking-water bottle to rinse the taste of the salt away, but I was still thirsty – day and night.

I had never seen so many elephants milling around everywhere. In fact, we had to keep a fire burning all night, to ensure they didn't inadvertently wander through the camp and, possibly, trample someone to death. Even with the fire, I could hear the elephants moving around nearby during the night. To make matters worse, there were no large shade trees anywhere near. It was one of the hottest, bleakest places I have ever come across.

But nothing could spoil the mornings, when I got up early to watch the elephants, literally hundreds of them, either at the salt pans or making their way there. When we shot the largest tusker we could find, we made sure that we did it well away from the salt pans, so as not to pollute their drinking water or the salt pan area.

I had found, on hunting trips, that one should always be prepared for the unexpected and my first trip to this area was no exception. It soon became obvious that, although there were plenty of elephants on the tsetse-free area by the river, there were no more big tuskers among them: they were mainly females with young elephants, and there was no choice but to cross the river into the tsetse fly area.

I had had no idea how bad the flies were going to be and I soon noticed that they seemed to swarm around me more than the Africans. I think this was because I sweated more, and that seemed to attract them. Anyway, they were thick on my back and nothing could stop them biting me continually on the neck and hands. Wearing a thick, long-sleeved shirt under my bush jacket protected my back but they still managed to bite my arms, which started to swell.

At first I had hoped that I would get used to the bites and the swellings would go down, but unfortunately this did not happen and I knew I would have to drive down to the Kigoma hospital to get treatment.

The timing was very bad because I had managed to shoot only one elephant with really good tusks and I still had four or five licences to complete, but treatment could not be postponed because the swellings were now so bad that I could not bend my arms. I decided to leave at 3 a.m., to avoid driving in the heat of the day – when the swellings always seemed at their worst.

Fortunately there was very little traffic on the roads, but I didn't relish the last bit of the journey as, although it was my first trip to Kigoma, I knew there was no road for the last few miles, so all the traffic had to use the railway track. The jolting over the railway sleepers was absolute agony and I couldn't get to the Kigoma hospital quickly enough.

At the hospital they found it difficult to believe the swellings were due to bites, but a course of Antisan pills soon brought the swellings down. I was advised never to go into the tsetse fly area again without taking a supply of Antisan tablets. I found the swellings were less troublesome on each subsequent trip and gradually stopped bothering me at all, but I always took the pills as a precaution.

As this was my first trip to Kigoma, I decided to stay a few days to convalesce and to see some of the local sights. In particular, I wanted to visit Ujiji, where Dr Livingstone had died, and see the Kaiserhof that had been built especially for the Kaiser's visit just before World War I.

I also managed a fascinating evening of fishing, going out in one of the small local fishermen's boats. They mostly used tilley pressure lamps, perched on the front of the boat to attract the masses of small fish. These fish were very like sardines, but smaller, and it was a local delicacy to have them fried whole and served up hot as a snack with the local beer.

It was an amazing sight every night on the lake near Kigoma to watch the hundreds of lights bobbing up and down in the lake. However, Lake Tanganyika had the reputation of being much more dangerous than Lake Victoria. It was long and narrow, so storms tended to spring up without much warning, building up quickly from both ends of the lake, and I was advised not to stray too far from the shore. But the weather was fine, and the fish plentiful, throughout my stay.

As at the Mwanza Hotel, the food was pretty unappetising, but the rooms were larger and better furnished. Although the standard was much better at the Kigoma Hotel than in Mwanza, it was still preferable (as in most places in Tanganyika) to find friends to stay with.

On this first trip, however, accommodation was not much of a problem because I was out a lot and I normally had only breakfast at the hotel. This was a fairly large repast, as I hadn't yet given up having the traditional fried English breakfast, and I didn't bother much about other meals. There was plenty of delicious fresh fruit available locally (including papaws, mangoes and bananas) and, in the heat, I much preferred to eat this during the day than to have a heavy lunch. In the evenings I drank plenty of beer and found that nibbling things like the little fried fish and other bar snacks was quite sufficient.

*

What always struck me very forcibly later, when I travelled to Albertville, Bukama, and other towns in the Belgian Congo, as well as to places like Usumbura, at the top end of Lake Tanganyika, in what was then Ruanda-Urundi (also under Belgian administration), was how much better the Belgian food and entertainment always was, compared to the British. Later Élisabethville, in the Belgian Congo's Katanga Province, became one of my favourite places to visit.

This made the tragedy of what happened later in the Congo, during their civil wars, all the more poignant. Although I had to go back to Katanga after independence, I never visited Élisabethville again, and always bypassed it when I had to go to Katanga to collect crocodile skins. In the end I had to give up going altogether, even though it was very profitable, when, not for the first time after independence, I was shot at by local bandits.

Normally bandits didn't bother me – I just put my foot down and went, if necessary, straight at them, knowing they were lousy shots. But on this occasion they must have had some renegade soldiers with them because, when I refused to stop for those on and beside the road, they opened up from some nearby trees and at least one of their bullets smashed into my windscreen. Luckily I was unhurt, and able to keep going.

Later on the road I met a convoy of Belgian vehicles and stopped to talk. They told me that, only the previous day, a Belgian couple had been murdered in about the same area where I had encountered the bandits. They said that every day things were getting worse and, on more than one occasion recently, their armed escorted convoy had been shot at. Most of them were moving out to nearby Northern Rhodesia.

Later, after moving to Northern Rhodesia, we were to get a stream of Belgian refugees, whole families who had got caught up in the violence, getting out of the Congo for good. They were often carrying all their possessions in their cars and glad to be safely out of the region as the civil war in Katanga got worse.

But this unnecessary violence was still in the future, unleashed by the stupidity of the UN and the colonial powers themselves, who turned against their own kind to try and curry favour with the communists and their socialist friends in the West.

I have always been glad that I made the most of those idyllic colonial days.

★

It was time for me to leave Kigoma and return to my elephant hunting camp on the banks of the Kagera river. I had been away for about a week but the Africans looking after my camp had managed very well and, as was usual in those days, I took it for granted that everything would be just the same as when I had left. I must say, once again, how honest the rural African was, unlike his urban brothers who had quickly begun to pick up all the faults of so-called Western civilisation, including theft, a crime unheard of in tribal areas during my days in Africa.

I had left the men with plenty of game meat, which was always plentiful in those days, and I expected them to exchange the surplus, as I did when in camp, for such local African produce as eggs and vegetables. Although they had managed well, I could see they were more than ready to start hunting elephants again.

The two local trackers had been going out while I was away, to keep an eye out for any good tuskers, and some had been seen not far from the camp the previous day. Ironically, now that I had my Antisan pills against the tsetse flies, the large elephants were returning to the relatively tsetse-free area where we were camped.

The next day we went out hunting early and soon came upon a herd with a good tusker. As usual, I was able to get close to him without any trouble and he was at the right angle for my favourite shot, just behind the ear. He fell the first time I fired, and never moved when we approached him, so I didn't think it necessary to give him another shot. We clambered all over him, to measure the tusks and to cut off his tail, but decided to leave him and return in the afternoon, when it was cooler. We had seen some signs of another herd before we came across him, so we marked the area well and went in pursuit of the second herd.

When we returned in the afternoon, however, we could find no trace of him. At first I just couldn't believe it, and made the men search the whole area, but then I concluded that I had just stunned him and that he had recovered later in the day. Eventually one of the trackers found signs of some fresh blood on the blades of grass leading to the river, so I just had to accept that I had made a bad mistake in not making sure he was dead by giving him an extra shot from my 9.3 Mauser at close range, as I normally did. It was a mistake that I never made again and it cost me dear in this instance, as it took three days' hard slog before we caught up with him.

But I had no option. In those days it was an accepted rule that any elephant you wounded had to be followed as soon as possible and killed, as there was no doubt that most deaths that occurred when hunting were caused by previously wounded elephants.

I understood, from the Tanganyika Game Department, that a lot of elephants were wounded by local African hunters using ancient muzzle-loaders. I had come across some of these guns when out hunting, and they certainly looked dangerous – more dangerous, in fact, to the hunter than to the elephants!

The wounded elephant had moved around in an almost complete circle and, when we at last came up with him, due entirely to the skill of my two local trackers, he wasn't far from the river and our camp. This time there were no mistakes. The rest of the safari went off without any hitches, and I still managed to fill the quota on my elephant licence and be back at the farm within the three weeks that I had allowed.

★

What I had begun to realise was that, no matter how much experience you had in hunting elephants and other big game, it was always possible to make a mistake that could prove fatal, and quite often, especially in the Kasulu-Kigoma area where there were plenty of elephants around, we came upon a herd unexpectedly when we were following a different one. Mock charges to warn us away were not unusual but, unless provoked, it was extremely rare for a real charge to be made. In fact, apart from the wounded elephant I had shot in the long reeds near my farm in the early days, I had only faced one real full-blooded charge out in the open. That had occurred in the same Kasulu area, on a later elephant safari, and once again I had been extremely lucky to survive.

We were at our camp by the river again and, no great distance from the camp, there were some quite thick clumps of trees that were often favoured by the bull elephants. We came up with a larger than usual tusker in the early afternoon, as he was moving across open ground to get to another clump of trees. So I ran ahead, with the African who held my wooden aiming-tripod, to get at the elephant before he moved into the next clump of trees.

I soon realised I wasn't going to get a good shot in before he disappeared, but there was a chance that a rear-end shot would make him turn and face me. Unfortunately, just as I was firing at him from my tripod, a drop of sweat got into my eye and I squeezed the trigger a bit too quickly. I must have just grazed his upper rear leg, but it was enough to turn him and provoke a full-blooded charge, with trunk up and bellows of rage. I knew it was extremely difficult to get an accurate frontal shot at his head, as there is only a very small vulnerable part in the front of the skull, so I decided to try a front leg shot at not more than thirty-five to forty yards away.

But I had a dud bullet when I fired and, in trying to reload fast, I jammed my 4.25 Westley-Richards elephant gun. Two bullets had jammed together as I tried to reload and I knew there was no way I could clear the blockage before the charging elephant reached me. I faced almost certain death in a few seconds, together with the African beside me, and I turned around as I heard the rest of my Africans coming out of the trees into the open space we were in.

In front was the African who was carrying my 9.3 Mauser rifle and I shouted to him to bring the Mauser as quickly as possible as my elephant gun was jammed, but he and the rest of the Africans were over fifty yards away and there was absolutely no chance of them reaching us before the elephant did. But they all came running towards us anyway, shouting and screaming and waving their spears. The elephant heard them coming and, to my relief and amazement, he veered off just in front of us, not more than fifteen or twenty yards away. Maybe he saw my Mauser rifle and recognised it as something dangerous – he could not know, of course, that the African had not been trained to use it.

This time, although everything seemed to happen so quickly, there was still time in the few seconds when the elephant was charging for me to think how ironic it was that I should die in the bush in a remote corner of Tanganyika when I had escaped from worse odds and situations against the Germans in Italy.

Looking back all these years later, I still find it amazing that none of the Africans even hesitated when I shouted to them about my elephant gun being jammed. If they had, I am sure that I would not now be writing this book. Every second was vital and the elephant would have completed his charge and killed us both before they came running and shouting. It is this kind of bravery that is so remarkable, as it comes from instinct and not from army training. They were all well aware that, had the elephant continued his charge, they would surely have been killed after the elephant had finished us off.

I hope something of my feeling for them is reflected in this book as they, and others like them in rural Africa, did not deserve the treatment they were later to receive under African socialism and all the half-baked ideas that their rulers have brought in from the communists and the socialists in the West.

Today's comparative scarcity of big game in East Africa is, in my opinion, another reason to blame the superpowers and the UN for pressing for premature independence. If the transition of power had been spread over a fifteen to twenty-year period much of the shambles that occurred could have been avoided.

Chapter Nine

Monitoring the Media Menace

It should be explained that when we came to Britain in 1983 neither of us had ever had any interest in politics. In fact, I had never voted in my life before I returned to Britain. My view of most politicians was excellently expressed by an old African chief, when we were discussing politics: 'They are like fleas on a dog's back, a necessary evil that has to be squashed occasionally.'

However, while I was recuperating from heart problems (in 1984–1985) I became aware that television, especially Channel 4, was escalating anti-South Africa propaganda programmes and news. My wife and I began to get extremely annoyed at the completely false and biased impression given of South Africa, and the almost complete lack of news about conditions in other parts of Africa. Eventually I decided to contact the war veterans' representative at the South African embassy, Bill Van Gass.

People who are not ex-servicemen will probably be unaware that the South African Legion is still a member of the BCEL (British Commonwealth Ex-Service League, formerly the British Empire Service League), and will be ignorant of its history. I quote from the British Commonwealth Ex-Service League's official brochure:

> What is the BCEL?
>
> The British Commonwealth Ex-Service League (BCEL) a registered charity, was founded as the British Empire Service League in 1921 at the instigation of Field Marshal Earl Haig and General Smuts. The inaugural Conference was held in Cape Town in that year and was attended by seven founder members from ex-service associations of the 'old' Commonwealth countries.
>
> The ex-service organisations of some countries that have left the Commonwealth are still members of the League at their own wish. [*my note*: this includes South Africa, one of the seven founder members.]

> This is entirely reasonable since it is a fact of history that the ex-servicemen they represent served the Commonwealth and Empire at a time when their own countries were still a part of it.

During my early conversations with Bill Van Gass, while we were discussing how British ex-servicemen could help their South African comrades-in-arms, he mentioned that his brother had been killed in action in Italy during the war. It was this, coupled with my anger about the mindless communist demonstrators outside the embassy, that was really instrumental in my getting together with other ex-servicemen to form TAAL, the Truth About Africa League, a British and Commonwealth ex-servicemen's organisation working for peaceful change in South Africa.

I have never forgotten the quite overwhelming hospitality of Durbanites during my first brief visit, nor how our troopship was sung into Durban harbour by that quite magnificent Lady in White, Perla Siddle Gibson. In the middle of 1989, when I first started this book, I decided to write to the mayor of Durban, asking him for details of the Lady in White. Included in the Appendix are the two photographs he sent me, as well as details of her career and Councillor D.W. Watterson's letter. Readers will note that one of her sons, Lieutenant Roy Gibson, was among the many South Africans who fought for Britain and were killed in Italy during World War II.

★

It became apparent, soon after I had helped to form TAAL (Truth About Africa League) in early 1986, that the media menace was far worse than any of us had hitherto suspected, especially in television, and that the communists, with their crypto-communist allies, had penetrated deeply into all areas of the communication business.

Leading the way was Channel 4, where openly communist film producers like Tariq Ali and Darcus Howe were churning out anti-South Africa propaganda programmes.

It became obvious to us that others of the same ilk in ITV wanted the propaganda campaign to be spread over all the networks, to make it seem more spontaneous. So Thames Television and the International Broadcasting Trust started the anti-South Africa campaign in October 1986 with *Spear of the Nation*, a very offensive eulogy of the ANC (African National Congress). Free booklets on this programme were published by Thames Television and the International Broadcasting Trust.

The whole programme was an excuse to launch a vicious attack on South Africa's war effort in the two world wars. It concentrated its attack on the anti-British pro-German/Boer element and deliberately excluded any mention of those Boers like Field Marshal Jan Smuts who, as prime minister, brought South Africa into World War II. Smuts was a friend of Britain and closely associated with our premier, Sir Winston Churchill, as well as being a valued adviser in our war cabinets during both the world wars. There were thousands like Bill Van Gass, the war veterans' representative at the South African embassy, who fought in the desert and in Italy with one of the South African divisions.

This travesty of a programme started the insults to South Africa's war dead and to surviving South African ex-servicemen. It was the equivalent of writing a book about Britain's war effort in which Churchill was ignored and pride of place given to Sir Oswald Mosley and his pro-German Fascist Party. This deliberately misleading programme started off TAAL's efforts on behalf of our ex-comrades-in-arms in South Africa and subsequent similarly vicious television programmes showed how necessary TAAL was becoming. The truth of the matter is that most people in Britain have been so brainwashed that they are far too scared to show any support for South Africa.

*

One of the most fascinating parts of TAAL's activities was investigating just how the media conspiracy against South Africa worked. Very few members of the general public have the time or the facilities to find out how an organisation like the Anti-Apartheid Movement (AAM) operates and where its almost unlimited funds come from. Ironically, two of its principal financiers are the communists and Church organisations.

The role of Archbishop Huddleston has already been mentioned and another key figure is Sir Richard Attenborough – both these men have appeared on the AAM platforms in Hyde Park. Attenborough is chairman of Channel 4 and openly employs communist producers like Tariq Ali and Darcus Howe. The many propaganda programmes about South Africa and apartheid conveniently ignore the ghastly plight of most of the rest of Africa, where murder, mayhem and mass starvation are common (a 1991 report states that there are 27 million starving Africans).

But where Attenborough really excelled himself was over his very one-sided film *Cry Freedom*. Regrettable as Biko's death was, it must be pointed out that Donald Woods's book, on which the film is based, is a dramatisation of events – and highly suspect to anybody who has lived in South Africa. One man who immediately saw the propaganda value of the film was, of course, President Mugabe of Zimbabwe. He receives well over thirty million pounds a year from the West to help keep his tottering Marxist state of Zimbabwe going, yet he paid five million towards the film's costs, as well as providing the film-making facilities in Zimbabwe.

A large number of TAAL's ex-service supporters, like myself, know Zimbabwe well and are completely disillusioned by the double standards of morality in the West, whose media must be aware of the wholesale massacre of thousands and thousands of unarmed Matabele by Mugabe's security forces (some reports reaching the Rhodesian Christian Group put the total murdered as high as forty thousand), but who seldom mention it.

TAAL's media-monitoring section feels there may well be a link between the recent noticeable increase in BBC programmes on South Africa (mostly very biased) and Michael Grade, who was head of BBC programmes before he joined Channel 4 as managing director. It would be interesting to hear how many readers share this suspicion!

The recent furore over Roland Joffe's film about Calcutta, *City of Joy*, shown on Channel 4's *Rear Window* programme, may well have been an indulgence for his communist comrades in West Bengal that communist producer Tariq Ali will come to regret – because it focused attention on the unpalatable fact that all foreign films made in India are heavily censored. Indeed, Mr Joffe stressed this when he was forced to agree to two Indian government censors being present at all the filming, to ensure that no politics or religion were included in the film.

This Indian censorship must detract from what is, in my opinion, the one great film produced by Attenborough – about the life of Mahatma Gandhi – and I would also remind people that Indian government financial backing was given for that film.

In 1986 Central Television came up with a *Viewpoint* programme *Back on the Frontier*. Their pamphlet on this film makes very interesting reading, as it lists all the anti-apartheid movements in Britain (including the African National Congress), as well as a forthcoming Granada television programme: *Apartheid*. This was in two parts and was to be fully networked, taking up the main viewing times on two successive evenings.

Among the other events listed, two were typical: *The 75th Anniversary of the Founding of the ANC* and *The 25th Anniversary of the Founding of 'Umkhonto we Sizwe'*, which is the ANC's military wing; the founder was Colonel Joe Slovo of the KGB and South African Communist Party.

Channel 4 got into the act, as usual, and the International Broadcasting Trust published a booklet on the channel's 1986 films on South Africa. This Trust describes itself as an independent charity linking education, television and the movement for world development, but it appears to have communist links. The Channel 4 films listed were: *South Africa: Witness to Apartheid*, *In Black and White*, *Mazimbu* (in Tanzania) and *The Two Rivers*. All four were anti-apartheid – and this was a comparatively modest year in the channel's propaganda campaign against South Africa!

In all our time in Britain (since we returned in 1983) we have only seen one television programme or film that could be said to reflect the true conditions in Africa. This programme was about Zaire and how Aids was spreading there. It was getting too near to the truth about the horrific conditions, however, and the television team were expelled from Zaire. To make up the footage, I presume, the British public were actually allowed a glimpse of the corruptness of most African leaders. They were showed how Zaire's President Mobutu had milked the country, amassed a huge personal fortune and purchased vast estates in Europe. What was not mentioned was how communist intervention had helped to create such appalling rulers all over Africa.

Over this period in the 1980s, television viewers in Britain may have noticed how the anti-South Africa propaganda campaign was steadily escalating. It was largely due to the courageous stand taken by our ex-PM, Mrs Thatcher, that sanctions against South Africa were not increased. To ex-servicemen, her stand was reminiscent of Churchill's in the 1930s, when he stood almost alone against the Nazis. Mrs Thatcher stood almost alone against an even greater menace: communism.

★

Part of the anti-South Africa propaganda campaign in 1988 was switched to the House of Commons, where an incredible seventy plus Labour MPs have had some kind of connection with the Communist Party. TAAL members felt obliged to send a letter to all members of parliament, demanding a stop to these insults to our South African comrades-in-arms. It was headed 'MPs insult South African war dead and surviving ex-servicemen'. The response and support from MPs was surprising and encouraging and, on 15th March, 1988, the *Daily Express* published my letter, 'A standard slur to old comrades':

> *Last week your Foreign Line had an article regarding certain MPs who wanted the Union Jack removed from the South African flag.*

Most ex-servicemen consider this a gratuitous insult too many. Britain was only too glad to accept the services of the 350,000 South Africans who volunteered to fight and die in World War II.

It is hoped, therefore, that as many ex-servicemen as possible will write to their MP registering their anger and disgust that such gratuitous insults to their dead South African comrades-in-arms should be allowed.

On 21st March, 1988, the *Daily Express* also published R. Bentley's letter, 'They honoured our flag':

Those MPs who want the Union Flag removed from the South African flag should visit the Somme area in France.

There they will find a place called Delville Wood, where of the 3,500 South African troops who fought there in July and August 1916, only 140 survived. They were an honour to the Union Flag.

These letters illustrate the anger felt by most ex-servicemen at the suggestion that the flag should be changed. Nothing could justify such an action and the communists, together with their socialist and Labour friends, miscalculated badly when it was proposed.

★

Another example of media bias was the way television and the national newspapers handled the Mike Gatting cricket tour of South Africa. The tour itself was relatively unimportant. What was of great importance was the intimidation, the threats of violence aimed at the two black British cricketers, de Freitas and Butcher. They were forced to withdraw from the tour in the face of threats to their families, as well as themselves.

This kind of intimidation is typical of how some trade unions enforce discipline on their members and the individual's rights are ignored. It is even more typical of the modus operandi of tinpot dictators.

If the ANC ever gets into power in South Africa, God help any African who does not agree with its policies! We have already seen newspaper reports of how the leader's wife, Winnie Mandela, openly encouraged the use of the barbaric 'necklace' to deal with her political opponents.

On Monday, 29th January, 1990, the *Daily Mirror* devoted its whole front page to Mike Gatting's cricket tour of South Africa, together with a long statement from the Labour Party's ex-leader, Neil Kinnock, asking the cricket players to abandon the tour. So far as I am aware, Kinnock's personal experience does not extend far beyond the humiliating night when a drunken Zimbabwean soldier stuck an automatic rifle into his guts and forced him and his party into a small hut at the airport, refusing to let them go for some hours – for no better reason than the fact that they had arrived there unexpectedly. Kinnock and his group were lucky that night, but I have never seen him show the slightest desire to help those less fortunate people who are detained in Zimbabwean prisons without trial – and frequently tortured. In my opinion, Kinnock would be much better employed curbing his militant supporters.

What gives some cause for hope and sanity, even after all the anti-South Africa propaganda being pumped out daily by the media in Britain, is the *Daily Express* readers' poll on 20th January, 1990, on whether Gatting's cricketers should stay in South Africa – 78.23% said they should carry on. These figures were reinforced by a Gallup poll at the end of summer 1989, which showed that two out of three Britons who responded favoured increased multiracial sporting contacts with South Africa.

*

What is not properly understood in Britain is that, although reforms are under way in South Africa, and have been for quite some time now, it is more necessary than ever for the reforms to be gradual, to avoid the shambles and starvation so typical of most of black Africa. The first priority must always be to maintain law and order, otherwise South Africa will become yet another disaster area.

What must be stopped is the ANC's methods of intimidating its opponents. The West has to get over the message that such barbaric practices as using the burning necklace will not, under any circumstances, be tolerated.

This is where ex-servicemen and women can do more, especially those who are World War II vintage and know the real conditions in India, Africa and the rest of the Commonwealth. Many are well aware that conditions have got a lot worse since the days of the British Empire. Most of the new rulers don't understand the concept of democracy and South Africa, with all its faults, is a paradise compared to most of the other African countries.

Hundreds of thousands of Africans from the so-called 'front-line states' still stream into South Africa to get work, mainly in the mines because one month's wages there are more than a year's wages in their own countries.

It is interesting to note that in the 1960s, when Dr Verwoerd was the prime minister of South Africa, he offered any of the three-quarters of a million

Indians in South Africa a free passage to India, together with a cash grant if they agreed to stay in India permanently. Only six took up his offers. The others preferred to stay, even though they had very limited political rights. A slightly different story to Uganda, where eighty thousand Indians were kicked out by Idi Amin – and all their property confiscated.

I believe that all the pious talk about apartheid from the Ramphals, the Ramsamys and their like, is to disguise their jealousy of South Africa's prosperity. Those of us who know India and Indians, and the many unsavoury facets of life there, wonder why they never mention the millions of unfortunate untouchables.

The African Commonwealth leaders are also so eaten up by greed and jealousy of South Africa that they will never admit that most of their own economic troubles are self-imposed and could have been avoided.

Those African leaders like Mugabe, Kaunda and Nyerere, who love to criticise South Africa and apartheid, don't worry about any kind of democracy in their own countries.

★

What most ex-servicemen despise more than anything else is the blatant double standards adopted over South Africa, well summed up by a letter published in the *Daily Express*, from a Mr P.N. Drew (from Ramsay on the Isle of Man), headed 'Lay off Gatting':

> *If at the time of the Moscow Olympics sport was above politics, when a boycott was called for, why then all this posturing and posing now over Mike Gatting's cricket tour of South Africa?*
>
> *Tweedledum Ramphal and Tweedledee Ramsamy are more than capable of doing all the whinging and whining on behalf of the Marxist African states, without all the sycophantic utterances from the sanctimonious, self-appointed and self-opinionated sports fraternity.*

This letter makes a mockery of British athlete Sebastian Coe's much publicised statement in Auckland, New Zealand, before the start of the Commonwealth Games, in which he condemned Mike Gatting and his team of cricketers for going to South Africa. My belief is that he made this statement in order to appease the very vocal black Commonwealth members who were threatening to ban Britain from the Auckland games.

Perhaps Coe had conveniently forgotten what happened at the Moscow Olympics, when Britain asked for a boycott because of the seriousness of the threat to world peace when Russia invaded Afghanistan. One might ask why it was all right for him to go to the Moscow Olympics, along with a lot of other British athletes, while it was wrong for Mike Gatting to go to South Africa.

Coe has already been criticised in some Conservative circles, and rightly so, and he should learn the valuable lesson that, even in politics, there are some who object to the double standards adopted towards South Africa.

What has to be stressed, here, is that nothing that happened in connection with Mike Gatting's cricket tour of South Africa was in any way spontaneous. It was a carefully planned exercise in intimidation, organised and paid for by ANC, AAM and other communist organisations.

There are also plenty of Church funds, from organisations like the World Council of Churches, to promote demonstrations and to pay for the world-wide propaganda trips of South Africa's political priests, like Tutu, Boesak and Chikane, as well as paying for all the mischief they are able to create in South Africa, knowing that their activities will be lavishly reported by the Western media.

The Mike Gatting coverage is an example of how they work together, and it should be remembered how the Labour Party leaders will always come out publicly with full support for South Africa's enemies and, of course, without any apparent concern for the two million or so South Africans of British descent, many of whom are ex-servicemen who fought for Britain in both world wars.

Some Labour MPs insulted the South African war dead, and surviving ex-servicemen, when they brought up the subject of the Union Jack on the South African flag. They have also shown that they would like to deny South Africans of British descent their automatic right to a British passport. Just about the only thing still worth something in today's Commonwealth is the fact that blood ties link together many of the people in Britain, South Africa, Australia, New Zealand and Canada. These family bonds were strengthened in both world wars, by the blood of servicemen who fought and died together in a common cause.

Surely it is not too much to ask that, today, we stand together against unscrupulous politicians who, to further their own ambitions, would willingly take away our South African comrades-in-arms' birthright. I am firmly convinced that the only way to stop these people is for the ex-servicemen to escalate their opposition.

Apartheid, or 'separate development' as it should be called, is nothing new to Africa. The tribal system is based on apartheid and still operates very successfully over a lot of Africa. My trips to Ruanda-Urundi (now Rwanda and Burundi) showed me one extreme example, where one tribe had dominated another for centuries. As it involves black and black, however, it is never mentioned in the UN.

It's the same in Malaysia, where the Malays were scared of being dominated by the local Chinese, who outnumbered them at one time, so brought in a very successful apartheid system against the Chinese. But, as it was brown against yellow, nothing was said by the Commonwealth or UN.

Fiji is another example, where the Fijians are threatened by the local Indians.

The list is endless.

So we come to the unmentionable in Britain. A voluntary form of apartheid, or separate development, is appearing in some British cities, those with a large immigrant population. Southall in London is just one example of what amounts to an Indian suburb within Britain.

★

So it is to my fellow ex-serviceman that I am appealing, as I feel he is able to discount most of what he reads in the national newspapers and sees on television, and because he will realise that most of the Commonwealth posturing is to draw attention away from Africa's real and desperate problems of overpopulation and starvation. These problems are caused mainly by bad farming methods and continue to get worse despite millions and millions of pounds of annual aid from the British taxpayer. The last thing anybody should want is for the same conditions to come to South Africa but, make no mistake, if the world forces a premature change of government on South Africa, and the Africa National Congress takes over, it will be the end of one of the last prosperous countries in the continent.

Disaster is what the communists and their socialist and Labour allies have already brought to most of Africa. We must not allow them to achieve their final goal, which is communist control of South Africa.

Up until now the ex-service voice has not been heard enough while, here in London, no matter what concessions South Africa makes, the anti-apartheid, communist-influenced voices of protest grow louder and louder the whole time and the Southern Africa Coalition was formed to pressurise the

Houses of Parliament to give the British public the impression that there is more support for anti-apartheid than is actually the case.

The well-organised left, the communists have been allowed things far too much their own way, and it is up to us, the ex-servicemen, to make sure that our views are taken into account, and to ensure that the mistakes in Rhodesia will not be repeated in South Africa.

What more people in Britain have to understand is why the colonial era was so successful, and why everybody benefited from *Pax Britannica*, with its system of indirect rule in both Africa and India, and how in Africa the tribal system flourished.

A great many of Africa's problems today have been caused by urbanisation and industrialisation, together with the Marxist policy of trying to destroy as much as possible of Africa's tribal life. This policy has to be reversed and more encouragement given for a return to an improved rural, tribal life before it is too late.

The local Africans, like many others I met during my travels in rural areas, represented all that is good about Africa. The tragedy is that we abandoned them to famine, corruption, misrule and economic disaster by not standing firm against the anti-colonial hysteria so carefully and cleverly nurtured by ambitious socialists and communists, who were never interested in continuing to develop the rural lifestyle of the majority of Africans. All such people are ever interested in is their own political career.

It is these unscrupulous socialists and communists who are the real enemies of Africa, and who have hindered its development by their propaganda against the colonials who lived in Africa. With all their faults, they brought about a peak of development by their vision, courage and endless toil, development that was so unnecessarily squandered by the colonial powers themselves when they turned against their own kind.

There are very few in Europe, or America for that matter, who have any idea of the communists' final goal in Africa. Some of their well-informed socialist allies in the West carry out their instructions by whipping up support about the evils of colonialism and the need for sanctions against apartheid, to disguise their real aims. It should never be forgotten that, as early as 1973, President Leonid Brezhnev made it quite clear what Russia's long-term goals for South Africa really were:

> Our aim is to gain control of the two great treasure houses on which the West depends: the energy treasure house of the Persian Gulf and the mineral treasure house of central and South Africa.

How well the anti-South Africa propaganda campaign, so cleverly manipulated by communist-funded organisations like the AAM has succeeded. This is shown by the attitude of the general public and most politicians in Britain, who are far too frightened to show any support for South Africa. If they do, they are accused of being racist – and they are all well aware of the treatment meted out to Mr Enoch Powell, when he tried to warn the British public of the dangers of allowing unrestricted entry to Britain.

The time is long overdue for those who spent most of their working lives in Africa to do more to question the whole very dubious attitude of the West towards South Africa, and to remember that over two million people of British descent will be involved in the final outcome.

The tragedy for South Africa was that she did not, at the time when it mattered, have a politician of international repute like Field Marshal Jan Smuts. He was a friend and confidant of Winston Churchill, and would never have succumbed to the euphoria of independence in 1961, like Prime Minister H.F. Verwoerd, who put apartheid on the new republic's statute books in the face of world opposition at a time when the USA was taking steps to dismantle racialist laws in the southern states and to enforce desegregation.

This maladroit timing, of course, played right into the hands of the communists, and enabled Moscow's man in charge of the African National Congress in South Africa, Colonel Joe Slovo of the KGB, to mount a formidable anti-apartheid campaign worldwide, which succeeded in getting partial sanctions against South Africa.

Thus the ANC and the Anti-Apartheid Movement helped to start a new era of racial bigotry. This coincided with the huge influx into Britain of hundreds of thousands of Hindus and Muslims annually, and the setting up of the Commission for Racial Equality, which spends millions of pounds of British taxpayers' money to stop the majority of the British population expressing their views about having multiracialism forced on them against their will.

★

When, as a mixed-race couple, we came to Britain in 1983 to get married, we were amazed at the hypocrisy in Britain over racial issues, and the almost complete ignorance about the real facts of life in Africa, especially about the conditions in most of black-ruled Africa. This is not surprising when one sees the obsession of the media, especially television, with apartheid.

A typical example of media bias is the current wholesale slaughter of black Christians in the south of Sudan by the black Muslims from the north of Sudan. Rarely is this mentioned, either in the national newspapers or on television. Yet we are inundated with stories about apartheid in South Africa.

A classic example of uninformed madness is the frequent communist AAM demonstration, with the red flag of the Communist Revolutionary Party being waved outside the South African embassy in London's Trafalgar Square. I questioned some of those demonstrating, and found that none of them had ever been to Africa, and they appeared to be quite unconcerned about the millions who had died there unnecessarily, due mainly to communist interference in African affairs. When I mentioned the fact that over 110 million had been killed by the Communists in Russia since their 1917 Revolution, the demonstrators just looked blank and mumbled irrelevant jargon about the workers being exploited.

A report in one of Britain's national newspapers sums up the incredible lengths to which the communists will go, and is typical of how they think they can exploit what they see as the weakness of democracy. It also shows the way the communists think they can manipulate public opinion in Britain and the unfortunate truth is that, through organisations such as AAM and CND, they are doing it very successfully.

This report appeared in the *Daily Express* on 23rd January, 1988, and was headed '"Police assault" case thrown out':

> An anti-apartheid protester who claimed that she was assaulted and stripped naked in front of laughing policemen had her case thrown out of court yesterday. Simone Dewhurst, 21, sobbed as the charges of false imprisonment, assault and malicious prosecution were rejected by the eight-man jury at Westminster County Court.
>
> Revolutionary Communist Party member Dewhurst accused Sergeant Benjamin Manders of making obscene sexual remarks at her and allowing police to leer at her as she stood naked in the charge room of Cannon Row Police Station.
>
> Dewhurst, of Bradbury Street, Hackney, was arrested on October 6 1986 during a demonstration outside the South African Embassy, in Trafalgar Square. Judge Percival Harris told the court: 'I was certainly considering sending the plaintiff's case to the Director of Public Prosecutions but this is a naive and immature woman and might have been manipulated by other forces.'

Once again the Revolutionary Communist Party is let off the hook! The British public is supposed to believe that these almost non-stop demonstrations are spontaneous.

★

It is my sincere hope that this book will do something to repay the debt I owe to those rural African tribesmen who showed me something of the real Africa before it was destroyed for all time by the stupidity and madness not only of the communists but by the policies of the West in Africa since the end of World War II.

The Destruction of a Continent heralded the start of a vital reassessment of what really went on in Africa after the end of the war that the media, especially television, have tried their best to conceal with a carefully nurtured anti-colonial campaign by the West's socialists, which the communists masterminded.

It is no coincidence that the real conditions in most of the independent African countries are carefully concealed from the public in the West while the evils of apartheid are reported in detail almost daily to divert attention from the misrule, corruption and economic disaster that have brought starvation, or worse, to virtually all the independent countries in Africa since the end of the war.

The Destruction of a Continent encouraged me to write this book, and it is my hope that others who have spent most of their working lives in Africa will be encouraged to write about their experiences there, as it is only in this way that others will get the real truth about Africa.

★

Another interesting, and little known, fact about UN interference in the internal affairs of a member state, South Africa, is that until they decided to bring in arms restrictions against South Africa it had no arms industry. Today, as a direct result of arms sanctions, South Africa has a thriving arms industry of its own and exports all over the world!

In the past, South African policy very sensibly restricted the sales of firearms to non-whites. Until, in October 1986, Thames Television and the International Broadcasting Trust produced their television programme and booklet *Spear of the Nation*, a history of the African National Congress, very few members of the British public would have been aware that non-whites who joined the South African Army in both world wars were allowed to serve only in a non-combatant capacity. To those of us who have seen something of tribal warfare in Africa this was a very sensible precaution, but the booklet *Spear of the Nation* twists the facts in a quite incredible way.

This is not surprising, as the account given was, unless I miss my guess, the work of KGB Colonel Joe Slovo of the South African Communist Party, the founder and leader of the terrorist wing of the African National Congress.

Despite all the Marxist media propaganda that is being churned out the whole time, the British public, especially ex-servicemen, will, I believe, still question why they are never given any facts about what is happening in the rest of Africa. They may also wonder why it should be necessary for the British taxpayers to pay out millions and millions of their hard-earned money annually in aid money to black-ruled Africa, where no improvements are ever reported. In fact, the starvation just seems to get worse.

Yet white-ruled South Africa, in spite of sanctions and apartheid, seems to be prosperous and successful. Could it just be possible that a large amount of the credit should go to the much-maligned five million whites, of whom over two million are of British descent? Many of them fought for Britain, as did the Afrikaners, in both world wars.

As the whites have survived in South Africa since 1652, isn't it just possible that, if they were left alone now, they might just manage to solve their own problems?

What is astounding to those of us who know the truth about Africa is the incredible double standard whereby South Africa is condemned for apartheid while the fact that there is no such thing as democracy in black-ruled Africa is completely ignored. It is African dictators like Nyerere, Kaunda and Mugabe, encouraged by the other megalomaniacs in the Commonwealth and UN, who shout the loudest for sanctions against South Africa.

Apart from our own courageous Mrs Thatcher, few people are prepared to stand up and say 'enough of this stupid nonsense', when millions are dying of starvation all over black-ruled Africa. How can democracy be said to work when most white politicians are scared of the black vote in their own countries? This comprises more than twenty per cent of the vote in the USA. In Britain it is much lower, but rising fast – and the politicians are afraid to face the true situation.

The Commonwealth is now controlled by the black vote and in the UN it has a powerful voice, far in excess of its real importance. So ex-servicemen have to wake up and realise they must start to use their 16 million votes before it is too late to stop the British megalomaniacs.

*

The Labour Party seems to have learnt nothing from the Salman Rushdie affair and its ex-leader, Kinnock, was quite happy to give pledges to India's Gandhi that a Labour government would relax present immigration restrictions and repeal both the British Nationality Act of 1981 and the Immigration Act of 1971. Presumably he would have been quite happy to give the same pledges to Pakistan and any other Commonwealth country that wanted it.

The contempt that the majority of the two million plus Muslims already settled here have for British laws was clearly shown over the Salman Rushdie affair but it should have been obvious from the start that Muslims could not be integrated fully into the Christian way of life. Britain's tolerance is regarded as weakness.

Iran, the instigator of much religious hatred, must have congratulated itself on the ease with which Muslim extremists were able to incarcerate the Archbishop of Canterbury's special envoy to Beirut, the unfortunate Terry Waite, along with the other innocent hostages. The West seems absolutely powerless, and tamely accepts all the insults that Iran and other militant Muslim regimes hand out. Only Israel seems to know how to handle these religious monsters.

Naturally the Muslims in Britain begin to think they, too, can flaunt British laws with impunity, with what seems to be the tacit support of the Labour Party. Here again, if anything is to be done to stop them, it will have to be action from ex-servicemen and women and their families, who number nearly a third of the British population.

Left-wing politicians helped to create the terrible suffering in most of Africa after independence and they will not be satisfied until they see ANC creating the same kind of conditions in South Africa, where coups, hunger, poverty and tribal warfare will become the norm, as in most of black Africa. Since independence was granted to many countries, Africa has become a continent tainted by its leaders. Corruption is an accepted way of life everywhere and only a fool or a communist can believe that the African National Congress will be any different if ever it comes to power.

Most people in Britain, and elsewhere in the West, make the mistake of thinking that their politicians care about the countless millions that are openly squandered and misappropriated annually in most African countries. In the UN money is wasted on an even larger scale. But there is a conspiracy to keep these facts from the Western taxpayer.

The bureaucrats are never satisfied, and already the EC is busy getting into the act; a further burden for the Western taxpayer. In June 1991, TAAL's media-monitoring section picked up an item that shows what lies in the future:

Euro MPs run up a £1m bill for jet trips

> European taxpayers face a bill of more than £1 million following a series of exotic trips by jet-setting Euro MPs. Top spenders were a group of 27 who flew back last night after three days on the island of Reunion in the Indian Ocean. They were there to discuss North Sea pollution.
>
> Last month the European Parliament's socialist group of 180 MEPs spent five days on the Greek island of Corfu. Christian Democrats met in Spain for five days and the Women's Rights and Development Committee flew to Lisbon. But one economy has been introduced – Euro MPs can no longer claim first-class travel.

Even Whitehall's African experts don't seem to understand that the smartly suited, English-speaking African politicians that they deal with have little in common with the inarticulate rural Africans who, with their tribal background, make up the vast majority of the African population.

★

This lack of understanding is true, also, of those in the hierarchy of the Church of England who delight in criticising South Africa.

Take that arch critic of apartheid and chairman of the Anti-Apartheid Movement, and one of television's favourites, the retired Archbishop Huddleston, who formerly held the very quaint title of Archbishop of the Indian Ocean – a place where most of the islands were previously French and Catholic!

His knowledge of South Africa was mainly restricted to his work in Sophiatown until he was recalled to Britain by his religious order and then sent to Tanzania, where he spent most of the 1960s. He must have seen the damage done by his friend Julius Nyerere's policy of communist collectivisation. This forced millions of rural African farmers into 'model villages' and caused a catastrophic drop in food production. Both Huddleston and Nyerere have appeared on British television recently, but neither will admit that any mistakes were made. They continue to blame the West for Tanzania's economic woes and there is, of course, never any mention of the millions of pounds sent there annually as aid.

★

The media in Britain take a great deal of trouble to disguise the workings of the communist and socialist conspiracy and the active connivance of the hierarchy of the Church of England and others. But occasionally they slip up publicly, as in the Viraj Mendis affair.

Even Labour MPs got into the act in the Houses of Parliament, shouting 'Sieg Heil' at Home Secretary Hurd when he refused to stop the deportation of Mendis, who had claimed sanctuary in a Manchester church. Up until then the media had had a field day but later, when Mendis admitted on television that he was a communist, and had never been in any danger in Sri Lanka, the media shut up fast.

It is interesting to note that it took thirteen years to deport this communist fraud and I think it is significant that there was never any demand for an inquiry into how many more bogus refugees there were in Britain.

The role of Manchester's Labour city council in the Mendis affair makes interesting reading. The council paid him £30 per week (total £3,500), as well as spending £5,000 on a publicity campaign, and £1,700 on coachloads of Church and communist supporters for a Gatwick demo. Father West flew with Mendis to Colombo and, presumably, the Church paid his expenses as well. In 1985 this same Labour council set up a Special Needs Trust for others like Viraj Mendis – it amounts to £100,000!

It doesn't take much imagination to realise that the Viraj Mendis affair is but the tip of an iceberg, and illustrates how democracy is abused by the communists.

★

To show the extent of the Church of England's involvement in political matters, there is no better example than Desmond Tutu's Birmingham fiasco. That eventually cost the Church of England in excess of £200,000!

The city-wide Christian Celebration, starring Archbishop Tutu, formed part of Birmingham's centenary celebrations as a city, and turned out to be a very expensive fiasco for the Church. The chairman of these so-called Christian celebrations was Bishop Colin Buchanan, who had to resign when the Church had to make good the loss of £200,000. The bishop had very foolishly overestimated Tutu's appeal when he hired Birmingham's National Exhibition Centre for two nights and Aston Villa's football stadium for a 'Tutu Day Christian Carnival'.

When the traditional St George's Day parade was cancelled, so it would not interfere with Tutu Day, this was the last straw for a long-suffering Birmingham public. To quote from one of dozens of letters:

> I could hardly believe my eyes when I read that the parade organised to honour our patron saint, St. George, on St. George's Day had been called off because of a foreigner.
>
> Recently my regard for the church has been greatly strained by the attitudes of some Bishops [by turning] St. George's Day into 'Tutu Day'. I am sure the majority of indigenous Birmingham people will not welcome this further visit of an evil trouble-maker.

This feeling was reflected by a spokesman for one of Birmingham's leading Roman Catholic parishes, who said:

> The Oratory parish is not supporting or attending the celebration because it is difficult to distinguish in one's mind Archbishop Tutu as a religious figure from Archbishop Tutu as a political figure.

The Church of England seems incapable of learning anything from these disgraceful fiascos, as is shown in the October/December 1989 issue of the *Christian Aid News*, which devotes most of its front page to the formation of the Southern African Coalition, with a large picture of its chairman, the Bishop of Coventry, the Right Reverend Simon Barrington-Ward, surrounded by members of such politically-motivated organisations as the Anti-Apartheid Movement and Oxfam (which is now under investigation for mixing charity with politics).

The good bishop, presumably carrying out his political duties for the Southern African Coalition, visited South Africa in September 1989, just a month before Christian Aid gave him front-page publicity. He said that Tutu, the trade unions, the Mass Democratic Movement and the South African Council of Churches all supported the Coalition's formation. This is not very surprising when one considers that all of them work together with the Communists and the ANC to overthrow the government of South Africa by any means possible, including violence.

Archbishop Tutu summed up how the political priests work, and shares their arrogant assumption that they know what is best for the masses, in this case mainly rural Africans, who will have far crueller rulers if ever the ANC gains power in South Africa.

> But you never go round in a liberation struggle asking the so-called ordinary people what to do. It is the leaders, the more politicised people, who take the decisions.
>
> *Rand Daily Mail*
> 22nd December, 1977

Doesn't this statement by Archbishop Tutu typify the attitude of meddling political priests like Archbishop Huddleston and those trendy interfering political bishops in Birmingham, Manchester and Coventry, who claim to represent the masses?

To the average person in Britain, it seems that these churchmen glory in publicity to the detriment of their clerical duties, and without any understanding of the long-term damage they are doing to the majority of the people in South Africa. Evidence of the damage they have helped to cause is seen in virtually the whole of Africa.

I have only one question to ask Archbishop Huddleston: why did he fail to speak out when he saw the suffering of the ordinary Africans in Tanzania, which was due to his friend President Nyerere's policy of communist collectivism on a vast scale?

Millions of rural Africans, like the ones I knew and admired so much in the Kakonko-Kibondo, Kasulu and Kigoma districts of Tanzania, were forced into 'model villages'. Their fertile farms were abandoned, thereby causing a massive drop in food production in the 1960s, from which Tanzania has still not recovered. These days the country has to be kept going by massive financial aid and technical assistance, like so many other African countries that were prosperous in colonial times.

Nowadays Zimbabwe is kept going by a few thousand white farmers, who are kept in Mugabe's Marxist state as economic hostages. If they leave permanently for South Africa they can take only $1,000 (Zimbabwean) with them and there are similar restrictions if they go other parts of the world. Nothing is said of the thousands of Matabele murdered in cold blood by Mugabe's Marxist troops.

Archbishop Huddleston and his Marxist and socialist allies in the West must be aware of these facts and of the risk of pushing reforms in South Africa too quickly, but they seem to ignore the fact that violence is the most likely communist solution in South Africa. Perhaps they will be satisfied when prosperous South Africa has been reduced to the same level of chaos, civil war, famine, misrule, corruption and economic disaster as most of the rest of black Africa.

Some priests have been courageous enough to speak out against the madness of this policy. One notable example is the Reverend Father Arthur Lewis (MA Oxon), a remarkable missionary of the Church of England who spent forty years in Africa, including many years in rural Tanzania, and who recently returned to Britain.

He finds time to be the honorary president of the Rhodesia Christian Group and the Good Hope Christian Group, as well as sending out his own newsletter about current affairs in Africa.

★

It is no coincidence that crime (virtually unknown in tribal areas), and all the other ills of Western civilisation, are multiplying fast in Africa. This is caused by a vast influx of rural Africans to the cities, with a large majority of the newcomers ending up unemployed, and kept alive only by UN food aid.

My experiences on my farm, in the remote Kakonko area of Tanganyika, brought this home forcibly as, travelling alone over the whole area, I never lost so much as a single round of ammunition, or anything else, when I left my lorry, tent and camping equipment completely unattended. The same applied when I was staying in an African village hut, the one normally used by the DO (District Officer) on his travels around the district.

When a local sub-chief asked me to shoot elephants that had been destroying his crops, in those days a common enough happening in the area, I often spent a night in his village, as he liked to show his appreciation by offering me hospitality. I found it a little embarrassing to accept the customary gifts of a chicken, eggs, and other delicacies, when I knew some of their food supplies had been destroyed by the elephants, but to refuse the gifts caused offence. In the early days I needed the money from the ivory for my farm, but an added incentive to go after the elephants was always the knowledge that the elephant meat provided the village with food for quite some time.

The rural standards of honesty applied on our farm as well, and rarely was anything locked up – unlike urban Mwanza, where there was a spate of burglaries just before we left.

But few Europeans, even South Africans, witnessed the African in his true tribal way of life and it is a tragedy, and a stain on our glorious Empire, that we allowed cleverly applied international pressure from the UN and communists to force the pace of African independence, with such tragic results.

The task for those of us who care about Africa is simple. It is to make more and more people in the West, especially ex-servicemen in the 'old' Commonwealth, aware of the dangers that face South Africa.

What is not generally understood in the West is that the political urban African activists form less than one per cent of the population. The African superbureaucrats, who are always so elegantly dressed and who drive smart limousines (the Mercedes-Benz is particularly popular), have nothing in common with ninety-nine per cent of the African population. They are far more avaricious and dictatorial than their colonial counterparts ever were.

★

No wonder that we are angry, those of us who have spent most of our working lives in Africa since the end of the war, and who have seen the unnecessary tragedy unfolding in front of our eyes. We witnessed at first hand the effects of the unholy alliance between the communists, socialists and certain elements in the Church.

Outside our home at Felixstowe

With my mother and grandparents

My prep school, Yardley Court, Tonbridge, Kent

School House, The King's School, Canterbury

With my sister Sylvia and
the nanny holding Paul

My father in the colonial
service in Nigeria

My father in the colonial service in Nigeria

My father in France

My father in the colonial service in Nigeria

My father in the colonial service in Nigeria

Troopship in Durban being
welcomed by the 'Lady in White'

DAILY EXPRESS Tuesday March 15 1988

A standard slur to old comrades

LAST week your Foreign Line had an article regarding certain MPs who wanted the Union Jack removed from the South African flag.

Most ex-servicemen consider this a gratuitous insult too many. Britain was only too glad to accept the services of the 350,000 South Africans who volunteered to fight and die in World War Two.

It is hoped, therefore, that as many ex-servicemen as possible will write to their MP registering their anger and disgust that such gratuitous insults to their dead South African comrades-in-arms should be allowed.

M. Walsh,
London W2.

Gurkha officers of 2/10 GR

2/10 Gurkha Rifles in Italy and Middle East

2/10 Gurkha Rifles in Italy and Middle East

Chapter Ten

Farming and Congo Travels

Our bartering, smuggling and transporting of salt was going smoothly and, although there was now no financial reason why I shouldn't have employed an African driver for transporting the salt, I liked doing the trip. In my Indian Army days with the 43rd Gurkha Lorried Brigade, I had got the taste of daily travel and, to be quite honest, the daily routine on the farm bored me a bit. Transporting the salt myself also meant I could do a bit of hunting en route.

I was extremely lucky to have someone like Rengli to run the farm for me, so I could get away frequently. On my regular trips to Uvinza, to collect salt from the mine, I would drive via Kasulu to get news of any large herds of elephants in the district, so my journeys served a dual purpose.

I needed quite a lot of salt myself, for preserving the crocodile skins, and transporting the district salt helped cut my costs, as I could carry my own half or one ton for free at the same time. There was very little traffic on the Tanganyikan roads in those days, so overloading my Ford diesel lorry didn't create any problems.

Everything worked out fine until one day I ran into some very heavy unseasonal rain. Since it was completely unexpected, I was not carrying with me the tyre chains I used for extra grip in muddy conditions. I had already passed Kasulu, on my way back to Kibondo, and I was finding it increasingly difficult to keep the heavily loaded lorry on the road.

The sensible thing to have done would have been to stop and sleep by the roadside until the road had dried out the next day, but it was a Saturday night and I was looking forward to joining some friends in Kibondo for drinks, so I decided to press on. I got away with it until I was only a few miles from Kibondo. Then, as I was going down a steep hill, the lorry started to slide, even in low gear, and I realised it would be impossible to negotiate the sharp turn near the bottom of the hill.

Fortunately I was on one of the few stretches of the road where there was no sheer drop on either side, and there was a convenient earth bank to steer the lorry into a little before the sharp turn: just after the turn there was another sheer drop on both sides of the road.

I had slowed considerably by changing down gears, but it was obvious that we were going to slide into the bank too fast for comfort, and the lorry could suffer considerable damage. One of my African farm workers was in the back, asleep on top of the salt, but there was no way I could warn him. I opened my bedroll on the floor of the lorry and, just before we hit the bank, I dropped to the floor, as I didn't relish the possibility of the steering wheel going through my chest, or glass from the windscreen smashing into my face.

We were lucky. The bank was wet and fairly soft, as it had only recently been dug, and we got off remarkably lightly. The African on the back was thrown right out of the lorry on impact, and woke up in the mud wondering how he had got there, but with no worse injuries than a few bruises. I got some quite bad bruises, but nothing broken either, and fortunately there was remarkably little damage to the lorry. In fact, apart from a smashed radiator and windscreen, together with some dents on the front wings, it was still roadworthy, which was a great relief. The odd sack of salt was damaged, but most of the load was intact.

I got a lift from a passing government truck and was dropped off at Peter Haynes's house, where my wife and I had been invited for drinks that evening. As usual, Peter helped me out and sent someone to collect the salt – and my African, who had stayed with the lorry.

My truck was towed into Kibondo for repairs and the radiator was patched up until a new one arrived. I had a spare windscreen at the farm, and this was fitted in Kibondo, but it was a long time before I overloaded the lorry again, and then only in the dry season. Most of my business – the elephant hunting, bartering, smuggling and salt contract – depended on keeping my lorry on the road, and it was not worth jeopardising everything by taking unnecessary risks.

*

Some time during this period I had acquired a Land Rover, which was very useful on the farm, and for the fairly frequent trips I was making to Usumbura (now Bujumbura) and other parts of Ruanda-Urundi (now Rwanda and Burundi). Both of these countries were administered by Germany until she lost Tanganyika to Britain at the end of World War I, and Belgium took over Ruanda-Urundi.

Prior to the independence of both these countries (in 1962) the Tutsi dominated the whole area and ruled over the local Hutu, as they had done for centuries. The Tutsi are impressive and reminded me strongly of the Masai in Kenya, since both tribes are very tall (fully grown men are usually well over six feet). Both are almost certainly of Nilotic or Nilo-Hamitic origin, and totally different to the local Hutu, who are of Ban origin. I quite often saw the Tutsi king, Mwanbutsa IV, in Usumbura, staying at one of the very good hotels there. At about six and a half feet tall, he was a very impressive figure.

Compared to Tanganyika, even the hotel food in Usumbura was very good and there were some excellent restaurants which served Continental food and wines. The town itself was very impressive and well laid out and I remember how the Catholic cathedral dominated the central area. The Belgian settlers had also developed some entertaining places on and near the lake shores – one even had a Saturday night dance with attractive, unattached Continental females, who worked locally or were the daughters of Belgian officials – it was all very unlike Mwanza and Kigoma in British Tanganyika.

Like Uganda, Ruanda-Urundi was, by African standards, an extremely prosperous country, with the same very fertile soil. Coffee and banana trees, in particular, were to be seen in profusion everywhere. It was just one more tragedy of Africa when the colonial era finished and the mayhem, murder, civil war, corruption, misrule and economic disaster started there, as well as in the Belgian Congo, with every encouragement being given by the communists and the West.

⋆

This tragic situation goes on even today, and the Western media give it a few lines in their newspapers as thousands of wretched refugees flee the country to the dubious safety of Tanzania and Kenya. There they become just another statistic of the starving millions in Africa that is the legacy of the interference of the UN, Russia, America and the rest of the West, in particular the Scandinavian countries. Apparently these people won't be satisfied until they have completed their work of destroying Africa by bringing the same conditions to one of the last prosperous areas, namely South Africa, which became a republic in 1961.

However, the envious eyes of newly independent states in the rest of Africa and in the Commonwealth, misruled and bankrupt, were quickly turned to ways of destabilising prosperous South Africa in the name of African socialism, a convenient smokescreen for communism and less likely to offend the delicate sensibilities of their European socialist supporters.

It was in these early days of the Republic of South Africa that the lack of a statesman with the international experience of someone like Field Marshal Jan Smuts was to be felt. He would never have made the mistake of bringing in apartheid laws at just the time that the United States of America was abandoning racial discrimination in its southern states. It enabled the communists and the UN to mastermind an anti-apartheid campaign of interference in South Africa's internal affairs, with ever-increasing help from the World Council of Churches. The backing of the WCC lends respectability to the communist cause and, at the same time, enables them to divert attention away from the truly appalling conditions in most of Africa. The media in the West always seem happy to help by concentrating their attention on the evils of apartheid, to the exclusion of worse evils elsewhere.

In this way the facts about countries like Rwanda and Burundi are always played down and rarely do the ordinary people in the West see any news or books that give a true account of the colonial era and how the colonial powers were, by their stupidity, largely responsible, with the UN, for today's tragedies in Africa.

*

When I travelled around Africa in those days, I took for granted the law and order of colonial times. Today it is impossible to travel safely by road to many of the places I visited. In those days the roads were well maintained, as they needed to be on the mountainous route from Kibondo to Usumbura.

There were few frontier or customs controls then and at night it was possible to cross the border at will either way, which is how most of the coffee was smuggled. The route was notorious for the mountain bit, that eventually dropped down to lake level (Lake Tanganyika) as you got near to Usumbura.

This mountainous stretch only allowed one-way traffic, as it was very narrow, with twists and turns most of the way, but there were lay-bys at intervals for emergency use. The road was open for twelve hours from one end, and then for twelve hours from the other end. About an hour before the changeover time, native drums would be sounded at the end that was due to open and anyone already on the road would know that they had an hour to complete their journey. If they could not get to the end in time, they could either turn round and go back to the beginning or pull on to one of the lay-bys and wait for twelve hours until the direction changed again. Once you knew the system, you planned your journeys according to the 'opening times' and it all worked quite well.

I only slipped up once, when I stopped off for drinks in Kibondo en route for Usumbura. The mountain road was open from my end from 6 p.m. to 6 a.m., so I planned to drive through the night. But I stretched my normal limits a bit by having one or two drinks too many 'for the road' – I had reckoned that if I pulled the canvas back off the Land Rover the cold wind would keep me awake.

This worked fine until I reached the really mountainous bit, at about two or three in the morning. I had to go fairly slowly on this twisty bit of road and I began to nod off. More than once I stopped at a lay-by to stretch my legs and make myself more alert. This did not help very much, however, and, as I did not relish falling asleep at the wheel (there were sheer drops on either side of the road of hundreds of feet), I pulled off at the next lay-by, only intending to snatch an hour or so of sleep. I had to pull the canvas over the Land Rover's frame, as I had seen leopards in the area on more than one occasion, and this, together with the blankets pulled over me, and the after-effects of the alcohol, made me sleep far longer and deeper than I had intended.

The next thing of which I was aware was the traffic from Usumbura passing by, and I knew that I had either to follow it back or to spend the whole day sitting in my Land Rover in the mountains. So I shaved, had tea and some breakfast and then joined the traffic, retracing the way I had come in the dark a few hours earlier and knowing that I would have to start all over again at six o'clock.

This was, of course, highly embarrassing, as I had arranged to meet some people in Usumbura and there was absolutely nothing I could do about it now.

In Africa you soon learnt to prepare for delays when travelling. I always carried enough food and water, as well as spare petrol, to keep me going for some time in an emergency. In remote areas a sudden rock slide or fallen tree blocking the road was not unusual, while a sudden tropical storm could make a river impassable for a few days. It was all part of the unpredictable charm of travelling in Africa.

Night travel was actively dangerous, as wild (and sometimes domestic) animals often wandered on to the road unseen, which could easily result in smashed radiators or windscreens for the unwary traveller.

So there were plenty of excuses I could use the next day, when I eventually reached Usumbura, but I never again made the mistake of travelling this very dangerous stretch of road after having a drink too many.

★

Looking back now at those carefree early years in East Africa, I am very glad that I made the most of every opportunity to travel and to hunt in those unspoilt countries and that, unlike a lot of my friends, I survived to write some of the truth about events in those remote areas of Africa.

It appears to me now that the Scandinavian socialist countries like Sweden and, of course, their communist friends, are beginning to reap some of the retribution they so richly deserve for the havoc and misery they brought to gullible African countries like Tanzania with their socialist theories. Not that this is much consolation to the starving rural Tanzanians, who have had to pay the price for the mad experiment of the 'model villages'.

Premier Ingvar Carlsson seemed incapable of learning anything from Sweden's economic problems, which were due to half-baked socialist schemes. Despite his country's troubles, he was quite prepared to continue paying from the Swedish public purse £20 million a year towards, as he so charmingly put it, the 'armed struggle' of the African National Congress, a communist terrorist organisation which will produce the same catastrophic economic conditions in South Africa as Sweden has already helped the communists to produce in all the African socialist countries.

Even in the 1950s it was obvious, from what was happening in Kenya with the Mau Mau, that there would be more and more demands for instant independence from all over Africa, with no regard for the welfare of the majority: the rural, tribal Africans. What did surprise us was the unseemly speed with which the major colonial powers caved in to the demands of so-called African Nationalists, who were so obviously unsuited and unprepared to take over the government of their countries and incapable of seeing that they were properly run.

It started in Ghana, when Britain, against the wishes of local tribal chiefs, allowed Kwame Nkrumah (in 1956) to hold pre-independence elections. This set the pattern for other African countries, who saw that wholesale intimidation, violence and bribery were quite acceptable to the colonial powers, who wanted out as quickly as possible.

In 1957 Ghana got its independence and Nkrumah became prime minister. In 1960 he became president. It took him less than ten years to wreck Ghana's prosperous economy, one of the many good things left him by Britain's well-run colonial service. By 1966 the Ghanaians had had enough of their hero and he was deposed in a military coup.

The African era of instability and chaos, with starvation thrown in, was just starting and (as shown in the table in Chapter Seven) there were sixty-eight successful *coups d'état* in Africa from 1963 to 1987.

What the continent obviously needed was not political speeches from Prime Minister Harold Macmillan about the 'wind of change' but someone to stand up and admit that the African countries needed a gradual transitional period, of at least fifteen years, to stand any chance of political stability after independence.

Unfortunately for Africa, Labour, socialist and communist pressure made sure she was never going to get that chance, and the tragic results are now there for everybody to see.

Incredibly, until the publication of *The Destruction of a Continent*, very little of the real truth about Africa was ever reported in the Western media. The very clever anti-colonial hysteria, so carefully nurtured by the communists and their socialist friends in the West, was largely responsible for this.

In the 1960s Prime Minister H. F. Verwoerd gave them a propaganda gift by institutionalising apartheid in South Africa, just as the reverse was happening, with a great deal of publicity, in the southern states of the USA.

Ever since then, the Western media have been obsessed by apartheid to the exclusion of the real tragedy of most of black-ruled Africa.

*

In Tanganyika by the mid-1950s, some of the local chiefs were already beginning to voice their anxiety over events that were taking place in Dar es Salaam, where Julius Nyerere had already formed his own independence party, Tanu (Tanganyikan African Nationalist Union).

We had seen the occasional Tanu representative in the district, but everything was kept very low-key in the early days, and Tanu's activities seemed to be restricted to distributing fairly harmless pamphlets.

Then one of these chiefs, who had some good connections in Dar, received some disturbing news about a new lot of European advisers, who had Nyerere's confidence. Evidently they were already advocating the 'model village', on communist collective lines, as the new solution to increase Africa's agricultural output.

These 'model villages' were also a very convenient way to break the tribal chiefs' power and undermine their local authority. This was the kind of madness that was produced by the 'wind of change' speech, and African socialism was accepted, or rather forced on, ignorant Africans as the way forward.

*

Forty years later, most African countries are beginning to admit the damage that socialist and communist doctrines did to previously prosperous agricultural systems worked out over many years of benevolent colonial rule. It can't even be much of a satisfaction to them to see the collapse of Russia and Eastern Europe's whole communist economic system.

However, current events in Southern Africa show that the Marxist regime in Namibia and Mandela's ANC in South Africa have learnt nothing from the hard economic facts in the rest of black-ruled independent African states. They still want to commit economic suicide by nationalising all big business in Namibia and South Africa.

Perhaps, this time, it is not too much to ask that Western countries refuse to encourage such madness? Or perhaps the socialists are not satisfied with all the havoc, chaos and starvation that they and the UN have helped to produce over the last forty years.

*

Although, at the time, I did not take the local chief's warnings very seriously, I did decide it would be sensible to take the precaution of extending my crocodile business into Northern Rhodesia. Then, if trouble did come in Tanganyika earlier than expected, I would have something to fall back on. The easiest way to expand seemed to be to explore the possibilities of the Belgian Congo, before going on to Northern Rhodesia. So I made a trip I had long wanted to take on the Congo and Lualaba river steamers that the Belgians ran so very efficiently.

It was quite a trip. First a drive from the farm at Kakonko to Kigoma, then across Lake Tanganyika to end up at Bukama, which was quite near the Northern Rhodesia border. In the dry season it was an easy day's drive to Kigoma, but it had to be coordinated with the infrequent steamer that went straight across the lake to Albertville.

In those prosperous colonial days, considerable amounts of local produce and other goods were sent between the Belgian Congo and Dar, via Lake Tanganyika, for import or export. It was much quicker, and far cheaper to use this east coast route rather than to use the West African route via Leopoldville.

Most of the steamers went right around the lake, but a few went directly to Albertville, on the Congo side of the lake. It took about a week to do the whole journey, and I hadn't the time to go all the way around Lake Tanganyika. But I timed it well, and everything ran to schedule on my first trip, so I left the next day, with the car on board, for Albertville.

Things do not always go so smoothly in Africa, of course, and I remember one trip in the rainy season when I got stuck on the road to Kigoma and arrived too late to catch the steamer to Albertville. This meant spending three very frustrating days in Kigoma while I waited for the next steamer.

From Albertville it was a good day's drive to Kabalo. Alternatively, it was possible to load the car from the steamer straight on to the train, which left that evening and linked up with the Congo river steamer the next day. On my first trip, I decided it would be safer to take the train, with the car, than to drive and take a chance of missing the river steamer.

No other river trip could give you such a feeling of the vastness of Africa as the Congo and its tributaries: huge expanses of water with seemingly impenetrable areas of water reeds, so vast that it was impossible to see any sign of land. The reeds seemed to go on for ever, but every now and again we would pass African fishing canoes coming out of the reeds laden down with fish, so we knew there must be hidden settlements somewhere near.

The river steamer was the lifeline for trade in this area. So we made frequent stops to load and offload goods and large quantities of dried fish, as well as to take on passengers. Although it was a slow trip, it was a fascinating one, and I never tired of making it. It was also rewarding gastronomically.

The Belgian captain and his wife, who supervised all the cooking on board, made sure the standard of Continental food and the wines were as good as in any restaurant in Europe, and the service was far quicker and more friendly than most.

I have forgotten how long the river steamer took to reach Bukama, but everything connected with the river seemed timeless. As we neared Bukama, the river opened up into what seemed like a vast lake and swamp, an area which was eventually designated as a game reserve.

*

The knowledge I gained on these trips was to prove invaluable after I had to move to Northern Rhodesia, especially after the trouble started in the Congo and we needed a route from Bukama via Kolwezi that avoided the Katanga and Rhodesian border posts and came out in Northern Rhodesia near to Mwinilunga, a small village near the border.

Even in those peaceful colonial days, a tribe that lived on the Lualaba River, the Baluba, had the fearsome reputation of still being cannibals whenever they got the chance.

On that first trip there was a senior Belgian Congo policeman on board who, at some time in a long colonial police career, had been stationed in the area. He had some pretty horrific tales to tell of murder and cannibalism.

At the time I discounted his stories as being a product of the excellent wine that was served on board the river steamer.

After the Belgian Congo troubles had started and UN troops had occupied Katanga Province, however, I remembered his tales when a whole UN patrol of Irish troops disappeared in the area without trace. I believe the odd army boot was found later, near the Lualaba River, but nothing could ever be proved against the Baluba.

I believe there were other mysterious disappearances of UN troops in the area, but the whole matter was hushed up. It was virtually impossible to follow the Baluba in the vast swamp and reed areas that they knew so well.

Whenever we visited the region, and had to sleep in the bush near the river, we made a point of having one European and one African awake as guards at all times. We might not admit that we believed the stories of cannibalism, but we preferred to ensure that none of us would end up in the Baluba cooking pots.

*

Leaving Bukama by the usual dirt road, it didn't take long to reach the immaculate and well-maintained tarmac roads built for Katanga's copper industry. It was like entering a completely different Africa, with plenty of Europeans and their cars on the roads.

Not far away was one of the Belgian Congo's largest military air bases at Kamina. Later, Belgian paratroopers had to be dropped there to stop the slaughter of civilians, including nuns, by the Simbas, who were even worse than their terrorist counterparts in Kenya's Mau Mau.

It was an introduction to one of the richest mining areas of Africa, one where big white businesses had completely taken over. Union Minière virtually controlled Katanga from the large mining centres in and around Élisabethville, Jadotville and Kolwezi. The road ran through the even larger Copperbelt in Northern Rhodesia, where large British and South African mining companies, like Anglo-American and RST, controlled not only the copper mines but the lives of most of the Europeans in the area. They led lives very little different to that in Europe or in the mining centres of South Africa, except for the fact that they were much better paid and there were cheap black servants available.

The trouble was that most of them knew nothing about Africa, and were just as easy to deceive as those living in Europe. Few could speak any African language, except some who had come up from South Africa, so they were generally completely taken in by Kaunda's smooth-talking, English-speaking UNIP representatives, and never understood that, like Tanganyika's Tanu, they really represented less than one per cent of the African population.

It hadn't taken the socialist, Labour and communist advisers from Europe to realise they could use the same tactics as in East Africa to break up British colonial rule all over the continent. But these were early days in the tragedy that was going to unfold all over Africa and few of us had any inkling of how, in the next twenty years, all these prosperous, well-run countries would be thrown into turmoil by the carefully planned, communist-fermented independence struggles that would stretch right down to South Africa's borders.

The 275,000 white settlers in Southern Rhodesia and the 75,000 whites in Northern Rhodesia (many of whom were miners on contract), were largely responsible for pioneering all the development in the two Rhodesias, but they never really had a chance once the colonial powers, including Britain, turned against them, and the large mining companies were rumoured to be contributing money to Kaunda's UNIP to safeguard their future interests.

In fact it was British colonial policy to make it difficult for settlers who wanted to migrate to the Rhodesias and it was mainly ex-servicemen who were prepared to go after World War II. If there had been any benefit for the majority of rural Africans, there might have been more justification for the short-sightedness and stupidity of the West.

South Africa would do well to remember that, even at this late stage, and also the fact that big business knows no loyalty except to making money. The sight of a planeload of South African industrial and mining magnates scrambling to be the first to appease the hierarchy of the ANC at Lusaka headquarters should not have surprised any who knew what happened in the Rhodesias.

Again, whatever their present protestations about liberalism, nothing can change the fact that it was largely business greed that created the problems of South Africa's huge African townships like Soweto. These made ideal breeding grounds for discontent for the communist agitators from the South African Communist Party and the African National Congress. Even now, after all this urban business development, nearly half of South Africa's African population still lead a rural life. This fact is, of course, always ignored by the ANC and its urban agitators.

Even at this late stage, there is still hope for saner views and reforms to prevail. Many South African whites now living urban lives, both Afrikaners and English-speaking South Africans, have Voortrekker or 1820 English settler ancestors, and there was a large influx in the years before and after the Boer War, and they understand Africa and its real problems. They know that the way forward is not Marxism or African socialism.

They will never be taken in by the smooth-talking Mandela and the rest of the ANC, who can only be far worse for South Africa than Mugabe has been for Zimbabwe. Mugabe is determined to have a one-party Marxist state and it would be very foolish to believe that South Africa will be any different if ever the ANC is allowed to take over the government of the country.

Anyone who thinks it is already too late for South Africa should remember that 275,000 Rhodesians under premier Ian Smith, an ex-Battle of Britain pilot with the RAF, defied the Western world and the communist forces of Mugabe and Nkomo for sixteen years. I am sure they would still be resisting now if extreme Western pressure had not been put on South Africa, so that it withdrew its support.

The same kind of pressure was put on Portugal to give up its African colonies of Mozambique and Angola, and with the same disastrous results.

So let nobody in South Africa or in the West be under any illusions about what will happen there if the Communists and Mandela's ANC ever get their way.

With the end of East-West confrontation and interference in Africa's affairs, there is now more hope that saner views of the reforms necessary in South Africa will prevail, and that the best interests of all the different races and tribes in South Africa will stand a much better chance of success.

But it would be very foolish to underestimate the internal communist threat in South Africa. It has been building up over the years and, whatever settlement is eventually reached, the threat from the Communists in places like Soweto will still be very real. It should be realised that the media in the West will always play down this menace while they concentrate on apartheid and the carefully manipulated protests in the African townships.

★

I still remember what a contrast there was between the affluence of the Copperbelt, with its abundance of goods and food, and the poverty of Tanganyika. All the main towns in the Rhodesias (Lusaka, Salisbury, Bulawayo, Kitwe, Gwelo, Ndola, Chingola, Umtali and Livingstone) bore a striking resemblance to Britain's middle-class suburbia, with very much the same immaculate gardens – although these were, of course, much bigger than in Britain.

But that certainly wasn't the Africa I knew and loved, and I knew then that, when and if I had to move from Tanganyika, I would miss the free and easy life. I also realised, even then, how lucky I had been to go to East Africa first, so that I was able to experience the real colonial-style life before it disappeared for ever. Fortunately most of Northern Rhodesia was still undeveloped and unspoilt when I moved there, as most of the development had centred on the Copperbelt and along the vital rail and road links with Southern Rhodesia and South Africa. Few who have not lived in this part of Africa can understand the almost complete dependence on these links and the trade with South Africa.

Despite the tears of Zambia's Kaunda and the shouting of Zimbabwe's Mugabe, nothing much has changed since those years, except that, through their stupidity, they have managed to impoverish their countries almost beyond belief, so that the promise of those prosperous colonial years has been almost completely wasted.

*

It really made very little difference which Rhodesian town you lived in, they were all very much the same. The only real difference was that of size. In fact, the only town with a real African flavour was Livingstone, and that was because it was near the Zambezi River. The same thing applied to the Victoria Falls village, which was on the Southern Rhodesian side of the border.

After Ian Smith's UDI (Unilateral Declaration of Independence), at which time we were living in Livingstone, the Zambian authorities, to discourage us from crossing over to Southern Rhodesia too frequently, used a huge stamp in our British passports – as it took up a whole page, the passports filled very quickly and we were put to the great inconvenience of making a trip to Lusaka in order to get new ones.

Another amusing example of African hypocrisy, which also shows how little the rulers really care about public opinion in the West, is often illustrated on television. We are shown Kaunda ranting and raving, when he is not weeping, about the need for more sanctions against South Africa and there, in the background, are the banquet tables in Lusaka with – large as life for all who know South Africa to see – bottles of South African wine, clearly visible on all the tables.

As Zambia relies on massive food imports from South Africa, it is a very safe bet to assume that a large proportion of the food being served at the Lusaka banquets has also been imported from South Africa – using South African Railways rolling stock, as Zambia has developed critical shortage of rolling stock since independence.

Even before we left Zambia for good, it was a standing joke in Livingstone about Kaunda replacing most of the railway drivers and other railway staff (who, before independence, were mostly experienced men from Southern Rhodesia or even South Africa) with the queerest bunch of incompetents from all over black Africa. They had managed to smash up a large proportion of Zambia's rolling stock long before we left in late 1969.

In fact, from friends we had on the railways in Livingstone, we heard that matters had become so bad that South African Railways had given the Zambians an ultimatum: that if all their rolling stock was not returned by a certain date they would stop all railway deliveries and exports of copper from South African ports. This would have crippled Zambia in a matter of weeks, rather than months, and I believe all the missing rolling stock was returned as a matter of urgency by Zambian Railways, who knew exactly how vulnerable they were.

*

Because communications were so much better in the Rhodesias, it was very much easier to organise my business. I arranged for the payments for my crocodile skins going overseas by rail, sea or air to be made on a letter of credit basis once delivery had been made to any main railway station or airport in the Rhodesias. This FOB (free on board) payment, once all documents had been delivered to the local bank, helped to develop the business in a much quicker way than had been possible in Tanganyika, especially with the extra crocodile skins that were coming in after my Congo trips.

Later, as the Rhodesian crocodile business expanded, we were able to cut down on the risks by air-freighting all the skins from any major airport in the Rhodesias, and we were paid out by the local bank on an FOA basis (free on aircraft).

Another great help was a weekly air service started by CAA (Central Africa Airways) from Nairobi, which stopped once a week at Tabora before going on to Lusaka and Salisbury. That made it possible for me to leave the farm at

Kakonko very early in the morning, catch the plane at Tabora that afternoon and arrive in Lusaka the same evening. Before this, I had to go via Kigoma and the Belgian Congo, and was lucky to do the round trip in under three weeks.

★

The Congo skins were, in fact, to prove a very mixed blessing, but that was one of the risks of dealing in a new area. The prices were normally so high that it made the risks acceptable.

At the start, everything concerned with the Congo seemed to be going very well, and it seemed nothing could interrupt the initial smoothness and profits coming from this new area. Unfortunately it took a long time, due to the distances involved, before the extent of a setback could be assessed – in those days, consignments of crocodile skins took three or four months to reach the tannery (by rail and sea) and the tanning of the skins was a process which took about nine months.

So it was only after this long delay that I learnt that the Congo was the habitat of two entirely different species of crocodile. One was the type found in East Africa, of Nilotic origin. The other was a gavial, only found by the crocodile hunters as they went farther west in the Congo but, to complicate matters further, there were some areas which had both varieties.

The whole problem with the gavials was only discovered after the first lot had been tanned. During the colouring process, it came to light that there was a small, central square of a hard substance in each scale area of the gavial crocodile's belly which would not take up the colour required. This meant the skin was useless except for cutting up, which entailed a huge loss on the finished product.

It was found that the smaller crocodiles had not developed the hard square and a new method of cutting these skins (called hornbacks) was worked out very successfully. It entailed cutting into the middle of the belly and using both sides of the back as well as the belly part, whereas for larger crocodiles only the soft belly part was used. The hornbacks saved us from total disaster, but nothing could disguise the huge financial losses involved as we had to accept much lower prices for the gavials – about sixty to seventy per cent lower than the Nilotic crocodile skins.

This, of course, meant that it was not worth the crocodile hunters going after the gavials, except the very small ones, and that meant hunting in the Congo was restricted: the farther west you went, the more gavials were found, and it just wasn't economical to travel the long distances involved.

Our problems were much worse than those of the hunters, as we had to guarantee prices for the skins before the hunters set out, and take our chance on how much we would get for them by the time the hunters returned. So, because of the time lag before we discovered the truth about the gavials and were able to pass on the news to the hunters, we had to pay the full 'Nilotic price' for gavials for a long time – and we continued to make a heavy loss until the whole mess was cleared up.

★

Instead of the easy move I had anticipated to Northern Rhodesia, therefore, with profits from the Congo assured for a long time into the future, we had to face some very heavy losses at the outset. This entailed a change of plans and I decided to make use of information I had received from Eric Nawotny many years earlier about a sure-fire area with plenty of Nilotic crocodiles.

The snag was that it was an area where crocodile hunting was not allowed, and that meant there were a lot of problems that had to be solved before I could decide whether it was worth taking the risk. It was also necessary to make a very careful choice of crocodile hunters to go with me, and to take only men who could keep their mouths shut.

Since others were involved, it was obvious that everything would have to be planned very carefully, almost on military lines, to ensure that everybody would get out safely. I made sure that there was an escape route, in case anything went wrong unexpectedly and one that could be closed off after we had passed, so that we could not be pursued by less heavily laden vehicles.

As some of those involved are still living in Africa, I cannot go into detail. Suffice it to say that everything went according to plan, even to the extent that we did, indeed, have to make sure we were not followed by temporarily closing one of the bridges on the bush road out of the area: we cut away the wood support, which collapsed the bridge after we had passed with our Land Rovers and trailers.

Whatever their suspicions, the authorities were never able to prove who had been involved and, looking back all these years later, it seems to me that it was a very minor misdemeanour when compared with the mayhem and bloodshed that was to take place in the whole area a few years later. But it was very satisfactory financially for all those who had taken part.

★

One lesson I learnt during those idyllic early years in Tanganyika was that the fewer Europeans you had around the better. While there were only a few of us, I never had the feeling that Europeans were in any way resented. In fact, in rural areas like Kakonko and Kibondo, the reverse attitude was always evident.

Most of us realised that the trouble we began to experience as independence approached was carefully manipulated by Nyerere's Tanu, a very, very small percentage of the Tanganyikan population.

It was also true that most Tanganyikans appreciated the law and order provided by Britain's colonial service. Some of the local chiefs were well aware of the dangers that would be created by Nyerere's Tanu, but few of them had any idea of just how disastrous his policies of African socialism were to prove for the millions of rural, tribal Africans whose traditional way of life was to be so needlessly destroyed by President Julius Nyerere and his socialist advisers from Europe.

Chapter Eleven

Uhuru: the Tragedy Begins

Uhuru is Swahili for 'freedom'. All over Africa in the 1960s, 1970s and 1980s, Africans were to learn, to their cost, the bitter truth: that freedom only applied to their new leaders and political associates. The majority of the people were to suffer untold oppression, hardship and even starvation.

It started early in Tanganyika. After independence in 1961, President Julius Nyerere forced millions of rural Africans to leave their homes and go into 'model villages', which resulted in a catastrophic drop in food production.

In the late 1950s increasingly disturbing stories of anti-white propaganda and intimidation of Africans in the main political centres by Tanu supporters were circulating even into rural areas. Although our district was too remote for them to bother much with us, it was becoming obvious that all rural areas would be drawn in sooner or later. In fact this started to affect me around early 1958, when I received increasing numbers of reports about Tanu's activities in rural areas and workers being told not to work on my farm on a part-time basis. I learnt that Tanu was telling the workers to ignore local chiefs as, in the near future – after independence – there would be sweeping changes.

I think that, subconsciously, I had already made up my mind to leave Tanganyika. For some time now, I had been putting off finishing my stone house on the hill and I think I knew, deep down, that I would never move into it.

I decided to call on one of the chiefs who, I knew, had been getting reports from Dar, and found that he was becoming increasingly pessimistic about Tanu's plans for independence.

Anyway, his advice, and the reports he gave me about Tanu's latest activities, made it clear that it could only be a matter of time before my part-time labour force would be intimidated into stopping work on the farm. So, having finally reached the decision to go, I arranged a last elephant hunting safari, for which I collected as many spare licences as possible.

That last safari (in 1959) seemed a good omen for the future: everything went without a hitch and there seemed to be more elephants than usual in the area.

Then I collected all the local crocodile skins, and returned to the farm for the unpleasant business of selling everything we were not taking with us. Last of all before leaving, we had the sad task of paying off a our African staff, including the ones who had done so much for me on my elephant hunting trips.

Before moving permanently to Northern Rhodesia, we had decided that we would have a holiday in Europe, going via Kampala (our nearest international airport), where I knew I would be able to sell the ivory and crocodile skins and book all the stuff we were taking to Britain by sea. I think it was only when they had helped me load the farm lorry for the last time that the Africans really believed we were leaving for good.

I had warned Rengli, our Italian farm manager, that we would be moving before long and he had left a few months earlier to take up another job.

I can still remember my huge disappointment at abandoning the unfinished stone house on the hill. It was the last thing I saw as I looked back to wave farewell to the Africans from the small bridge close to which I had so nearly been killed by the wounded elephant in my early days on the farm.

That last sight of my unfinished house really brought home some of the hard facts about Africa. I had actually arrived about forty years too late to realise my dreams on the farm. The turmoil rapidly developing all over the continent made sure of that, but I have never regretted my attempts to do so. Far far better to have tried and failed than not to have tried at all.

It was a unique period in Africa, and in British colonial history, and it is because of my experiences in Tanganyika in those wonderful years before independence that I am better qualified than most to write a true account of the terrible mistakes that were made in granting premature independence to so many countries.

*

Pressure from the UN and the communists does not excuse the folly of the major colonial powers, including Britain, in not seeing that there were sufficient safeguards to protect the rural masses of Africa. Nothing that has happened in any way excuses the mistakes that have led to so much misery and starvation all over Africa, right up to the present time.

On the long journey to Kampala I had plenty of time to reflect on my idyllic years in Tanganyika, and how I had been privileged to meet a lot of the pioneers, people who had achieved a great deal without most of the trappings of so-called civilisation. I knew, from my wartime experiences in Italy, just how thin the veneer of civilisation really was, and it was tragic to see so many of the pioneers being driven out of Africa in the chaos that came with independence. So many of their achievements were destroyed in the mindless violence that followed.

Perhaps my army years helped, but I never felt that the lack of modern facilities was in any way a burden. Many of them are superfluous anyway, as I discovered when I eventually returned to Britain, perhaps for good, in 1983.

There was no electricity in most of Tanganyika (so no television), no daily newspapers or modern cinemas, but we lived life to the full. Not for us the second-hand information gained from the media (as in Europe and America), which fill the masses with completely false impressions and values fostered by mass production, and extolling the dubious advantages of Western civilisation.

In my opinion it is the individual who counts: the fact that something is big does not necessarily mean that it is good.

★

It took me thirty-five years of living in Africa before I really began to question the whole madness of most of the fabric of modern life in the West, where most people seem to have lost their way and have no values at all. Those they do have are over-influenced and distorted by the media, especially television. The fact that the congregations of Christian churches are constantly shrinking is hardly surprising when you see the concrete jungles of the large cities in which so many people have to live, so completely divorced from nature and the real values of human life.

Yet the West appears to be trying to promote the same urban way of life in Africa, despite the fact that it inevitably leads to mass deprivation. The tribal African is misled into believing that he will be better off in a city than in pursuing his traditional, rural, way of life.

The politicians do not seem to have the courage to tackle the real problem of Africa (and much of the rest of the world), namely overpopulation.

What is the point of repeatedly mentioning Prince Charles's interest in the environment when, on his 1990 trip to Africa, television news reports showed him asking an obviously impoverished African woman about the size of her family and looking pleased, rather than appalled, when she said she had twelve children? Doubtless this was royal protocol, but showing it on TV does nothing to help the cause of sensible birth control.

Just imagine that enormous family multiplied all over Africa and the need for curbing the population explosion becomes obvious. The number of people in Africa must not continue to multiply, because they cannot be fed and starvation will spread even further through the continent. Not even prosperous South Africa can manage the existing rate of population growth, which is expected to double the present 28 million within the next twenty years!

Organisations like the UN and the Commonwealth, and even the Church, should long ago have started to tackle the problem, rather than wasting time on the evils of apartheid and holding innumerable expensive conferences all over the world that seem to achieve nothing. Instead of wasting millions of pounds financing terrorist organisations to fight the South African government, the money should have been spent on paying African families not to have more than one or two children.

To us, as a mixed-race couple, nothing sums up the trivia of the media's approach to racial problems better than the television programmes, especially those on Channel 4, although recently the BBC seem to be getting into the act, too. People taking part in programmes which are meant to deal with ethnic minority problems seem to enjoy picking over the suppurating sores of racial hatred so much that no progress is ever made and the programmes end up seeming contrived, petty and pointless.

About the only times the public get genuine ethnic minority feelings being shown on television are when there are some unrehearsed news items – like the Muslim anger over Salman Rushdie's book. Race relations, or rather race hatred, have been turned into a thriving business in Britain. There is now a government department (which, like the Commonwealth, costs the British taxpayer millions of pounds annually) to tell people how they must behave towards the ethnic minorities. Some Labour councils in London have even appointed politically orientated teachers to instruct the children how to treat their ethnic minority classmates.

It is mainly the hypocrisy of our politicians (and Labour must take most of the blame) that, aided and abetted by the media, has created this ridiculous and potentially dangerous racial situation in Britain.

It was the Labour Party which encouraged the huge post-war influx of immigrants, and we have already seen some of the problems that one group, the Muslims, created over the Salman Rushdie affair. This is just one example of what can be expected in the future, as the proportion of people belonging to ethnic minorities increases.

Since my wife and I came to Britain in 1983 we have never seen an unbiased and truly factual programme about South Africa and rarely are the British public allowed to see what conditions are really like in the black-ruled African states, nor the scale of the genocide that began in the early days of independence and continues unabated to the present day.

Nobody who has lived in South Africa, especially a mixed-race couple, can be unaware of South Africa's faults, so believe me when I say that, when compared to the murderous excesses of black-ruled Africa, these faults pale into insignificance. Yet very few politicians, with the notable exception of Mrs Thatcher, have the guts to state the facts, for fear of offending the UN, the Commonwealth and the very vocal minorities in the West, including Britain.

Now that Russia's interest in Africa is on the wane, following the recent developments in Eastern Europe, it will be interesting to see how long it takes for the rest of the world to come to its senses and show a more intelligent interest in South Africa's very complex multiracial problems. If they don't, South Africa will decline and experience the ghastly conditions already common elsewhere in Africa: famine and semi-starvation, civil and tribal wars, corruption, misrule and economic disaster.

★

The tragedy of the whole senseless situation is that very rarely do those who have spent most of their working lives in Africa return to Britain or the West and, of those few who do return, most are well-indoctrinated colonial civil servants, who rarely have knowledge of both black-ruled Africa and South Africa. This suits organisations like the UN, the OAU (Organisation of African Unity) and the Commonwealth, who have a vested interest in seeing that the Western taxpayer does not learn the truth about the appalling way in which annual aid is squandered and misappropriated by most of Africa's rulers.

This is why I keep coming back to the importance of *The Destruction of a Continent*, which reveals, for the first time, something about the UN, and how international aid is continually squandered on a vast scale.

The campaign against Mrs Thatcher was carefully fermented by some in her own party and the media, as it suited their purposes to have someone much less outspoken in the driving seat. But, in my opinion, it will be a disaster for Africa if she leaves public life entirely, as her frankness and courage have inspired others to speak out about the real facts in Africa.

We all know what happened to another Conservative politician, Mr Enoch Powell, who (in the late 1960s) had the guts to speak up about the madness of allowing mass immigration into Britain, in his famous and prophetic 'rivers of blood' speech. Yet even the subsequent Handsworth race riots, and the hacking to death of a London policeman by a mainly black mob, have done little to change the minds of those who favour immigration.

I should perhaps mention that, until my return to Britain in 1983, I had never voted in my life. I am not a Conservative, although I did vote for Mrs Thatcher because of her opposition to sanctions against South Africa. I find certain aspects of Conservative policy obscene, in fact: how can it be right for top businessmen to earn hundreds of thousands of pounds annually while thousands of homeless young people are allowed, or rather forced, to sleep on the streets of London and other big cities and to beg for a living during the day?

*

Many people in Britain know that the Church of England is one of the largest property owners in the country, but do we ever see any protest campaigns about how few of its resources are used to help the homeless? The answer is, of course, an emphatic and disgraceful 'no'. But, encouraged by the former Archbishop of Canterbury, Dr Runcie, in all the finery of his high office, we saw most of the hierarchy of the Church (equally splendid in all their church finery) spending a great deal of their time criticising, financing and sometimes actively organising apartheid activities in Britain and overseas.

In fact the *Christian Aid News* of October/December 1989 had the Right Reverend Barrington-Ward, Bishop of Coventry, on its front with many of the communist-front UK organisations. This Church of England bishop likes to dabble in politics and is the chairman of the recently-formed Southern African Coalition (SAC) – a front for the Anti-Apartheid Movement and the African National Congress, which has close links to Tutu and the South African Council of Churches, whose general secretary, the Reverend Frank Chikane, has a brother in one of the top jobs in the ANC.

The extent to which these arrogant Church of England bishops are prepared to go to is again best illustrated by Archbishop Tutu's Birmingham visit, which had Bishop Colin Buchanan as chairman of the city-wide Christian celebrations. Birmingham's church people were left with a bill of over £200,000 to pay because of this fiasco, but there were no apologies from

Bishop Buchanan – and calls for Archbishop Tutu to make good the loss were ignored.

The terrorist links are played down, but considerable amounts of Church funds are given to African terrorist organisations, while the welfare of British people living on the city streets is conveniently ignored by the Church.

Archbishop Trevor Huddleston, who frequently appears on television and at all the anti-apartheid political rallies in Britain, as one of the figureheads of the movement, was a bishop in Tanganyika during the 1960s. As a close friend of President Julius Nyerere, surely he must have been aware of the damage caused by Nyerere's policies of African socialism (or, rather, communist collectivism) to millions of rural Tanzanians who, presumably, Huddleston went there to help.

But never does the good archbishop criticise his friend's policies and at one point, on television, he even tried to blame Britain for Tanzania's economic woes, rather than admit that there is something wrong with African socialism (or communism).

Is it any wonder that support for the Church of England has now dropped to an all-time low? Is it really too much to ask these well-paid clerics to devote more of the Church of England's possessions and wealth to the care of the poor and homeless? It would be fitting for them to show some practical form of sympathy for the plight of the growing number of British poor, instead of giving the impression that they are only interested in high-profile media propaganda targets like the Anti-Apartheid Movement and Southern African Coalition, while ignoring what is happening elsewhere in Africa and the rest of the world.

Another classic example of completely unnecessary interference in matters that do not really concern the Church (and which ended in complete embarrassment) was the case of Viraj Mendis – again there were no apologies from the Bishop of Manchester or the others involved.

Viraj Mendis was a communist who posed as a refugee from Sri Lanka and fooled the Church of England into giving him much-publicised sanctuary in a church in Manchester. He managed to avoid deportation from Britain for thirteen years by saying his life would be in danger if he were returned to Sri Lanka.

Manchester's Labour-run city council compounded the folly of the Church by spending, or rather misspending, over £10,000 of ratepayers' money on Viraj Mendis.

In 1985, using ratepayers' money again, the council set up a 'Special Needs Trust' for cases such as Mendis. Over £5,000 was spent on a publicity campaign for Comrade Mendis and £3,500 was spent on providing him with a £30 weekly wage, over and above what he was getting from the Church. A further £1,700 was spent to take coachloads of militant supporters to Westminster and to Gatwick for demonstrations on the day he was deported. The Church sent Father West to Colombo with Comrade Mendis. Unfortunately, this publicity stunt backfired badly in Colombo when Comrade Mendis admitted, on television, that he had lied about his life being in danger if he returned to Sri Lanka. Nothing more was heard from the Reverend Father Henry West or Comrade Mendis.

*

There have been other widely publicised television extravaganzas laid on for the gullible British public, who are shown other Sri Lankan Tamils like Mendis coming to Britain to seek political asylum. What the public are rarely told is that the Tamils in southern India are openly backing their fellow Tamils in Sri Lanka and there is, therefore, absolutely no need for any of the Sri Lankan Tamils to seek refuge in Britain. They can quite easily go to India – to the province of Tamil Nadu – but there is no political capital to be made out of this.

However, the activities of the trendy pinkish prelates in the Church of England pale into insignificance when compared to the biased output of Channel 4 under the chairmanship of Sir Richard Attenborough. His feelings about apartheid cannot be doubted, but I feel that he has used his position to indulge this personal obsession – by scheduling a stream of very inaccurate anti-South Africa television programmes, made by communist producers like Tariq Ali.

What annoys me most about Sir Richard Attenborough, however, is that he accepted five million dollars from Mugabe towards the expenses of filming *Cry Freedom*, as well as film-making facilities in Zimbabwe.

I cannot believe that he was unaware of the fact that Mugabe is receiving millions of dollars in aid from the West, to which the British taxpayers contribute vast amounts annually. Surely it must have been obvious to Attenborough that the money he was being given had come out of the aid money? Yet this abuse of taxpayers' money produced no protests from the Western media.

The death of Steve Biko at the hands of the South African authorities was, of course, appalling, and Donald Woods's account of the whole affair made a very good story on which to base the screenplay for *Cry Freedom*. But it would be nice to think that, in the interests of a more balanced view of Africa, Sir Richard would next turn his attention to making a film which exposes far worse malpractices on the part of black rulers.

I suggest that his benefactor, Mugabe, would be a good subject to start on – surely the massacre of tens of thousands of Matabele by Mugabe's security forces would be a strong dramatic theme? The highly reputable Rhodesia Christian Group would, I am sure, be very happy to supply the basic material for a screenplay – although it is difficult for them, because of news censorship in Zimbabwe, to confirm reports that put the number of Matabele murder victims at over forty thousand.

★

No one really knows the extent of the communist-socialist conspiracy against South Africa, but it is pretty obvious to me (with the help of TAAL's media monitoring) that there is collusion between some of the hierarchy of the Church, the communists and the media in the West. From certain reports, it is reasonable to suppose that this unholy alliance is much more extensive than the authorities in the West are prepared to admit.

One example of the deviousness of the Western media was shown by the television news recently, after Nelson Mandela's release, when he was seen meeting ANC's hierarchy in Lusaka. Viewers may have noted that there was one white man present and would, I am sure, be interested to learn something about him.

He was Joe Slovo, a very unsavoury member of the South African Communist Party and, much more importantly, a high-ranking KGB staff officer, the founder and (from 1985–1987) the chief of staff of Umkhonto we Sizwe – the terrorist arm of the ANC. For masterminding the terror campaign in South Africa, Slovo was promoted by the KGB from major to colonel – some reports indicate that he has since received further promotion in the KGB.

Slovo publicly praised Umkhonto's 'Young Lions' – it was they who devised the notorious, barbaric 'necklace', to dispose of any fellow blacks in the South African townships who did not agree with the ANC's policies. The arms of the victim are bound with barbed wire, the hands are hacked off, a diesel-filled auto tyre is then placed around the neck and the victim is burnt alive. It is to these barbarians that the unholy alliance would like to hand over South Africa!

Ironically, Slovo was born in Lithuania (in 1926), and one wonders how he viewed Russia's recent attempts to intimidate Lithuania in its fight for independence. Probably he was so well indoctrinated that he could accept every change in his masters' policies, but he must have wondered whether he would be able to achieve his objective of masterminding the ANC takeover of South Africa.

With the present situation in Russia and Eastern Europe, South Africa has been given a much-needed breathing space as, without Russian aid and arms – not to mention the Cuban troops – the ANC is no longer in a position to create a Namibia-type military-terrorist situation on South Africa's borders. Hence the ANC's agreement to start talks with South Africa. It should be remembered, however, that this apparent willingness to negotiate does not make the ANC any less dangerous, and it tries (secretly) to escalate township disturbances and violence, in order to embarrass the South African government.

Every episode in the South African townships is reported in detail by the media in the West, who largely ignore the genocide, mayhem, unrest and mass starvation in black-ruled Africa. Long-term Russian policy is unlikely to have changed, however, and I believe that Soviet strategy is still as set out by Leonid Brezhnev, when he said the Russian aim was to gain control of the Persian Gulf, central and Southern Africa.

The unsavoury Slovo was little different to the British traitors that the Russians used to further their plans: Blunt, Philby, Burgess, Maclean and others less well publicised. Before fleeing South Africa (he has since been able to return), Slovo had been a Johannesburg lawyer, another of the left-wing products of the London School of Economics.

Incredible as it may seem, Slovo was given a British passport and, some day, someone is going to have to explain why he was allowed to travel as he pleased between London, East Berlin and Odessa, presumably planning the ANC terrorist campaign in South Africa with his KGB bosses.

Stupid as the British Secret Service may appear, especially after the *Spycatcher* affair, it is stretching the imagination a bit far to believe that the top brass knew nothing at all about Slovo's activities. Perhaps they were ignorant of the fact that Comrade Slovo was a high-ranking KGB officer, but they must have known that he had an office in Euston, made regular trips to East Germany and Russia, and was reputed to be a Soviet citizen. They must also have known that he was the chairman of the South African Communist Party and constantly manipulated the ANC, helping it to further Russia's aims by organising terrorist activities in South Africa.

There may have been reasons for allowing the odious Slovo to continue his activities on British soil, if only to keep an eye on him, but I am sure that most members of the British public will be as puzzled as I am as to why he was given, and allowed to retain, a British passport.

★

Knowledge about what really happened in Africa after the end of the war is restricted mainly to those who lived there at the time. There can be absolutely no doubt that the communists, socialists and their allies in the West were largely responsible for one of the biggest and most damaging confidence tricks in history, using colonialism and apartheid (which is practised all over Africa on a black against black basis) as a convenient justification for bringing about untold damage, devastation and starvation to countless millions of innocent, rural Africans – all in the name of progress and African socialism.

Only now, forty years later, are the poor Africans beginning to understand the extent of the damage so needlessly caused, with the active connivance of the colonial powers themselves.

Of course the hard-pressed taxpayer in the West was never told any of the truth, nor how unnecessary this continual drain on his income really was, nor how little control there was of how aid money was spent in Africa. It was not in the interests of the bureaucrats in the UN and elsewhere to demand an inquiry into the vast amount of aid being misappropriated by Africa's political leaders. After all, it is not their money and they have little interest in protecting the hard-pressed taxpayer in the West.

Not even North Sea oil can pay for Britain's huge contribution to all this completely unnecessary bureaucratic expansion, with the EC to follow, and it is no coincidence that the majority of British citizens are now much worse off than they were ten years ago.

It is only the suspicion that the Labour Party would make matters worse that kept it out of power, but the sad truth is that the Conservatives have served the interests of few except the wealthy. But Mrs Thatcher was a leader of world repute and she understands at least something about what has to be done in Africa. Not that African affairs are of much concern to the average British voter, whose main interest is in voting for the party that makes him, personally, better off.

It seems that most of the ordinary voters believe that nothing can be done to improve matters. This is quite untrue, but no improvement will come from either of the two main parties in British politics unless there is a great deal of pressure from a formidable, but hitherto silent, body of voters: the sixteen million British ex-servicemen and women who, with their families, account for nearly a third of the total British population. For far too long, ex-servicemen have accepted the old idea that their organisations should not be involved in politics. Until the communists came along that might have worked fine, but in today's world it is nonsense.

The communists, Labour's militant left and left-wing prelates of the Church have combined with the media to manipulate every sphere of life in Britain, including so-called peace and anti-apartheid movements, since the end of World War II, while we ex-servicemen have stood idly by and watched them destroy just about everything for which we fought.

The communists and their sympathisers have very effectively destroyed much of the African continent since the war. Warnings about the communist menace from ex-servicemen such as Ian Smith were largely ignored in Britain, where politicians like Sir Harold Macmillan waffled on about the 'wind of change'. Wasn't he informed that the communists were taking full advantage of the colonial powers' decision to pull out of Africa and abandon their own kind in the Rhodesias and East Africa?

It should also never be forgotten that, after the shambles and shame of Suez, it was largely American pressure that brought about the betrayal and abandonment of the Rhodesias. The present propaganda campaign in the West against South Africa is only a continuation of that policy.

The suffering and starvation all over Africa, that has worsened annually as a result of communist activities, does not seem to worry the media or their allies in the Church in the West and in South Africa.

Archbishop Desmond Tutu provides an example of how Church funds are used for non-religious purposes. He lives, like all high prelates of the Church, in a fine palace and, with a seemingly clear conscience, he travels around the world at the Church of England's expense, demanding more sanctions against South Africa. His allies in the ANC do precisely the same, even though they know their activities mean starvation for more and more of the ordinary people of South Africa. These anti-apartheid journeys are always very well publicised by the Western media.

Dr Mangosuthu Buthelezi, chief minister of Kwazulu and president of Inkatha, represents over six million Zulus and is one of the few sane voices coming out of South Africa, yet he is all but ignored in the West when he says, repeatedly, that sanctions are not in the best interests of the Africans in South Africa. Before it is too late, the outside world should listen very carefully to his words about the present situation in South Africa, and not be misled by communist propaganda in the West. I quote from *Clarion Call*, Inkatha's official magazine (volume 3, 1989):

> The outside world must be careful in likening South Africa to pre-independence countries like Zimbabwe or Mozambique... A great many people regard South Africa as some kind of blown-up version of these countries. They see revolutionaries in exile returning home to become a Government returned from exile and they make the analytically fatal error of judgement of looking at white society in South Africa as they looked at white society, say, in Zimbabwe.
>
> White South Africa is not dominated by expatriates who can be repatriated or who have somewhere to go when the going gets tough. South Africa is, for whites in the country, an end-of-the-line country. It is a live, do or die country...

People like Kinnock, Ashdown, Huddleston, Barrington-Ward, Tutu, Jesse Jackson, and even Gorbachev and his Cubans, would do well to remember these wise words. They would also be wise to remember that there are over one million British South Africans who are entitled to hold a British passport and have the right to live in Britain. There are about another million South Africans who are of British descent, many from as far back as the 1820 settlers. There are also thousands of ex-servicemen from two world wars, both British and Afrikaner, such as the late Field Marshal Jan Smuts, who deserve the wholehearted gratitude of both the sixteen million members of ex-service families in Britain and the hundreds of thousands of ex-servicemen from the old Commonwealth countries of Australia, Canada and New Zealand.

★

There has never been enough appreciation of the importance of South African servicemen's voluntary contribution to Britain's victories in both the world wars, and it is obvious that the politicians need to be reminded of the sacrifices of those brave South Africans. Only their fellow ex-servicemen in Britain can do this effectively.

South Africa's President de Klerk had the courage to start the process of reconciliation by releasing Nelson Mandela, and it is now up to ex-servicemen to see that South Africa gets the support it so richly deserves from Britain and the West.

Let me also remind the politicians that most of the sixteen million who comprise the ex-service families dislike fair-weather friends and political opportunists.

The real value of the Commonwealth today lies in the ties of kith and kin that were so shamefully betrayed in Rhodesia, and the bonds that were built up in the bloody battles of two world wars by the fighting men and women of the old Commonwealth countries. At last there appears to be some realisation of these facts in *Legion*, the official Journal of the Royal British Legion (the November/December 1989 issue). I quote from page 3, 'Silent for too long' (NEC is the National Executive Council):

Comment

> It is also the aim of the NEC to bring to the attention of national and local authorities the depth of feeling of the men and women who have served in the armed forces and their view that they have been silent for too many years.
>
> Her Majesty's Government has long given the impression that it regards ex-service men and women as an aged and dwindling number, undeserving of major priority. We have certainly never been seen as part of the electorate who might need more of the nation's money and resources than is presently allocated. It surely cannot be a surprise to the government to learn that ex-service men and women number with their families, including the shamefully neglected pre-1973 war widows, some 16 million – nearly a third of the total population. In only one of the 50 years since the end of the Second World War have British sailors, soldiers and airmen not been asked to sacrifice their lives.

It shouldn't surprise ex-service men and women to learn that this untypical pressure from the Royal British Legion produced results very quickly for the pre-1973 war widows, who should not have been discriminated against in the first place, when the politicians began to see the importance of the ex-service votes. This kind of pressure has to be applied more often.

I therefore appeal to the sixteen million to help stop the madness of what is happening in Africa. We must demand an immediate end to the remaining sanctions against South Africa, and then see that a new policy of cooperation with the country is started in Europe and America, so that this last prosperous Christian bastion in Africa gets the chance to carry out the reforms that are necessary at a pace that will not create chaos.

There will never be a better time for South Africa to solve its problems than now, with Russia and East Europe in such turmoil that they do not have the time or the money to interfere in African affairs.

The ANC is, of course, well aware of the position, but it is encouraged by its supporters in Europe and America to believe that, by increasing internal violence in South Africa, it will get political results. It is up to ex-servicemen and women to see that our politicians stop playing party politics over South Africa. We must voice our disapproval of the way members of the Labour Party, the Kinnocks in particular, have been encouraging Mandela and the rest of the ANC in continuing to believe that they can achieve their political aims by violence.

Much more encouragement must be given to moderate African leaders like Dr Buthelezi.

*

The communists may have had to give up their plans for a military victory in South Africa with the departure of the Cubans, but they still actively used other methods to obstruct the steady and sane reforms being carried out by President de Klerk. On Easter Monday, 1990, for instance, Nelson Mandela was used as the excuse to stage a so-called 'concert' – a television programme of outright communist propaganda – on BBC2. This disgraceful spectacle lasted for four and a half hours, and was given world coverage by the BBC.

Isn't it time for as many as possible of the sixteen million ex-service families to protest strongly about the outrage I'm sure they feel about such misuse of the money they pay in annual TV licence fees?

My own anger is intensified by the fact that this programme was aired over the Christian Easter holiday. What a time to glorify a man who is a highly trained communist terrorist, and one whose followers have killed so many of their fellow blacks in South Africa!

Why do we allow the media, especially television, to publicise all the activities of Mandela and his communist friends, rather than the millions of Africans who follow moderate leaders like Dr Mangosuthu Buthelezi? Many of the latter hold genuine Christian beliefs, but their views are seldom represented on our television screens.

As I listened to Mandela speaking, and heard the baying of the mob, I reflected on how well the communists had learnt from Hitler and the Nazis when they were allies in the early part of World War II. I noticed the Kinnocks were in the audience, apparently enjoying the spectacle and happy to give the Black Power salute.

Another link in the conspiracy to promote Mandela's aims was provided by the presence of US presidential hopeful Jesse Jackson. He actually had the temerity to go on television and blasphemously compare Mandela to Christ! I am sure the American viewers will react appropriately when asked to vote for the Reverend Jackson in the future.

The genuine aspirations of the majority of Africans are not best served by the communist aims of Mandela and the ANC, and that is why much more publicity has to be given to the damage caused by African socialism, which is only another version of communism. From Mandela's Easter 1990 speech in London it is obvious that he has learnt nothing from the mistakes that were made in other parts of Africa.

★

While vast publicity was being given to Nelson Mandela's visit to Britain, the Kremlin made the staggering admission that it had been the Russians who had been responsible for the notorious Katyn massacre.

I find it significant that the media barely acknowledged this statement, despite the fact that it was the first time that the Kremlin had admitted guilt for the mass murders (in April and May 1940) of the cream of the Polish Army, when over fifteen thousand officers were killed at Katyn, near Smolensk in Russia. The Poles were prisoners of war, captured in 1939 when Germany and Russia both invaded their country and divided it between them.

The Russians had always denied responsibility for the massacre, insisting that it was the Nazis who had killed the Polish officers, so this new Kremlin announcement was truly newsworthy, yet it received little more than a mention. Even if there was insufficient time to produce a proper television documentary, surely the very least that should have been done was to interview the Polish community leaders in Britain, who include many of the brave Poles who fought for Britain in World War II.

I recently lunched at the large Polish ex-servicemen's club in London, with a Kiwi author, Ron Jeffery, who had an exceptionally hazardous war fighting with the Polish Underground in Warsaw. His book, *Red Runs the Vistula*, describes his war experiences and I'm sure that he would have been very happy to lend his help to a programme about Poland in general and the Katyn massacre in particular.

Surely such a programme, or at the very least an extended news item, would have been much better suited to the Christian spirit of Easter than the appalling Mandela circus? Certainly this would have been appreciated by British ex-servicemen, who make up nearly one third of Britain's population.

*

The socialists and communists in Europe were already conspiring with the UN to destroy what had been built up during the years of colonial rule and it was becoming increasingly obvious (after the Suez fiasco in the 1950s) that they would succeed in their aims.

But what angers me most is the hypocrisy of the superpowers, especially Russia. Between them, they have destroyed most of colonial Africa, and are indirectly responsible for destroying much of its wildlife, yet they have the gall to accuse the Africans of destroying the game! They conveniently forget that they supplied most of the military hardware that was responsible for the indiscriminate slaughter of the animals.

The Russian Kalashnikov AK-47 is the perfect weapon for Africa's rugged conditions and able to withstand the rough handling it gets from poorly-trained African troops and terrorists. It fires 7.62 mm bullets, either singly or in rapid bursts as a machine-gun. It is an extremely accurate weapon up to four hundred yards and superior to anything of the same type produced by America or the West. There are now literally millions of AK-47s in circulation in Africa.

It is this superpower hypocrisy that was able to convince the West that it was colonialism that was the main threat to Africa after the war. In fact it was the communists, who also ensured that very little of the real truth about Africa ever got out.

The UN has squandered millions of pounds in its propaganda campaign against colonialism, with the help of the Communist bloc and Third World countries, knowing that after the Suez fiasco the Western colonial powers had lost the will to resist and were quite happy to abandon their own people in Africa. Thus most of the advances made in colonial days – modern methods of agriculture, Western technology and sensible economic progress backed by law and order – were lost in the course of the civil wars and general mayhem that followed independence.

What the West was never told was how a few socialist-Marxist urban Africans, many mission-educated, with their European advisers of the same ilk and UN-Russian support, stage-managed the takeover of their countries, with disastrous consequences for most of the tribal Africans who, for the past thirty or forty years, have been reduced to starvation and worse over most parts of ex-colonial Africa.

Few people in the West were interested in the fact that the smart-suited Africans they saw on their television screens had nothing in common with the large majority of rural, tribal Africans. Indeed, few Europeans in Africa ever met any rural Africans and the urban Africans they met were normally house servants – or similar. The few Africans educated in the West cannot have been very impressed with Western civilisation, with ever fewer active Christians and a culture that seemingly revolved around drugs and pop stars, while urban decay escalated and there was a soaring crime rate.

It should not surprise the West that most of the African leaders, although many of them received their early education in mission schools, should see communism as their ally, especially as it supplied the Kalashnikov AK-47 and other military hardware which they deemed necessary to promote their cause. These armaments came in very useful in the many civil wars and when it was necessary for the leaders to oppress their own people.

⋆

The Western media always tried to give importance to Macmillan's 1960 'wind of change' speech in Cape Town, while trying to gloss over the importance of the shameful debacle at Suez in the 1950s, when the world's two greatest colonial powers were humiliated by Egypt.

Those who served in Egypt during World War II and afterwards will remember their feeling of utter disbelief when they heard the news of the ignominious withdrawal of the British and French troops from Suez.

Eden had been in Churchill's shadow for too long to withstand American pressure to withdraw, and his ill health did not help, but what really rubbed salt into the wounds of British and French military pride were the later magnificent victories of Israel over Nasser's Egypt, although the Israeli troops were heavily outnumbered by the Egyptian forces.

The damage to British and French prestige in Africa was irreversible, and was exploited by African politicians like Zambia's Kaunda – who called Britain 'a toothless old lion'.

As America and the West pay most of the UN bills, it would have been easy in those early days for the colonial powers to have insisted that the UN took over the supervision of all African colonies for a period of at least fifteen years, to ensure their orderly progress and stability during the years leading up to full independence. This could still have been done after it had been seen how quickly Kwame Nkrumah managed to ruin the economy of Ghana, after its independence in early 1957.

But, even after forty years of misery and starvation under Marxist/African socialism and military dictators, it is obvious that nothing has been learnt by those mealy-mouthed politicians in the UN, who still allow the Communist bloc and Third World to dictate policy in Africa, the latest addition to this madness of Marxist/African socialism being Namibia, in late 1989.

The UN, who actively support the ANC, would like to have this bankrupt madness extended to the Republic of South Africa, and it is up to all of us, especially ex-servicemen, to see that it does not succeed.

*

As our journey continued, and Lake Victoria came into sight for the last time, I realised I was much more upset at leaving the farm than I was prepared to admit.

We had intended to visit friends in Bukoba on our way to Kampala but, now we were actually en route, all we wanted to do was to get this last East African trip over with as soon as possible. We preferred to make a clear break with the whole area, which held so many happy memories of the last few years, and to start our holiday in Europe as soon as possible before returning to live in central Africa – Northern Rhodesia.

I had no trouble in getting high prices for the ivory in Kampala, and the crocodile skins also sold well. I arranged for our heavy luggage to go by sea, and we spent a short time in Entebbe, on the lake shore not far from Kampala. I liked the town – it always reminded me of Mwanza, which was at the opposite end of the lake.

There was one last thing to do before we left for Europe. At the airport I parked the Ford lorry that had served me so well on the farm and posted the keys back to the Land Bank in Dar. So ended the first part of my thirty-five years in Africa.

I had some forebodings for the future of this most lovely and unspoilt part of Africa, which had been progressing so favourably in the very stable conditions under the law and order that colonial rule provided, but none of us believed that things in Tanganyika (now Tanzania) and the rest of East Africa would deteriorate so quickly.

President Obote was bad enough for Uganda, but who could have foreseen the mad tyranny of Idi Amin (from which the country has never recovered)?

Who would have anticipated that Tanzania would still be suffering from the effects of African socialism under Nyerere? In the short term, Kenya got off with the least damage, as its main problem was on a smaller scale: having to contend with the notorious corruption of the Kenyatta family.

*

As I write, I can still hardly believe that I am back in London, just completing the first part of my book – about Tanzania, or rather the Tanganyika Territory, as it was in those days – and about to start on the second, about the Rhodesias.

I have no intention of going into detail about my personal life, except where it is helpful in explaining how my book came to be written, or where it is necessary for continuity. If I hadn't married an Indian girl, for instance, I would never have returned to Britain. We had to come here in order to marry, as mixed-race marriages were not allowed in South Africa at that time (1983). I am pleased to say that that law has been changed, as part of the reforms now taking place in South Africa.

I sincerely believe that it was more than just fate that brought me back to Britain, however. I was lucky to survive problems with my heart in 1984 and 1985, just as I began to realise how necessary it was that a true account should be written of what really happened during those fateful and tragic post-war years and how few people had my long experience (from 1948 to 1983) of life in East, central and South Africa. I was also given a rare opportunity to compare the Africans' rural and urban ways of life under colonialism, before those prosperous days were swept away for ever by the foolish excesses that followed African independence.

Like most of my contemporaries in Africa, I laughed at the stories about the 'red menace' there. Since returning to Britain, however, I have been both amazed and disturbed at the extent of communist influence in the media, especially television. Neither my wife nor I has seen a really balanced programme about South Africa since we arrived.

*

Reflecting on my first eleven years in Africa, I remember my first impressions vividly. I shall never forget that amazing sense of wide open space and a freedom so different to overcrowded Europe, especially Britain, nor my first railway trip of two and a half days from the capital, Dar es Salaam, to Mwanza on the shores of Lake Victoria. It all gave me a very good idea of the vastness of Africa.

Today most travellers arrive by air and miss the pleasure of leisurely conversations on the train with some of Africa's old hands. I remember how impressed I was by the speed with which they put away their brandy!

I had, of course, been used to sleeping under a mosquito net, suitably camouflaged, during my army days in India. A net was also a necessity in Tanganyika in those days, although I still came down with malaria many times during my eleven years there.

Shortly after my arrival I did my first road trip from Kenya's capital, Nairobi, to Mwanza – and had my first experience of getting stuck in the mud during a fierce tropical storm. But it was worth every inconvenience, after spending the night at Musoma, to get my first sight of the magnificent, unforgettable Serengeti Plains.

In those days, in the late 1940s, it was still possible to spot just about every type of animal from the main road that ran near to the game reserve. Standing on the roof of the pick-up truck, you could see hundreds of thousands of different animals, stretching as far as the eye could see across the plains. It was a truly incredible sight and you could drive through the various herds without worrying the animals at all, they would move no more than a few yards, just enough to let your truck get through.

I was lucky enough, during my first trip to the Serengeti, to see a pride of lions making a kill. They were completely uninterested in the fact that they had a human audience close by.

It wasn't long before the lure of being able to hunt near the boundaries of the Serengeti reserve became too strong for me to resist. I still remember the thrill of my first hunt, when I killed my first wildebeest, zebra and impala. We sat around the campfire that first night, eating a large part of the impala's leg at one sitting and then sleeping on the ground in the African bush, with the fire going strong to keep the lions and jackals away. It was sheer magic and I have never regretted killing even the elephants, as we never wasted anything, unlike the rich, well-fed European and American tourists, whose main interest was in acquiring game trophies as symbols of their success. These were, in fact, often shot for them by their 'white hunter' guides.

★

My first opportunity to get to know the rural Africans came in the 1950s, when I farmed and hunted in the remote Tanganyikan district of Kibondo-

Kakonko. It is because I was one of the few lucky Europeans to get this chance that this book is important to those who want to know the truth about Africa during the turbulent post-war years.

Unless you have actually slept in an African village as a guest, taken part in the villagers' discussions, noted the lack of crime (although the people were extremely poor), and experienced the almost embarrassing hospitality, I know it will be difficult for you to understand my anger and distress that the West has allowed the virtual destruction of this way of life: one that suited the tribal African so well.

*

I had always considered myself pretty fit as, because of the back trouble that was a legacy of my wartime paralysis, I always did my yoga exercises to strengthen my back muscles. But I remember how amazed I was at the toughness and the endurance of the local Africans during my elephant hunting trips, and how easily they coped with twelve hours' walking, or more, if we were on the track of a really large elephant.

I, like them, never stopped to eat during the day, but I did carry water (to be precise, one of the Africans carried my flask and two bottles of water), but they drank nothing and, at the end of the day, seemed totally unaffected.

Although I made a point of never showing how tired I really was, I could not go on for more than three or four days at a time before taking a day off: I usually made an excuse to see the local game guard or sub-chief in the area, while the men continued to scour the area, looking for large tuskers.

It was an unforgettable sight to watch them chop up a whole carcass in a matter of hours, some of them working from inside the elephant – nothing was ever wasted.

There is no doubt that, if the traditional lifestyle had not been broken up by the communists (for which the West must also bear responsibility), and the whole of Africa had not been flooded with unnecessary firearms, there would never have been the wholesale slaughter of big game.

These facts are, of course, never mentioned by any of the do-gooders in the present Save the Elephant campaign, and it is about time that the blame is placed where it belongs: on the Russians, the Americans and the other large arms suppliers in the West, including Britain.

*

The real tragedy of Africa after the Suez fiasco was that there wasn't an international politician, someone of the stature of Churchill or Smuts, to insist that the UN take over, and sort out, the mess that it had helped to create. Only experienced statesmen like Smuts and Churchill had sufficient understanding of the British Empire to realise that the problems of the Indian subcontinent were totally different to those of the African colonies.

India was a vast country of great commercial value to Britain, but there were immense problems created by clashes between the Hindus and the Muslims. The solution that was finally reached was to divide the area to form two countries, India and Pakistan, at the time of independence in 1947. Because of the religious strife, the whole process had to be completed quickly.

Africa, apart from the Union of South Africa (which, in any case, was a self-governing dominion), was of little or no commercial or political value to Britain and there was absolutely no need for the unseemly haste with which the colonial powers abandoned their colonies there, with such disastrous results for the rural Africans.

★

Like many of my contemporaries who had volunteered to fight for the British Empire during the war, I felt that I had every right to make the most of the remaining years of the rapidly dying British Empire, and I am happy to say that I enjoyed every moment of my eleven years in Tanganyika, except at the very end, when I had to leave my farm.

Appendix Two

PERMIS DE VISITE
BEZOEKSVERGUNNING N° 12
VISITOR'S PERMIT

NOM / *NAAM* / FAMILY NAME: M. / *M.* / Mr/Mrs/Miss WALSH

Prénoms / *Voornamen* / Christian names: Michael

Nationalité / *Nationaliteit* / Nationality: Britanique

Lieu et date de naissance: / *Geboorteplaats en datum:* / Place and date of birth: 27/9/1923

Venant de: / *Komende van:* / Coming from: Texeira de Souza

Accompagné de: (chauffeur, serviteur): / *Vergezeld van:* (*autobestuurder-dienstbode*): / Accompanied by: (chauffeur, servant):

Est autorisé à se rendre à: / *Is gemachtigd zich te begeven naar:* / Is authorised to travel to: Dilolo à Eville en transito

Le titulaire du présent permis doit avoir quitté les Territoires du Congo ~~Belge et du Ruanda-Urundi le,~~ 27/4/65

De titularis van onderhavige bezoeksvergunning moet het grondgebied van Belgisch Congo en van Ruanda-Urundi verlaten hebben voor:

The holder of this visitor's permit must leave the Territories of the Belgian Congo and Ruanda-Urundi before:

Par le poste frontière de: / *Langs de grenspost van:* / By the frontier post of: Dilolo-gare

Document présenté pour obtenir le présent permis et établissant que le bénéficiaire sera réadmis dans le pays d'où il vient:
Aard van het document dat werd voorgelegd tot het bekomen van onderhavige bezoeksvergunning en waaruit blijkt dat belanghebbende terug in het land vanwaar hij komt zal toegelaten worden:
Document produced to obtain this permit proving that the holder will be readmitted to the territory from wich he has come:

Sceau / *Stempel* / Seal — Délivré à / *Afgeleverd te* / Given at: Dilolo — le / *de* / on: 24/4/65

(État du Katanga — Service Immigration)

Le Préposé: (Nom): (Signature): Mutunda Alphonse
De Aangestelde (*Naam*): (*Handtekening*):
Officer in charge (Name): (Signature): [signature]

Remarque: Il est interdit au titulaire du présent permis de visite de se livrer à aucune activité lucrative au Congo Belge et au Ruanda-Urundi.

En quittant les territoires du Congo Belge et du Ruanda-Urundi, le titulaire est tenu de remettre le présent permis au préposé du poste de sortie.

Opmerkingen: *Het is aan de houder van deze bezoeksvergunning verboden, een winstgevend beroep uit te oefenen in Belgisch-Congo en Ruanda-Urundi.*
Bij het verlaten van het grondgebied van Belgisch-Congo en Ruanda-Urundi is de titularis verplicht onderhavige vergunning aan de aangestelde van de uitgangspost af te geven.

Remarks: The holder of this permit is prohibited from taking paid employment in the Belgian Congo or Ruanda-Urundi.

The holder is required to surrender this permit to the officer in charge of the immigration post at the point of departure from the Belgian Congo or Ruanda-Urundi.

MICHAEL WALSH
THE GAME SKIN & CURIO SHOPS
WIDENHAM

P.O. Box 206
UMKOMAAS

PHONE: 69

African Game Skins
Display & Sale
AT
PARK HOTEL
HONG–KONG
IN CONFERENCE ROOM 11TH FLOOR
FROM
13th to 17th November inclusive
Hours 10 a.m. to 10 p.m.

EXHIBITION & SALE
Rare
AFRICAN GAME SKINS
including handbags, briefcases etc.
Hyatt Regency (Jade Room) Dubai 3-5 Feb inclusive
The Centre Hotel-Abu Dhabi 7-10 Feb inclusive
Intercontinental Al Ain 12-14 Feb inclusive
AFRICAN GAME SKINS
229

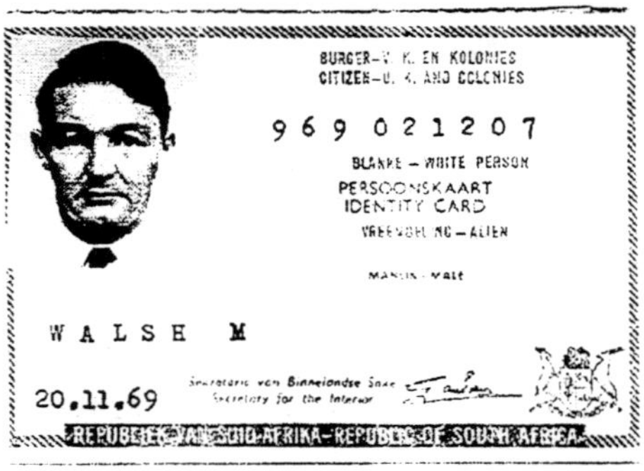
CITIZEN–U. K. AND COLONIES
969 021207
BLANKE – WHITE PERSON
PERSOONSKAART
IDENTITY CARD
WALSE M
20.11.69
REPUBLIEK VAN SUID-AFRIKA–REPUBLIC OF SOUTH AFRICA

REPUBLIC OF ZAMBIA
NATIONAL REGISTRATION CARD
Signature

Appendix Three

MAP OF OUR FARM & THE KAKONKO AREA IN THE 1950s. ("TANGANYIKA TERRITORY")

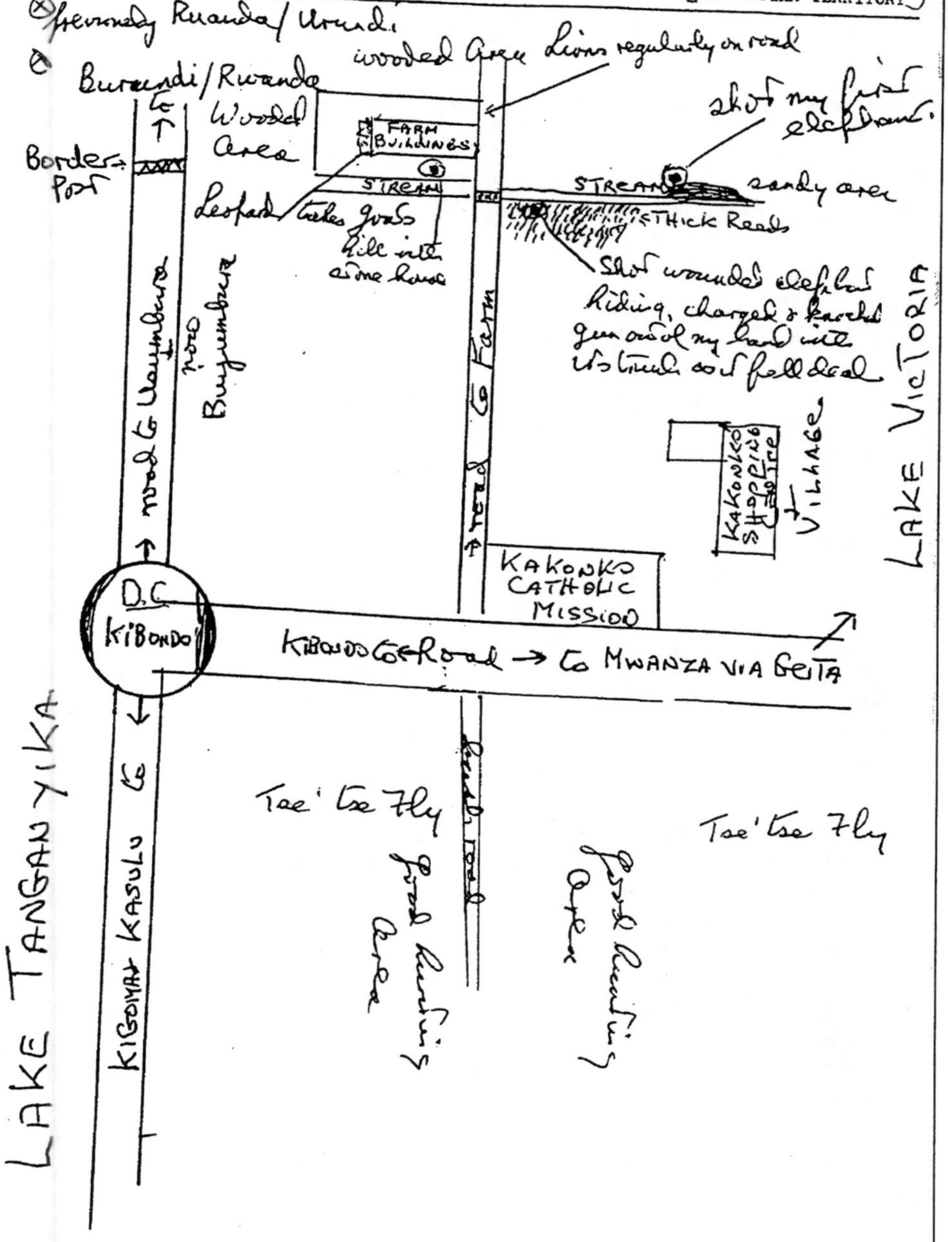

TRUTH ABOUT AFRICA LEAGUE

TAAL TAAL

A British & Commonwealth Ex-servicemen's Organisation Working for peaceful Change in R.S.A

Bishop Paul Ruzoka,
Kigoma Diocese,
Tanzania. East Africa.

15 November 1990.

Dear Bishop Ruzoka,

It was indeed a great surprise to hear from you after all these years & I was extremely sorry not to have been in London when you were here from 22-24 October as there is so much I want to talk about . In fact your visit to Kakonko Parish prompted Father Yves Laforest to reply to my letter & he gave me news of your family & your father Chief 'Mzee' Ruzoka, who gave me so much help when I was getting the farm started in the mid 1950s especially over part-time work on the farm (not officially allowed) while we were getting started. In fact it was a messenger from your father who guided me to the first elephant I had ever shot & only a few minutes walk from the farm down by the small river. Although all this happened 35 years ago I still remember every detail .

You may remember that Peter Haynes was then the District Commissioner in Kibondo, he was ex-Kenya, do you know when he left Kibondo ? He was also very helpful to me & gave me the Uvinza salt contract & I used the farm lorry a 4/5 ton Ford Diesel to transport the bags of salt from Uvinzo to Kibondo. This money not only helped me pay the farm wages but I also picked up local information about elephants in the Kasulo/Uvinza districts, when later I went shooting elephants there as well.

You may be interested to hear that my family has quite a few connections with Africa & that my father was in HM's Nigerian Administration. Most of his service was in Northern Nigeria & he spoke fluent Hausa. He was in Nigeria from 1919 to 1943, when he retired to U.K. My mother's family arrived in South Africa in the 1870s & her father served all through the siege of Kimberley in the Boer War. During WWII I first saw Africa, 10 days in Durban, before going on to India & OCTU there & eventually ending up in Italy in '44 &'45 where I served with 43 Indpt Gurkha Lorried Bde. It was only after I returned to UK in 1983, after 35 years in Africa, that I began to understand how privileged I had been in having the opportunity to get to know the ~~XXXX~~ rural African really well & that something had to be done about the appalling ignorance in the West about what really went on in Africa. After heart troubles in '84 & '85 I therefore helped start TAAL in early 1986 with others who had spent most of their lives in Africa.

With kind regards
Yours sincerely
Mike Wals

All communications to be addressed to: The General Secretary

BISHOP'S HOUSE
P.O. BOX 71
KIGOMA
TANZANIA
Tel. 143

Prot:

02 - 03 - 1991

Mr. Mike Walsh
Victory Service Club,
63 - 79 Seymour Str.
LONDON W2 2HF

Dear Walsh,

Thank you very much for keeping in touch. I received both letters: of 15th November, 1990 and the last one of 4th February. Unfortunately, I had just returned from Mwanza when I got the last one. Otherwise, I could have tried to find out from some old priests of Mwanza who might know where Gerald Chopra went after leaving Mwanza. Nevertheless, I shall be writing to someone in Mwanza who might help and let you know as soon as I get some information leading to Gerald's whereabouts.

I was at Kakonko mid-February. Fr. Laforest is fine but I am afraid he might not have the photographs of "Katengera ruins" yet. However, he was thinking about doing it. It is not easy really because the place was abandoned for long time now. Even my parents are no longer in Nyarusange. They migrated farther south towards the sourse of that famous river, Ruhwiti!
Some games have taken charge of what was once a growing settlement.
In any case, I shall remind him to see to it as soon as possible.

Lastly, I am enclosing one photograph taken ~~at~~ during my installation in Kigoma on February, 25th last year. I hope you can still recognize Mzee Ruzoka together with my mother.
I am anxiously waiting to read your book that has something to say about my own locality.

With best wishes and prayers,
+ Ruzoka
Paul Ruzoka

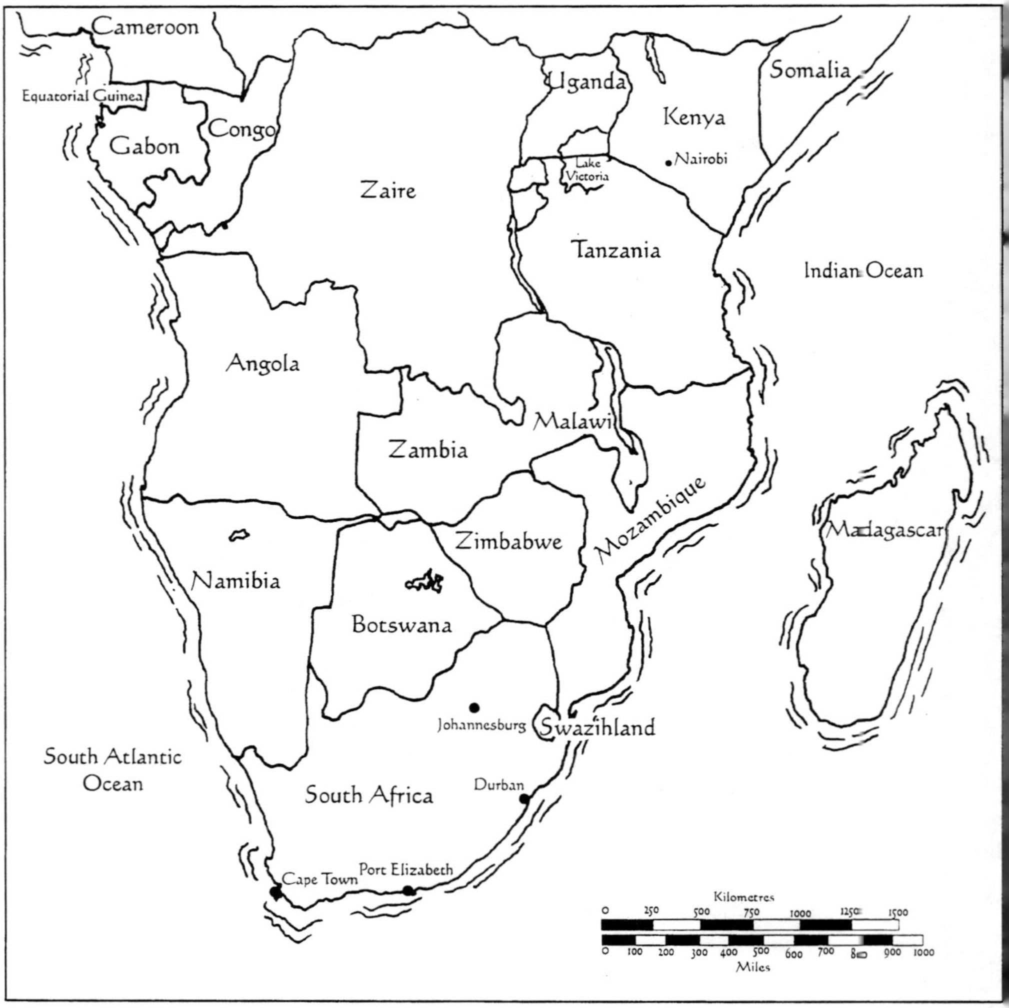

Equatorial and Southern Africa

My route from Ndola and Livingstone to Botswana Game Industries in Francistown

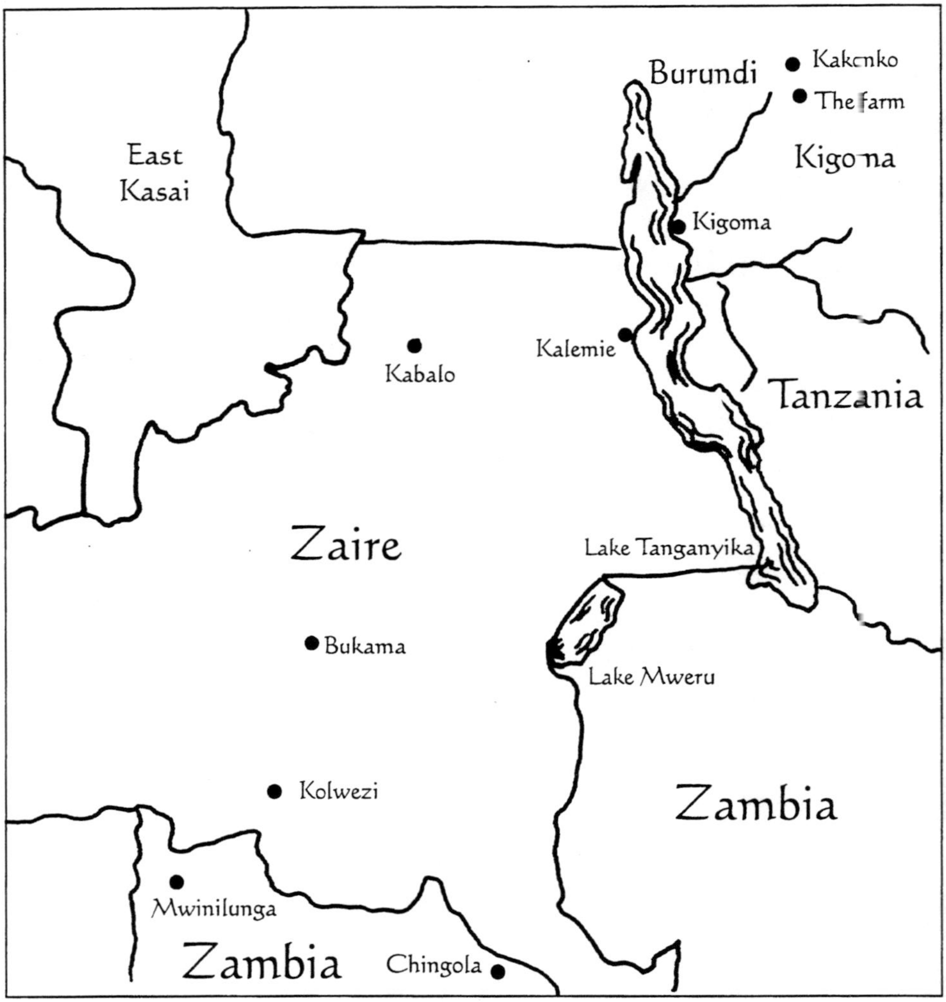

Journey in East Africa 1948 – 1983

Part Three

Central Africa: 1959–1969

Chapter One

The Federation of Rhodesia and Nyasaland

Returning to Europe, and later to Britain, in the late 1950s, I found no reason to change my opinion that life was far better in Africa. I soon missed the tropical sun on my back – in fact, without it, I felt only half alive.

My wife, Betty, did not have the same enthusiasm for Africa, especially as she had the type of fair skin that could not stand the sun. She went back to her parents in Wales and I began to make arrangements for returning to Africa on my own.

We parted amicably. There had been faults on both sides but I was grateful for all the help she had given me in East Africa and certainly a bachelor's life there had had few attractions. I knew in 1948, before she came out to join me, that I was drinking far too much and there were enough hazards to life in Africa without having a drinking problem as well – I had seen how tragically things could turn out for those who were unable to cope and I knew Betty's presence had helped me not to go the same way.

Things were different in the Rhodesias, however, and I quite fancied a year or two as a bachelor there. Neither of us was in a hurry to remarry so it was left that we would just wait out the three-year separation period that was necessary for divorce in Britain at that time. There were no snags and, after the three years had passed, I received notification that I was a free man again.

*

I knew that, wherever I eventually decided to settle in Northern Rhodesia, I had to start in Lusaka, since that was the main base for crocodile hunters in both Rhodesias. All the necessary arrangements for letters of credit and other forms of payment had already been established there, during trips from Tanganyika, and I had friends to stay with until I found a place of my own. So, as soon as I had sorted out my affairs in Britain, I headed back to Africa and found that Lusaka had become quite a boom town since the Federation of Rhodesia and Nyasaland had begun (in 1953).

A priority on arrival was to finalise plans with one of my ex-service crocodile hunters, who was keen to come with me on crocodile hunting trips to the north, where the right type of crocodile, the Nilotic and not the gavial, was still available in large numbers. But the creatures had to be shot without any kind of official permission, which entailed careful planning of a back-up route, in case a speedy exit should be required.

With all the expenses of starting a new life in Lusaka, I needed a quick trip fairly urgently to raise some funds. My finances were not exactly flourishing because I had lost a lot more money than I could afford in the casinos at Nice and Monte Carlo.

When I had first visited Lusaka (from East Africa) it had been little more than a one-street town, important mainly as a rail centre for the prosperous Copperbelt. Cairo Road, which was the major street, ran through the middle of Lusaka, leading north to Broken Hill and the Copperbelt and south to Livingstone and Bulawayo or, where the road branched off at Kafue, to Salisbury.

Now, on my return, I scarcely recognised the place. There were new office blocks, new industrial areas, new blocks of flats, a new hotel (The Ridgeway) and plans for an Inter-Continental Hotel. It was certainly not a place I would have chosen to live in if there had not been good business reasons for doing so, but the same could have been said of almost every other town in Northern Rhodesia. The exception was Livingstone, because of its magnificent location near the Victoria Falls and Zambezi River, and that was where I moved after I remarried.

I don't think anyone could have gone to the Rhodesias in those heady days without marvelling at what our pioneering ancestors had achieved and understanding something of the dreams of Cecil Rhodes. It was his persistence and initiative that had brought both Northern and Southern Rhodesia into existence.

World War II gave many ex-servicemen, like myself, the opportunity to see India and other parts of the British Empire, thus enabling them to have much more understanding of the incredible achievements of the men who had helped to establish and run it. Rhodes, Livingstone and Lugard are part of our glorious colonial history in Africa, just as Clive of Plassey and Warren Hastings are a part of our colonial history in India. James Brooke (the original 'White Rajah' of Sarawak) and Thomas Stamford Raffles (of Singapore) are but two of the colourful characters who contributed to our colonial past in other parts of the world. The history of such men has always fascinated me.

★

Sadly, few in post-war Britain had any real understanding of the responsibilities that went with running an immense empire. This was especially true of Africa, where the lack of education of most of the rural people meant that they were easily exploited by the urban African politicians, who were not interested in the welfare of the tribal people. They were only interested in pleasing their communist masters, with disastrous results for most parts of newly independent Africa.

Britain's enlightened policies had been responsible for the Federation of Rhodesia and Nyasaland in 1953. During talks in London ten years later, however, the politicians destroyed their own excellent creation.

The prime minister of the Federation, Sir Roy Welensky, had been given a promise by Britain that the federation would continue, but carefully prepared disturbances in both Nyasaland and Rhodesia, together with Labour and Commonwealth pressure, were sufficient to force a change in British government policy that was to have disastrous results, as it heralded the end of what would have been an excellent chance of building a truly multiracial society in Central Africa. The Federation of Rhodesia and Nyasaland could have been as important to Central Africa as the Union of South Africa (in 1910) was to Southern Africa.

Instead of having a federation with an economy second only in importance to South Africa, we now have three little tinpot African countries: Zambia, Zimbabwe and Nyasaland – badly run and virtually bankrupt, without even the pretence of a democratic system of government – and that now costs the British taxpayers millions in aid! How right Zambia's President Kaunda was to call Britain 'a toothless old lion'.

He knew, after Suez, that Britain would not make a stand on the question of the federation. His communist advisers would have pointed out that the 275,000 British settlers in Southern Rhodesia and about 90,000 in Northern Rhodesia meant nothing to most British politicians, nor to most of the people in post-war Britain. No one in Britain had much interest in a lot of trouble-making Africans who weren't even grateful for the aid they were getting from the British taxpayers, nor were they very concerned about the few thousand British settlers.

The local and overseas newspapers also played their part in lulling most of the British Rhodesian settlers into a false sense of security so that, right up to 1963, most of them refused to believe that a British government would betray them.

Only one man I talked to in the early days did not believe the British propaganda, and he was the father of Denis Gaunt, one of the crocodile hunters I met in Lusaka.

John Gaunt was our local MP in Lusaka and a retired Northern Rhodesia district commissioner. He was a most unusual politician, who actually took a genuine interest in people and was prepared to help whenever he could. From his days in the colonial service in Northern Rhodesia, John knew the country extremely well and he took the no-nonsense approach that was necessary in the political set-up in Northern Rhodesia during the ten years of federation, from 1953 to 1963.

One evening in the early 1960s, at his house, I asked John Gaunt what kind of future he saw for the Federation of Rhodesia and Nyasaland. I was later to remember how accurately he had predicted the later actions of the British government when, in 1963, it repudiated its promises to the prime minister of the federation, Sir Roy Welensky. By killing off the federation, they played right into the hands of the communists, with tragic results for the whole of central Africa.

*

Looking back all these years later, I still find it difficult to believe just how stupid the British government, and Western countries in general, were. Their apparent ignorance of conditions in Africa was quite amazing and I shall never understand how they could have been taken in by the Marxist-socialist nonsense which most of the African leaders spouted but barely understood.

To those of us who lived through the completely unnecessary tragedies in East and central Africa after the end of the war, the most disturbing part of the whole sorry mess is that, it is obvious even now that few of the politicians in the West have learnt anything from the tragic mistakes of the past.

A meeting in Dublin of all heads of EC governments showed this clearly when Mrs Thatcher, then premier, got very little support when she asked the EC to lift sanctions against South Africa as a reward for the very courageous efforts of President de Klerk to seek a solution to South Africa's problems with the ANC's leader, Nelson Mandela.

*

Part of the propaganda campaign backed by communists, the Third World, the UN and the ANC is to try to compare the Rhodesias with South Africa. The comparison is absolute nonsense, because there were only about a third of a million white settlers in the Rhodesias, while South Africa has five million whites, together with about a million Indians and about three million Coloureds. The Dutch first settled in South Africa well over three hundred years ago, whereas the British had been in the Rhodesias for less than a century. A better comparison is with Algeria, where French settlers (and others from Europe) numbered one and a half million before independence (in 1962).

Although the period of European settlement in Algeria had been much shorter than in South Africa, the colonists had used their relatively short tenure to develop the land there and had produced a very prosperous area from what had been mainly unused land – very much as the Jews had done in their homeland of Israel.

Despite a treaty signed between France and Algeria, promises that settlers would not be victimised or dispossessed were not honoured and the number of Europeans dropped from 1,500,000 to 100,000 within a very short period of independence being granted.

There is a salutary lesson here for the five million or more Europeans in South Africa. The gullible liberals need to be made aware of the sort of people employed by the UN, as epitomised by Kurt Waldheim – a former Nazi intelligence officer who held the position of Secretary-General of the UN for ten years.

*

A great many ex-servicemen are aware of the way the Russians operate and their anxiety at the gullibility of the West is expressed in a letter from TAAL (Truth About Africa League), sent to Prime Minister Mrs Thatcher just before the Commonwealth heads of government meeting in Kuala Lumpur, Malaysia, in October 1989 (see Appendix for text of letter).

It should be remembered, especially in Africa, that although former Secretary-General Waldheim was eventually exposed (after he had left the UN) there are others still in the UN who also played their part in destroying Africa during the post-war period of decolonisation. It is these people who combined with the Russians, the Chinese and all the socialist movements in

Europe in a relentless propaganda campaign to destroy the Federation of Rhodesia and Nyasaland in 1963.

Kaunda's UNIP (United National Independence Party), which had little support outside urban areas like the Copperbelt, was instructed to cause industrial unrest and that was coordinated with similar disturbances in Nyasaland, to give the erroneous impression overseas that the majority of Africans wanted independence.

As in East Africa, this was complete nonsense, as the rural African had little or no idea of what independence meant. But Kaunda and his socialist advisers, especially in the Labour Party in the West, were well aware that, after the humiliation at Suez, there was little likelihood of Britain being able or willing to withstand all the combined communist and socialist pressure at the UN.

Kaunda, a very shrewd politician, was able (with Britain's help) to destroy the Federation of Rhodesia and Nyasaland and, in so doing, to destroy the last hope of moderate Europeans and Africans for a truly multiracial society in central Africa.

Gallantly as the Rhodesians, led by Ian Smith, fought against the communist forces of Mugabe's Zimbabwe African National Union (Zanu) and Nkomo's Zimbabwe African People's Union (Zapu), there was never any doubt about the eventual outcome. Incidentally, there were more black Rhodesian soldiers fighting for Prime Minister Smith's government than white, after the Rhodesian leader (from 1964 to 1979) was virtually forced into declaring UDI (Unilateral Declaration of Independence), in 1965.

For fifteen years, against all the odds, Prime Minister Smith's government in Rhodesia stood virtually alone in the world, except for help and support from the Republic of South Africa. When South Africa itself succumbed to world pressure and threats of sanctions from the UN (then under the control of communist puppet Kurt Waldheim), the inevitable end was in sight for gallant Rhodesia. With Whitehall's help, the stage was set for a Marxist takeover of Rhodesia by the communist-backed Zanu under Mugabe, in 1980. So Rhodesia became Zimbabwe – and another milestone in the betrayal of the tribal Africans who make up the large majority of the population, by the erstwhile colonial power, Great Britain.

What a triumph for evil and communism! And no one played a more important role in this continuing African tragedy than communist puppet and former Nazi intelligence officer Kurt Waldheim.

So black African nationalism triumphed, with the aid of the communists in central Africa, and the scene was set for black nationalists to fight white nationalists in South Africa.

How important Waldheim was to the communist plans in Africa was shown by their successful efforts to get him appointed to a second five-year term in the UN, so that he could continue to mastermind plans to conquer South West Africa, using Cuban troops in Angola to help Swapo fight the South African forces in Angola and SWA. This was achieved in 1989, when South West Africa became Namibia.

★

It is interesting to note that South Africa gained very little when it succumbed to UN and world pressure and ceased to support Rhodesia. The AAM (Anti-Apartheid Movement), the communists and the Church made sure, through their relentless propaganda campaign against the country, that sanctions and other financial pressures were later imposed on South Africa anyway. President de Klerk's reforms brought some softening of the sanctions policy, but it is highly probable that it was only the collapse of communism in Eastern Europe in the latter part of 1989 that helped to make this possible.

TAAL's letter to Mrs Thatcher gives the reader some idea of how seriously many ex-servicemen with experience of Africa view the Waldheim conspiracy with the communists. The devastation that has been caused in Africa by this unholy alliance must be brought to the notice of the public in the West. They are only rarely given the full facts by the Western media but, even at this late stage, further damage to the last prosperous Christian country in Africa, South Africa, could be avoided if more people in the West, especially ex-servicemen, began to realise just how the communists operate, and just how dangerous the UN can be.

There is no doubt that the sixteen million members of ex-service families mentioned in the Royal British Legion's magazine of November/December 1989 (see Appendix) must stop sitting on the fence and insist that Britain and the EC take a more sensible attitude towards South Africa.

This action is not only for the two million South Africans of British descent, many of them ex-servicemen who volunteered to fight and, if necessary, to die for Britain in two bloody world wars, but also for the millions of poorly educated rural Africans who have been so mercilessly exploited by their mainly Western-educated African rulers.

This completely unnecessary African tragedy cannot be more eloquently or truthfully described than in *The Destruction of a Continent* (Chapter Two – 'From Vasco da Gama to Kurt Waldheim'):

But when the African colonies were dismantled and demolished, it was due to neither exhaustion nor conquest. It was due neither to rivalry between the colonial powers nor to any decline in their military and industrial powers. The African colonies were demolished not by the Africans themselves, as many believe, but by the colonial powers themselves when they were still building a new world in Africa. The African colonists were destroyed at the peak of their development by a new breed of men and women, different from anyone the world had ever seen before. They were the crusaders for a new world free of imperialism and exploitation. They did what no one did before: they turned against their own kind.

They indoctrinated a whole generation of Africans, who went to Europe to study, about the evils of Capitalism. They taught the Africans to hate the whites, and encouraged them to take up arms and destroy the colonials' empires in Africa. Intoxicated by the preachings of Marx and Lenin, Africans mobilised all their forces to demolish a world they had learnt to hate and despise. With the same energy the colonial powers had devoted to build a new Africa, they set about tearing apart all that the colonials had accomplished.

Under pressure from the UN, exposed to relentless propaganda from the socialist movements in Eastern Europe, England, Germany, Holland and Scandinavia, and confronted by guerrilla warfare and open hostilities, the colonial powers were eventually forced to dismantle and leave their colonial empires they so painstakingly had built up in Africa.

The rapid decolonisation of Africa had been, and still is, a traumatic experience for the continent's own black population as well as the millions of white settlers, immigrants, and colonials who were uprooted, displaced, and forced to leave the parts of Africa they had built up and believed to be their own. That the well-organised colonial administration was often replaced by total chaos, and that the relatively peaceful conditions under colonial rule were replaced by unrest, revolutions, and civil wars, were of little consequence for those who at any price wanted to wreck colonial rule in Africa. The price was high, and the continent was swept by racial wars in North Africa, the Congo, Mozambique, Angola, and Rhodesia; savage civil wars in Nigeria, the Congo, Somalia, and Chad; and military invasion by Tanzania into Uganda, Ethiopia into Somalia, and Libya into Chad.

The key figure in the decolonisation of Africa was Kurt Waldheim, Secretary-General of the UN from 1972 to 1982, who demonstrated the same enthusiasm in tearing down the colonial system as the settlers had shown in building it up.

Flirting with any pro-Marxist organisation in Africa, like SWAPO in Namibia, and always recognising any terrorist organisations fighting against colonial rule, like the liberation movements of Angola, Mozambique, Guinea Bissau, and Cape Verde, Kurt Waldheim is unique in the history of Western civilisation as the only man with high position and power – and he had plenty of both – who consequently and with great vigor [sic] supported any struggle, whether military, political, or economic, against his own kind, the European communities in Africa.

It is symbolic that when Kurt Waldheim addressed the OAU meeting in Addis Ababa in 1973, not a single word was said to praise what the white man had done in Africa during the last 300 years, but assurances were given to continue the efforts to decolonise Africa and to 'liberate' the territories still ruled by white minorities.

The UN is also unique in being the only known large-scale international organisation that took part in dismantling and demolishing the economic, political, and social systems of most of the continent without trying to substitute it with anything else. The last invaders of Africa – the UN and the international bureaucracy – represent a system that has built nothing to replace what they so effectively have helped to destroy.

The road from Vasco da Gama to Kurt Waldheim has been a long and difficult one. What started as an era of accomplishment and continued as an age of building and construction, has ended as a period of disintegration and chaos.

The Destruction of a Continent illustrates why Africa is in its present terrible position and puts the blame where it belongs: on Kurt Waldheim. This man, a former Nazi intelligence officer suspected of involvement in massacres in Yugoslavia and probably blackmailed later by the Russians, used his UN position to help the so-called freedom fighters destroy what had been built up in Africa over the last three hundred years.

⋆

Although the multiracial Federation of Rhodesia and Nyasaland was only allowed to exist for ten short years, it was long enough to show what could be achieved when all the races combined, when there was a stable government that was able to maintain the law and order that was necessary for all races to progress peacefully.

The standard of living for Africans was improving the whole time, as local industries boomed and created the demand for industrial power that culminated in the imaginative and well-planned building of one of the world's largest dams, Kariba, which harnessed the power of the mighty Zambezi river and led to Lake Kariba being created.

I visited Lake Kariba on numerous occasions, and also had friends who were involved in Operation Noah's Ark: the rescue of animals that were trapped on a number of islands as the water level rose after the completion of the dam.

Even South Africa began to realise that, with the completion of the Kariba Dam, the federation could, in the future, pose something of an industrial threat if it continued in the same imaginative vein. But the success of the federation scared venal African politicians almost out of their wits, both in the federation and outside. It was quickly seen as a threat to the vast amounts of aid money that less efficient regimes received from the UN and socialist countries in Europe.

So a partnership with the communists came about, to make sure the federation was not allowed to continue, as had been promised by Britain, for a second ten years.

It is now history how well the evil conspiracy succeeded as, after the shame of Suez, Britain was not interested in standing firm on any colonial matter. It has to be said, here, that I believe it was a mistake to send Roy Welensky to London to negotiate with the British Establishment. They change little over the years, and still seem to go largely by the old school tie – and Sir Roy was from a different background, as demonstrated by one of the remarks made about him at the time: that he was 'fifty per cent Polish and fifty per cent Jewish and acts as if he were one hundred per cent British.'

Sir Roy Welensky was a brilliant and respected politician in the Rhodesias, but the British Establishment would never forget that he was not one of them. He had actually been a boxer and an engine driver on the Rhodesian railways in his youth! The way they broke their promises to him about the continuation of the federation is typical of how they act towards those they believe to be gullible.

It would, I think, have been different if Lord Malvern (ex-Southern Rhodesia PM, when he was Sir Godfrey Huggins) had gone to London. He understood the British class system, with its dirty tricks and broken promises.

It is a great pity that today's South African politicians, especially Afrikaners, do not understand the British Establishment better.

That great imperialist Cecil Rhodes understood the problem very well and the theme of his Rhodes Scholarships should be copied by Afrikaner industrialists, so that aspiring Afrikaner politicians will get some understanding, from their time at Oxbridge, of how to handle British politicians. There is a lot of sense in the old army adage, 'Know your enemy.'

It was snobbery and an obsession with the British class system that caused a great deal of unnecessary trouble throughout the British Empire and helped to frustrate so much of the good work carried out in Africa. The Colonial Office in London rarely listened to advice from people on the spot unless it happened to fit in with their post-war policies for African independence, regardless of the consequences.

The Matabele under Nkomo were to find this out in a tragic way when the Marxist Mugabe sent in his notoriously brutal security troops to murder tens of thousands of them, as a lesson to his opposition. When Nkomo came to London to protest, he got nowhere with British politicians.

When the Rhodesian tragedy was drawing to its inevitable conclusion, Lord Soames was sent out (in December 1979) as British Governor, to give a completely false veneer of democracy to Mugabe's election victory in March 1980. The whole election procedure was rife with intimidation, as is usual in Africa.

In true African fashion, Mugabe's Zimbabwe is now a one-party Marxist state. So much for democracy in Africa!

Chapter Two

Some Journeys and Deaths

While I had been employed by Booth's as their manager in Mwanza it had been difficult, if not impossible, for me to get away for any length of time, apart from reasonably frequent trips to Nairobi, both on business and for pleasure – usually when I played cricket for the touring team from Tanganyika. So when Ken Lee (DFC) and myself were chosen to represent Mwanza at the East African Chamber of Commerce meeting in Kampala, we both jumped at the chance to get away. It was decided that we would do the trip by car, and make it a worthwhile journey by travelling the whole way around Lake Victoria.

Ken Lee had taken over from John Miles as manager of the United Africa Company in Mwanza. We were meant to be in competition in the hides and skins business, but we never let that bother us and cooperated as much as possible. We decided to use Ken's company car, a Chevrolet, as it was much more comfortable than my company's pick-up truck. His wife had relatives at Geita, and we spent the first night there.

Since most of Geita's traffic went towards Mwanza, we could get very little reliable information about the road the other way, and it was to prove the most difficult stretch of our journey around the lake. Some of the wooden bridges were so bad that we had to rebuild them partially before we could cross, and it took us the best part of a day to reach the main dirt road to Biharamulo and Bukoba – and we were very thankful that Ken's car had suffered no worse damage than a few dents and one ripped tyre. We knew we were very lucky to have got off so lightly, especially as one bridge had had only two sound planks and, as Ken had crossed at speed to get up the steep bank on the other side, we had seen that one of the planks had split almost in half. So there would have been no going back for a second attempt if he hadn't got it right the first time.

From Biharamulo onwards we had a comparatively easy and enjoyable drive, through some of the richest areas of East Africa. There seemed to be coffee trees and bananas everywhere and the local Africans were noticeably much more prosperous than the ones around Mwanza.

Coffee provided about twenty per cent of Tanganyika's income from exports. In Uganda it played an even greater role, contributing about sixty per cent to the country's exports. The Buganda area was one of the wealthiest in Africa, and nowhere was this more apparent than it was in and around Kampala. We were privileged to see one of the colonial showpieces of Africa at the height of its prosperity.

★

Little did any of us realise that, very soon after independence, all this prosperity would end with the advent of another evil tyrant – the notorious Idi Amin who, apart from the infamous mass murders he committed, devastated the economy and put back development in Uganda to such an extent that the country has still to recover.

Nobody in the West appeared to give a damn and the whole area was virtually handed over to that UN monstrosity, the New International Economic Order (NIEO), an arrogant, supposedly charitable UN organisation that no one in Africa wanted.

★

After a very pleasant time in Kampala, we experienced the only really sour note of the trip. This was on the way back, when we reached the Mara River, intending to cross on the ferry to Musoma. We arrived at about 2 p.m. and sent an African canoe across with a message to come and fetch us. Our messenger returned saying the owner was too drunk to come, so we had to spend a very unpleasant night about a mile back from the river and the lake. The mosquitoes were really fearsome and made it very difficult to sleep. Neither of us had mosquito nets with us and, after that night, I never again travelled without one. When the ferry did arrive the next morning there were no explanations or apologies – par for the course when travelling in Africa.

This incident could not spoil the trip for us, however. How pleasant, peaceful and prosperous everything was in those long-gone idyllic colonial days!

The biggest hazards on Africa's dirt roads were the truly appalling local drivers, at the wheels of vehicles which would never have been allowed on the roads in Europe.

The most dangerous part was overtaking in clouds of dust during the dry season – it was just about suicidal to try passing except on a long straight road where visibility was good. The local lorry drivers, however, thought nothing of overtaking on blind corners and you just had to learn to make allowance for this and other cowboy driving. On our trip around Lake Victoria, however, we passed only one fatal accident – on the Bukoba-Kampala stretch of road.

My first experience of just how lethal travelling on African dirt roads could be for Europeans used to tarmac and roadworthy vehicles happened shortly after I arrived in Mwanza, when a young airways employee was tragically killed on the road to the airport. He had been riding his motorcycle at night and misjudged a lorry coming towards him with only one headlight on – he took it for another motorcycle and was decapitated when he went through the lorry's windscreen.

I met very few people in Africa who had not had their share of accidents. The most common, as I found out when I turned over in my pick-up, was misjudging the slope and slippery surface at the side of the road when trying to overtake. I was lucky, and got away with a bit of concussion and some pretty bad bruising. On two occasions passing lorries sideswiped me in the wet weather and the drivers didn't stop (they were probably driving unlicensed vehicles), but I was fortunate enough to escape serious injury.

All these hazards were accepted as one of the risks of living in Africa. It was always reckoned that once you had survived the first year of driving in African conditions you would have learnt enough to keep out of bad trouble in the future. That reminded me of Italy with the Gurkhas – if you lived through the first month of active service, you had a pretty good chance of surviving the rest.

★

Another disconcerting thing I discovered, on my hides and skins travels in the Lake Province, was how quickly a dried-up river bed can become a raging torrent. Shortly after my arrival I was out with my Arab selector, Mohamed Kader, in the Shinyanga district. On our return, although we had seen little rain, we came to one river bed that had risen so quickly that a lorry had got stuck crossing and the force of the water had turned it on its side and pushed it about fifty yards downstream. We had to wait all night for the water to subside sufficiently for us to get across safely.

Stray domestic animals were another hazard and I had my share of smashed radiators and windscreens from hitting goats or sheep that had wandered on to the road. Later, when we moved to Livingstone, I made it a rule never to drive at night, except in an emergency, or travelling very slowly.

In those early days many of the roads in Southern Rhodesia had two narrow concrete strips down the centre for vehicles' wheels, so you could maintain quite a good speed so long as you had the road to yourself. Every time you encountered traffic going either way, however, you had to make room for the other vehicle by leaving the strip and driving on the gravel or earth sides of the road. In wet weather, in particular, the change of surface made it difficult not to skid – especially when you had been taking advantage of the concrete strips to drive fast.

I took especial care near game reserves or parks after Mitch Spence's wife was killed one evening as they returned from Bulawayo. Even though they had passed the most dangerous area for game, around the Wankie Game Reserve, there was, in those days, still plenty of game around everywhere and one of the larger antelope jumped right through their windscreen and broke Mrs Spence's neck as it hit her, killing her instantly. What was especially poignant was that Mitch, who had run a very profitable curio business at the Victoria Falls for years, had only recently got married.

When we lived in Livingstone, during the Sixties, we regularly visited the Victoria Falls Casino for a meal and an evening out, and one night we returned home only about an hour before another Livingstone resident hit a hippo on the road. Unfortunately he had been travelling at speed and, after impact, the Volkswagen he was driving caught fire. He was trapped, and burnt to death before anyone could free him.

Living, as we did, in small European communities in Africa, such tragedies always struck us very hard, as we all knew the people killed – very different to the impersonal life of most city dwellers in Europe and America.

*

The son of one of the American crocodile skin tanners with whom I did business, Joffe of Messrs Fleming Joffe, was coming to Africa on his honeymoon and wanted to do a little business at the same time. I offered to drive the Joffes around and to visit some of the centres in the Rhodesias from which I got some of their crocodile skins. As luck would have it, we ran into a very bad tropical storm on the strip road between Bulawayo and Livingstone.

Normally this would have created few problems, but I was staying in Salisbury at the time and going through one of my bad financial periods so I had put off having a new exhaust fitted until I received (from overseas buyers) some outstanding payments for crocodile skins. There were a few holes in the exhaust, but that did not bother me – I simply opened both front windows, and that took the smell away.

In the back of the car, a Ford Cortina, the fumes were worse and Joffe's wife complained a bit on the way from Salisbury to Bulawayo, but I passed it off as the heat and petrol fumes from other cars. The storm the next day really finished things for her, however. With the front windows closed against the rain, she opened one of the rear windows and the fumes got so bad that I had to open my front window again, although that meant I got soaked.

This incident, together with skidding off the road, was the last straw for Mrs Joffe and she insisted that they fly from Livingstone to Lusaka and back to Salisbury, leaving me to come on alone by car. This actually suited me fine, as I didn't then have to put up with her continual, if justified, moaning.

As it turned out, the trip was a very good one for me. I was able to have more talks with Mr Oza, who owned Oza's Emporium, the largest general store in Livingstone. He sold just about everything except food, and had most of the European business in the area tied up. As Livingstone was a very popular local holiday resort, and near to the Victoria Falls, he had a really flourishing business and was easily the wealthiest Indian retailer in Livingstone. As well as the emporium, he owned a large ivory and skins business, and handled a considerable number of crocodile skins.

From previous talks, when I had been in Livingstone exporting crocodile skins, I knew he was very interested in expanding his business in Barotseland. That fitted in very nicely with my own plans, but a major stumbling block was getting him to purchase a new long-wheel base Land Rover before I would agree to taking a short-term job with him to get the business in Barotseland organised.

Mr Oza had already exported crocodile skins to Messrs Fleming Joffe, and I knew he would be quite impressed if I brought the son of one of the owners to see him. During his talks with Mr Joffe and myself, I was pretty sure that Oza had at last made up his mind and would agree to my purchasing a long-wheel base Land Rover in Salisbury, which I would then drive to Livingstone.

So it turned out, and that led to one of the most interesting periods of my life in Africa, because Barotseland, including the area from Livingstone up the

Zambezi to Barotseland, was one of the most untouched and picturesque parts of central Africa.

★

While I finished my business in Livingstone, which included making some arrangements for accommodation when we moved there, the Joffes were enjoying the Victoria Falls and other tourist attractions, so they were in no hurry to leave. Eventually they flew to Lusaka, where I met them, but they didn't want to stay long, as they were now anxious to get back to Salisbury as soon as possible.

That suited me, because there were many crocodile hunters in Lusaka and I certainly did not want Joffe to meet them. I was glad, in fact, to see him and his wife leave Salisbury on their way back to the USA, because I was taken up with the hassle of moving to Livingstone.

Livingstone was, of course, ideally situated for my business, but until the threat of independence in Northern Rhodesia, I had not seriously considered moving. Being on the Zambezi River, and with easy access to Barotseland, Botswana, the Caprivi Strip and the bottom (southern) end of Angola, Livingstone had the added advantage of being the best place to be if, after independence, it became necessary to leave in a hurry, as the Belgians had had to leave Katanga.

We had seen those unfortunate Belgians from the Congo streaming into Northern Rhodesia, most of them with only the clothes they had on and absolutely penniless. So those of us who knew the unpredictability of the Africans were already taking precautions in case a speedy departure became necessary.

★

At the first sign of carefully manipulated civil disorders in Nyasaland and, to a lesser degree, in Northern Rhodesia, the completely pusillanimous British government panicked, just as it had done so shamefully at Suez and went back on promises given to Welensky. This very effectively destroyed the last hope of any true multiracial settlement in central Africa and led inevitably to Ian Smith's UDI.

That was just what the communists wanted, and they shrewdly worked out that when American and British pressure forced South Africa to stop supporting Smith, the Marxist Mugabe would take over. That, combined with the presence of their forty thousand Cubans in Angola and Mozambique, would almost complete the communist line which cut South Africa off from the rest of the continent.

To those of us who know Africa and the East, it was the disaster at Suez that decided Africa's post-war future and, for that matter, the colonial Far East in such places as Vietnam. The world's two most powerful colonial powers, France and Britain, were publicly humiliated by Nasser's Egypt, a defeat made worse by the low opinion most people, especially ex-servicemen, had of the Egyptians at the time.

Training in the Indian Army, especially in the Gurkhas, was based on instilling the theory of loss of face into every officer, and it was instrumental in saving my life in Italy during the war, as well as when I was hunting elephants in Africa.

People who have never lived outside Europe, however, may find it difficult to understand the importance of not losing face in other parts of the world. Ex-prisoners of war of the Japanese found out the hard way what their captors thought about this very important concept.

The Japanese considered that it was a total loss of face for a fighting man to allow himself to be captured and such people were not, in their eyes, entitled to any sort of consideration. What is more difficult to understand is why they treated those innocent children, women, old men and disabled who had the misfortune to fall into their hands almost as callously as the fighting men.

To this day I will not willingly buy anything that I know to be made in Japan, because of the way they treated their British and Commonwealth captives.

*

It was no use politicians like Harold Macmillan thinking they could change the shame of Suez by making speeches about the 'wind of change' in Africa. The USA can consider itself lucky that the US shame about Vietnam was balanced by the USSR's shame over Afghanistan. I feel, in fact, that Mr Gorbachev's liberal policies were influenced a great deal by the events in Afghanistan.

Labour's left and the communists were not slow to point out to African leaders like Kenyatta, Nkrumah and Kaunda that all it needed for independence was a bit of anti-British propaganda, and violence when their policies were opposed. They made it known that they would add their support in the West and at the UN, with virulent speeches about the evils of colonialism.

Thus these evil men, later headed by suspected Nazi war criminal Kurt Waldheim (while he was Secretary-General at the UN from 1972 to 1982), were able to use the carefully planned violence in the Central African Federation (mainly in Nyasaland but sporadic violence in Northern Rhodesia also helped) to manipulate public opinion in both the UN and Britain. The Tory government bowed to the pressure, broke its promises to Welensky, and ended the Central African Federation of the Rhodesias and Nyasaland after its ten very successful years, from 1953 to 1963.

Thus ended a bold experiment, with a true multiracial and economic base, that could have been used to show South Africa that moderation could pay even in the violence of Africa. Today, to those of us who know and love Africa, there is a very strong case for indictment against these evil men from both the UN and the Commonwealth. It seems they are still not satisfied with the unnecessary misery they have brought to most of black-ruled Africa: famine, civil wars, corruption, misrule and economic disaster.

★

Because of a series of disgraceful and gutless policies, we have several very vocal little tinpot countries, and several African leaders with delusions of grandeur. The worst is the murderous Marxist Mugabe who, because he is black, can, with complete impunity, murder thousands of his political foes, the Matabele, who are one of the offshoots of South Africa's famous warrior tribe, the Zulus.

The Matabele have always despised the Mashona, and terrorised them in their tribal wars before the arrival of the British in Salisbury (in 1890), in much the same way that the Masai in Kenya fought their traditional enemies, the Kikuyu. The Matabele fought the British in the First Matabele War (in 1895) and then again in the Second Matabele War (1896–1897). In the days of the Zulus' tribal domination, the Matabele moved up from Natal, conquering the area of western Zimbabwe and driving out most of the local Mashona.

Nowadays, with the UN's tacit stamp of approval for black-on-black violence, African leaders like Mugabe, a Mashona, know they can settle old tribal scores with complete impunity.

When Mugabe sent his notoriously brutal 5th Brigade into Matabeleland there was hardly a protest from the West, the OAU or the UN. In fact, if the highly respected Rhodesia Christian Group in London hadn't received reliable information from sources in Matabeleland, very little would have been known about the extent of the massacres. The murderous death toll has been put as high as forty thousand Matabele.

Zimbabwe's 5th Brigade was originally trained by a North Korean communist military mission in Zimbabwe. When I wrote a letter to the Foreign and Commonwealth Office, protesting about a British military mission in Zimbabwe training Marxist Mozambique army officers, as it would appear that we in Britain condoned the massacre of forty thousand Matabele, I received the following reply from a minister:

> ...The British Military Advisory Training Team in Zimbabwe who replaced the North Koreans have been widely praised for their major contribution to a blending of a strong, united and disciplined army from the disparate group which previously existed...

That we get any uncensored news out of Zimbabwe is due mainly to two remarkable men and their Rhodesia Christian Group: the honorary president, Reverend Father Arthur Lewis (MA Oxon), and the director – W. Denis Walker. Father Lewis was a missionary in Africa for forty years, and is one of the few Church of England priests who are prepared to speak out against the official cover-up.

If there is any hope at all for changing these attitudes, it is due to one of Britain's greatest prime ministers, Mrs Thatcher, who almost single-handed stood firm about the Commonwealth demands for sanctions against South Africa. The Falklands War tested her to the full, and she restored British pride, in far more difficult circumstances than Suez.

★

The three great lakes of central and East Africa – Lake Victoria, Lake Tanganyika and Lake Nyasa – played their part in helping me to develop my crocodile business. This was especially true of Lake Tanganyika as, unlike Lake Victoria, roads around the lake were practically non-existent and being able to use the lake steamers to transport vehicles, equipment and crocodile skins played a vital role.

In retrospect, I am glad that I made full use of the very enjoyable steamers which operated on all the great lakes. I often managed to take time off from business, to complete trips on and around these beautiful lakes, and I always found these leisurely voyages extremely enjoyable. Especially relaxing were the sundowners I consumed on deck during the balmy tropical evenings and the short visits I made to Bukoba, Entebbe and Kisumu before returning home to Mwanza on Lake Victoria.

Later, in my Kibondo-Kakonko farming and hunting days, I often went from Kigoma to Albertville, Usumbura and Mpulungu on Lake Tanganyika, and travelled on Lake Nyasa up to Nkhata Bay.

One thing that has always interested me about the great lakes is the little-known part they played in World War I in Africa. In fact it was on Lake Tanganyika, in June 1915, that the first German warship, in any theatre of war, was captured and converted to British use.

British forces had brought up the motor vessels, *Mimi* and *Toutou*, armed with a three-pounder gun and machine-gun, with naval personnel that came via Cape Town by rail to the Katanga border (the Belgian Congo), then via river and rail to Lake Tanganyika. The Germans knew nothing of this, as the boats were taken there in parts and reassembled on the shore of Lake Tanganyika. Within a day or two of launching, they captured the German armed steamer *Kingani*.

The following year another German ship was sunk, and two others driven ashore. The last German vessel on Lake Tanganyika was scuttled later that same year, 1916, thus enabling General Smuts to move his South African and British forces into Tanganyika (then German East Africa), having already successfully completed the conquest of German South West Africa.

However, due to the very difficult terrain and the excellent leadership of the very resourceful and resolute German officer von Lettow Vorbeck, the German East African forces were able to hold out until the Great War finished on 11th November, 1918.

In fact, it is believed that von Lettow's forces fired the very last shots in the war two days later – on 13th November. After blowing up the Northern Rhodesia government offices in Kasama, von Lettow followed a Northern Rhodesia police unit to the Chambashi river pontoon and, on 13th November, started firing at them from the north bank of the river.

Owing to a fault in the telegraph system, the district commissioner at Chambashi heard of the end of the war only then, and sent von Lettow a message to that effect. On hearing the news, von Lettow immediately surrendered.

In Nyasaland there had been less activity on the lake, as the Germans only had one vessel there, the *Hermann von Wissmann*. At the outbreak of the war, in 1914, this ship had been undergoing repairs in the harbour of Alt Langenburg. British forces in Nyasaland were informed of the outbreak of war before the Germans and sent the gunboat *Gwendolen* to ensure that the repairs would not be completed. The engines of the German vessel were put out of action, and the German officers and crew were captured before they even knew war had been declared! The Germans continued trying to repair the *Hermann von Wissmann*, as it was the only vessel they had on Lake Nyasa, but, in a further amphibious raid, British forces put her out of action for the rest of the war.

On Lake Victoria the position was different, as British forces from Kenya and Uganda dominated the situation, both on land and on the lake. The only action that occurred was some desultory shelling of Mwanza and Bukoba before British land forces moved in to capture Bukoba (in June 1915 from Kampala in Uganda). About a year later the British forces moved from Kenya to capture Mwanza (in July 1916).

Most German settlers in Tanganyika had hoped that, if they did nothing, the British in East Africa would leave them alone. But von Lettow Vorbeck, then a colonel in charge of all German forces in Tanganyika, had other ideas. He considered it his duty to tie down as many British and South African troops as possible, fighting a guerrilla-type war in the Tanganyikan bush so that the Allied troops could not be used against Germany in Europe. This job Colonel von Lettow did brilliantly. He must have been an infuriating foe for General Smuts, as he would never stand and fight, but continually moved around the countryside, causing immense trouble to the troops who were chasing him in unpleasant tropical conditions which caused far more medical problems than German bullets.

Over 150,000 British and South African troops were involved, but they never managed to defeat or capture von Lettow until he eventually surrendered, two days after the war had ended, to the British district commissioner in Northern Rhodesia.

Truly a remarkable man! When I arrived in Mwanza (in 1948), there were Africans there who still remembered him. He was the best type of German officer, admired greatly by even his wartime enemies – rather like General Rommel in World War II.

It was only when I started researching some South African history for the last part of my book that I began to understand just how lucky it was, for both Britain and South Africa, that there were South African leaders like Jan Smuts and Louis Botha with the wisdom, foresight and courage to put aside personal feelings and bring South Africa into World War I on Britain's side.

If I had been an Afrikaner who had experienced what Britain did in the Boer War of 1899–1902, I am sure that I would have volunteered to fight for the Germans. Few in Britain understand the debt we owe to those two great Afrikaner leaders for the fact that their country did not join the Germans and for the peace and prosperity that have prevailed in South Africa for the last ninety years – in such sharp contrast to conditions in the rest of Africa. Are we going to allow the communists to destroy this prosperity now?

Chapter Three

Lusaka and the Crocodile Business

Lusaka, in those boom years of the Federation of Rhodesia and Nyasaland (1953 to 1963), was the centre of the crocodile business, Livingstone being the only other town handling large numbers of skins. I found settling into Lusaka easy as, on past trips to buy and export crocodile skins, I had made plenty of friends there and was able to stay with some of them while I got myself organised.

As a boom town, Lusaka had all the usual faults of too-rapid development and, apart from business facilities, had very little to recommend it as a place to settle.

During my previous trips, however, I had noticed an area only a mile or two south of Lusaka that had looked ideal for me. This was the area bordering the Makeni Road. It was unfashionable, a bit run-down and completely away from the development zone of Lusaka, consisting largely of smallholdings a few acres in size. I felt one of them would be just right for me. It was not far from the main road between Lusaka and Salisbury, Livingstone and Bulawayo, but most important of all it had a good (and very private) track that ran along the edge of the whole property.

A derelict house by the Makeni Road entrance put most people off, but the private track led to fairly spacious cowsheds and other outbuildings that had been used as business premises by the previous owner, who had now moved his dairy to a farm a few miles further up the Makeni Road. There were lots of fruit trees on the property: the oranges, lemons, guavas and papaws were particularly good, and I never had to buy any fruit while I lived there. It had a borehole with a pump for water, and a large metal storage tank on the ground which could double as a swimming pool in the hot weather. The whole place was perfect for my needs, as I could see that it could be converted, without any great expense, to provide living quarters as well as business premises.

A crocodile hunter friend called Johnny Young, and his Polish wife, lived a mile or so up the Makeni Road and he knew the owner, an Afrikaner farmer, well. So the whole deal was quite simple to arrange and the necessary alterations to the building took little time.

The cowsheds had sloping cement floors, open at the back but with solid brick walls at the sides. A wall in the middle, which had separated the cows from a large office and storerooms, made it easy to convert the building into my living accommodation. Opposite the cowsheds was another office building which was close to the water pump, and I felt that would be ideal for visiting crocodile hunters to stay in overnight.

But the greatest advantage of all, so far as I was concerned, was the complete privacy. My nearest neighbour was over half a mile away, so I had no inquisitive colonial civil servants nearby to take an interest in my activities. Most of them lived in a central area called the Ridgeway. A large hotel, imaginatively named The Ridgeway Hotel, had been completed there shortly before I moved to Lusaka.

I had learnt, from my Mwanza days, just how dangerous nosy, gossipy people could be and, although my friends and I often drank, wined and dined at the popular Woodpecker Inn in the Ridgeway area, we kept well away from most of the civil servants. The steadily dying colonial way of life had little attraction for most of us.

Looking back now, I don't think I appreciated just how lucky I was to find so secluded a place so close to town. We had firearms that needed testing before going out hunting and it would have been impossible to do this in any of the residential areas of Lusaka, and streams of crocodile skins coming in at all hours would undoubtedly have caused speculation and complaints from neighbours. Had I been in town, simply using the premises for commercial use would probably have caused complaints.

Although there had been electricity for years in Lusaka itself, it had not yet reached the Makeni Road area. I didn't mind – using tilley lamps brought back pleasant memories of my early days in East Africa and of my time farming at Kakonko.

*

Very soon the realities of life in rapidly developing parts of Africa were brought home to me in a very unpleasant manner and I was reminded of a saying of the old hands in Tanganyika, about getting the best out of Africa by choosing to live in a place with few Europeans around. They had found that more Europeans normally meant more trouble for all.

None of the Africans who handled or hunted crocodiles (most of whom were from Tanganyika) were keen on housework, so I had to employ a local man from Lusaka, and he was left behind to look after the property while I was away.

Only a few months after I had moved in, I went on a hunting trip to Angola and the Belgian Congo with an ex-Indian Army friend and hunter, Hugh Charnaud. His parents owned a tea estate in Ceylon (now Sri Lanka) and I still remember the taste of the tea that his parents sent him: I think he told me it was the first picking but, whatever it was, it was so strong and tasty that the blended stuff sold by the big tea companies appeared to have no taste at all.

When Hugh and I got back from the trip, we reached Makeni Road in the early evening and found there was no sign of my house servant. I entered the bedroom and saw immediately that he had stolen just about everything that was easily portable: including my sheets, blankets, pillows, some of my clothes, drinks and cigarettes. The room was almost empty. Fortunately there was an open veranda between the bedroom and the lounge-cum-dining room, and I had always kept the latter locked as some of my tin boxes were in there, still unpacked, so many of my belongings had escaped the thief, but I had to borrow such basic requirements as blankets, pillows and sheets from Hugh. He, with one of the local hunters who had arrived shortly after us, arranged for all the crocodile-hunting Africans (who had no liking at all for the smart-alec urban Africans of Lusaka) to start a search for the thief in all the local African townships.

It took them a day or two to track him down, but they did so late one afternoon. One of them stayed nearby to keep an unobtrusive watch on his hut until we came later in our Land Rovers. We timed our arrival for about two in the morning, when we knew everyone in the township would have settled down for the night.

In the event, we surrounded the man's hut and pushed open his door before any of the occupants woke up. There was a half-empty bottle of my whisky and cigarettes by his bed on the floor, and I woke him none too gently as he lay on my blankets and sheets. He had been using my new Ronson cigarette lighter, a birthday present from a girlfriend which had been given to me just before I had left on the safari.

We whites could not give him the hiding he so richly deserved, but the Tanganyikan Africans did the job very effectively, then we took the thief and my stolen property to the central police station in Lusaka. I kept back an unopened bottle of whisky and my cigarette lighter. The rest of my stuff, I knew, I would not get back until after the case came up in court.

*

Those of us who knew Africa felt that this sort of crime wasn't entirely the fault of the urban African. In the boom years that followed the end of the war, Europeans streamed into Africa, mostly on well-paid, short-term contracts that required them to stay only a year or two. The vast majority came primarily to acquire a nest egg for when they returned to Europe and very few had any interest in, love for, or understanding of Africa. Most never even bothered to learn how to communicate with the Africans in their own language.

Many of the urban Africans picked up a few words of English, in order to get a job with the Europeans. They had to work very hard but saw their bosses living what was, to them, an incredibly rich and wasteful type of life. In the evenings they could see many Europeans drunk outside the bars in Cairo Road, Lusaka's main street, picking up the African prostitutes who were flocking to the boom towns on the Copperbelt and to Lusaka. This was before the era of Aids, but most of the women had venereal diseases, and the whole scene was a very poor advertisement for the Western way of life.

So the urban African couldn't really be blamed for trying to take advantage of this type of European, whom he was increasingly coming to despise – egged on by nationalist politicians like Kaunda. The trouble was that those Europeans who did love Africa and want to make it their home were tarred with the same brush and, eventually, were to lose everything they had worked for over the years.

Those of us who had been brought up with the traditions of the colonial service, or with the Indian Army (especially the Gurkhas), despised the 'contract Europeans' who were causing so much damage in Africa, and blamed them rather than the urban Africans for the growing crime rate.

This is not to say that we never got drunk, of course, but we did try to be discreet. In places like the Mwanza Club, for instance, after some of the Saturday night dances, we made sure that the African and Indian members of the staff had been sent home before we let our hair down. Certainly the hot climate increased our libido, but we kept it amongst ourselves.

I feel that most of the expatriates who made a display of themselves were the colonial equivalents of the modern lager louts who have given English football supporters such a bad name. Like the modern hooligans, the indiscreet drunks of colonial times cared nothing for the damage they were doing to the reputation of their country.

★

On the business side, I knew only too well that the good old days of no competition were over and the ease of travel in the Rhodesias, compared to East Africa, wasn't going to help me either. There were two large hides and skins firms from Port Elizabeth (Hollanders and Lurie), who had branches in Bulawayo and, on my earlier trips from Tabora to Lusaka, the news of the number of crocodile skins that were starting to come into Lusaka must have filtered through to them. Hollanders started to send their number two in Bulawayo on regular trips to Livingstone and Lusaka.

Later, when I had moved to Livingstone, I got to know the number two (Gerry Levinkind) quite well – and their Bulawayo manager, Salinger. In fact I found them both quite useful on occasions, when I wanted to sell in either Livingstone or Bulawayo. After I had moved to Livingstone they weren't competitors in the areas I then concentrated on – Barotseland and Angola.

But in Lusaka it was a different story and I found experienced crocodile hunters like Hugh Charnaud, Hannes Wieuwouldt and Mike Weston were starting to export for themselves, as they had seen how easy it was for me, using an irrevocable letter of credit, with money paid out when I delivered either to the aircraft or to the railway station in Lusaka.

Fortunately there were still enough crocodile skins coming in from my old areas in the Belgian Congo, Angola and even Tanganyika but, as conditions in all these areas began to deteriorate (in the 1960s), it became increasingly dangerous to travel there, with all the civil disturbances and the complete breakdown of the law and order that had been the norm in colonial days.

I knew the time was coming when I would have to move from Livingstone. The upper Zambezi River area, from Livingstone to Barotseland and beyond, was just about the last unexploited area and the distances involved, combined with the lack of roads, meant that it was not worth my competitors' time and expense to go. In those early days I had little idea how inaccessible the area really was, but I also underestimated how lucrative it was to be for me when, eventually, I made the move to Livingstone.

With hindsight, I think I should have made the move earlier. But in those days none of us anticipated that the Federation of Rhodesia and Nyasaland would end in 1963, nor how quickly events would move thereafter. Zambia was given its very premature independence in 1964. As in Tanzania, it took the new ruler, President-for-life Kenneth Kaunda, only about five years to wreck the economy of Zambia.

Having seen what had happened to the Belgians in the Katanga Province of the Belgian Congo, I had no intention of being anywhere but Livingstone when Zambia got its independence.

*

There were plenty of colourful characters in the crocodile business. Although, after all these years, I have forgotten some of the names, I still remember quite a few.

In Lusaka there were Danny Young (whose brother had helped me get the Makeni Road property), Mike Weston (ex-army and Nyasaland), and Hannes Wieuwouldt. I knew Hannes did not like me taking his wife out when he was away, but I did feel he was going a bit far when he accused me of stealing one of his crocodile hunting boats, complete with the outboard engine and other bits and pieces. Fortunately, when the police came around, I was able to find the receipt and deed of sale he had given me. There was also Denis Gaunt, whose father was our local MP during the time of the federation, and who helped me over my immigration problems.

I had had permanent residence in Tanganyika and I had just moved down to Northern Rhodesia on a temporary resident's permit, one I had used on my business trips from Tabora. But I hadn't bothered to renew the permit and the border officials got a bit stroppy with me when I was returning from a holiday in South Africa. They gave me three days to put things right and, without John Gaunt's intervention on my behalf, it could have been very awkward for me. Anyway, thanks to John Gaunt's help, I got my permanent residence through very quickly.

Another friend was Jeff Widekind, who had a farm at Mumbwa, not far from the Kafue River, and who hunted crocodiles in the surrounding area. He had a thatched rondavel-style farmhouse of a type that always appealed to me, as it fitted so well into the African background. It was like my very first house in Mwanza, and I always enjoyed staying there when I visited him. He had been a London stockbroker who had been forced to move to Africa for health reasons – he had only one lung and needed the high altitude and clean air.

Quite a few miners from the Copperbelt tried crocodile hunting at various times, but few lasted for long. Notable exceptions were Hank and Charlie Holloway, who were very successful and kept hunting for years. In the end, I believe, Charlie became very religious and could be seen preaching in all the Copperbelt towns.

In Livingstone there were some hunters with whom I am still in contact today. John Seaman is one. I used to stay with him in Livingstone long before I eventually moved down there. He gave me much-needed advice about local conditions and never refused to help, even on an occasion when there was trouble with the Livingstone police over some crocodile skins that I had been storing at his house.

Later, when John moved to Mongu, the capital of Barotseland, he was invaluable to me while I was setting up my business there, for he had many local contacts and often bought skins on my behalf. John has spent most of his life in Africa. His father owned trading stores all over Botswana, and John now owns and operates a crocodile breeding farm at Maun, which borders on the Okavango Swamps in Botswana. Anybody who wants to see the real, still completely unspoilt, Africa before it disappears for ever could do worse than take a safari at Okavango, and should find a visit to the crocodile farm of great interest. John had started a safari business and lodge which his wife Ursala continue to run at Camp Okuti, Private Bag 047, Maun, Botswana.

John Seaman and I met up again many years later, after I had moved to Durban, in Natal. Once again he was able to give me help, by mediating over a financial dispute with Peter Becker, the managing director of Botswana Game Industries in Francistown.

When my present wife, Joyce, and I left South Africa in 1983, John Seaman came to Johannesburg Airport to see us off.

⋆

Lolly Sussens and his Polish wife had been in Livingstone for a long time when I moved there. As well as his hunting and crocodile skin business, he was involved in the very lucrative tourist trade. His company, Greenaway Launch and Taxi Service, operated tourist launches on the Northern Rhodesia side of the Zambezi River and a fleet of taxis and minibuses that ran trips to the game parks and other local places of interest. Lolly sold all his businesses at exactly the right time: shortly before the border between Northern and Southern Rhodesia was closed to tourists.

He then bought one of my favourite hotels in Africa, and one the most picturesquely sited – on the banks of the Chobe river in the border area between Botswana and Northern Rhodesia. In fact, one bank of the river was Northern Rhodesia's border and the other bank was Botswana's border, and there was an antiquated ferry on the Zambezi River which the hotel guests had to take to and from the hotel.

The Chobe River Hotel had its main hotel buildings right on the banks of the Chobe River, but a large number of rondavel-type huts had been built in the spacious hotel grounds as bedrooms. Whenever I was going to Katima Mulilo, I would break my journey to spend the night in one of the rondavels.

There were no restrictions on travel in those days and I could pass through South Africa's Caprivi Strip en route to Katima Mulilo, then return to Zambia and continue to Senanga and Mongu (in Barotseland), without even bothering to take my passport.

Some years later I heard from friends that Lolly and Ala Sussens had sold the Chobe River Hotel and moved to the eastern Transvaal, but it was only when I read a letter about the Sussens Game Lodge (in the February 1989 edition of *Focus on South Africa*, which is published in Cape Town), that I was able to contact them again. For readers who want to view game and also hear some stories about the real Africa, I recommend a visit (Lolly and Ala Sussens, PO Box 289, Hoedspruit, 1380, E.TVL, South Africa).

In August 1993, I stayed with the Sussens for a week; a truly marvellous experience of the real Africa. One morning I couldn't get the door of my rondavel open. An elephant had been eating outside and pulled down branches that blocked my door. At night an armed escort went with me to the rondavel as there were lion and leopard footmarks in the sandy ground outside. It was better than the Kruger National Park (thirty miles away).

★

Another Livingstone crocodile hunter who comes to mind is Dick Burton, another long-term resident there, who eventually decided he needed a change and got a job with a brewery in Dar. He knew I had lived in Tanganyika for quite a few years and, with a young family, he was a bit anxious about conditions and stability there.

I told him that, for Europeans, Dar was the best place to be as, if trouble came, they could get away quite easily by sea. My recommendation was tempered by a proviso about the very hot and sticky weather there, since not everybody could cope with it.

Julius Nyerere had been knocked off his presidential perch, but only briefly, as the Royal Marines had been called in quickly to reinstate him. That had been in the early days of independence and Nyerere had, by this time, had plenty of opportunity to dispose of any opposition – as is normal in all black-ruled countries in Africa. I told Dick how shrewd Nyerere was, and how he had wangled more international aid for Tanzania than any other country in Africa, by using his system of African socialism as a model for all the socialist countries in Europe and the UN to help.

None of these countries like Norway, Sweden, Denmark, Holland, even Germany and Britain, as well as the UN, are now prepared to admit that the whole business of African socialism has been a dismal failure.

To his credit, Julius Nyerere admitted some of this in his 'Arusha Declaration', ten years later (in 1977). But he has listened to his Chinese and socialist advisers from Europe for so long, and has been given so much aid money, that he is quite prepared to cover up the inefficiency and corruption of his government departments, so long as the aid money continues to flow in.

So, with the socialist and UN madness over aid to Africa continuing unabated, Dick Burton and his family probably had a long stay in Dar. Maybe they are still there.

★

In Chobe, apart from the increasing numbers of African and Coloured crocodile hunters, who were each selling me a few crocodiles every trip, there was Lolly Sussens at the Chobe River Hotel.

With the hotel to run, Lolly had less time to devote to the crocodile business, but his shortfall was offset by the increasing number of skins that I was getting from another hunter there, 'Dup' du Plessis. By the time I left Zambia (at the end of 1969), Dup had completed his house on an island in the river not far from Chobe. I often wonder how long he managed to stay – I am sure that he would have been forced to move eventually by the increasing numbers of terrorist gangs in the area.

Tony Butts of Choma, which was, in those days, a prosperous European farming area about halfway along the main road between Lusaka and Livingstone, had a string of African trading stores on or near the Kafue River. His place was quite a drive off the main road and, when going there, it was necessary to stay for at least one night. But he was one of the most successful hunters in the area and the trip was always worth while.

★

Since I had moved down to Northern Rhodesia, another new area had opened up on Lake Nyasa, the last of the three great central African lakes. Peter

Gurney had invited me down, and we arranged to meet at Ryall's Hotel in Blantyre, almost as famous in central Africa as Meikles Hotel in Salisbury. I remember we had a mostly liquid lunch at the hotel and left later than was wise for the trip down to the lake.

Peter had offered to give me a lift, so I could enjoy the countryside, and I left my Land Rover at the hotel. We got a few sandwiches for the journey from the hotel.

Nyasaland is, I think, one of the most attractive countries in Africa, with a fascinating variation in scenery down to the lake. As we approached, there were various signs about the need to be careful of elephants and sure enough, as dusk began to fall, we had to wait for quite considerable lengths of time to let several different herds cross the road.

The whole area reminded me, almost painfully, of East Africa, and I was not disappointed when, later that night, we eventually got to our destination, Fort Johnstone. This was a small place, but it did boast a district commissioner and a little airfield. We stayed at another of my all-time favourite hotels, a most attractive thatched main building with separate thatched rondavel-type bedrooms in the grounds, right on the shores of Lake Nyasa. Early every morning I had to take only a few steps in order to enjoy a swim in a protected part of the lake opposite the hotel.

The whole atmosphere of the place was very similar to East Africa. In Nyasaland, as in Tanganyika and Botswana, there were very few Europeans, and it had the same easygoing attitudes that I had liked so much in Tanganyika.

There were other hunters who were connected with the flourishing local fishing industry, but it is Peter Gurney and his tragic death that I remember most. Evidently he was under his boat in the lake, carrying out some repairs to the bottom of the boat when, it is thought, he suffered a heart attack and drowned before he could be pulled out of the water.

The only other death I heard of in those days was of a hunter called Wilmot in Botswana who, on one of his crocodile hunting trips there, forgot to take the usual serum with him and died from a poisonous snake bite.

The low number of deaths was quite remarkable, considering all the risks and mishaps that could occur while out hunting crocodiles in a wet and slippery boat. It was not unusual for a supposedly dead crocodile to come alive unexpectedly in the boat and most crocodile hunters and their African crews had, at some time, fallen in a river or lake amongst the reptiles, with nothing worse happening to them than a very complete soaking – but it was truly amazing to see the speed with which they could get back in the boat!

It was only many years later, after we had moved permanently to South Africa, that I read about the death of another friend from those years of the federation (1953 to 1963), a pilot called 'Rusty' Russell. I had met him through Hannes Wieuwouldt, and he had flown a lot of the crocodile hunters around. By the time he died, he was a very experienced pilot, but he ran into a very bad storm in hilly country and died when he hit a hill only a few feet from the top.

*

There were some very inexperienced pilots around in those days, and I bumped into one of them on one of my trips to Livingstone. He had just flown up from Botswana and wanted to see something of Barotseland, and to get some flying practice in as well.

Since I needed to go to Barotseland on a skin-buying trip, I offered to show him around while I did my business, but he was to pay all the flying expenses. I noticed, at the time, that he had a double-the-normal-size chequebook that he tended to flash around a bit too much, but I took it to be part of the image he was trying to project as the owner of an almost new Cessna aircraft.

I had arranged for us to spend the night at Katima Mulilo with 'Old Man' Finaulty, although we landed at the Sesheke airfield in Zambia, on the opposite bank of the Zambezi River.

In those days Old Man Finaulty handled just about everything in the whole area, including aviation fuel, and my pilot paid for everything by cheque, which included getting some extra cash for the trip. Finaulty accepted this form of payment because he assumed the pilot was a friend of mine.

On my next trip to Barotseland, however – about two months later – Finaulty showed me the cheque, a South African one, which had bounced and been sent back to him by his South African bank. He was pretty furious with me and told me not to bring any more such customers to stay with him. He also asked me to investigate ways of getting his money back.

Later I was to find the pilot had done the same thing in Balavale, which also reflected on me as I had been with him. Fortunately I had not associated with him much in Livingstone, as I later discovered he had bounced a lot of big cheques there – and all over Zambia.

On that first trip with him I had noticed that he rarely used a map, but I wasn't unduly worried because I assumed the reason was that I had told him that if we followed the Zambezi River it would be impossible to miss Sesheke, Senanga and Mongu, and that Balavale shouldn't be too difficult to find, although it was near the Angola border. But we had strayed away from the river, as we had detoured to follow a herd of elephants, and he panicked a bit before we eventually found Balavale. Although some of his landings were a bit hairy, we had got back to Livingstone without any real dramas.

On the way, I had told him that I was going to Ndola the following weekend and he offered to fly me there for free, so that he could get some more flying experience. I naturally jumped at the offer.

It was, of course, a very different matter navigating our course to Ndola, which was in the middle of the industrialised Copperbelt area. There were a number of towns en route that all looked the same from the air and a map was a necessity. He started to panic around Broken Hill: I had been dozing when he woke me and said he was going down to get a good look. It was only when I saw a mine that I realised he didn't know where he was.

I told him the best thing to do was to look for a small private airfield, as there would be hell to pay if he got through to Ndola Airport and said he had lost his way. A little later we saw an airfield that looked fairly accessible, near the railway line and with some buildings. It turned out to be Kapiri Mposhi, on the main road to Ndola, but landing wasn't easy, as it was only a small emergency airfield that doubled as a football field, and it took him two attempts to get down without hitting the nearby buildings. Some of the locals had come out of the pub and were clearly amazed to see us. They were even more amazed when we told them we were lost, but they recommended that we should follow the main Lusaka to Ndola road (which ran past the pub).

We took off with great difficulty, only just missing the roof of the nearest building. I could see his nerves were finished, as were mine for that matter, but luckily there were no delays in getting permission to land at Ndola Airport. He made an appalling landing but at least we got down in one piece. I left him at the airport, trying to explain why we were two hours later than our flight plan from Livingstone, and turned down his offer of a return flight.

The following week I was quite happy to take the scheduled Central African Airways flight back to Livingstone. About two months later, after I learnt about the bounced cheques, I asked friends in Botswana to find out more about the pilot. They discovered that the Cessna was not yet his, as it was still being paid off on hire purchase but, before anything further could be done, I heard on the local grapevine that he had died in a plane crash.

*

It was becoming increasingly obvious that the ever-growing numbers of crocodiles being shot or trapped was beginning to affect the balance of nature.

In fact the local fishermen, mainly Africans, were complaining that their catches of small fish like bream were being affected by the ever-increasing numbers of barbel, a much larger fish that feeds on the bream and other small fish. Previously, the crocodiles had kept down the barbels and the smaller fish had been able to survive in larger numbers.

The Northern Rhodesia Department of Game and Fisheries became so alarmed at the situation that they brought in an expert from Britain to carry out a survey of what was happening to the fish in the two largest rivers, the Zambezi and the Kafue.

His subsequent report confirmed what had been suspected: that the ever-decreasing crocodile population was no longer sufficient to control the barbel, who were now increasing alarmingly, at the expense of the bream and other small fish that they fed on.

Stricter controls on crocodile hunting were brought in, but it was obvious that the long-term answer was to encourage crocodile breeding farms. What helped to accelerate this policy was that it was becoming increasingly difficult for the well-organised, successful hunters, like Hugh Charnaud and the Holloway brothers, to find new areas where there were still plenty of good-sized crocodiles. They were used to bringing in three hundred and fifty plus crocodile skins from each safari but the shortage of reptiles meant that they were having to look farther and farther afield. This added considerably to the cost of the safari. They had to go to neighbouring countries to the north, where hunting was becoming more and more dangerous as the chaos caused by independence was getting worse the whole time. Inevitably, with Zambia's independence in 1964, the number of crocodile skins being brought in by European hunters decreased dramatically.

This drying up of my sources had brought about my move to Livingstone before independence, as supplies of skins from African hunters were not affected and increasing numbers were coming in from Barotseland. As I distributed my crocodile hooks to the local hunters, I found the number of skins began increasing without any of the competition that now prevailed in Lusaka and Bulawayo, the main centres for the dwindling number of crocodile skins that were coming in.

Today there are crocodile breeding farms spread all over central and South Africa. Victoria Falls and Lake Kariba are the main areas, with two or three in Natal and Botswana. I have already mentioned the Okavango Swamps crocodile farm of John Seaman. Natal's crocodile farms are a more recent event and, shortly before I left South Africa in 1983, I spent a whole day with a friend, Peter Watson, on the site of his proposed crocodile farm near

Maidstone, going over his plans. I was able to put him in touch with John Seaman, so he could get supplies of crocodile eggs and baby crocodiles flown in from Maun in Botswana.

Peter opened his crocodile farm to the public in 1984. It is near Maidstone, on Natal's north coast road to Kwazulu, an easy half-hour drive from Durban and a very pleasant way to start a trip to Natal's Kwazulu game reserves at Umfolozi, Hluhluwe, St Lucia, Mkushi and Ndumu.

★

Few people outside the crocodile business have any idea of the cost and work involved in organising a successful crocodile hunting trip and, even in the early days, it was a pretty expensive business – and with no guarantee of success. There were many risks in the business and even the most successful hunters had some trips that were a complete failure.

At least one long-wheel base Land Rover and a large trailer were needed to transport the crocodile hunting boat, as lorries were normally unable to get into the hunting area without getting stuck or, worse, breaking down. The boat itself had to be constructed of strong metal and have at least two 25–30 hp outboard engines.

Bags of salt for preserving the skins had to be carried as well as, of course, rifles, ammunition, gaffs and all the camping equipment. Space also had to be allowed for at least five or six Africans, who had to be skilled at their jobs. The ordinary local Africans, if there were any in the hunting area, could be used for unskilled jobs like manhandling the crocodile skins, but recovering the carcasses was an acquired skill.

The most difficult job of all was gaffing the crocodile after it had been shot, and making sure that the belly was not damaged, either by this process or while it was being dragged into the hunting boat. Gaffing was quite an art in fast-flowing rivers like the Zambezi and Kafue, and the success of the hunt depended to a great extent on the recovery rate of the African gaffers. Even in the lakes, there were only two or three minutes to secure the creature before it sank, so an awful lot depended on the skill of the Africans.

The same sort of skill was required by the Africans who handled the skinning and preserving of the crocodile skins after they had been brought ashore. Just one cut in the belly part of the crocodile meant an enormous loss to the hunter and it was essential that skins with as little damage as possible be sent overseas.

It was mainly the East African blacks who handled the skilled work, as they had a lot more experience than the Rhodesian Africans. A bonus was always paid to them, based on the number of crocodiles they skinned and cleaned without any damage and, once this became understood, it was quite remarkable how quickly the quality of the crocodile skins improved!

Most European hunters used a strong hunting lamp that worked off a battery, which meant a portable battery charger had to be taken along as well for night hunting. The light was reflected in the crocodile's eyes in the water, so only a head shot was possible, which avoided damage to the belly skin. It was easy to calculate the size of the crocodile from the width between its eyes.

Later, in Livingstone, when I was getting increasing numbers of crocodile skins from African hunters in Barotseland, I experienced the same trouble with damaged skins as I had done in the early days in Tanganyika. As had been the case there, a lot of unnecessary damage in the smaller skins was caused by the animals being speared to death to save ammunition. It was, again, difficult to get across to the African hunters why a skin with a hole in the belly was worth less than half of the value of the same skin with no hole. Again, of course, the bonus system ensured that quality improved in the end. In the meantime, I was lucky to be able to get rid of some of the damaged skins to Hollanders, and to some of the Indian dealers in Livingstone.

Chapter Four

Salisbury, Livingstone and Ndola

Although everything was going reasonably well with the crocodile business, I had some personal problems over my plans to remarry in Northern Rhodesia. My wife-to-be, Eve, had to get her divorce finalised before we could marry and, with things getting more than a little awkward in Lusaka, I decided it would be better for all concerned if I made a temporary move to Salisbury. My business could be run easily from almost anywhere in the Rhodesias.

In many ways I thoroughly enjoyed the Salisbury interlude, during which I used a central telephone answering service to handle all my business calls while I had a good look around Southern Rhodesia. I hardly knew the country at all as, before moving to Northern Rhodesia, I had been there only once; when I flew to Salisbury for a couple of days, to buy a large load of crocodile skins.

We were in Ndola when Eve's divorce came through, and we got married there, but not long afterwards we had to start making plans to move down to Livingstone as the political scene in Northern Rhodesia, especially the Copperbelt, got worse.

I knew only too well how completely unpredictable all black-ruled countries were, and that we might have to move again – over the border into Southern Rhodesia (only a few miles from Livingstone) – at very short notice.

Looking back now, I can see we were very lucky to have been given about six very good business years in Livingstone before things became absolutely impossible in Zambia and we had to leave.

★

Salisbury became one my favourite towns in the Rhodesias, clean and small enough to have no traffic problems in those days, early in the 1960s. Everything revolved around the Meikles Hotel and its huge lounge, with the old-fashioned cane furniture that was so popular in hotels all over the British Empire. It was seldom that you went in there without meeting someone you knew.

When we wanted a change of scenery, our favourite places were the very central BESL club, or one of the other ex-service clubs. Pubs in the suburbs also abounded and one of my favourites was the Quorn Hotel.

The Rhodesians in those days were very much like the South Africans I had met in Durban when our troopship called there en route to India, and their hospitality, especially to ex-servicemen, was very reminiscent of my days in Tanganyika. I stayed with ex-service friends until I found a convenient central flat for what would be my last interlude of bachelor life before I remarried.

Life as a single man was pretty hectic, and the pace did begin to tell: I wasn't as young as in my Cairo and London days just after the war. So I enjoyed visiting the Eastern Highlands (via Umtali), the Kariba Dam and Wankie Game Reserve, in between my working trips for crocodile skins.

★

One of my girlfriends, Lesley, had the same kind of colonial background as I did. Her parents had also worked on the west coast of Africa before retiring and buying a fruit farm in Sussex or Kent (I forget which). Her sister had married a sugar farmer in the Hippo Valley area of the Fort Victoria region. The farms there were small by African standards, but well irrigated, and individual white farmers had developed each farm from scratch. It was Ray Stockhill (later knighted) who had masterminded and developed the sugar industry in the region.

Lesley and I drove down from Salisbury and arrived after dark. It was quite a job finding the farm at night, as it was set among the sugar fields, and the high cane didn't help visibility. It was difficult to spot the farm signs on the dirt roads, too, because of the amount of dust around. However, with the help of a friendly local farmer, we eventually made it.

We spent a fascinating few days there, and I liked everything about the place, as it was very reminiscent of Tanganyikan farm life. The large thatched house, with its high ceilings and verandas, brought back happy memories, but I kept quiet about my misgivings for their future. Lesley's brother-in-law was a South African and I often wondered, later, what had become of them. Two thirds of the white population left Rhodesia after independence and, unless he made an early departure, he would have lost just about everything. Anyone leaving Zimbabwe and settling in South Africa could take with them only $1,000 (Zimbabwean) of assets or money – not quite what the 1979 Lancaster House Agreement had in mind.

So you could say that the few thousand white farmers who have stayed in Zimbabwe are economic prisoners. With all the shortages and mismanagement so typical of newly independent African countries, the remaining farmers still manage to produce more than fifty per cent of Zimbabwe's food and tobacco.

*

What always surprises me about Rhodesia (and most of Africa, for that matter) is how little we know about its history before the arrival of explorers like David Livingstone in the middle of the last century. Nothing brought this home to me more vividly than my first visit to the Zimbabwe ruins.

I am convinced that the ancient city of Zimbabwe was built by people who had some connection with Pharaonic Egypt, probably Arabs or one of the African tribes that mixed with the Hamites and still have a Hamitic language, such as the Hausa of northern Nigeria – who, we know, moved there from the Sudan.

On a personal note, I find it interesting that my father spent most of his colonial career in northern Nigeria and it is recorded in the Nigeria staff lists that, in 1932, he passed his intermediate standard language examination in Hausa. I know that, if he were still alive, he would be very interested in my theories about the Hausa – or some similar Hamitic tribe.

It is known that there were metal-working skills in the Zimbabwe region centuries ago, probably also learnt in the days of the Pharaohs, and this explains why the people who had established themselves in Zimbabwe travelled down the east coast of Africa: they were in search of gold and other precious metals. None of the local Bantu tribes had ever built in stone before, so the stone ruins must have been the work of people who originated outside the region.

That there were ancient gold mines in Rhodesia is well known and, from very ancient times, there were tales of Ophir and King Solomon's mines. It is accepted that these unknown people came up the Zambezi River and, even though the jungles have long since destroyed all traces of buildings, it is probable that stone forts were constructed en route as staging posts for those taking the gold out to Egypt or Arabia.

Zimbabwe was almost certainly the capital of these outsiders, and no one knows why or when they left (if, indeed, they did leave). All we have today are the very impressive stone buildings of the Zimbabwe Ruins: but they are undeniable proof that there was a sophisticated civilisation here prehistory.

In Wilbur Smith's enthralling novel *The Sun Bird*, the local Bantu are motivated by greed and jealousy. They rise up and destroy the 'gold people', only to find that they haven't the necessary skills or organisational ability to carry on the gold-mining business. This theme is typical of real-life Africa. Maybe something of the sort happened in the original Zimbabwe, as it is happening again today.

Certainly there is a parallel in what was allowed to happen in black-ruled Africa after the war, when the Africans were encouraged by the communists and socialists to rise up and destroy most of what the white pioneers and settlers had built up during their hundred years or so in Africa. What they could not destroy now lies rusting away all over black Africa as, no matter how much UN, Church or other charity aid money they receive, they cannot organise and run things without those white men, the majority of whom they have driven out of Africa.

★

Some years after we had been forced to move to South Africa, I witnessed a modern scenario that reminded me vividly of my thoughts at the Zimbabwe Ruins: we were travelling on the Rand and saw hordes of African miners streaming out of one of Transvaal's gold mines at the end of their shift.

The gold mine was in the area of the Golden Arc, which stretches from Welkom to Evander – what a prize that would make for the Communists and the ANC! South Africa has sixty-three per cent of all the gold reserves in the West and, no matter what the Communists say about reforms that are being forced on them by their economic failures, the dangers to South Africa are still there.

Few in the West are fully aware of what the pioneers achieved, not only in South Africa, but all over Africa. It is a criminal waste that, through ignorance and communist and socialist propaganda, the West has allowed most of the colonial progress to be destroyed by Africans since the end of World War II.

I am just as proud of my mother's South African connections (her father was at the siege of Kimberley) as I am of my father's colonial service in the Nigerian administration. There is absolutely no doubt in my mind that those of us with such close African connections have to do much, much more to counter the communist conspiracy and the Western media's very biased reporting of events in South Africa.

There is, without any doubt, a great deal of largely silent support for South Africa in Britain – especially from the sixteen million ex-servicemen, women and their families. It must always be remembered that two million South Africans are of British descent. Many of these are ex-servicemen, like my cousin, Jack Cordingley White, who served with the South African Air Force in the last war and was awarded a DFC.

It is not widely known that about a million South Africans still have the right to a British passport – a very unwelcome fact to many British politicians, especially Labour MPs.

But a major problem, even in South Africa, is the very real lack understanding about just how bad things are in black-ruled Africa, where democracy is unknown. The smartly dressed Wa-Benzis, who are seen on Western television so eloquently pleading in English, French or Portuguese for more aid money to maintain their Mercedes-Benz lifestyle, in no way represent the real Africans. While they posture in the West, ninety-nine per cent of the ordinary Africans starve, because of the gullibility and ignorance of the West and the incredible incompetence and greed of the Wa-Benzis.

It is, therefore, vital that those who have spent most of their lives in Africa should write books giving a true and unbiased account of the lives there and how conditions have changed with independence. There are, at present, far too many books by authors (mostly of the left in British politics) who, after only a few weeks in Africa (often they are journalists or politicians who are there as guests of the ruling regime), look on themselves as experts on African affairs and give highly biased accounts that can only mislead their readers or audiences in the West.

I estimate that the two million South Africans of British descent have, on average, about four relatives each living here. If I am right, that makes a total of about eight million people in Britain who have links of kith and kin with South Africa, although a great many of them have not kept in touch in the past. In view of the communist conspiracy against South Africa, how important it is that these family links between Britain and South Africa should be revived, maintained and strengthened – with the maximum of publicity possible – to counter the continual anti-South Africa propaganda of the communists and socialists, through the very biased and misleading reporting of the Western media.

I have found that, since helping to start the Truth About Africa League (TAAL) in early 1986, there has been a marked improvement in the awareness of our MPs about the debt owed to South Africa and her servicemen and women of two world wars. Details of those killed and wounded were sent to politicians.

In March 1988, when certain left-wing Labour MPs wanted the Union Jack removed from the South African flag, TAAL's letter to all MPs made ex-service disgust and anger quite clear at this insult to their South African comrades-in-arms.

The service links, built up in the bloody battles of both world wars, are extremely important and more must be done to ensure that they are strengthened. These efforts must be combined with attempts to promote the younger generation's family links all over the old Commonwealth: Canada, Australia, New Zealand and South Africa.

★

We knew anything could happen in newly independent African countries and now, with a family, we wanted to be near the Rhodesian border. We had no intention of leaving Zambia in the way the Belgian settlers had been forced to leave Katanga – in a hurry and being able to take only those possessions that could be packed into their cars.

Our decision to move to Livingstone proved a wise one in more ways than we could have imagined, because Zambia soon developed the same kind of food shortages as other newly independent African countries. What had been taken for granted in the well-run days of the colonial era changed completely due to African incompetence and corruption. Even a simple matter like importing various foods became a complex matter, with bribery being necessary before an import licence could be obtained.

It wasn't long before we were forced to make regular buying trips to Bulawayo to buy our food supplies. In Rhodesia, even after UDI in 1965, there were no shortages, except for petrol, which had to rationed due to the British naval blockade outside Beira.

★

It is difficult to find unbiased books about what really happened in the Rhodesias and Africa in any of Westminster's libraries – and this is probably true all over Britain. But it is very easy to find slanted accounts.

One fairly recent (1986) addition to the plethora of books I dislike is *The Road to Zimbabwe – 1890–1980*. This is no different to all the others, although the author says in his introduction that it is not an account of black nationalism or white racialism. I find it impossible to relate his account of events to what was the reality for those of us who actually lived there. There is not even a hint of the role played by the socialists in Europe, and the far left of the British Labour Party, in furthering communist aims in the Rhodesias and in so many other African countries.

Perhaps this is due to the fact that the author, Mr Anthony Verrier, was a senior associate member of St Anthony's College, Oxford, from 1967 to 1974. He is now a journalist and broadcaster, whose knowledge of Africa appears to have been gained when he attended the August 1979 Lusaka Commonwealth Conference. Later he witnessed something of the events that led to Zimbabwe's independence.

The reader is, therefore, advised to compare this academic's account with that of two other academics, who both spent over twenty-five years in Africa – Dr Karl Borgin and Kathleen Corbett. I refer again, of course, to *The Destruction of a Continent*. I find it significant that this book is not readily available in Westminster's libraries and has to be specially ordered.

*

The harsh fact about Africa over the past thirty or forty years is that most of the newly independent countries, including Zimbabwe, have become incapable of ruling themselves. Whatever authors like Verrier, the Western media, the Commonwealth and the UN say, that fact will have to be faced soon.

Look at Liberia, which became independent in 1847. The elite in the capital, Monrovia, were mainly freed slaves from America who, in 1847, easily took over control from the locals. More recently, Sergeant Doe promoted himself to general when he took over in a military coup in 1980, but he was killed in the civil war which has virtually destroyed the whole country – it never had sufficient stability for real development to be possible.

This is a good example of why it is so important that the truth about Africa be told: so that the same tragic mistakes that were made in the Rhodesias during federation are not repeated in South Africa, where they would be on a much larger scale.

One thing which must be clearly understood is that there was nothing spontaneous about the civil unrest in the federation. It was mainly confined to Nyasaland and the Copperbelt and was carefully planned by the communists and their socialist and far-left allies in the West, so that the Western media could give the impression that there was a great deal of African opposition to the federation. This was completely untrue – most of the population had no interest at all in politics. Kaunda's UNIP deliberately caused the trouble on the Copperbelt and Banda's Malawi Congress Party did the same in Nyasaland.

The outcome of a continuing federation would have been a strong multi-racial economy in central Africa that would have brought peace and stability to the whole area. Instead, we have three little tinpot countries which are completely dependent on outside aid, and which are going backwards instead of forwards.

*

People like Verrier will, of course, never give any credit to Rhodesian politicians like Huggins and Welensky, even though it was they who had the foresight to push for the building of the Kariba Dam on the Zambezi. It is easy to understand the fury of Welensky at the gutlessness of the British politicians, who were afraid to upset the very vocal far left and their communist connections.

After the shameful Suez debacle in 1956, any chance of Britain taking a firm stand on Africa was finished, as was the federation, and Macmillan's 'wind of change' speech (in February 1960) only reflected this change of policy which, as history has shown, turned out so disastrously for most of newly independent Africa.

It should be noted that Mr Verrier, with his Oxford University background, likes to mention in his book how provincial everything was in Salisbury (now Harare) and how parochial he and the British politicians found all Rhodesian politicians, including Huggins and Welensky.

British politicians, and people like Verrier, forget that it was just such provincials, not the Whitehall Establishment, who suffered extreme hardship and took incredible risks, fighting (and often dying) to build up the greatest empire that the world has ever known.

The Whitehall Establishment, and bureaucrats everywhere, would be wise to remember that British provincials once rose up to protect their hard-won liberties in Britain. If Cromwell had not succeeded in curbing the Royal Establishment of his time, it is very doubtful whether the world would later have had the great benefits which arose from *Pax Britannica*.

It would be very unwise to underestimate the damage that Waldheim, Ramphal, and others like them, have done in Africa, and to appreciate the fact that this damage is not restricted to Africa. One tragic event in London in the

Eighties should have brought home just how thin the veneer of civilisation in Britain has become. I refer to the appalling incident when a largely immigrant London mob brutally murdered a British policeman. PC Keith Blakelock was hacked and stabbed to death: there were over fifty wounds on his body! Personally, I found it all too tragically reminiscent of how Mandela's ANC murders those of its fellow Africans who do not agree with its communist aims.

It would be as well to remember that up to the mid-Sixties Britain had only about forty to fifty thousand of these immigrants. It is mainly due to the far-left part of the Labour Party that there are now about five million of them – mostly of alien religions and with no real understanding of the British way of life.

Whitehall was quite prepared to spend millions of pounds on the Commission for Racial Equality, but offered no reward money for information leading to the arrest of PC Blakelock's killers. If money had been offered, the violent immigrants might have got the message that they could not murder London's police with impunity. I believe the politicians, who have created the present situation where the incidence of violent crime is rapidly rising, should bring back the death penalty for murders of policemen.

Nothing shows better the contempt of such left-wing councils as Haringey for those British policemen who keep law and order in today's multiracial London than an article in the *Daily Express* of 15th October, 1990: 'Fraud probe dropped – Broadwater £100,000 cannot be recovered':

> A probe over £100,000 given by a left-wing council to a group trying to free convicted police killers has been called off.
>
> Fraud Squad detectives have told Haringey Council they cannot find out what happened to the money – despite a six-month inquiry – because so few records were kept by the Broadwater Farm Defence Campaign.
>
> And councillors have been warned that civil action to recover the money is unlikely to succeed because of the lack of receipts.
>
> The campaign, which still receives money from the council, was set up to demand the release of Winston Silcott and two others convicted of killing PC Keith Blakelock during the Broadwater riot in North London five years ago.
>
> But last year the District Auditor recommended police should be called in when council bookkeepers discovered money had been handed over without any checks. Cash and loans had simply been given

> to individuals and large, unexplained payments made for airline tickets and home decorating.
>
> Council leader Toby Harris admitted last night:
>
> 'We simply don't know what happened to the money. The cash may all have been used entirely properly but it is not explained in accounts.'
>
> The missing money was dished out between 1987 and 1989. This year the council is giving the campaign £47,000 and Mr Harris said grants were rigorously checked.
>
> But Tory Andrew Mitchell said: 'It's scandalous. I am convinced that not enough has been done to identify the guilty parties. Many worthwhile charities are being starved while this campaign puts money to unknown uses.'

This is just one horrifying example of how law and order is breaking down, and the blame has to be placed where it belongs – with the politicians and the bureaucrats.

Since the 1960s, the politicians in Britain have appeared to be doing their best to turn London into an alien, polyglot city, where one is more likely to hear Arabic or Hindi spoken than cockney.

London is now rapidly becoming as dangerous as New York, where, all too frequently, law-abiding citizens are murdered for little more than their wristwatches. In many areas of London half the population (the women) feel unsafe and are afraid to go out alone at night, as muggings and sex crimes are becoming more and more commonplace.

More and more ex-servicemen who remember Britain's 'finest hour' and who helped bring about Britain's victory in World War II, are beginning to wonder how long Britain's provincials (who still make up the majority of the British people) will tolerate the present ever-deteriorating situation.

During the Gulf War, many Muslims made it quite clear that their loyalty lay with their fellow Muslims in Iraq, not with Britain. Many other immigrant Muslims were on Britain's side, of course, but it is worth pausing to consider whether that would have been the case had Iraq's aggression been against a Christian country rather than another Islamic state.

No one except a complete fool could believe that our politicians were unaware of the possible future dangers of religious and racial mixing on a large scale, but the lessons of Ireland and the IRA were ignored. The same is true of the Jews who, over the centuries, have been persecuted all over Europe. Only one Conservative politician had the guts to warn the nation of the folly of allowing millions of immigrants into Britain. In his famous 'rivers of blood' speech, Enoch Powell forecast the problems that would arise if the newcomers failed to integrate. He was correct, but his only reward was to be branded a racialist.

It was all very reminiscent of the way Winston Churchill had been treated in the 1930s, when he tried to warn the nation of the dangers of appeasing Hitler and Mussolini.

Nothing shows better the contempt of politicians for the wishes of the British people than the fact that a referendum on the issue of immigration was never held, although the whole lifestyle of the nation was being changed.

The politicians' attitude becomes completely incomprehensible when one considers that many of them must have realised that, in most of the trouble spots of the world, the conflicts are based on religious and racial issues, for instance in the Middle East, Israel, India, Cyprus, Sudan, Ethiopia and the Philippines – to name but a few.

There is a limit to the strains that can be put on any society. As they read about the ever-growing crime rate and the ever-increasing number of incidents caused by racial tension (which the Commission for Racial Equality love to publicise), the ordinary people must wonder what has gone wrong and where it is all going to end.

The answer is simple. It is the politicians and bureaucrats who are to blame, because they refuse to face the facts – they suffer from the same sort of selective blindness that caused the successive tragedies in Africa after the end of World War II.

*

There are many people in Britain who, like me, believe the only sensible approach towards immigration would have been to continue a policy of slow assimilation – a policy which had worked successfully over the centuries as Britain had absorbed hundreds of thousands of refugees and immigrants, and they had fitted into the religious and social life of Britain without difficulty.

Opening the floodgates to alien cultures and religions is another matter and has an entirely different effect. When immigrants arrive a few at a time they make a real effort to integrate. When they arrive in crowds, however, instead of trying to fit in with the existing order, the newcomers cling to each other, gather in the same area and retain their old customs, refusing to adapt to their new environment and creating ghettos. Many do not even bother to learn the language of their new home.

That the whole fabric of Western civilisation is under threat cannot be disputed, and nowhere is this malaise better illustrated than in the capital of 'the land of the free'. Every day in the streets of Washington, DC, within sight of the US government buildings, drug-related murders are taking place, and the forces of law and order are powerless to stop them. Decent citizens do not venture on to the city streets after sunset and there are some no-go areas even in daylight hours.

★

Is it any wonder that those of us with years of experience in Africa (unfortunately there are far too few of us returning to Britain), who actually witnessed the virtually crime-free lives of tribal Africans whether in Tanzania, Barotseland or Botswana, now question the values of the West and its rapidly disintegrating crime-ridden civilisation?

The urban, politically-orientated, Western-educated Africans that the Western leaders meet represent less than one per cent of the African population. Since most of these African gentlemen have been well indoctrinated with the teachings of Marx and Lenin by their friends in the West, it is hardly surprising that so many Western writers, like Verrier, tend merely to reflect these views.

It is what authors like Mr Verrier leave out that is so telling for those who know the full story. President Nyerere of Tanzania, for instance, is regarded by Verrier as the pivotal figure among the African presidents at the 1979 Commonwealth Conference in Lusaka and Nyerere's disastrous agricultural policy, based on communist collectivism, is dismissed in a few words by Verrier: 'Nyerere was troubled by the collapse of his economic experiment.'

At the 1979 Commonwealth Conference there were twelve African countries that had been given independence by Britain in the late 1950s and early 1960s. Mr Verrier fails to mention that the financial burden of their independence is still borne by the British taxpayer. The only ones who have benefited from this situation are the new African elite, the Wa-Benzis, who have personally pocketed millions of pounds of aid money.

In this regard Mugabe is no different from any of the other African leaders – he relies heavily on Western aid, especially from Britain. When Sir Richard Attenborough approached him, seeking permission to film *Cry Freedom* in Zimbabwe, Mugabe not only granted full facilities for the filming itself, but also financed the project to the tune of five million dollars – despite the fact that Zimbabwe was, as usual, in acute financial difficulty.

It should never be forgotten that Mugabe, who was apparently so outraged by the death of one individual at the hands of the South African authorities, is the same person who was quite happy to let loose the North Korean-trained 5th Brigade on Nkomo's supporters in Matabeleland in 1982 and 1983. It will probably never be known exactly how many thousands of Matabele were murdered in cold blood but, according to reports received by the highly reputable Rhodesia Christian Group, it is probable that the figure of forty thousand is very conservative.

According to Mr Verrier's version of events, it was the British High Commission in Salisbury which, through its unhelpful attitude, was responsible for Mugabe's decision to allow the North Koreans to train his 5th Brigade of ex-Zanla troops. This would be laughable if it weren't so tragic. Genocide is now prevalent all over Africa, and has been ever since the end of the colonial era.

The Ndebele or Matabele, although numerically far fewer than the Mashona (now known as Shona), were related to the South African Zulus. They had dominated the Shona long before the days of Rhodes and the British South Africa Company. So, after Zimbabwe became independent, the Shona (Mugabe's tribe) were not slow to take revenge, by slaughtering thousands of their old enemies, the Matabele.

★

It is interesting to see the cleverness of Western socialist and communist propaganda, whereby the Western media hardly ever report on the black genocide all over Africa, but continually bring up the sixty-nine Africans who were killed in the South African township of Sharpeville in 1960. It is noticeable, however, that they seldom give the background of events that led up to the Sharpeville deaths.

The ANC and PAC were organising a series of countrywide demonstrations to get overseas publicity. One of these was about the passbooks which had to be carried at all times by all non-whites. The Africans were ordered to go to police stations all over South Africa without their passbooks and thereby invite arrest. They were to try and provoke as much trouble as possible, for the consumption of the Western media.

Despite a great deal of provocation, the police in most places managed to disperse the crowds without resorting to the use of firearms. Sadly, the policemen on duty at Sharpeville were inexperienced and unable to handle the pressure – they panicked and opened fire without waiting for orders from their senior officers.

A similar African mob had, shortly before this, run amok in Durban. They had hacked and stabbed at any policeman, white or black, who had been unfortunate enough to get in their way. If that event is remembered, it is not difficult to understand why the inexperienced policemen at Sharpeville lost their nerve. What they did was tragic, certainly, but hardly the callous massacre that is usually portrayed by the media.

★

What few in the West seem to understand is the latent savagery of Africa, or rather urban black Africa. Things in London may have been changing for the worse recently, but it must be understood that the Trafalgar Square poll tax riots were like a vicar's tea party compared to the excesses of the Mau Mau in Kenya, the Simbas in the Congo and, more recently, the ANC's necklacing of African political opponents.

The ANC's policy has not changed since the 1960s and it is still doing everything it can to undermine the authority of the South African police, with the active assistance of the Western media who, with Western socialists and the communists, have done all they can to further the aims of the ANC. Authors like Mr Verrier merely take this process of communist disinformation about Africa a stage further, in order to disguise the fact that it wasn't black nationalism that triumphed in Rhodesia but communism.

It wasn't even a simple issue of black fighting white, as Verrier tries so hard to make out. In actual fact, four out of every five soldiers fighting Mugabe's Marxist Zanu were black Rhodesians.

The loyalty of white Rhodesians to Britain was never in question. When Britain faced war with Hitler's Germany, Rhodesia (in proportion to its population) sent more volunteers to fight for Britain than any other country in the British Empire.

In the period of Bishop Abel Muzorewa's visit to the Lancaster House Conference in London (December 1979), Mugabe's Zanu was making every effort to intimidate and influence black Rhodesians. After the ceasefire on 28th December, 1979, as all Zanu forces were starting to return to Rhodesia, the campaign of intimidation was able to operate quite openly – regardless of the presence of the Commonwealth Monitoring Force and, at the end of January 1980, the Commonwealth Observer Group. Like Mr Verrier, none of these Commonwealth personnel spoke either Shona or Matabele, but a small matter like that never stopped any of them believing that they were experts on Africa, and Rhodesia in particular.

★

In the usual Marxist tradition in Africa, Mugabe's Zanu, having won the election, changed the system and now only allows one man, one vote – for the only political party: Zanu. The other parties, including Nkomo's Zapu, have been banned.

Despite millions in annual aid from Western sources (Britain alone gives both Zambia and Zimbabwe about twenty-five million pounds annually), Mugabe's Marxist Zimbabwe followed the usual African independence pattern. Kaunda had taken only a few short years to wreck the prosperous colonial economy handed to him by Britain and Mugabe is doing his best to bankrupt Zimbabwe. His 1988 budget shortage amounted to seven thousand million Zimbabwe dollars, despite the massive Western aid. It's not surprising when you consider that he was prepared to gamble five million dollars of his aid money on *Cry Freedom*.

The tragedy of Africa today is that the false prophets of socialism and communism have managed to destroy most of the progress made in colonial times.

I felt I had glimpsed something of this truth, as well as the grandeur of Africa, when I visited the Matopo Hills to see where Cecil Rhodes was buried. When Rhodes died (in 1902) the twenty-mile route from Bulawayo to his Matopos grave was lined the whole way by the Matabele, silent in their respect for a truly great man. Many of them would have remembered how, almost single-handed, he had brought an end to the Matabele rebellion in those same Matopo Hills. In 1896, Cecil Rhodes, unarmed and with only three companions, had had a meeting with the rebellious Matabele Indunas, and persuaded them to agree to end the rebellion (in which more than a hundred settlers had already been murdered), provided that he settled their grievances. This Rhodes did, after days of talks, and the Matabele rebellion ended, saving Rhodesia from a lot more bloodshed.

As I travelled around the continent, I always remembered that I, like all the other settlers and travellers, owed my safe passage in even the remotest parts of Africa to those heroes of the British Empire like Cecil Rhodes, who made *Pax Britannica* a reality for millions all over the world.

It is obvious that Western countries, especially their media, have learnt nothing from the misery, strikes and starvation that the false prophets have already caused for millions of ordinary Africans, and that they are not interested in finding a peaceful solution to South Africa's problems. In fact, it could be said that they encourage the bloodshed that has already started there.

It is these attitudes that make it so important that more unbiased books on Africa should be published relating the personal experiences of authors like Dr Karl Borgin and Kathleen Corbett. Their book inspired me to write down my own experiences in East, central and South Africa, and I hope that my book will inspire others to do the same.

There is far too little appreciation of the heroic role played by the early pioneers who helped to build the British Empire in Africa, and thus gave Africa the much-needed impetus it required to take it into the twentieth century.

This book is intended, among other things, to be a tribute to all those who played their part in making this possible: missionaries, settlers, HM's colonial servants, soldiers, policemen, traders and so on – all heroes in their way – who helped to create the British Empire in Africa and elsewhere around the world.

The false prophets would do well to remember that it is easy to destroy, but not to create, especially in Africa.

★

Much as I liked Salisbury, and Southern Rhodesia in general, I knew the time for me to return to the north was overdue, for both personal and business reasons.

Once I had fixed my personal arrangements to meet Eve at Kafue, so that we could go on together to Livingstone, all I had to do was to collect (in Salisbury) a new long-wheel base Land Rover – on Mr Oza's behalf. As well as Oza's Emporium, he ran a thriving ivory and skins export business and, on one of my trips to Livingstone, it had been agreed between us that I should work for him in developing his hides and skins business in Barotseland.

At that time no Indian businesses were allowed in Barotseland and part of our deal was that he gave me free use of the new long-wheel base Land Rover, and paid all my travelling expenses while I was in Barotseland. This agreement had fitted in with my future plans very well, although I hadn't been ready to move to Livingstone at that stage. Now I was.

I knew from reports from crocodile hunters that there was virtually no competition there, as Livingstone was still pretty much isolated from the rest of Northern Rhodesia and the distances involved, together with the state of most of the dirt roads (or, rather, rough tracks), kept most people away.

★

Eve and I settled into Livingstone quickly, and I was soon making the arrangements for my first visit to Barotseland. I remember vividly that first trip (in the early 1960s) as, in its way, it was just as exciting as some of my earlier Tanganyika and Congo trips from my farm in the Kakonko-Kibondo district. My expectations were more than fulfilled, as the whole area was almost completely undeveloped and still unspoilt, with the majestic Zambezi River never far away.

On the first stage of my journey, especially when I was on the flat areas near the Zambezi River, there was no actual road at all. I merely followed the tracks of lorries and buses – making sure I kept out of some of the worst potholes. Those, if taken at speed, could easily have broken the Land Rover's springs, especially when I was carrying a heavy load of wet-salted crocodile skins.

During the course of the trip I had to use two ferries to cross the Zambezi: one at Sesheke and the other at Senanga. I knew that, with a few detours to shoot the odd bit of game for the pot (on that first trip there were plenty of guinea fowl and other small game, mainly antelope, about), I would be lucky to reach Sesheke before dark and, when I did get there, I still had to locate the government rest house where I planned to spend the night.

★

From the Livingstone Museum and Livingstone's Library, I had learnt that the Lewanika (the king of the Lozi tribe) had met the British South Africa Company's representative, a Mr Lochner, at Sesheke late in 1889. This was at about the time that the Pioneer Column marched on Mashonaland to complete the conquest of what was to become Southern Rhodesia.

The Lozi, like a lot of other tribes, had long been troubled by the very warlike Matabele who, on several occasions, had raided and looted them. So the Lewanika was keen to obtain British protection against the Matabele.

Mr Lochner had been sent to arrange the treaty, as Rhodes's company had a royal charter to do this. In June 1890 the treaty was duly signed and one of the clauses it contained was that a British Resident should be appointed in Barotseland, to keep the peace. But these were turbulent and dangerous times and the resident magistrate in Salisbury, a Mr Hervey, who was appointed as the first British Resident in Barotseland, was killed in the Mashonaland and Matabeleland rebellions.

It was about seven years before his replacement, a Mr Coryndon, arrived in Barotseland and in 1900 the Barotseland-North Western Rhodesia Order in Council declared Barotseland to be a British Protectorate. In 1902 the final seal was put on all these arrangements, when the Lewanika visited England to attend the coronation of King Edward VII.

The treaty stayed in force until 1969, when it was arbitrarily cancelled by Zambia's President Kaunda, who renamed Barotseland the Western Province. The reason for Kaunda's action was anger caused by the support that the Lozi had given to Harry Nkumbula's opposition party, the ANC (African National Congress, but not the same organisation as South Africa's ANC), in the December 1968 election, when opposition to UNIP was still allowed.

A lot of the ANC's support came from the Southern Province and there had been violent incidents between ANC and UNIP supporters at Livingstone and elsewhere in the Province.

In typical African democratic fashion, Kaunda threatened to cancel ANC supporters' trading licences (he managed to get rid of whites in the same way: I was told in 1969 that if I did not take a Zambian passport I would not get a trading licence in 1970), and to dismiss all ANC members from the civil service and police force. In that same year, he virtually sacked Zambian Chief Justice Skinner (originally appointed by Kaunda himself) and the two remaining British judges, Evans and Wheelen, for daring to question his presidential authority. Then UNIP supporters were appointed to Zambianise the judiciary.

In 1972, having finally silenced all opposition in Zambia, this doyen of African presidents declared a 'one-party participatory democracy'. Chairman Mao must have been proud of his pupil!

*

That first night at the government rest house in Sesheke, as I sat on the veranda drinking a few tots of whisky (the surest and pleasantest way of keeping malaria away), I pondered what we owed to pioneers like Lochner, who had come to Sesheke in 1898, only about seventy years before, to sign the treaty with the Lewanika, as Cecil Rhodes's (so, indirectly, the British government's) representative, and how we all tended to take for granted everything that had been built up by the pioneers.

In all my travels in Barotseland, I never bothered to lock the door of the rest house or my Land Rover, being rightly confident that nothing would ever be stolen. What a contrast to so-called civilisation where, in all the big cities of the Western world, the crime rate rises every year: notably car theft, robbery with violence, burglary and all drug-related crimes. Can anyone wonder that those of us who really know Africa question Western values?

The tragedy of the post-war years was that Western politicians had so little knowledge of Africa that they were completely unable to tackle its problems realistically. The same applies, of course, to the UN.

In consequence, the rural African has suffered all over the continent, regardless of whether he lives in a rich country like Nigeria or a poor one like Tanzania or Mozambique.

★

As this was my first trip to Barotseland, I intended to spend at least two or three days in both Sesheke and Senanga before going on to Mongu.

It was necessary, apart from being courteous, to call on the local chiefs, who could be very helpful in promoting one's crocodile skin business in the area. Most locals made their living from fishing in the Zambezi River, where fish were still very plentiful.

Apart from the odd Coloured hunter, few of the locals had any experience of using hooks for catching crocodiles, but most of the local fishermen had stories about being bothered by the reptiles while out on the river. Indeed, when we went down to the river a few miles from Sesheke, I was very surprised to see quite a few crocodiles by day – this was now most unusual further down the Zambezi River – in areas that had been regularly visited by European crocodile hunters, right down to Feira, near the Mozambique-Rhodesia border.

In the course of conversations with local chiefs and African businessmen, it soon became clear that one man controlled most of the business in the area, even though he lived on the other side of the Zambezi River, at Katima Mulilo in the Caprivi Strip, which was administered by a South African district commissioner. In those halcyon days, no one bothered with borders and it was possible to drive in and out at will. Old Man Finaulty had trekked up there from South Africa in the days of the ox wagon.

He was indeed a character, one of the pioneers, known all over Barotseland and Northern Rhodesia. He was away on my first visit but, over the years, I got to know him well. He was extremely hospitable and I spent many a night at his place later, after we returned to Livingstone before Zambia got its independence in 1964.

There was hardly any business activity in the area in which Old Man Finaulty was not involved. He had a very well-stocked general store and a butchery, as well as a string of African stores in the districts on both sides of the Zambezi. There were also a small sawmill and a very thriving hides and skins business. Amazingly he ran all the different businesses himself, as he was a bachelor. Later he was joined by a cousin, Doug Finaulty, and Doug's wife.

There was an important Wenela (an organisation which arranged African contract labour for the South African mines) staging post with quite a number of European recruiting staff, and this, of course, brought in a considerable amount of business for Finaulty.

One thing I have never forgotten is the pack of dogs that Finaulty kept outside his house at night. On one of my later Barotseland trips I had decided to try the alternative route to Katima Mulilo, via Chobe in Botswana. A few drinks and lunch at the Chobe River Hotel had delayed my departure and I didn't arrive at Finaulty's place until well after dark. When I got out of the Land Rover, and even though I had left the headlights on, I was immediately surrounded by his snarling pack of dogs. Deciding discretion was the better part of valour, I got back into the Land Rover very quickly and, until Finaulty came out himself and called them off, they wouldn't let me through.

Evidently there were quite a few Wenela lorries, with urban African drivers, who passed by frequently carrying Africans to the Wenela camp, and they all knew he handled large sums in cash. His store had been robbed once, but the thieves very wisely kept well away from Finaulty's house – and I don't blame them, having seen his fearsome pack of dogs in action! After that visit, I always tried to arrive in daylight.

*

It was on the first trip that I met some men who had been hunting in the border area between Barotseland, the Caprivi Strip and Angola. After hearing their glowing descriptions of the amount of game that they had seen, I decided to follow the route they had taken.

It was only a rough track, and it was sometimes difficult to know whether you were in Barotseland or the Caprivi Strip, especially when you were following herds of game. Not that it mattered in those days, as it was long before South African troops moved up to Katima Mulilo and movements on both sides of the border were curtailed. I never saw another vehicle in the area at all, and only occasional Africans.

In fact, the only things to worry about, in certain parts, were the tsetse flies, which were pretty fierce and hungry.

★

Later, after moving back to Livingstone, I met a representative of one of the tobacco companies (BAT, I think) who had visited Sesheke and heard about a load of ivory just over the Angolan border. If I had known how difficult it was going to be to get there, I don't think I would have gone.

Anyway, we had to leave the Land Rover in the bush while we took a trip in a heavily laden African canoe, in which it was impossible to move, for fear of capsising. The journey lasted well over an hour and we could see plenty of crocodiles lurking in the reeds as we went by. I have never been so glad to set foot on dry land again!

It was a pretty wild part of Angola, but we stayed very comfortably in the Portuguese government outpost for a day or two while we talked business. The Portuguese had proper boats, so I made it a condition of the deal that they should deliver the ivory to the Caprivi Strip, Sesheke or Livingstone. I certainly wasn't going to push my luck too much by doing the return trip in an overloaded African canoe!

Because of the fascination of the area, and the distances involved, I invariably stayed longer in a district than I had anticipated before leaving Livingstone. Looking back now, I'm not surprised that Mr Oza, back in Livingstone, sometimes got a bit exasperated at the lack of news from my end. When I returned to Mongu, I often found telegrams from him asking for news of my progress.

★

Despite Kaunda's many promises to develop Barotseland, the new West Road from Lusaka to Mongu was still not finished when we left Zambia at the end of 1969, but it was one of the few that could be used all year round. Most of the roads in Barotseland were usable only in the dry season and a Land Rover was an absolute necessity at other times. In some sandy areas where tracks ran near to the river it was necessary to use sand mats to get through, as it was not unusual for them to have been so badly churned up by heavy lorries that not even a four-wheel drive Land Rover could get a proper grip in the soft sand.

It was also, of course, absolutely essential to carry plenty of water and food at all times. In the event of a major breakdown, it was sometimes necessary to send an African on foot to get help and, as that could entail him walking a considerable distance, it could be two or three days before help arrived.

The road to Senanga, and then on to Mongu, was normally in much better condition than other stretches of the road. The most difficult part was north from Mongu to Balavale, as very little traffic used this route beyond Kalabo – I almost always had to use a compass on the final leg. In Kalabo there was an independent European trader, one of the very few allowed by the Lewanika. Elsewhere in Barotseland, Sussman Bros & Wolfson, a South African firm whose local head office was in Livingstone, had a virtual monopoly on the retail trade.

Most of the Sussman stores had African managers, except in Mongu, where they had several European staff. These not only ran their large Mongu store and butchery, but were responsible for supplying and checking on the smaller stores spread all over the north of Barotseland. Head office in Livingstone looked after the stores in the south.

Before we left Zambia, at the end of 1969, there was already talk of Indeco (Zambia Industrial Development Corporation), taking over Sussman Bros & Wolfson's business in Zambia and Barotseland, as Kaunda started the same sort of disastrous policy as his friend Julius Nyerere of Tanzania: African socialism (really Marxism in disguise). Kaunda called it 'African humanism', and *The Quotations of Chairman Mao* was being distributed all over Zambia.

★

Senanga was an attractive little place, but it soon became obvious that Mongu, with the Lewanika nearby at Lealui, dominated most of the business in the north. Sesheke, because of its position near to the Caprivi Strip's Katima Mulilo, dominated most of the business in the south. Mongu was, of course, much bigger than Sesheke, and boasted a very pleasant European club. Cars (Central African Road Services) had a large depot there, with a bus and transport service that ran people and goods to Lusaka and the Copperbelt.

A visit to the Lewanika was obligatory for all Europeans visiting Barotseland. When I went to see him I was wearing a reasonably respectable safari suit and scarf, and I was somewhat surprised to find him in formal British morning clothes – even more surprisingly, he seemed completely unaffected by the hot weather. Tea and biscuits were served and he was very interested in the latest prices of ivory, as he controlled most of the hunting that went on in Barotseland.

In fact, if any of the Lewanika's Lozi subjects shot an elephant in Barotseland, by tradition one tusk had to be handed over to the Lewanika or his representative. Also by tradition, leopards are considered royal game, as they are in most parts of tribal Africa, and the skin had to be handed over to the Lewanika.

That this traditional way of life continued for about seventy-five years after Barotseland became a British Protectorate is a great credit to Britain. Both Queen Victoria's British Resident and Queen Elizabeth II's British Resident must have witnessed the same thrilling spectacle: the annual move of the Lewanika and his staff, by royal barges, from the palace on the Zambezi flats shortly before the Zambezi River flooded the whole area, as it does each year.

British television recently recorded this annual move, so viewers will have learnt something of the pageantry of African tribal life, which is now being so tragically destroyed all over Africa by the socialists and communists, who wish to destroy all the old tribal traditions, because they see them as a threat to the Marxist philosophy.

It is to be hoped that, with the recent collapse of the Soviet Empire and the end of the Cold War between the two superpowers, it will be possible to save what remains of the tribal traditions.

*

The Zambian elections gave a very good indication of how the new socialist autocratic African leaders, like Kaunda, would act when they were opposed in a democratic election.

In Zambia's second election, in 1968 (it took President Kaunda eight years to turn Zambia into a one-party state), the Lewanika's Lozi people in Barotseland made it quite clear what they thought of Kaunda's UNIP, with its bunch of mainly urban Africans.

Even when UNIP mounted a special campaign in Barotseland to get more support there, using the full force of its powerful political machine and money, it was able to win only twenty per cent of the vote in Barotseland. Out of approximately one hundred seats in Zambia, Barotseland was given ten seats and Kaunda's UNIP won only two of them – Harry Nkumbula's opposition party, ANC, won the other eight. In Zambia as a whole that percentage was reversed and UNIP obtained roughly eighty per cent of the seats, but Kaunda was not happy to have such a large opposition party.

He cancelled the treaty with Barotseland that Britain had signed some eighty years before and renamed the Barotseland region 'Western Province'.

Such actions are typical of African tyrants in the post-colonial era, who pay lip-service to Western-style democracy but actually treat it as a joke.

Britain's reaction to Kaunda's outrageous behaviour was also typical: almost complete silence! In the continuing farce of today's Commonwealth, we allow the tyrants who rule countries like Nigeria, Zimbabwe, India and Pakistan, to criticise any support that is given to South Africa over sanctions, while we continue to fill their begging bowls with millions of pounds of annual aid.

The time is surely long overdue for British taxpayers to tell the government that enough is enough. We should make it clear that we expect action to be taken at the UN, and within the Commonwealth, to stop all the Third World tyrants, who seem to think that they have the right to bad-mouth Britain while happily accepting millions of pounds of aid money from us every year.

Sometimes it is very difficult to understand why it was necessary to appease such tyrants, even given the excuse of the Cold War. Now that appears to be a thing of the past, it is time to deliver the message that we have had enough – and the sooner that message is given to all the Third World tyrants the better it will be for everybody in the West.

★

I always enjoyed my trips to Mongu (which reminded me of my early years in Mwanza), especially when it was possible to include some wild duck shooting – as it was on that first visit. Soon, however, with business calling, I had to complete the final leg of my trip: to Balavale.

It was only then that I realised I had considerably underestimated the difficulties. I certainly hadn't expected the road to be as bad as it was – on some stretches it disappeared almost entirely – and I was very glad I had a new Land Rover in tip-top condition. Its staying power in four-wheel drive was tested most of the way from Kalabo to Balavale.

It was more than fortunate that, at the insistence of a Mongu friend, I had borrowed his sand mats. Without them, I would most certainly have been in a lot of trouble. After that first trip I purchased my own mats, and never set off without them.

I began to wonder how Mr Oza would react when he saw the condition of his new Land Rover. It had been impossible to avoid scratches to the bodywork and one of the tyres was badly cut when I had to negotiate one of several river beds which had been repaired with loose stones. The journey was an experience I enjoyed, but I was still glad to arrive at Balavale without any really serious mishaps.

Balavale was an interesting little place near the Angolan border and, with the increasing chaos and dangers of travelling in Katanga and other parts of the Congo in the early 1960s, it was obviously well worth my while to investigate the possibilities of entering Angola via the road from the Copperbelt to Balavale.

At first the Portuguese at the Angolan border post were not very friendly, as they had recently had some trouble with Rhodesian crocodile hunters. I gathered it was something to do with them trying to smuggle out ivory and crocodile skins via a bush track.

When I returned with a bottle of whisky, to help smooth things over, they were more relaxed, and introduced me to some Portuguese hunters, who were also visiting them. These hunters were very interested in finding out what our ivory and crocodile rates were like and it transpired that the prices we were paying were much higher than they could get in Angola or from the Balavale dealers.

It was obviously going to take time to organise a way of doing business with them, however, as it was only possible to collect their crocodile skins from well inside Angola. Otherwise our dealings would upset the Balavale crocodile skin dealers, especially Serrano, a Portuguese who had the biggest store in Balavale, as well as handling a lot of the crocodile business. I had hopes of buying skins from him in the future, as well as from Dick Bailie (who also operated from Balavale) and I knew they would not take very kindly to my buying skins from some of their local Portuguese hunters. So I decided that it would be wiser to postpone any action for the time being but that, in a few months, I would organise a trip into Angola and take the matter further.

All too soon it was time to start the return journey to Livingstone.

As I was so many days overdue, I had to make much shorter stops at Mongu, Senanga and Sesheke on the way back and I must say that, after all the hazards of the trip, I was glad to get back to Livingstone without any serious damage to the Land Rover.

I don't think Mr Oza ever fully appreciated the kind of battering that even a Land Rover had to take on a journey right across Barotseland, from Livingstone in the south to Balavale in the north. Over the next few months he was to get quite a lot of extra business from my Barotseland visits, but I can still remember his face when I eventually arrived back in Livingstone after that first trip and he saw the state of his new long-wheel base Land Rover, which now looked far from new. It was an accepted fact in Barotseland that the life of a Land Rover, even one carefully driven, was about two years or, with luck, three years – after that it was wise to get a replacement.

I made many more journeys across Barotseland, but none ever had quite the charm of that first memorable trip, when everything was new to me.

Mr and Mrs Oza were a charming couple and I still remember the excellent curries I had at their house. After a few months, there was a parting of the ways, but there was never any ill feeling on either side.

When we later returned to Livingstone (before Zambia's independence at the end of 1964), we continued doing business with the Ozas until we left Zambia for good, at the end of 1969. I heard later, on the grapevine, that they eventually moved to Britain and I hope that, one day, they will read my book about those very happy years in Africa.

★

With Angola in mind, Ndola (on the Copperbelt) seemed a good place to be based, so Eve and I moved there.

On our way to Ndola I had arranged to see Hugh Charnaud in Lusaka, because it was obvious that an undertaking there needed someone of his calibre. It was becoming increasingly clear that conditions in Angola were going to get just as dangerous as in the Congo, so it was necessary to start organising our move as soon as possible.

While we were in Ndola, Eve's divorce finally came through, and we got married there in 1963. We spent our honeymoon in Beira, one of our favourite holiday spots. On this occasion, we stayed in the Estoril's main hotel building. Later we came to prefer the chalets right on the beach as, being self-catering, they were ideal for the children.

Beira's beach was one of the safest in Africa, and children could play in the shallows in perfect safety, but what I liked most of all was being able to get up early in the morning and, with only a short walk, plunge straight into the warm sea. There were neither roads nor any of the other hassles of many of South Africa's holiday resorts, which were far too built-up and sophisticated for my liking. The package tour and plastic mentality had already managed to spoil a great deal of South Africa's natural beauty, by trying to make it just like Europe and America.

I still have fond memories of my favourite lunch on the beach: a few lagers first, then delicious prawn samosas (brought to you on the beach from the only restaurant allowed there). I have never, before or since, tasted such excellent samosas; both the pastry and the prawns were out of this world. After the prawns we would finish off with some of the local fruit: papaws, bananas and oranges. Beira was well known for its unpolluted waters and the excellence of its seafood and I don't think I have ever tasted better prawns piri-piri. The local lobsters were also excellent and, by European standards, all the seafood was extremely cheap.

★

Today, like so much of Africa since the colonial era, Beira has become a ghost town wrecked first by the Marxist Frelimo and later by Renamo in the civil war that has raged in Mozambique since independence in 1974. Again it is the rural African that has suffered starvation and hardship, due mainly to the gullibility of the West and the incredible inefficiency of the UN, whose personnel seem to think their job means hanging around the Polana Hotel in Lourenço Marques (now Maputo).

Even in the days of the Portuguese, the roads were pretty appalling, but at least they were always safe to travel on, by day or night (the only way to travel now is in military convoy, with Mugabe's troops providing the armed escorts – but even this is no guarantee of safety), and many times we travelled all through the night from Rhodesia in order to get to Beira in time for an early morning swim.

Lourenço Marques was, of course, very popular with South Africans, but it never had beaches to compare with Beira. On occasion, however, we did dump the children with relatives in Rhodesia and fly to Lourenço Marques for a week's stay at the Polana, a superb hotel in the best colonial style, like the Victoria Falls Hotel. But I found the Portuguese used olive oil in their cooking to an extent that was a bit excessive for my taste.

Recently we watched one of the usual propaganda-type TV films about Africa which are so beloved by Western socialists. It interested me mainly because it was about Mozambique and featured the Polana Hotel; and the international communist, socialist and UN personnel who, between them, played such a big part in wrecking prosperous colonial Africa. It seems they have now made the Polana their headquarters.

The hotel bills are, of course, paid by the Western taxpayers and I remember wondering then: now that the Cold War is over, how long will it be before these taxpayers will start exerting pressure on their governments to stop the wasteful activities of the UN? They should insist on getting results for their money by sending to Africa only people with African experience, either from the West or from South Africa, who, as in colonial days, understand the way of life in the African bush, know the local African languages and lead by example, with the help of the local African chiefs.

The rural African, like his counterpart in the West, is still the backbone of the country, not the city slicker. Furthermore, he is not a fool. In the last forty years or so of independence, he has seen retrogression in every sphere of his life, caused mainly by the ideological madness of his leaders and their efforts to break up the tribal system which the colonial era so wisely fostered.

Now he sees those same communist-socialist fanatics, who fooled his leaders and brought untold misery and starvation to newly independent Africa, in dire economic distress in their own countries – even in Russia itself.

Is it too much to hope that the West has learnt something from the mistakes made in Africa during the past forty-five years, since the end of World War II? Will it now begin to have some understanding of just how unnecessary it was to grant independence to countries in Africa who hadn't the slightest interest in maintaining any form of democratic government in their newly independent countries?

Now the pressure of the Cold War has been removed from the international scene, there is even less excuse for making the same mistakes all over again, this time in South Africa.

There must be more understanding in the West of the difficulties facing President de Klerk, not least from some of his own people. What is needed is a more sympathetic approach to the natural fears of the Afrikaner people who have seen the shambles and starvation in most newly independent African countries to the north and have no reason to suppose that, if ever a black majority government takes over in South Africa, it will be any different to the ones which have been so disastrous elsewhere.

It is important to understand that it is not simply a matter of money. By 1988, Nigeria (because of its oil) had a slightly higher gross national income than South Africa – yet it remains a complete economic mess, due mainly to misrule by its military dictators, and the universal corruption which means that absolutely nothing can be accomplished without everyone involved being bribed.

★

Back in Ndola, our plans for Angola were quickly finalised and Hugh Charnaud and I were soon off to Luso, the provincial headquarters of Angola. Our plan was to purchase crocodile skins from the Portuguese hunters I had met during my trips in Barotseland and also to get crocodile hunting licences from the Luso authorities.

I found my letter of introduction from John Gaunt, then Ian Smith's UDI minister of mines, came in extremely useful, as British passports were not very welcome, but nothing could speed up the Portuguese government officials.

Officialdom in most parts of colonial Africa was pretty slow, but the Portuguese in Angola were in a class of their own and Luso was truly a place of *bado kidogo* (Swahili for 'after a little while' – which, in practice, normally meant a long time!). It is similar in concept to the Spanish *manana*.

Eventually, however, we got the licences we wanted. In the meantime we had managed to purchase quite a number of crocodile skins from (mainly) Portuguese hunters, as well as getting more than expected in the Balavale district. We had what we thought were all the permits, invoices and veterinary licences necessary to get the skins to Northern Rhodesia, but we had not finished with Portuguese red tape yet. We discovered this only when we went to a local bank just before leaving, to confirm that there would be no difficulty in transferring some of the money back to Luso for further purchases on our next trip.

Imagine our surprise and anger when the bank manager told us we could not transfer any funds unless we had a special export licence from Luanda, which normally took six to eight weeks to obtain – and he assured us that it would not help to speed matters up if one of us were to fly down to Luanda. So there was nothing we could do except return to Northern Rhodesia without the skins. This put our plans back by about three months and meant we had to do an extra trip of hundreds of miles across some of the worst roads in Africa. The cost, not to mention the wear and tear on the vehicles, was considerable, but fortunately the profit on crocodile skins was large enough to justify the expense.

After that lesson, we applied for our export licences well before they were actually needed. There were never any checks on whether or not we already had the skins, so all we had to do was to fix the dates on the invoices to match the export licences – just another example of how to manoeuvre round red tape in Africa.

*

While we were developing the crocodile business in Angola, the political scene was hotting up all over the continent.

Civil wars raged in Zaire, Angola and Mozambique, with the communists and their Western socialist allies masterminding the anti-colonial insurrections everywhere they could. After Suez and Algeria, they knew that both Britain and France had lost the will to fight.

Tanzania became independent in 1961, and Uganda in 1962, and Zaire had already achieved independence (in 1960), so the stage was set for the communists and Western socialists to turn their whole attention to the CAF (Central African Federation) and to organise civil unrest in the three countries which formed the federation: Northern Rhodesia, Southern Rhodesia and Nyasaland.

This they did so successfully that Britain was quite happy to go back on its promises to Sir Roy Welensky that the CAF would continue. So it came to an end, after ten very successful years, in 1963. This effectively ended any hope of a strong, multiracial federation, which could have been built into a very strong economic force, as a counter to the industrial might of South Africa.

*

By the beginning of 1964, it was obvious that we would be returning to Livingstone much sooner than we had expected, before Zambia's independence on 24th October, 1964. We wanted to stay in Zambia for as long as possible, but we had no illusions about black independence and we were only prepared to stay in a place from where we could get over the border quickly if it became another Congo – and that meant Livingstone. Naturally we hoped that we would be able to stay there for a reasonable time, and we were lucky enough to get about six successful years before things in Zambia became totally impossible.

Although I had known things would be good from a business point of view, and I had been building up my Livingstone crocodile skin business even before we moved there – with a lot of help from John Seaman who, among other things, put me up whenever I visited Livingstone – I was surprised by how much business we actually got from Barotseland. Part of this was due to the trips I had made on Mr Oza's behalf before we moved to Ndola.

But nothing could disguise the fact that our days in Africa, at least black-ruled Africa, were numbered, as it was soon obvious that Kaunda would be just like all the other despotic African leaders, so we had to make the most of the few years left. But I have always considered myself very lucky to have had twenty-one glorious years in the old Africa before we were forced to leave, at the end of 1969.

Chapter Five

Livingstone and Barotseland

On one of our Angolan trips, just before I moved to Livingstone, Hugh Charnaud was taken ill suddenly during our journey back to Northern Rhodesia, and I had to drive all night to get him to Lusaka for medical attention. As it was going to take him a day or two to recover, he asked me to stay on for a while to finalise some business matters. I wanted to get home, but I was also extremely interested in the methods used by Hugh's Africans in preparing his skins for export. I knew that if he had not been ill I might never have found out how it was done.

We all knew the vast profits crocodile tanners were making overseas, and we were always looking for ways of increasing our own profits. Up to now none of us had found a way of retaining the extra inches after stretching the skins, but Hugh had done it – and kept the secret to himself.

By this time everyone was air-drying the wet-salted crocodile skins, to save on air-freight charges to Europe and America, but there was still sufficient moisture in the skins to make stretching very ineffective: the skins were measured across the soft belly to the first hard horn on either side. I discovered that Hugh had devised a new type of metal scraper with a handle that made the final cleaning and scraping much easier and much more effective and avoided the risk of any holes in the skin. Using his slow, regular, stretching method still involved quite a bit of manual effort, but it retained most of the stretch indefinitely. That made a difference of four to five inches on each medium and large skin and, with the price at over £1 per inch, this made a considerable extra profit for us on each month's consignment of crocodile skins.

However, it was only after we had moved to Livingstone, and I had trained my team of Africans to cope with commercial quantities, that I began to realise the possibilities in handling other dealers' skins as well as our own. I gave a demonstration to one of the largest Indian dealers. He was impressed, so I had a proper legal agreement drawn up, whereby we would handle two thousand of his crocodile skins and we would share the extra inches on a fifty-fifty basis.

After the success of that first contract, I made similar arrangements with other dealers. The whole operation was, of course, on a one-off basis since, once the dealers had learnt from us how it was done, they could do it themselves at the end of the contract. So I wouldn't agree to any contract that was for less than two thousand skins.

What pleased me most was that quite a number of these crocodile skins were being sold to our opposition, Hollanders and Lurie. These large overseas hides and skins dealers had local head offices in Port Elizabeth and branches in Bulawayo. When they had large overseas contracts to fulfil, they had an irritating habit of putting up crocodile prices in Livingstone and Lusaka, which made it difficult for exporters to get the supplies that were needed.

I had become quite friendly with Gerry Levinkind, Hollanders' buyer, who regularly came up north to buy crocodile skins and, when it suited me I sold him skins myself. When in Bulawayo, I had also visited their warehouse and met Salinger, their Bulawayo manager. I had seen some of their skins being packed for export and I could tell, from the wetness of some of the piles, that they were not stretching their skins.

To the best of my knowledge, up to the time I left Zambia (at the end of 1969) neither firm had any idea of what was happening.

It was a very well-kept secret, and it was only years later (after we had moved to Natal's south coast and were touring Rhodesia on business) that I learnt on the grapevine that one of the overseas tanners had noticed that he was getting less inches from a certain crocodile exporter and had started investigations to find out why. I never heard the outcome, but I knew, from the prices we were paid overseas, that the tanners there could well afford to make up for any shortage out of their large profits.

The contract scheme for stretching seemed to set the pattern for everything I touched in Livingstone during my final halcyon years there. The gods certainly seemed to be smiling on everything I did. As the sun set on the British Empire I knew I couldn't expect many more years, and I was determined to make the most of the ones that were left.

*

A further bonus towards increasing our business in Barotseland occurred when John Seaman's firm, Messrs Sussman Bros & Wolfson, decided to move him to Mongu, and John was able, on the side, to buy skins on my behalf.

When large numbers of skins were available, he would let me know and I would then fly up to Mongu.

I still enjoyed the more leisurely trips to Barotseland with my Land Rover and trailer, but I found business was increasing so rapidly that I could seldom spare the time and I usually had to plan shorter trips – to Chobe or to Sesheke.

It was on one of my early trips to Sesheke and Senanga that I found out how much time could be wasted if you had trouble with your vehicle. My Land Rover's engine packed up not far from Sesheke and it had to be towed to Finaulty's place at Katima Mulilo, where it was found that major repairs were needed – which meant they had to be carried out in Livingstone. So my trip ended abruptly.

With Finaulty's help, the Land Rover was loaded on one of the barges that came up with supplies from Livingstone and he then took me over to Wenela, which was in radio communication with Livingstone, and arranged a charter flight for me with the Livingstone Flying Club for early the next morning, as there were no commercial flights scheduled from Sesheke for three days. In all the rush, nobody thought about letting the South African district commissioner know that a light aircraft would be using his airstrip early the next morning.

Finaulty took me to the airstrip after the plane had circled over his house and, after chatting to him for a few minutes, the pilot took off. We circled once or twice, waving to Finaulty, then, as we flew on our way, we saw the dust of a Land Rover speeding towards the small airstrip. But it was only on my next trip that I found out it had been the South African DC, absolutely livid with Finaulty for allowing the plane to land and take off without his permission. Old Man Finaulty had been unruffled, however. He had merely told the DC that I was a personal friend of his, and nothing more was said.

I find it amusing to imagine what would have happened if the incident had occurred a few years later, when Katima Mulilo was turned into a forward base for the South African Army and a new airstrip was built to take South African Air Force planes.

We had scant respect for borders in those days and, when I came to Katima Mulilo via Chobe, I never thought twice about detouring into the Caprivi Strip and doing a bit of hunting there on the way to Katima Mulilo whenever I felt like it. I don't remember ever seeing another vehicle on any of my trips. I had, in fact, had no idea there was a DC at Katima Mulilo until Finaulty told me.

*

Most of us realised that things would change after independence (at the end of 1964) and that the inhabitants of the Southern Province, especially Livingstone, would be singled out by Kaunda and UNIP as supporters of Rhodesia and suspected spies. The local newspapers were normally full of this kind of UNIP propaganda, and Chairman Mao's Little Red Book was appearing all over Zambia.

A lot of the hatred was vented on those Africans in the Southern Province who still supported Kaunda's old boss, Harry Nkumbula, and his ANC (African National Congress, but nothing to do with South Africa's ANC). Kaunda had broken away from the ANC and had then formed UNIP. Barotseland was the other ANC stronghold and, even after four years of all-out UNIP propaganda and promises there, ANC won eight out of the ten Barotseland seats in the next (1968) election.

That was the last election in Zambia where any opposition was allowed. In 1972 the country became a one-party country, like Russia, and Kaunda was made president for life. As usual, these events were barely reported in the British press, which much preferred to concentrate on apartheid in South Africa.

It is also rarely mentioned that the hard-pressed British taxpayer contributes nearly £30 million a year to the support of the dictator, President Kaunda, a man who detains political opponents without trial for as long as he pleases. On the rare occasions this happens in South Africa, there is an almost universal outcry from the Western media.

★

What most of us did not expect, however, was the petty venom that soon made it impossible for us to go out at night in Livingstone without finding UNIP officials and supporters looking for trouble in all the hotels, restaurants and other public places – especially in the bars. Shortly after independence I witnessed one of these incidents in the bar of one of Livingstone's better hotels.

I had noticed a half-drunk UNIP official at one end of the bar, as I came in for a quick beer, and I carefully kept well away from him. Eventually he managed to provoke a reaction from one of the Europeans near him, who told him to shut up, whereupon the UNIP official called the police and told them he had been insulted. The eventual outcome was that the unfortunate European was given twenty-four hours to get out of Zambia and his wife was left behind to pack up all their belongings and follow him at a later date. Few such incidents were reported outside Livingstone, but we all knew what was going on.

Quite a few of our friends had moved over the border before Zambia got its independence, and we had already fallen into the habit of spending almost every weekend in Rhodesia, at Victoria Falls. During the day we swam, and had lunch by the pool, at the Victoria Falls Hotel. In the evening we either had dinner there as well or went to the recently opened Victoria Falls Casino, to dine and have a gamble.

It was to counter this habit, adopted by many white Zambian residents, that UNIP brought in a special immigration stamp. Every time we crossed the border, they used this special stamp – it took up a whole page – and it wasn't long before both our passports were full. Then we were put to the inconvenience of applying to Lusaka for new ones, or of having extra pages added to the existing ones.

*

The petty British bureaucrats in Salisbury also seemed to delight in making travel difficult for all and sundry. After Rhodesia's declaration of UDI the British Consulate in Salisbury had been closed, but an additional page was eventually added to my passport by the British High Commission residual staff (in August 1966) and I think it makes interesting reading (see Appendix).

I needed the extra page for a Portuguese visa to go to Beira. The British residual staff, who were a pretty unhelpful bunch, seemed to take great delight in telling me that the Portuguese wouldn't accept a page added to the passport and, unless I could get Portuguese approval first, they wouldn't give me the extra page. I don't think they expected to see me again. What I didn't tell them was that I had a letter of introduction to the Portuguese (Angolan) authorities from John Gaunt, now the minister of mines in Ian Smith's UDI government.

John's letter did the trick and the Portuguese consul-general gave me a personal note to take back to the British residual staff. I had also showed him my passport which contained plenty of Mozambique and Angola stamps from my many previous trips.

I did, of course, derive great satisfaction from going back to the British bureaucrats and asking for the extra page for my passport. I added that I wanted it immediately, as the charming Portuguese consul-general had agreed to wait for my return so that we could get on our way to Beira early the next morning.

That added page was to come in very useful on later occasions, as all I had to do was to cut the tape at the back of my passport and add a few more pages as and when I needed them. I did not want all my trips recorded in my new British passport and was especially anxious to avoid the special Livingstone residents' stamp that took up a whole page.

Those of us who were in Africa long enough soon learnt ways of countering the stupidity of most local regulations.

★

Even with the constant provocation, we were determined to stay in Livingstone as long as possible, and we witnessed the whole rotten mess develop in Zambia, a mess which had been created mainly by gutless British politicians, scared of communism and pressure from the UN. The troubles really started when Kenneth Kaunda began to speed up the Zambianisation of all public services, regardless of the fact that a lot of the Zambian appointees were not qualified to do the jobs. So it wasn't long before cracks began to appear in the whole infrastructure.

I saw more of what was happening than most of the Europeans, because they were mainly restricted to the larger towns or were in the copper mines, whereas I travelled all over the country.

The first thing to become noticeable was a lack of maintenance on the rural roads, which began to deteriorate fast, and it wasn't long before this neglect spread to the main roads leading to the Copperbelt. For the first time, I began to see huge potholes – even on the tarred roads – with PWD (Public Works Department) vehicles and other equipment just abandoned by the roadside.

At independence the Americans had given Zambia twenty-five brand new ambulances. It wasn't long before I began to see them smashed up in the countryside: some wrapped around trees, others overturned – all abandoned. I believe it took the (often drunken) drivers only a year to write them all off!

If Kaunda had had the sense to stick to Zambianising only the public services, the damage could have been limited but, by early 1968, he had decided to restrict the trading activities of all expatriate businesses, in other words, those owned by Europeans and Asians. In January 1969 twenty-six major foreign-owned companies were forced to sell fifty-one per cent of their shares to the Zambian government. New trading licences for non-Zambians were issued only in the ten main urban centres, most of which were in the Copperbelt.

These new restrictions were disastrous for the rural Africans in most parts of Zambia, as it had been the Asian traders who had dominated the businesses in most of the small towns. When nearly one thousand Asian stores were forced to close, it seriously disrupted the whole way of life in rural areas. Whatever their faults, the Asian traders had kept the rural economy moving and also financed a lot of the small African farmers until their crops came in.

The Indian traders had made a good profit from buying the local crops and skins from the Africans, and another good profit on the goods they sold in their retail stores. A lot of them were wholesalers as well, supplying and financing small shops run by Africans in the surrounding villages.

During my travels I learnt that this system worked well on the whole, but there was one major complaint: some of the more unscrupulous Indians insisted on bartering. If an African brought in some hides and skins, for example, the Indian trader might insist that, in lieu of cash, the African must accept payment in the form of goods from the Indian's store – at a value set by the Indian. Of course the African realised he was being cheated, but there was very little he could do about it as, in most cases, he would have had a very long journey to reach another trader.

Many of the Indians did, of course, trade honestly and the ones who abused their position could have been controlled quite easily by Kaunda's government – or even expelled. But it was not necessary to expel all the Indians from the country – they had actually provided a much-needed service to the rural African communities.

Kaunda had confidently expected Zambians to come forward and buy the ownerless stores at knock-down prices but, once again, his Marxist advisers' lack of knowledge was to prove disastrous. The rural Zambians knew the hard work and organisation needed to run the Indians' businesses successfully, and they were not interested in taking them over. The few who did like the idea of owning a business fancied something like a bar or tearoom in Lusaka or one of the Copperbelt towns. The last thing they wanted was the hard work of running a shop in a rural area. So nobody bought the once-prosperous stores – and small communities all over Zambia suffered.

⋆

Kaunda loved to talk about humanism and the African socialist policies so rigorously enforced by his friend Julius Nyerere, with tragic results for millions of rural Africans in Tanzania. Nyerere was the darling of the socialists and far left in Europe, and Tanzania has been given more aid than any other country in Africa.

Kaunda's humanism applied only to his urban supporters in the Copperbelt, Lusaka and the other large towns. He couldn't have cared less about Barotseland, the Southern Province and the other rural areas, where he had very little support.

It is interesting to note that that it was after the UNIP conference in 1967, at which President Nyerere was a guest speaker, that the restrictions on expatriates started and Zambianisation was pushed ahead rapidly, without any regard to the damage it was doing to the country. Totally unsuitable UNIP supporters were given jobs in the public service because of their loyalty to UNIP rather than their (often non-existent) qualifications for the job.

All the transport services suffered, but none more than the railways which were vital to Zambia's survival. They became an absolute shambles, due to the prejudice and folly of Kaunda and UNIP. Living in Livingstone, which was an important railway depot, we had a lot of South African and Rhodesian friends who worked for the railways. They were all forced to leave what is now Zambia Railways and most transferred to either South African Railways or Rhodesian Railways. There was absolute chaos when a motley crew of only half-trained railway men came, from all over Africa, to replace them.

Most, if not all, of the senior railwaymen who had maintained discipline had left and drunken engine drivers smashed up their trains almost nightly. Rolling stock which belonged to Rhodesia and South Africa was stranded all over Zambia. Eventually both South African and Rhodesian Railways issued warnings that they would not allow any more trains into Zambia unless their rolling stock was returned to them without delay.

This caused complete panic in Zambia, because most of its copper still went by rail via Rhodesia. The rolling stock was returned!

All this unnecessary expense was hushed up as, in the end, it was the poor unfortunate taxpayers in the West who would have to pick up the bill for Kaunda's expensive prejudices.

★

It is a fact that most African rulers are far more racialist than most of the Afrikaner politicians in South Africa. Kaunda's treatment of the Asians when, at a stroke of the pen, he closed nearly a thousand of their stores in rural Zambia, was little better than the behaviour of that murderous maniac Idi Amin towards the Asians in Uganda.

Their methods contrasted sharply with Dr Verwoerd's actions in South Africa, when he wanted to get rid of some of South Africa's Indians. They were offered free passages together with some financial inducements to return to India permanently. Only a handful of Indian families took up his offer. They knew, only too well, how bad conditions really were in India, and how much better off they were in South Africa – despite the discriminatory laws.

It should be mentioned that organisations like AAM, and the communist elements in the Commonwealth, make a great fuss about Indian traders in South Africa not being allowed into the Africa Reserves in the rural areas, but there is a very good reason for this. As I have pointed out about the Zambian Indians, it was very easy for the unscrupulous among them to take advantage of the economically naive rural Africans.

It is very easy for people in the AAM, and other such organisations, in the safety of their comfortable Western homes, to criticise the South African government, as they do regularly with their red flags outside the South African embassy in Trafalgar Square. It was the antics of these people, who angered me with their ignorant nonsense about Africa, that contributed greatly to my determination to write this book about what I personally saw and heard during my thirty-five years in Africa.

*

Most of the trouble in Africa since the end of World War II, as I have mentioned before, has been carefully organised by the communists. But this in no way excuses the actions, or rather inaction, of the great colonial powers, Britain and France. After their humiliating experiences at Suez and in Algeria, their main concern was to get rid of their colonial responsibilities in Africa as soon as possible, and they did so without any regard for either the European settlers or the majority of rural Africans.

It was conveniently forgotten, especially by Britain, that the settlers had been encouraged by previous governments (from the days of the 1820 settlers in South Africa) to go to Africa and bring law and order to countries that had been devastated by the slave trade and by tribal wars that precluded any kind of normal life for millions of Africans. In what was to become Rhodesia, for instance, the Shona were so frightened of the raiding Matabele that they had abandoned their villages and were living in caves in the mountains.

The bravery of the early British settlers is usually forgotten today, and I am proud that I can record just what we all owe to the Pioneer Column of 1890. I don't think it is widely appreciated just how much Africa owes to Cecil Rhodes and the small body of men who made up the Pioneer Column, worthy successors of Oliver Cromwell's men.

There was a squadron of four hundred mounted men, under the command of Colonel Pennefeather (which was later to form the nucleus of the British South African Police in the Rhodesias), to protect the first two hundred pioneers chosen by Cecil Rhodes. They represented as wide a range of trades as possible. Rhodes had insisted that every man should have South African experience and a proportion of Afrikaners were included in the two hundred.

Fresh in everybody's minds must have been the events of the Zulu War of 1879, only eleven years before, when the Zulus inflicted on British forces one of the worst disasters in British colonial history: over a thousand British troops and their attendant forces were completely wiped out by about ten thousand Zulu warriors at Isandhlwana in Natal, South Africa.

For the Pioneer Column to reach its final destination, Fort Salisbury, it had to pass through territory controlled by the Matabele, relatives to the Zulus. The British South Africa Company of Rhodes had an agreement with the paramount chief, Lobengula, but it was by no means certain that he could control the eighteen thousand Matabele warriors, as they were seething with discontent and really wanted to repeat the Zulu success with their own Isandhlwana. But their tribal traditions of military discipline held and the Pioneer Column was allowed to proceed on its slow journey to Fort Salisbury – and the start of the Rhodesias, North and South.

One of Cecil Rhodes's greatest legacies to Rhodesia was the building of the railway from Mafeking, in South Africa. It reached Bulawayo in 1897 and brought much-needed help to the town during the Matabele rebellion then. It could be said that it was Rhodes's offer to build the railway line that had influenced the British government to grant the charter to his British South Africa Company.

By 1902 the railway had reached Salisbury, but the Boer War delayed further construction of the line to the north, and Rhodes's death in 1902 meant he never lived to see the spray of Victoria Falls from a railway carriage, as he had intended.

Rhodes's dream of a railway line all the way from the Cape to Cairo was never to be achieved, but what a magnificent dream and what a magnificent man!

Without his drive and vision, there would never have been two prosperous Rhodesias to be handed over so prematurely to black majority rule, or rather misrule, by a British government: Northern Rhodesia (Zambia) in 1964 and Southern Rhodesia (Zimbabwe) in 1980.

Most British taxpayers are unaware of just how many millions of pounds are poured into these two socialist-Marxist countries every year to keep them going. It is seldom mentioned that all this mess could easily have been avoided if, in 1963, the British government had honoured its promises and let the Central African Federation under Welensky continue, rather than giving in to communist-inspired pressure.

But, after Suez, there was never any real hope of a stand from any British government.

*

There is absolutely no doubt in my mind that the military events in Africa at the end of the nineteenth century helped to influence Kaiser Wilhelm II and his advisers in their fateful decision to challenge Britain and France. That resulted in World War I and then the Russian Revolution – which was the start of communism as a world menace.

Military Events in Africa

1879	Natal, South Africa. Zulu War, Isandhlwana. One of the worst disasters for the British Army in all its long colonial history.
1880	Majuba Hill, South Africa. First Anglo-Boer War. Victory for Boers.
1885	Sudan. General Gordon killed at Khartoum, due to delays in sending the British relief force. Khartoum was not retaken until 1898.
1899–1902	Second Anglo-Boer War. 500,000 British troops needed to defeat 30–35,000 mainly mounted Boer troops.

Germany was one of the few European countries to have actively supported the Boers, and the Kaiser would have received regular reports from Windhoek (capital of the new German colony, South West Africa) of the early reverses of the British Army in South Africa – until Field Marshal Kitchener was brought in as commander-in-chief.

Much would have been made of the fact that it took a force of 500,000 British troops to defeat Boer forces that never exceeded 35,000 (mainly mounted troops) and the Kaiser would have questioned the British will to fight. The Germans would also have expected a repeat of their victory at Sedan in 1870, where the French were decisively defeated and Emperor Napoleon III was captured. He was later deposed.

The Kaiser must have felt confident that his well-trained army would defeat both Britain and France.

It was only twelve years after the second Anglo-Boer War that World War I began and set in motion the chain of events which was to lead inexorably to the shattering of Rhodes's dreams for British Africa. They died as surely as a generation of British, French and German youth, in the unnecessary slaughter on the muddy fields of Flanders. That led indirectly to the Russian Revolution in 1917, and the start of a worldwide communist campaign of subversion and propaganda of unprecedented proportions, to which the mainly illiterate Africans were particularly susceptible.

My father, who went through the whole of the war in Flanders, probably survived only because he was wounded four times (and therefore missed some of the fighting while he was being treated), and he would never discuss the ghastly conditions in the trenches. But I remember one remark he made and, although he was referring to Britain, it can be applied to France as well. He said: 'You cannot expect things to ever be the same again, when most of the best of a generation have been killed off in France.'

*

How well the evil of communism has succeeded all over Africa since the end of World War II, culminating in 1989 when the communists took over Namibia, thus completing the isolation of South Africa – their final target.

It would be a very grave mistake to believe that events in East Europe and in Russia itself, have in any way changed the long-term goal. Massive aid to Angola continues, and news about the delays in the withdrawal from Angola of about thirty thousand Cuban troops is ignored by America and the rest of the West.

Dr Jonas Savimbi and Unita have been abandoned, both by the West and by South Africa, and a combined Soviet, Cuban and MPLA offensive is being mounted against Dr Savimbi – with minimal media coverage in the West.

Any reader wanting to see beyond the media propaganda should take note of KGB Colonel Slovo, Chairman of the South African Communist Party, who was always on hand to pass on Moscow's instructions to Nelson Mandela. There were reports that Slovo was promoted to general for his murderous activities as chief of staff of ANC's terrorist wing, Umkhonto we Sizwe.

The time is long overdue for the West to face up to some unpleasant facts about Africa, especially about how the communists and sections of the Western media have conned the public by not revealing how appalling conditions in Africa have become since the different countries have become independent. Due to incompetence, corruption and misrule, famine is constantly increasing all over Africa.

Even the rapid spread of Aids has not checked the population explosion and the UN, despite spending billions of Western taxpayers' money, has done nothing to help control the situation.

Whatever South Africa's faults, the West simply cannot afford to let the same mistakes be made there. This must be made quite clear to Mandela.

The West is finding it difficult enough to feed the present masses starving in Africa. Communist violence and misery must not be allowed to spread. It is no coincidence that Mandela and the Communists want sanctions against South Africa to continue, while moderate African leaders like Buthelezi (leader of the Zulus and Inkatha) have, for a long time, wanted them to end. They know, just as Mandela does, that it is the ordinary Africans who suffer most from sanctions.

Unpalatable facts have to be faced and, if South Africa is not to go the way of the rest of Africa and become a further burden on the Western taxpayer, then the five million whites (over two million of whom are of British descent) have to be supported. Reforms can go ahead only as long as they do not affect the general well-being of the country, and law and order must be maintained at all times.

With Russia facing its present internal difficulties, South Africa and the West have been given an opportunity to carry out reforms without any unnecessary rush.

I hope that my readers, especially ex-servicemen, women and their families, will realise that nothing appears to have been learnt from the disastrous mistakes made in the 1960s and that there is now a need to speak up, to protect the two million or so British South Africans, as well as the Afrikaners who were Britain's allies in two world wars and the millions of non-political rural Africans. Our politicians must get the message that we will not permit a repetition of the shameful betrayal of the Rhodesias to happen in South Africa.

★

Shortly after returning to Britain, after thirty-five years in Africa, I watched a television programme that summed up the stupidity, ignorance and arrogance of the media in the West. The programme was about Lord Fenner Brockway and his interference in the affairs of Uganda during the colonial era, when he was promoting the communist and socialist plans for immediate independence there. The programme stated that when Fenner Brockway went there, shortly after independence, crowds of Africans lined the streets cheering his arrival.

The promised communist and socialist Utopia was, of course, very short-lived, but there was no mention of that fact in this TV eulogy. What I wondered was how many of those cheering gullible Africans had survived the terrible years of that madman Idi Amin. The skulls of his murdered victims were more than enough to have lined those same streets in Kampala and, regrettably, they would have been a far more fitting symbol of Ugandan independence.

The extent of the folly that was encouraged by the communists and their socialist and Labour friends in all the newly independent African countries is almost unbelievable, and neither the British government nor the UN had any interest in seeing that the real truth came out of Africa. All this folly and unnecessary expense was, and still is, paid for by the long-suffering Western taxpayer.

★

One of the pleasures of writing this book has been renewing contacts from my years in Africa, as well as tracing my mother's relatives in South Africa. One of my greatest surprises was learning that the son of the local chief, Mzee Ruzoka, who helped me so much while we were getting the farm going in the mid-1950s, is now the Catholic bishop of the Kigoma diocese, Bishop Paul Ruzoka.

I think it well worth while to include two paragraphs of a letter I wrote to him, as I feel it is very important that we all keep, and extend, the contacts we made when in Africa:

> It was only after I returned to the UK in 1983, after thirty-five years in Africa, that I began to understand how privileged I had been in having the opportunity to get to know the rural African really well and that something had to be done about the appalling ignorance in the West about what really went on in Africa. After heart troubles in '84 and '85 I therefore helped start TAAL, in early 1986, with others who had spent most of their lives in Africa.

It is of course one of the tragedies of Africa that so few Europeans, and this includes residents in South Africa, ever get to know the African in his proper rural surroundings where crime and all the other imported urban African problems are virtually unknown in rural African areas. If this book I am writing does nothing else at least I hope to get this message across in Europe.

★

The Destruction of a Continent makes a point of saying that, although the British were excellent colonists, there was one great flaw in how they treated the local population in their colonies, in other words, as second-class citizens. To a lesser extent this was also true in the dominions (colonies that became self-governing and were no longer controlled by Whitehall).

This attitude was bound up with the past in Britain, and the ridiculous class system that continues even in modern times. Coming back to Britain after thirty-five years in Africa, it was easier for me to see why the British acted the way they did after Suez (1956).

The Establishment had little or no involvement in building up the empire, and Africa was no different – the only Establishment name that comes to mind as being personally involved is Lord Delamere in Kenya. The majority of settlers were British provincials, whose forebears were the backbone of Cromwell's victorious armies. Unfortunately Cromwell did not live long enough to really change the system in Britain and, with the restoration of the monarchy, most of the robber barons got back their estates – and more.

The richest man in Britain today is that Establishment figure the Duke of Westminster who, amongst other things, still owns a lot of very valuable land in central London. The Church of England is, incidentally, also one of London's largest land owners.

Life in the colonies offered a total change of values for those bold enough to take the very real risks involved. It could be hard getting started but, once you were established, it was a free and easy existence compared to Britain – and whether you became established depended almost entirely on your own efforts (plus a little luck). No one outside the colonial service was interested in a settler's ancestry or personal history. You didn't even have to be British to get to the top – as Sir Roy Welensky showed in Rhodesia. It was only with the English Establishment in England that Sir Roy had any problems.

Politics, at least at the upper level, is about self-interest and, when it was expedient to do so, the British were quite prepared to abandon their settlers:

about 275,000 in Southern Rhodesia and about 70,000 in Northern Rhodesia, together with thousands more in East Africa, mainly in Kenya, but also in Tanganyika, Uganda and Nyasaland.

I always thought ex-servicemen like myself were the luckiest, as the services taught us to be resilient and to plan for any eventuality. I was determined that no tinpot African dictator was going to make me leave until I was ready to go, which I was at the end of 1969, when our plans to move to Umkomaas (on Natal's south coast in South Africa) were completed.

★

Many people in the West will find it difficult to believe the extent of the manipulation of the news from Africa, especially South Africa, by the Western media.

That is why I found the Foreword to *The ANC Method – Violence* by Peter Worthington, a Canadian journalist who has known Africa since the 1960s and covered the Congo when it got its independence from Belgium, of great interest. Few in the media have ever had the courage to speak out about media manipulation in covering news from Africa, especially South Africa.

In fact, I have seen only one television programme, since returning to Britain in 1983, which even hints at the real truth and tragedy in Africa. It started off as a mild documentary about Zaire and the Aids problem in Africa, with some criticism of the hospitals in Kinshasa – I have personally seen a lot worse during the course of my travels in independent African countries. The fun really started when the television crew were deported by Mobutu's bunch of police thugs – after that the programme developed into a fairly interesting exposé of just how corrupt black African leaders really are, Mobutu in particular.

I'm sure that many of the British viewers would have been quite shocked at hearing about the millions Mobutu has milked from his long-suffering African subjects – we were shown some of his magnificent estates in Belgium and elsewhere. The despotic Mobutu was so angry at these revelations in Belgium that he ordered all his students there to return to Zaire!

I am extremely grateful to Peter Worthington for his permission to quote his Foreword in full, as I am confident it will open more eyes to the realities of Africa that are so frequently obscured by the media:

The first time I came to South Africa was in 1960. I was a journalist for the old *Toronto Telegram* – fresh from covering the Congo, which had just got independence from Belgium.

The Congo was in chaos and dangerous – South Africa orderly and safe. At the time the Canadian Prime Minister John Diefenbaker had just made moves that resulted in South Africa quiting [sic] the Commonwealth and becoming a Republic and the Afrikaans and English population were at odds over what the future held. And yet at the time as a Canadian with no experience with, or exposure towards the policy of apartheid I was appalled and offended at the attitudes and policies of South Africa.

I even preferred the chaos of the Congo to the discrimination of South Africa and I wrote as much in my newspaper. At the time although Afrikaner and English South Africans disagreed with each other they all seemed to favour apartheid as a policy. I would estimate that 85% of South Africans generally supported the policy of apartheid.

When I returned to Canada I even made speeches opposing apartheid and on occasion appeared on the same platform as Harry Belafonte, deploring the policy.

Now some 27 years later, I found the country still the richest and most civilised in Africa yet with one dramatic difference. This time instead of ordinary South Africans generally favouring apartheid, most white South Africans seemed opposed to it.

In fact, I would say the percentages of 25 years earlier had been reversed. Now 85% of the white population disapproved of apartheid, recognising it as obsolete, unworkable and to be dismantled.

The only question is how?

Comparatively speaking, as fast as attitudes and policies are concerned, South Africa of the '80s bears little resemblance to South Africa of the '60s.

But what offends me now as an individual and as a Canadian, but most particularly as a journalist, is the lack of recognition and understanding in the West of what exactly is going on in the whole of Southern Africa today, not just South Africa.

When one looks at the evidence that unfolds daily, for all to see who want to see, there is a war going on, not against apartheid, but against South Africa itself.

I'm afraid I am convinced that the Western media, Western politicians, academics and all too many church figures are not so much

> interested in a peaceful solution to South Africa's problems, but want bloodshed and an overthrow of the system at any price, and the installation of another form of government, even if it ends up being a Marxist regime.
>
> I mostly blame the media for what can only be described as disinformation about South Africa. Instead of going where the story takes them, that is, of honestly reporting events as they see them, too many media people are reflecting what they think their audiences or editors want to see, hear, read, or what they personally believe should be the case.

It is interesting to note that Mr Worthington devotes a whole page of his book to 'Moscow's man in the ANC'.

This, of course, was Colonel Joe Slovo of Moscow's KGB. There were some (unconfirmed) reports that he was promoted to general for his work as head of the South African Communist Party and the only white sitting on the ANC's Executive Committee. He was there for a very good reason: he coordinated the flow of strategy decisions between the ANC, SACP and the Soviet Union.

Slovo was born in 1926 in Lithuania (one of the Baltic states that came under the control of Moscow and have only recently regained their independence), and went to South Africa with his parents in 1935. Since he received almost all his education there, one would have thought that he would have had some loyalty to his adopted country – but not so. While studying at the University of the Witwatersrand, he joined the South African Communist Party and he worked for it until his death in 1995.

During the years that Mandela was in jail in South Africa and the African National Congress was an illegal organisation operating from Lusaka, Slovo was the real power behind the president of the ANC, Oliver Tambo.

Slovo's ruthlessness was shown when he controlled the Special Operations Group, the elite members of the ANC military wing, Umkhonto we Sizwe. They were responsible for numerous indiscriminate attacks on civilian targets in South Africa, when innocent women and children were killed in places like supermarkets, and in any easy target in rural or urban areas of South Africa. Landmines, limpet mines and sophisticated car bombs were willingly and indiscriminately supplied by the Russians. In recognition of Slovo's murderous activities, he was awarded the Order of Lenin in 1986.

What was significant was that, after Nelson Mandela's release from prison, and the unbanning of the African National Congress and the South African

Communist Party, the Communists no longer thought it necessary for their man, Slovo, to stay in the background.

There is no longer any need to conceal the role that the communists have played in bringing this victory about just as they have done in Namibia, where their man Sam Nujoma took over in 1989.

Many viewers must have noted the sudden appearance of a white face among the black hierarchy of the ANC, and how he appears near to Mandela during television appearances. ANC meetings are now being thoroughly covered by the Western media, as they attempt to give the impression of overwhelming support in South Africa for Mandela and the Communists.

It should come as no surprise that we rarely see any of the moderate black leaders in South Africa, like Chief Mangosuthu Buthelezi, despite the fact that he is the representative of close to seven million Zulus and their Inkatha movement.

However, nothing can disguise the stupidity of the Communists and Mandela when it was decided that the two black leaders should not meet to discuss the senseless killings in Soweto and other black townships. When we eventually get an impartial summing up of these tragic events it will be recorded that Chief Buthelezi, who has always favoured non-violent methods to achieve change in South Africa, was always ready to meet Mandela to try and stop the ANC-Inkatha murders. These were tribal killings between Xhosa and Zulu.

★

I wish to make it clear that, although I lived for about thirteen years in South Africa, after twenty-two years in the black north, I never had the slightest interest in South African politics. I worked in Durban for some years, but (for most of them) I lived in Umkomaas, a small, quiet, very attractive village on Natal's beautiful south coast, and I cannot remember ever discussing politics with anyone, either there or in Durban.

I always insisted on keeping my British passport, and never had a vote anywhere in Africa, including South Africa, but I cannot say I ever felt deprived.

Quite a few of the English-speakers I met in Natal had very little time for the Afrikaners. Few of them had ever been to the black north and they were stupid enough to believe that if the blacks took over in South Africa they would still enjoy the same kind of law and order as under the white Afrikaner government.

I rarely, if ever, bothered to tell them about the realities of the black-ruled north, or about the atrocities committed by the Mau Mau and the Simbas. It now seems to me quite incredible that, in those peaceful days, I had, myself, never heard of communist villains like Slovo, Tambo, and the like, nor been acquainted with the ANC, AAM, CND and the host of other peace movements (like the World Peace Council) that have proved such useful propaganda organisations for furthering the aims of communism, as communist activists have successfully penetrated them at all levels.

Few of us in Africa had any idea how powerful these people were in the West and, with plenty of help from organisations like the WCC, they were able to launch an international campaign to free Mandela that proved irresistible.

While the Western media happily built up the Mandela myth, the truth was completely ignored: that Mandela was not a political prisoner. In 1985, in a letter to an American newspaper, Amnesty International made the position quite clear:

> A political prisoner is a concept created by Amnesty International by which the organisation means a person who has been arrested because of his views, colour of skin, ethnic origin, language or religion, and who does NOT *use*, or *incite violence*. In 1964 Mandela was charged with sabotage, and he was sentenced to life imprisonment. Amnesty ascertained that Mandela had participated in planning acts of sabotage and inciting violence, so he could no longer fulfil the criteria for the classification of political prisoners.

What was not mentioned by Amnesty International was the size of the arsenal found in an ANC hideout just outside Johannesburg in 1963, which was to be used in large-scale terrorist attacks against civilian targets in South Africa:

210, 000 hand grenades
48,000 landmines
50 tons of explosives

Documents found at the same time clearly showed the involvement of Moscow, China, Algeria, Czechoslovakia and East Germany, and proved that they were financing and actively backing a communist revolution in South Africa.

*

That Mandela has not changed his communist views must be made more obvious to all in Britain and in the West, and much more has to be done to see that the usual communist misery and chaos is not allowed to take over in South Africa as it has done in so much of the rest of Africa during the last thirty years.

The propaganda machine of the Western media tries to treat South Africa as if it were another Rhodesia, but that there were 'only' 275,000 whites in Southern Rhodesia and South Africa presents a problem of far greater dimensions. There are over two million people of British descent in South Africa, and to them must be added three million Afrikaners and other whites, three million Coloureds and one million Indians. Harsh facts just have to be faced: the West cannot afford a Mandela-Communist takeover, followed by the chaos and starvation that is typical of the black-ruled countries.

A letter Mandela wrote to ANC supporters in January 1990 was later published in the South African press. It called for ANC-SACP nationalisation of the mines, banks and other major industries in South Africa when the ANC come to power.

> The nationalisation of the mines, banks and monopoly industries is the policy of the ANC and a change or modification of our views in this regard is inconceivable. In our situation, state control of certain sectors of the economy is unavoidable...

wrote Mandela, who asked that his statement receive the widest possible publicity.

In revolutions, especially communist-inspired revolutions, symbols are very important. This is why the campaign for the release of Mandela was so important to the communists, and why all their socialist and media friends in the West were asked to help.

Mandela's release was not only a signal to the communist revolutionaries that they had won. It was also a signal to millions of black moderates that the revolutionaries had the South African government on the run. A lot of the five million whites in South Africa are beginning to believe that the ANC-SACP will win in the end. With the Russian Communist empire disintegrating fast, I believe South Africa will be given a final chance to sort out her problems in a manner more beneficial to South Africans of all races.

★

It is appropriate, at this stage, to question why successive British governments were willing to allow the destruction of all Cecil Rhodes's plans for Northern and Southern Rhodesia, and why the largest empire that the world had ever seen was unable to secure a British dominion in South Africa after winning the Anglo-Boer War of 1899–1902, instead of letting British control slip away to the Boers.

It has never been explained why Britain was quite willing to commit half a million British troops to defeat the Boers in 1902, but then failed to ensure that there would always be a British majority in the Union of South Africa, before it granted dominion status in 1931. The historic Balfour Declaration of 1927 defined a dominion as an autonomous community within the British Empire.

It is inconceivable that the British Establishment was not aware of the hatred and bitterness of a great many of the Boers. They, quite rightly, felt that it was impossible to forgive the destruction of their farms and the deaths of their women and children in British concentration camps during the Anglo-Boer War of 1899 to 1902.

It must have been anticipated that dominion status would lead to republic status once the mainly Afrikaner National Party came to power, as it did in 1948 when Dr Malan defeated Field Marshal Smuts's United Party. What followed then was inevitable and, in May 1960, the National Party leader, Prime Minister Dr Verwoerd, called for a national referendum on the republic issue, which was won with a very narrow majority – only 74,580.

On 31st May, 1961, therefore, South Africa became a republic outside the British Commonwealth. The carnage of World War I may explain the lack of moral fibre shown by British governments in the period between the two world wars, but the reasons for British failure to send enough British settlers to South Africa to ensure British rule go far deeper into the British way of life and the class system in Britain.

The British Establishment may have supplied a lot of the money to finance the building up of the British Empire, but it was the provincials who did the hard work, the fighting and the dying, often in very harsh conditions, all over the world. It is no coincidence that popular heroes like Clive of Plassey and Warren Hastings were both persecuted by the Establishment, largely through jealousy of the huge wealth that they had acquired in India.

Later, in South Africa, Cecil Rhodes would suffer in the same way as the British Establishment hadn't the vision to back his plans for a Cape to Cairo railway, even though Rhodes himself, via his British South Africa Company, financed most of the costs of the early development in Rhodesia, including building the vital line from Mafeking to Bulawayo.

The railway to Bulawayo was completed in two years, and the first train steamed into Bulawayo on 19th October, 1897. It was Rhodes's foresight and drive in wanting the railway completed quickly that probably saved his Rhodesian dream during the Matabele rebellion.

What was not understood then was that, although the provincials had built the greatest empire the world had ever known, the control of it was not in their hands but in those of the British Establishment, and it was Whitehall who controlled colonial policy. This is the main reason for the unnecessary tragedy of Africa since the end of World War II, when Britain and the other great colonial powers abandoned their own kind and left Africa to the misery of African socialism and communism.

Not even the self-governing colony of Southern Rhodesia could be saved, as the communists and their Western socialist allies spread the evil message of racial hatred all over Africa. Only the dominions from the days of the great British Empire (Australia, Canada, New Zealand and South Africa) were comparatively safe, as they were self-governing.

Unfortunately the new rulers of South Africa after the 1948 elections (the mainly Afrikaner National Party under Dr Malan) were far too honest, and sorely missed the international experience of one of South Africa's greatest statesmen, Field Marshal Jan Smuts. They played right into the hands of the communists and their Western socialist allies when they brought in the apartheid laws.

It is only people like myself, who travelled widely through Africa before, during and after the independence process, who have seen that, even with its apartheid laws, South Africa is a paradise for blacks when compared to most of the independent black-ruled African countries. India and some other countries in the Commonwealth are little better. In most places chaos and starvation, due mainly to corruption, have become the norm since *Pax Britannica* became a thing of the past after the end of World War II.

Having seen the appalling mess in most of black-ruled Africa, I feel that it was fortunate for South Africa that the Afrikaners took control in 1961. They have made mistakes but, had anyone else been in power, there would, by now, probably be nothing left in the country that would be worth arguing about.

★

These truths are, of course, never discussed at Commonwealth meetings, nor at the UN, where the communist conspiracy against South Africa was openly aided by people like Waldheim (UN Secretary-General from 1972 to 1982) and Ramphal (Secretary-General of the Commonwealth for far too long a period).

It was fortunate for Britain that, in the late Seventies, the Conservative Party, as well as the British Establishment, moved with the times very much more effectively than the Labour Party and the trade unions, and appointed Mrs Thatcher as their leader. Her greatest achievement, in my opinion, was that she restored national pride, something lacking since the shame of Suez in 1956, although I believe that it is mainly ex-servicemen who can understand best the magnitude of the task undertaken by the British prime minister in retaking the Falkland Islands from the Argentinians, especially in view of the great distances involved.

It was a great pity that it was too late to save most of Africa from the evils of communism. Let us pray, however, that there is still time to save South Africa from communism while Russia has to concentrate on all the problems connected with the break-up of its own empire.

*

It is obvious that the international bureaucrats of the European Community are going to be responsible for Britain being faced by a great deal of unnecessary expense in the future, expense over which it will have only minimal control. The same will apply to non-financial decisions that will affect our present way of life.

Mrs Thatcher showed us what had to be done, before she was so ungallantly forced to resign after eleven distinguished years at the helm. As with the Commonwealth, she had to fight for our rights just about single-handedly, but she did show the way forward.

I feel it is going to be up to British pensioners, with many ex-servicemen and women, to see that effective action is taken. Age has its advantages, and we are the only section of the British community that has the time to carry out a full-time campaign for our rights – we pensioners number over eleven million in Britain. Did we save Europe in World War II only to hand over our sovereignty to European bureaucrats?

Two recent television programmes have shown that pensioners are beginning to be aware of what could, and should, be done. The first featured a newly formed pensioners' rights campaign meeting in Carlisle, Cumbria. The second was about the Grey Panther movement in Germany. The Grey Panther's organiser, a woman, is a member of the German Parliament, fighting for German pensioners' rights. She has already started a very interesting self-help housing scheme for members, who band together to get bank finance. After converting a large house the members have individual accommodation, as well as company, the protection of numbers and nursing care if necessary.

Eventually, by linking all pensioners' groups in Europe together, good ideas like this could be pooled, and the combined pressure of pensioners would have to be listened to by the bureaucrats who, one day, will control Europe.

Although the modern constitutional monarchy in Britain plays a vital role in holding together the traditional British way of life, ever-increasing numbers of citizens are beginning to question not only Britain's role in the Commonwealth but the British monarchy's role as well.

There has to be a complete reassessment, not only about the aid money that Britain gives to Africa, but also about the role of the UN in Africa. Mrs Thatcher was bitterly resented in some quarters because she had the courage to defy many of the petty dictators in the Commonwealth, who think they can behave like gangsters in their own countries and then attend the biennial Commonwealth Conferences and adopt a high moral stance about South Africa.

When Fiji (no longer in the Commonwealth) had to adopt a racially-based system to protect her own Fijian citizens against the Indians imported by the British (who now outnumber the Fijians), nothing was said at the Commonwealth Conference, even though the Fijian system is now institutionalised.

Malaysia, the hosts of the 1989 Commonwealth Conference, have the same problem with their Chinese population, and have had to bring in discriminative legislation.

The silence is understandable, since so many members of the Commonwealth, especially those from Africa, have guilty secrets that are carefully concealed from the Western media.

Perhaps the most galling aspect of the whole Commonwealth farce is the way in which these very devious leaders keep their begging bowls out, even while they continue to criticise Britain.

I have described these Commonwealth Conferences as resembling the Mad Hatter's tea party, because the unrealistic atmosphere and the views expressed always remind me of *Alice in Wonderland*. Some day – very soon, I hope – the British taxpayer is going to bring them all back to earth with a very painful bump.

*

Readers may, perhaps, have noticed that, every few months, some British government minister will casually announce the latest gift of millions of pounds of aid money to Africa. The last announcement I heard concerned the Sudan, where the Muslim government in the north is currently butchering thousands of Christians in the south.

The UN, dominated by the communist and African countries, spends millions of pounds on anti-South Africa activities but ignores the atrocities in the Sudan, just as it ignored Liberia in 1990, where Africans were butchering each other for months on end. It is time something was done to get priorities right.

Eritrea is another war zone in Africa, as it has been for many years. Largely due to the civil strife, there is now another famine and Britain has already given about thirty million pounds in aid money. What she should do is get together with other Western powers, the UN and the Organisation of African Unity to see that the fighting is stopped before further aid is delivered.

Such civil wars in African countries are allowed to drag on for far too long, and the whole UN system has become an expensive farce – reforms are long overdue.

It is part of the whole UN madness, and a disgraceful waste of money, that aid funds are given to people who misuse them. But it's not UN money, just the Western taxpayers', so why should they worry?

Under Waldheim, UN policy was to spend millions of pounds annually on the Secretariat's Centre Against Apartheid. It had a large permanent staff dealing only with South Africa, and it gave financial support to the Special Committee Against Apartheid – which also spent millions annually on anti-apartheid campaigns all over the world. So, in effect, the West was paying for the communist propaganda campaign against South Africa.

Literally thousands of British pensioners retired to South Africa after a lifetime of work in East and central Africa. They could, and should, have been employed by the UN on short-term contracts, which would have saved the Western taxpayer millions in airfares and other unnecessary expenses for jet-setting UN officials. But until pressure is brought to bear on the UN nothing will be done.

Now the same sort of crazy bureaucratic expense is being extended to the European Community. Some way has to be found to curb the power of the bureaucrats, and a first essential step should be a campaign to cut down both their numbers and their expenses. For example, there are seventy-five British

Euro-MPs, and we should insist that the same number of MPs be dropped from the House of Commons.

It is proposed that the armed forces should be cut by about thirty per cent and I feel the same criteria could, more usefully, be applied to the various Commonwealth bodies that are supported by the British taxpayers.

The number of bureaucrats in the UN could also be reduced dramatically without anyone outside that organisation even noticing the difference.

Chapter Six

The End of the Colonial Era

Even before Zambia's independence (in 1964), it was becoming obvious that our greatest problem would be getting our money out of the country when we were ready to move down to South Africa.

From President Kaunda's speeches, it was clear that the whites in Zambia were going to have to pay more and more for his spending sprees, and that it was just a matter of time until he nationalised the copper mines, banks and other big businesses.

Fortunately for most of us he held off until August 1969, then he 'invited' the two large copper-mining groups to sell fifty-one per cent of their shares to the Zambian government. The state also claimed the rights to all minerals and then issued foreigners with twenty-five year exploitation leases.

To cover the other industries that were to be nationalised, the Industrial Development Corporation (Indeco) was formed. It soon became common knowledge that the banks were next on Kaunda's list. When they were taken over, in 1970, the Finance Development Corporation (Findeco) was formed as well.

We left for South Africa at the end of 1969, so we had about six years in Livingstone before we were forced to move.

*

In the early 1960s, I had a chance meeting in Livingstone with Peter Becker (a white hunter from Kenya), which was to help solve the problem of getting our money out of Zambia. Peter mentioned that he was looking for a suitable place to start a tannery in what was then the British Protectorate of Bechuanaland (which, in 1966, became the Republic of Botswana). It had one great advantage for us: it used South African currency. Kaunda was trying to stop trade with South Africa, but this was one loophole he could not close, because he knew his black brethren there were due to get their independence.

I wondered, later, if I had extolled the virtues of Francistown to Peter too much as, like most towns in Botswana, it was a pretty ghastly place. But, for his purposes, it was ideally situated (see Appendix for map) being reasonably near to some of Botswana's best game areas, such as Ngamiland, as well as having a reasonable road to Bulawayo. More importantly, Cecil Rhodes's railway from Mafeking in South Africa to Bulawayo ran through Francistown, so it was easy for me, later, to re-route some of the skins to South Africa whenever necessary.

Peter Becker was unaware, of course, that I had my own reasons for wanting him to open a commercial tannery in Botswana. I became one of his first, and very enthusiastic, customers while he was still in his old tin shed. Later he moved to palatial premises (more than 3,600 square metres), cleverly converted from what had been a dairy and creamery.

By the time Peter registered his company, Botswana Game Industries, in 1966 (for more details, see Appendix), Kaunda and UNIP had managed to wreck most of the colonial commercial structure in Livingstone. Food shortages, unheard of in the colonial era, became a normal part of life and we were forced to make monthly shopping trips to Bulawayo to purchase basic essentials. We found Macey's was one of the best-stocked shops with the cheapest prices.

Even before Zambia's independence, I had begun to realise that there would be quite a demand from expatriates leaving Zambia for the more exotic tanned skins. I was being kept pretty busy at the time by my continually expanding raw skin business: crocodile mainly, but lizard, python and other easily available raw skins were also very profitable. So I didn't bother to do anything about tanned skins until after my meeting with Peter Becker in Livingstone.

In those days I had no idea that the profits on exotic skins were even larger than on raw skins but, before Botswana Game Industries opened, with the single exception of Umtali Leather in Rhodesia, there were no tanneries outside South Africa that handled exotic skins on a commercial basis.

Umtali Leather, to whom I had sent a few skins for tanning as a favour to friends, had a good selection of zebra skins and some very attractive variegated hand-thonged mats: made from small pieces of skin from all the antelope available in Southern Rhodesia, for example impala, springbok, wildebeest, lechwe and tsessebi. But the range of game skins was very limited compared with what was on offer from BGI once it had expanded its business after moving to its new large premises.

★

Kaunda started making racialist verbal attacks on whites in Zambia, reserving his most venomous remarks for those of us who lived in Livingstone and elsewhere in Zambia's Southern Province, which, like Barotseland, had always supported Harry Nkumbula. Nkumbula was the former leader of Zambia's African National Congress, from which Kaunda broke away to form his own party, the United National Independence Party (UNIP).

It has always seemed to me that Kaunda's Zambia, like East Africa, provides a typical example of Western hypocrisy about Africa. The Western politicians are quite prepared to accept African racialism, and there were never any protests about Kaunda's treatment of Asians and few about his treatment of Europeans. But South Africa's apartheid has been reported ad nauseam in the Western media.

Look at the scene at the beginning of 1991: Liberia completely devastated by civil war and famine; Somalia's civil war continuing and all Europeans having to be evacuated from the capital, Mogadishu; civil war in Sudan also continuing. In Eritrea, Ethiopia, Angola and Mozambique, all ruined by civil wars, there were twenty million Africans facing starvation yet again.

★

President Kaunda's racialistic speeches acted as a spur to me and I lost no time in visiting the newly established Botswana Game Industries in Francistown. The trip was certainly not wasted.

BGI was housed in what was little more than an old tin shed, but the lack of proper premises had certainly not affected the quality of the tanning. This was of an extremely high standard, and the quality of the skins was as good as, if not better than, those produced in South Africa and Europe.

Although Peter Becker and I have had our differences over the years, I have always admired what he and Bodo Mucho (his expert Swiss tanner) have built up from such humble beginnings.

After they moved to their present spacious premises, Bodo's talents as taxidermist could be displayed to the best advantage. His fully mounted animals were really superb, and he had the knack of capturing the look of the animal, so it seemed to be alive in its own environment. BGI's range of mounted animal heads was also extremely impressive, from the small steenbok's head to the huge head of the African buffalo.

I remember that, after all my own displays and sales in Zambia, I got pretty blasé about the effect they had on first-time customers, most of whom had never seen anything like them before. But, with regular displays every year, the novelty had worn off for me.

*

Later, after a few years in South Africa, I was getting pretty bored and decided to give Bahrain and the United Arab Emirates a go with this kind of game skin display. Unfortunately the newspaper cuttings and picture are the only ones I have left and the picture has faded a lot. There is no mistaking the impact of my first displays in the Middle East as the newspaper's headline shows: 'Botswana fair takes Dubai by storm.'

In 1975, to pay for a holiday in the Far East, I held the same sort of display and sale of game skins at the Park Hotel in Hong Kong, which had the same kind of effect.

I must say that the Chinese officials with whom I came into contact were a real pain in the neck, starting with customs, who made a real meal of clearing my skins: I had to go there in person before I could get any action at all. Then I discovered the reason they wanted to see me personally: they expected bribes to be paid before clearance was granted – but I was not prepared to go along with this and, in the end, I got my clearance without doing so.

After all that hassle, I wasn't best pleased when I had a visit from some Chinese municipal official who wanted to close down my display. He said I hadn't got some licence that was needed to sell. To hold him off, as he was calling almost every day, I implied I would give him a present at the end of the show, based on my turnover.

I was booked to leave the hotel on 19th November, but when I learnt (from one of the girls at the reception desk) that he had checked when I was leaving, I got everything packed up and sent off on 18th November, and moved out of the hotel the same day. I was only sorry that I could not be there to see his face when he came round for his bribe on the 19th and discovered that I had left a day early.

The game skins display and sale had proved very successful, however, and I continued to supply some Chinese wholesalers in Hong Kong for quite a long time afterwards. Especially popular were the circular springbok mats made from ten to twelve skins and backed on red or black felt. Zebra skins, pouffes and cushions were also in great demand. I was asked to return, but I never had any intention of doing so – the distances involved and the bureaucratic hassles just did not make it worth while.

The Gulf was a very different business proposition: most Arabs are very fond of game skins, there was plenty of money around and I could visit several towns within relatively short distances. On my first trip I did three displays: starting in Dubai for five days, then on to Abu Dhabi for another five days and ending up in Bahrain for a final five days.

I always like to mix business with pleasure, so I spent a few glorious days in the Seychelles on the way back and I was away for over a month in all – I remember I only just made it home in time for Christmas.

The above trips were, of course, a good few years in the future, but they all stemmed from my first trip to Francistown. The proceeds enabled me to send the children to Durban University, where, I am happy to say, they both got degrees.

*

My future plans depended to a great degree on Botswana Game Industries being able to supply well-tanned skins in commercial quantities. After that very first trip in the 1960s, I was entirely satisfied that Bodo Mucho and Peter Becker were capable of doing this, and I never had any complaints about the quality of their game skins.

So as soon as I got back to Livingstone, I completed my arrangements for a display shop in the foyer of the Fairmount Hotel. In those days it was the best-run and best-sited hotel in Livingstone, on the main road from Lusaka to Bulawayo, via the Victoria Falls.

Later the Inter-Continental Hotels group built a hotel near the falls. I always felt it was a great pity that they did so, as it meant there was a great increase in traffic in the area, but at least they didn't build a skyscraper, so the scenery remained unspoilt.

I couldn't be bothered to open a real shop in those early days in Livingstone, but the passing business I got from the display shop (I sometimes opened it at weekends if I felt like it) did surprise me. A lot of its success was due to the hotel owners, Dave Hebbenshaw and his wife, as, when the shop was closed, they passed on my home telephone number to prospective customers. At that time I always kept a large stock of the more popular skins at my house and could supply customers from there.

Dave and his wife would also pass on to my many customers on the Copperbelt and in Lusaka details of when I was holding my next displays and sales in their areas. Initially I used the Edinburgh Hotel in Kitwe and the Ridgeway Hotel in Lusaka. Later, when the new Inter-Continental Hotel opened in Lusaka, I switched to that.

Some years later, after we had moved to Natal, I met Dave Hebbenshaw's daughter in Durban. It was in the 1970s, not long after I had purchased a curio shop, African Curios and Carvings, from 'Aussie' Frolich on Durban's Esplanade. She told me her parents had been forced to leave Livingstone, and were still having difficulties in getting payment for the Fairmount Hotel.

I always felt sorry for people like the Hebbenshaws, who spent years building up and running a business, in their case the best hotel in Livingstone, and who were pressured into leaving without getting full compensation for their efforts.

The same happened all over the British colonies in Africa, including Zimbabwe in 1980. A country should be judged by how it treats its nationals, and the British record in Africa after Suez was an absolute disgrace.

The British government gave the wailing and weeping Kenneth Kaunda millions of pounds of aid money, which he frittered away, but it hadn't the guts to demand complete protection for the British in Zambia.

I was fortunate that I had learnt my lesson early, in Tanganyika, and I was prepared for the worst. Even so, I was extremely lucky to be able to use Botswana to get a lot of my money out of Zambia, as well as the tanned skins that I was later able to sell from the game skin and curio shops that we started in South Africa in the 1970s.

⋆

It cannot be stated too often that the disasters which have taken place in Africa since the end of World War II, were due mainly to the granting of premature African independence – and that was brought about by pressure from the communists and the UN (which is also communist-influenced), combined with pressure from their Western socialist supporters in organisations like CND and AAM.

A fairly new organisation called the Southern African Coalition (SAC) gives some idea of the involvement in Africa of so-called liberal churchmen. It has a bishop as chairman (the Right Reverend Barrington-Ward), just as AAM has another rabble-rouser from the Church of England as president (the Right Reverend Huddleston). Sitting in palatial mansions provided by the Church, these people seem to want to create the same kind of communist havoc in South Africa that they helped to create in other parts of Africa, when the well-organised British colonial administration disintegrated into chaos and corruption.

The peaceful, progressive days of *Pax Britannica* were replaced by communist revolutions in the name of African socialism. The West has paid hundreds of millions of pounds for these disastrous mistakes, and it seems it will continue to do so for the foreseeable future.

Brutal military regimes like that of Idi Amin in Uganda were accepted, while the communists, socialists, and their allies in the churches, concentrated on apartheid in South Africa. Mass killings all over Africa were virtually ignored, and continue unabated in the Sudan, Mozambique and other countries to this day. But we seldom see our religious friends bothering about anything but apartheid, and the Western media encourage this mad, one-sided attitude.

There is, of course, no mention of any kind of regret for the disastrous dismantling of the colonial system, whereby plenty was replaced by famine in most of Africa. Can anyone in Britain wonder at the anger we expatriates felt as we witnessed the senseless destruction of all the progress made during the colonial era?

Some day the prelates will have to pay for the suffering they have caused all over Africa. Something has to be done to stop them, and the communists, from spreading the same kind of chaos, corruption and starvation in South Africa.

At the start of 1991 we were inundated on television by the annual pleading from charities for African famine relief; over twenty million pounds wanted immediately for six countries in Africa: Liberia, the Sudan, Eritrea, Ethiopia, Angola and Mozambique.

Yet the UN and the Organisation of African Unity do nothing (except for a Nigerian peace force sent to Liberia in August 1990 after most of Liberia had been destroyed) and are quite incapable of maintaining law and order in Africa. In early January 1991, another civil war started in Somalia, which will probably have to be added to the list of African countries destroyed by internal strife.

Surely the time cannot be far off when Western taxpayers will demand results, and an end to the present waste of their money by the UN and OAU. They must demand progress reports and accounts from all the charities about their expenses, and about how aid money is spent in Africa.

*

From my very first display and sale of tanned game skins, it was obvious that I had greatly underestimated the requirements of expatriates leaving Zambia and sometimes, in the early days, it was difficult for me to meet the demand. It was the expensive rugs with mounted heads (especially male lions with a good mane) that were the most popular and, on more than one occasion, I sold out of zebra skins and had to get further supplies sent from my stocks in Livingstone.

It was, therefore, particularly annoying when, at one of my early displays and sales at the Ridgeway Hotel in Lusaka, I was given an example of how Kaunda's Zambian hierarchy felt they could act.

One of Kaunda's aides asked me to supply two rugs (I have forgotten now whether lion or leopard was wanted), with fully mounted heads, for some state function that Kaunda was giving for some African leaders at State House (in colonial days it had been Government House). I was not at all keen on dealing with government officials, but I told him that if he came back with a purchasing order I would supply him with the rug mounts. I thought I had got rid of him, but he came back later with the necessary purchasing order and I gave him an invoice, which he said would be paid within ninety days.

Ninety days later I had not received the payment and, when I phoned State House, I could get no sense out of them. I could do nothing else until my next Lusaka display – about six weeks later.

Eventually, about five months after the original transaction, I got on to one of Kaunda's secretaries and was given some long rigmarole about a misunderstanding – didn't I want to present the two rugs to the president as a gift? As tactfully as possible, I said that I ran a business and that the two rug mounts had been invoiced and must be paid for – or returned in the same condition in which they had been taken.

The secretary could not make a decision and I was asked to phone back later the same day. When I did phone back, I got some underminister, who apologised for the misunderstanding. He said the mounted heads had been wanted only temporarily, for one of Kaunda's state functions, and would I please come and collect them the next day? I said I would, and asked him to advise the armed guards of my visit. This he promised to do.

Next day, however, the guards at the main gates knew nothing of my visit and I was kept waiting for over half an hour while they checked up. When I eventually entered State House, I saw that one of the rugs was still being displayed, just off the main entrance hall. Fortunately, although both were a bit dusty, they had not suffered any real damage.

It looked to me as if Kaunda's aide had earned himself some kudos for getting the rug mounts for the state function, where I believe they were very much admired. Certainly there had never been any intention of paying for them. One of the excuses I was given was that there was an economy drive going on in Zambia and it wouldn't look right if such luxury goods were purchased!

*

There was a sizeable demand for exotic skins in Johannesburg and I supplied quite a few to some of the city's leading furriers. Being able to send the skins directly from Botswana to South Africa was a great help.

One day I saw a really beautiful kaross at Derbers (one of Johannesburg's best furriers). It was hanging in the background to enhance a fur display that they were putting on. The design of the kaross and the quality of the hand-stitching were truly exceptional. The white skin background was made from pieces of wolf skin, with tigers as the motif of the kaross, the figures of the tigers being made up from pieces of tiger skin.

It was supposed to have originated from the area of Afghanistan and I managed to acquire it after Derbers' fur show was over. I used it regularly as the background for my Zambian displays and, although I received some very high offers, I always refused to sell it. Just before we left Zambia for good, I sent it off to Umkomaas, described as a carpet.

Eventually I sold it to Zell's – opposite Ivy's in Durban's West Street – they were the two biggest curio and skin dealers in Durban. It was too big and opulent for the customers I was then getting in my four skins and curio shops in Natal. Later, when I began to give displays in the Middle East, I regretted having done so, as I knew I would have been able to sell it to the Arabs for more or less any price I named.

*

During my years in Africa I never found it difficult to make money, but holding on to it was a different matter. After my first eleven years, in Tanganyika, I had no illusions about the final outcome of the communist and socialist madness that was sweeping through most of Africa, but I didn't see any reason then to change my way of life.

Looking back now, I must have presented an easy target to the Belgian Count. I believe his title was genuine – I have forgotten his name, but it isn't important.

I first met the Count when he came to one of my Kitwe displays in the Copper Cabin in the Edinburgh Hotel. He purchased a few skins and we got talking and discovered that we had mutual friends in the Belgian Congo. There was nothing unusual in his behaviour, except that he stayed longer than was usual for a first acquaintance, and we had a few beers together while I continued to sell my skins. He would have seen that I was taking in quite large sums of money.

Normally, when I was having a display and sale, I didn't finish working until about ten at night – even later at weekends. He had some business to do in Kitwe and suggested that, when he returned later that evening, we should have dinner together.

Over dinner the Count mentioned that he worked for an outfit called IOS and that, if I needed to get cash out of Zambia, he could arrange it if I invested my money with the company. He explained that IOS was an international mutual investment company that paid high interest on the money invested. I was a bit dubious, and said I would think it over: I wanted to check up on him. The people I asked confirmed that they had found him quite reliable to deal with and the next day I was really convinced when he showed me that he had, himself, invested in IOS.

At the start I gave him about £750 to invest, to see if everything went through smoothly. It did. So, at later displays and sales in Kitwe, I gave him much larger amounts and, with his help, I opened a Swiss bank account. This turned out to be very useful, since I could have the final payments for the raw skins I was exporting paid straight into Switzerland and thus bypass the Zambian banking system, on which I had had to rely in the past. It was all too good to last, however, and IOS was eventually unable to pay the high interest it had promised.

Some time in the 1970s, after we had moved to South Africa, IOS went bankrupt and the American who had started the company was jailed in Switzerland. But that didn't get back the money I had invested, and hundreds of thousands of people lost most of their savings.

I had amassed several thousand US dollars in my Swiss bank account from the final payments on raw skins. Some time after we had moved to South Africa, I wrote to my Swiss bank, asking if they thought it okay to invest most of that money in IOS. They wrote back saying that IOS was earning well, as it had done for years, so I went ahead and invested most of the rest of my money there.

It was less than a year after this that IOS collapsed and investors lost most of their money, including me. Luckily my shops were doing well, so I wasn't dependent on IOS, but I had worked damned hard (from 10 a.m. to 10 p.m. and later), to earn my money, and I didn't appreciate some unknown American crook losing most of my savings.

★

When I had started putting on displays, I had found the Zambian media a bit of a nuisance. They wasted a lot of my time with idiotic questions and wanted to interview me and, quite frankly, the last thing I wanted was personal publicity. I knew people in the Game Department were watching my activities so, to forestall trouble with them, I went to see them and showed them my invoices from Botswana Game Industries, together with all the necessary export-import permits and veterinary permits.

As I related earlier, I had had some previous trouble with the Zambian Game Department and had been lucky to get off lightly because the resident magistrate had also been at The King's School and knew me. The last thing I wanted was for the Game Department to take a renewed interest in my business.

I was persuaded by a Livingstone drinking buddy, Stewart Campbell (ex-Game Department), to take him along to cope with the media. At the time he was between jobs and I thought he might be useful, as he had some tourist and curio experience as well as knowing some of the media people. I paid for his hotel and travelling expenses and, at first, he did prove very helpful in handling the media for me. He liked to give the impression to the radio and TV people that it was his show and, for the reasons I have given above, I was quite happy to go along with this. So I stayed in the background as much as possible, content to take the money that was rolling in.

Campbell was also helpful with the selling, as I had no previous sales experience. I even put up with paying his drinks bill, which amounted to about a bottle of whisky a day, but we fell out when I refused to pay for his girlfriends' drinks as well. He was shaken by this as he had thought he was indispensable.

It was quite amusing on my first display and sales visits to Lusaka and Kitwe after I had got rid of him. The media people came around to see what had happened to him, as they were missing the free drinks he liked to dispense on my behalf. I did my own advertising in the newspapers, giving the dates and places of my displays, so I didn't need television and I kept my answers as vague as possible. I let them get the impression that I was just running things until Stewart Campbell came back, and that I was sorry I hadn't the time to give them any free drinks, and so on. It was interesting to note that this made no difference to my sales which, in fact, increased.

The day after I returned to Livingstone from the first trip without Campbell, I was visited by a European police officer and a representative of the Game Department. I knew both of them socially, and they were much more embarrassed than I was as they searched my house. I was furious, as I was keeping things very legal – with permits from Botswana and elsewhere.

They found nothing illegal as I always made a point of clearing everything possible before I went away. I never kept raw skins at my house, anyway, only the legally imported tanned skins from Botswana Game Industries and other tanners, such as Umtali Leather in Southern Rhodesia.

Since they had found nothing, I thought that would be the end of the matter. But they reappeared in the afternoon – could they now inspect the commercial premises, which I hired from Zambezi Saw Mills? Again nothing illegal was discovered, but I began to wonder what was making them so determined.

I had, in actual fact, hired further premises secretly, using the name of a trusted friend, and the authorities knew nothing about that. When hunters brought in dubious skins, these were kept well away from my house and from my official business premises, and only a few hunters knew of the existence of my other store. There was far too much at stake to take any risks, and I had no intention of being forced to leave the country before I was ready to go.

After the searches there were profuse apologies, but I was determined to track down whoever had tipped off the police. It took me some time to find out, from a police officer who was leaving Africa, that it had been Stewart Campbell. I could only be thankful that I had not given him any details about the unofficial side of my business.

Campbell, in the meantime, had had some difficulties of his own and had left Zambia in a hurry. Perhaps it was as well that I did not discover his treachery sooner, and had time to calm down a bit before I ran into him again.

Some time later I learnt that Stewart Campbell was working for some Rhodesian safari company around Wankie. I was told that he still visited the Victoria Falls Hotel on occasion, and I let it be known that I had a small present for him.

Although Eve and I spent most weekends at the Victoria Falls Hotel, Campbell managed to keep out of my way for quite a time. One day, however, not long before we were to leave Zambia for good, we were swimming in the hotel pool and about to have lunch, when a friend tipped me off that he had just seen Stewart Campbell in the hotel foyer with some of his safari clients.

I ran around the grounds to the car park, as I always kept his 'present' in the car, then I entered the hotel. Stewart Campbell was still in the foyer, with his back to me, so I was able to approach him unobserved and I still remember his face when I gave him the present – a specially tanned skunk skin – and told him, in no uncertain terms, why it was appropriate.

His American clients just looked on in amazement, and I often wonder what explanation he gave them.

*

Every year it became increasingly clear that Kaunda would not be satisfied until he had driven most of the white settlers out of Zambia, and I found it very depressing to drive along the main road from Livingstone to Lusaka and to see all the abandoned farms.

Like most of Kaunda's so-called African socialist reforms, it was never the rural Africans in Zambia who benefited. Kaunda was greatly influenced by Tanzania's Nyerere and his Arusha Declaration of January 1967. In that same year Nyerere was guest of honour at the annual UNIP Conference in Zambia, and it was no coincidence that in the following year, 1968, Kaunda started to Zambianise European businesses and to close eight hundred and fifty Asian-owned stores and businesses all over Zambia.

It was a clear indication that our days in Zambia were drawing to an end. So, later that year, we went down to Natal's south coast and purchased a house in Umkomaas, which was to be our home for over ten years. It overlooked the golf course and had outstanding sea views, too. A bonus was that a junior school for the children was less than a mile away, in pleasant rural surroundings.

We could not move immediately, however, as we knew it would take some time to make the necessary discreet arrangements to get some of our belongings out of Zambia, to obtain a fair price for those we would be leaving behind and to complete the transfer of our money and tanned game skins via Botswana.

I had had more than enough of the nonsense of Kaunda's Zambia by now. It was, for instance, still impossible to go out for a drink in any of Livingstone's hotels without coming across some drunken UNIP official looking for an excuse to pick an argument and get you deported immediately. But I was more than ever determined to leave only when I was ready financially – I had set a provisional date of departure for mid-1969.

I must admit that I had not wanted to go to South Africa – I had favoured moving to the Victoria Falls, but, thank goodness, I listened to my wife. If I had not, we would have had yet another black dictator to deal with in Zimbabwe – the Marxist Mugabe, who was far worse than Kaunda – about ten years later, and we wouldn't have been able to take our money to South Africa, as Mugabe restricted departing residents' assets and money to one thousand Zimbabwean dollars. But at that time (early 1970) it looked as if Rhodesia had everything under control, even sanctions, and the country was booming under Ian Smith.

I had met quite a few Portuguese troops in Angola, even going on patrol with them, and I knew some of the officers did not like having to do more than one tour of duty in Angola. But none of us had any idea that they would collapse so quickly when a left-wing *coup d'état* in Portugal (in April 1974) led to the communists taking over in Angola and Mozambique. This was disastrous for Rhodesia and, almost overnight, changed the war situation, adding over a thousand extra kilometres of hostile frontiers for terrorist bases.

Worse was to follow, in 1975, when South Africa withdrew its troops from Rhodesia, under intense pressure from the West. It was the beginning of the end for gallant Rhodesia, although it took the communists another five years to triumph completely.

*

In 1980 Rhodesia ceased to exist and Mugabe took over in Zimbabwe. I was glad to be established safely in Umkomaas, on Natal's beautiful south coast. It sometimes reminded me vividly of my youth and summer holidays spent in Felixstowe, on England's east coast. I was actually born in old Felixstowe, and I still remember being taken down steps which led between cliffs to the beach below. On reflection now, I am extremely glad that we were able to bring the children up in such idyllic surroundings, far away from the Western drug scene.

That the last eighteen months before we left Zambia for good were going to be very difficult was obvious. When we had moved to Livingstone in 1964 it had been easy to rent a house from South African Mutual but now, after independence, it was almost impossible, as just about everybody wanted to sell and get out.

When South African Mutual announced that it was selling all its houses, I found I had no option but to buy somewhere to live. I managed to find a fairly large house with a lot of spare ground. Then I bought a railways house very cheaply, took it down in sections and, using PWD foremen at weekends, put it back together again on my property. So I now had two buildings together, forming what I hoped would be an attractive proposition for some large company when the time came for me to sell.

Fortunately I was right and, in 1968, I was able to sell the whole property, at a good profit, to a building firm. They had a road contract in Livingstone and, for security reasons, wanted to keep all their European staff together. They used the large lounge, and my study next to it, as a mess and the rest of both buildings as sleeping quarters.

There was such a demand for tanned skins and accessories in Livingstone, due largely to the publicity generated by my displays in Kitwe and Lusaka, that I found I could not cope with the ever-increasing number of people who visited our house on their way out of Zambia. So we were forced to open a shop, next to Livingstone's only cinema, in the Capital Theatre building on the main street going to Victoria Falls, Bulawayo and South Africa.

From the pictures of the shop (see Appendix) it can be seen that we offered handbags (frame, drawstring and shoulder), briefcases, pouffes and cushions, as well as such smaller skin items as purses, wallets and key cases.

It was this shop that gave me the idea of what I should do for a living when we had to go to South Africa at the end of 1969, although I rarely had time to visit the shop, which was run by very reliable European staff. When I had to collect the money, or see to something personally, I made a point of going after hours as, during opening hours, there were too many UNIP officials about requesting (in effect demanding) donations for UNIP funds, which I always suspected went straight into their own pockets.

I managed to sell the shop to an American missionary, who wanted a business for his wife and, most important, he agreed to take any game skins I had not sold when we left for good at the end of September 1969.

After selling our property, we were lucky enough to find a place to rent on a short-term basis, while we made arrangements for most of our furniture to be sold, as well as my Land Rover and trailer. All my remaining raw skins also had to be sold in Bulawayo during that last month before our departure for South Africa.

⋆

Officially we were going to South Africa on our annual six weeks' holiday, so we both asked for (and got) our usual two months' re-entry permits to Zambia: without a re-entry permit I would have had to have tax clearance.

There was one last hurdle before we could leave. I had already sent off two railway consignments of trunks, containing prize skins and most of our smaller belongings, and I had had to pay heavy bribes to get them out. But we still had so much stuff on the roof-racks that I prayed that the customs officers on duty would include one of the two who had previously taken bribes for consignments of my skins going to Johannesburg – and my prayer was answered.

When the man came out to examine the car I could see he was a bit shaken at the amount we were taking. But I had slipped him his usual retainer, and I could see that he was prepared to accept my story that we were going on a camping holiday and needed all the extra stuff we were carrying.

It is pointless to describe the relief I felt as we pulled in at a riverside chalet (on the Rhodesian side of the Victoria Falls) which we had booked for the next few days, because, for those accustomed to life in the West, it would be almost impossible to understand the pressure of living in a place where one rash word could mean being put over the border (minus nearly all one's possessions) at twelve hours' notice.

We spent the next day at the chalet, a pleasant place on the banks of the Zambezi, repacking everything. I arranged for five or six of the larger suitcases and cartons to go by passenger train from Victoria Falls to Umkomaas in Natal.

One night during our stay I got a bit drunk when I was at the Victoria Falls Hotel bar with some Rhodesian friends. Some American tourists, hearing me talking about Livingstone, asked for my opinion of Zambia – they seemed a bit taken aback at how venomously I replied.

Drunk as I was, I soon realised that the Americans, like so many in the West, had been so brainwashed by the media that they were incapable of understanding what was happening in independent African countries.

It would have been pointless to explain that, after six years of keeping my mouth shut in public in Zambia, it was a relief to be able to say exactly what I thought about Kenneth Kaunda, UNIP and the whole sorry mess I had left behind.

★

Before I sum up my twenty-two years in East and central Africa, and what I think has to be done to try to clean up the mess created mainly by the communists and the West, there has to be some understanding of just how widespread the deliberate cover-up is, and how effective the disinformation about black Africa has become. Not even the large charities are immune, with Oxfam and Church charities being among the worst offenders.

One television programme about refugees in Africa and the charities working in Ethiopia (or somewhere in that area) summed up the incredible stupidity and waste of effort that goes on all over Africa. Viewers were shown a large refugee camp, and a great deal of footage was devoted to showing how water had to be carried by trucks to the camp from the nearest water supply – fifty miles away. This is madness on Africa's dirt roads!

Why wasn't the refugee camp sited near the water supply? Then, with a bit of drive, the refugees could have been put to work to make the camp self-sufficient in food supplies; to begin with, fruit and vegetables could have been planted. These refugee camps appear to be almost permanent fixtures, so more must be done to make them self-sufficient in food. Apart from solving the problem of how to get supplies to the camps, working to grow their own would give the refugees some self-respect.

Another television programme illustrated the madness of some of Kaunda's actions in Zambia. He likes to blame Rhodesia's UDI for all Zambia's economic troubles but they are mainly self-inflicted because he drove out a large proportion of the white farmers but did nothing to assist African rural farmers.

Yet viewers are shown a bunch of Europeans, Irish I think, who were sent out from Europe at great expense, with large and expensive farm machinery, to grow crops commercially in Zambia. There was, of course, never a mention of the cost of this madness. All I could think of was the farce of the Groundnuts Scheme in Tanganyika.

It cannot be stressed too often that there is no need for the annual famines that occur in most parts of Africa. A very simple first step would be to make cassava a compulsory crop, as it was in Tanganyika in the colonial days.

Mention has already been made of how the media used *Cry Freedom* in their campaign of propaganda against South Africa. Much the same applies to the film *White Mischief*. The film gave the impression that it depicted the way white settlers in Kenya (and elsewhere) acted. The truth is that there were a few degenerate British Establishment remittance men in Kenya's Happy Valley, but they were not typical. Most of the white settlers were ordinary, hard-working farmers, businessmen, government officials and so on. There were, incidentally, quite a few Afrikaner farmers in Kenya, especially around Eldoret.

The majority of the hard-working Kenya farmers, as in the Rhodesias, had built up their properties over the years completely from scratch or from very small beginnings. Most considered themselves to be Africans and they felt dispossessed and bitter when the colonial powers turned against them in the vain hope of saving Africa from the evils of communism.

★

Too few people in the West seem to understand that the smartly suited Africans, mission and often university educated, who are seen so often on our television screens and at the UN have absolutely nothing in common with the large majority of their fellow Africans. Most of the rural Africans have been reduced to near starvation by the incompetence and corruption of most of their leaders.

It has to be accepted that the UN has been a complete failure in Africa for the past thirty years (from the time most of the African countries got their independence). The communists, with their socialist allies in the West, as well as the Commonwealth and other Third World countries, have tried very successfully to conceal just how badly the UN has failed in Africa.

Now that the Gulf War is over, the West has to face up to some home truths about Africa and start to listen to those of us who have spent most of our lives there and know the truth about the unnecessary tragedies that have occurred there since the end of World War II.

The UN has to be restructured to curb the communist and socialist nonsense about a 'new world order' (such gibberish is just as common in the West). Action has to be taken to stop the Communist bloc manipulating the UN – as it has done for the past thirty years, with the help of the Third World countries.

The figures given below are from the main UN budget for 1984–1985, and show just why the present system cannot be allowed to continue:

Description	Total Countries	Percentage of UN Budget Paid
West and Japan	24	74%
Communist states*	16	18%
Latin America**	33	4%
Asia**	35	3%
Africa**	51	1%
Total UN member states	159	100%

*China, East Europe, and so on
**119 Third World states pay only 8%

From these figures it will be seen how ridiculous it is that the West and Japan pay seventy-four per cent of the UN budget, while the 119 Third World countries (including tiny island groups like the Seychelles, Comoros, Mauritius and São Tomé) pay only eight per cent of the UN budget and the fifty-one African countries pay only one per cent.

From the noise these insignificant countries make at the UN, however, anybody not knowing the real situation would assume that it was they who paid the seventy-four per cent and the West and Japan who paid the eight per cent. The time is long overdue for the Third World countries, especially the fifty-one African countries, to be cut down to size and made to face facts.

During the past thirty years, while the UN has been squandering billions of the West's money in Africa, the population there has more than doubled. During this period, especially from 1972 to 1982 (while Waldheim was the Secretary-General), the communists were able to manipulate the UN to such an extent that hundreds of millions of dollars were squandered in anti-apartheid activities against South Africa: one of the few prosperous countries left in Africa.

Western politicians have to be forced into action at the UN. They must point out to the Third World and the communists that, in the West, if a person or business goes bankrupt money cannot be poured in year after year unless results are achieved – and they must make it clear that the same criterion must be applied to UN aid money where African countries are concerned.

No UN aid will be given unless there is compulsory planting of anti-famine crops like cassava. No grandiose UN scheme will be considered, let alone implemented, until the African country is self-supporting in food. Most UN aid must go to rural African farming schemes on a small-scale basis only.

A vigorous birth control system has to be brought in immediately: the current norm (six to eight children) just cannot be sustained. Financial rewards should be given to parents who have no more than one or two children.

Any African country that requests aid must produce a provincial plan to encourage rural growth, with proper estimates of how long it will take for the area to become self-supporting in essential food. Then VSO and other aid organisations must be used to check on annual progress.

This is just a bare outline of what has to be done, but the waste at the UN cannot be allowed to continue.

*

The Gulf War showed very clearly the madness and greed of both the communists and the West, in that both had been only too willing to supply Iraq with its formidable array of military hardware and deadly chemicals.

It has to be said that, although we won World War II, we most certainly lost the peace, due to our own stupidity, and the quickness of the communists to exploit Western weaknesses, not only in Africa but all over the world.

Now, with the communists in disarray, the West has been given another chance, not only in Africa but at the UN as well. The war in the Gulf has been won and it is up to all ex-servicemen to see that Western politicians take advantage of this opportunity to end the domination of madmen like Saddam Hussein. This may well be the UN's last chance of saving Africa.

Someone of the calibre of the old leaders like General MacArthur and Field Marshal Smuts should be appointed as UN supremo in Africa, with the responsibility of stamping out the civil wars that are destroying the continent. Nairobi, with its temperate climate, would make excellent headquarters. To avoid corruption, only retired army, colonial, business or farming people (with some personal knowledge of Africa) should be appointed to decision-making positions.

A brigade of Gurkhas, paid for by the UN, should be more than sufficient to handle most local insurrections or attempted coups. Until the Gurkhas leave Hong Kong in 1997, a battalion or so would probably be sufficient and, in any emergency, more Gurkhas (and paratroops) could be flown in from

Britain. The mere presence of the Gurkhas in Africa should deter most of the troublemakers.

★

The present situation in Africa is absolutely ridiculous. Some African countries, like Ethiopia, the Sudan and Mozambique, where civil wars have been going on for years, are spending more than a third of their total national budgets on arms, while simultaneously getting millions of dollars in aid from both the UN and international charities.

With Russia sidelined, these civil wars should be stopped immediately, even if a special UN force has to be sent to guard and feed the refugees. All UN aid to these countries should be stopped until their expenditure on arms is cut to less than ten per cent of their total national budgets.

Senior representatives of the Organisation of African Unity (about fifty African states are members, as they are of the UN) must go with UN forces, in order to enforce the UN ruling of no civil wars, and to get the message across that all aid from the UN will stop unless the civil war is ended immediately. It is amazing that the UN has not already brought pressure on the OAU to see that this is done.

I know, from my extensive travels all over Africa for thirty-five years, that the rural Africans who make up the majority of the population want law and order restored to the way it was in the colonial era – they are the ones who suffer most from the present lawless situation. Their lives are difficult enough, battling with the elements to feed their large families.

It is up to ex-servicemen, and their organisations, to press for action at the UN.

The other priority is Africa's population explosion, and it is vital that the UN supremo in Africa be given funds to start a vigorous birth control campaign, so that Africa will have a chance to prosper in the next century.

On holiday with the children, Sylvia and Jean, in Natal and in Southern Rhodesia

Betty and myself in Mwanza, Tanganyika

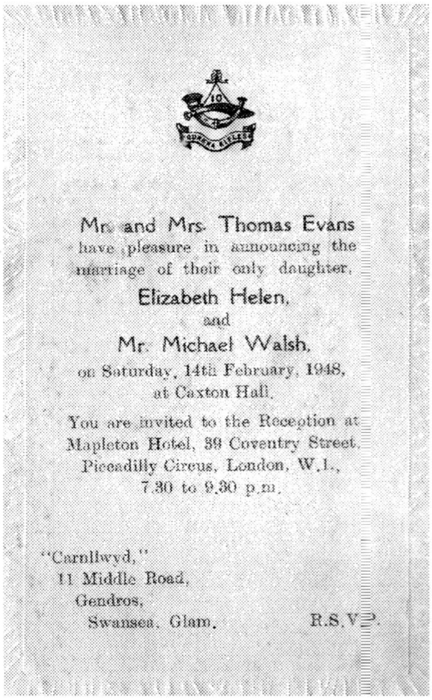

Mr. and Mrs. Thomas Evans
have pleasure in announcing the
marriage of their only daughter,
Elizabeth Helen,
and
Mr. Michael Walsh,
on Saturday, 14th February, 1948,
at Caxton Hall.

You are invited to the Reception at
Mapleton Hotel, 39 Coventry Street,
Piccadilly Circus, London, W.1.,
7.30 to 9.30 p.m.

"Carnllwyd,"
11 Middle Road,
Gendros,
Swansea, Glam.

R.S.V.P.

My present wife, Joyce

My present wife, Joyce, and my daughter Jenny

My first game and curio shop in Livingstone

Mwanza, Tanganyika, 1951

Livingstone in the mid-1960's

Appendix Four

TO WHOM IT MAY CONCERN.

This is to certify that Mr. Michael Walsh is proceeding to Mozambique accompanied by his wife, Mrs. Evelyn Ruth Walsh and that they are respectively the holders of United Kingdom Passports Nos. C.125085 and D.533118.

Both documents have insufficient space for further visas and the purpose of this letter is to confirm that there is no objection to the Portuguese Consulate-General at Salisbury endorsing this document with the necessary visas.

6044

Visto bom para viagem a PORTUGAL (Mocambique)
Visa good for travelling to PORTUGAL (Mocambique)
Válido para uma só viagem o permanencia de 7 [illegible] dias.
Available for one journey and permanency of 7 [illegible] days.
Utilizavel dentro de 120 dias a contar da data da sua concessão. 20. AUG 1966
To be used within 120 days from date of issue.
Este visto não dá direito à fixação de residência nem ao exercício de qualquer actividade, excepto a puramente comercial.
This visa does not entitle the holder to fix residence nor to carry out any activities other than those purely commercial.
Consulado Geral de Portugal em Salisbury
pelo O Consul, Geral, 20. AUG 1966

50$00 SERVIÇO CONSULAR
50$00 SERVIÇO CONSULAR

CONSULADO GERAL DE PORTUGAL SALISBURY

HERNANI JOSÉ DIAS
VICE-CONSUL

Pagou ao cambio de 80$00 a ... de £ 1/5/ Segundo o n.º ... da tabela, ficando esta importancia lançada no ... de receita sob o No. ... 9 2 5 8
Pagou mais a importancia de £ 7/6 segundo o n.º 13 da Tabela

THE BRITISH HIGH COMMISSIONER SALISBURY

BRITISH HIGH COMMISSION
RESIDUAL STAFF, SALISBURY.
19.8.1966.

ZAMBIA IMMIGRATION
13 SEP 1966
KAZUNGULA

ZAMBIA IMMIGRATION
12 SEP 1966
ROAD
KAZUNGULA
Exit

PROV. DE MOCAMBIQUE
POLICIA INTERNACIONAL
2 AGO 1966
AEROPORTO-MAVALANE
ENTRADA

PROV. DE MOCAMBIQUE
POLICIA INTERNACIONAL
28 AGO 1966
AEROPORTO-MAVALANE
SAIDA

ZAMBIA
IMMIGRATION
29 SEP 1966
ROAD
Exit KAZUNGULA

STATION COMMANDER
B.P. POLICE, Kazengula

STATION COMMANDER
29 SEP 1966
B.P. POLICE, Kazengula

BOTSWANA GAME INDUSTRIES CATALOGUE

FOURTH EDITION

Botswana: The African Colossus

Lying at the centre of Southern Africa, the Republic of Botswana is a landlocked country of some 220,000 square miles with a 1976 population of about 720,000.

Botswana is dominated by the famous Kalahari Desert which occupies four fifths of the country and is the home of large numbers of game and the few remaining bands of nomadic Bushmen hunters. In sharp contrast to the surrounding desert the Okavango swamps in the remote northwest corner of Botswana, where a major African river drains into a unique internal delta, comprises 6,500 square miles of streams and lagoons, rich in wildlife. Most of the population live in the eastern part of the country. This is a region of rocky hills, thick bush and ephemeral sandrivers, but a sufficient rainfall produces good pasturage for livestock.

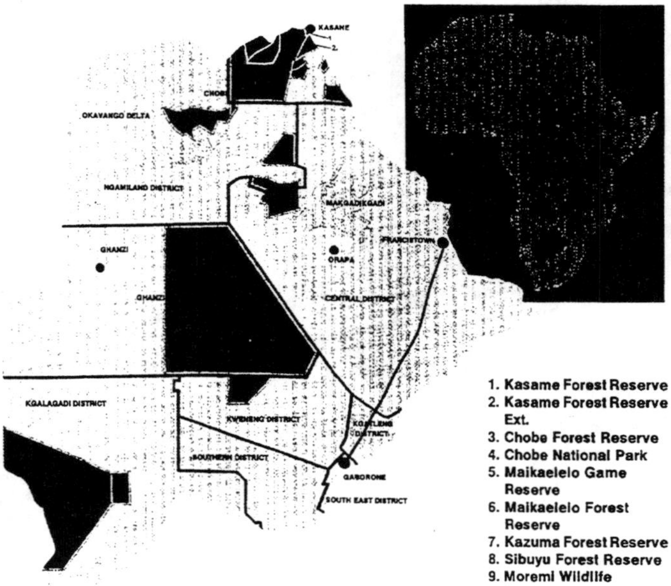

1. Kasame Forest Reserve
2. Kasame Forest Reserve Ext.
3. Chobe Forest Reserve
4. Chobe National Park
5. Maikaelelo Game Reserve
6. Maikaelelo Forest Reserve
7. Kazuma Forest Reserve
8. Sibuyu Forest Reserve
9. Moremi Wildlife Reserve
10. Nxai Pan National Park
11. Makgadikgadi Pans National Park
12. Central Kalahari Game Reserve
13. Kutse Game Reserve
14. Gemsbok National Park
15. Mabuasehube Game Reserve

THE GAME SKIN SHOP

P.O. BOX 576

LIVINGSTONE.

CAPITOL THEATRE BUILDING,
MOSI-O-TUNYA WAY.

Phones: Shop: 2329
Res: 2609

DISPLAY AND SALE

KITWE:

AT: EDINBUGH HOTEL (COPPER CABIN) 21st to 24th MARCH 1969 (inclusive)

LUSAKA:

AT: HOTEL INTER CONTINENTAL (ZAMBESI ROOM) 27th to 30TH MARCH (inclusive)

10:00 am to 10:00 p.m.

* * * * * * * * * * * * * * *

TANNED GAME SKINS

Complete range of lion, leopard, zebra, serval cat, civet, springbok; also karosses, and circular and half-circular fireside mats as well as square and oblong bedside mats. NEW LINE variegated game skin mats stitched in squares.

NEW ELEPHANT POUFFES AND FOOT STOOLS

CUSHIONS IN ZEBRA AND SPRINGBOK

HANDBAGS: Crocodile, lizard, leopard, cheetah, ostrich & zebra.

New range of drawstring bags in springbok (from K8:00)

ORDERS TAKEN FOR MOUNTED SKINS

* * * * * * * * * * * * *

VISIT US WHEN NEXT IN LIVINGSTONE - NEAR THE CINEMA

THE GAME SKIN SHOP

The place for wildlife in modern Africa

The great herds of Southern Africa have passed into legend.

At the turn of the century, springbok migrating in their millions would take 3 days and nights to pass one spot.

And a single herd of elephants covered the plains, far as the eye could see, in a coat of grey.

But man advanced. Wildlife retreated.

There was mass and wanton slaughter. Hunger of poor tribes competed with gluttony of poachers.

Whole species were wiped out or reduced to a few, sought-after specimens. Governments intervened, made laws and restrictions. Game Parks were established.

These measures helped. But hunger cannot be reasoned with.

The only long-term solution was to demonstrate to the people of Africa the long-term benefits of game conservation.

Man and wildlife integrated

The founders of Botswana Game Industries believe that wildlife has a better chance of survival when integrated with man's land use, rather than when it is a barrier to that use.

Game must become part of the local economy, promising future growth and prosperity.

Then it will be protected from extinction: as the fur trade in Canada demonstrates.

In Scotland the grouse moors are conserved through use. And in Africa the inland fisheries are being successfully developed. Fishermen learn the most effective catching techniques, how best to preserve, market and profit from their catch. At the same time, they understand the need to conserve breeding stocks.

Preserving the balance

Botswana Game Industries is run by conservationists.

They are committed to protect wildlife from indiscriminate hunting.

They are also committed to the rural people of Botswana.

To show them how the surrounding wildlife can be to their economic benefit.

So the company puts to best use the products of scientific culling the game administration.

Botswana Game Industries has a tannery and a world famous taxidermy studio. It trades in ivory and manufactures many items from game trophies.

The company is at the service of hunters, manufacturers and gift seekers.

It only purchases trophies that have been acquired legally.

An independent wildlife research consultant has been commissioned by the company to keep a watch on its conservation activities.

If any evidence indicated that trade in the products of a species might jeopardise its survival in Botswana, the company would cease to handle them – irrespective of whether other bodies held the same view.

Growth through conservation

Botswana Game Industries (Pty) Ltd was formed in 1966.

The company is one of the biggest employers in Botswana and one of the country's largest exporters.

To date, Botswana Game Industries has spent over $4 million (U.S.) in Ngamiland and $1.5 million in the Western State Lands. In the next 5 years more than $8 million will be spent in these areas on raw material purchases. This money goes directly to the lowest income groups of Botswana.

"Growth through Conservation" is a policy that benefits those people whose need is greatest. It demonstrates to them the value of wildlife. And it gives the animals their permanent place in the African continent.

From an old tin shed...

Botswana Game Industries started in 1966. It was the first company to register after Independence. The company's original "factory" and head office was an old tin shed, barely 72 square metres. Today, Botswana Game Industries has a tannery in Francistown covering over 3 600 square metres.

HOTEL
INTER•CONTINENTAL
LUSAKA

P. O. Box 2201,
LUSAKA.
Zambia.
Central Africa.

22nd August, 1969.

TO WHOM IT MAY CONCERN

This is to certify that Mr. Michael Walsh, the Hides and Skins Exporter, P. O. Box 576, Livingstone, Zambia, has been holding, since the opening of the Hotel Inter-Continental Lusaka, regular displays and sales of game skins. We have had many compliments on the quality and variety of these displays.

Victor Lima

V. R. Lima,
FOOD & BEVERAGE MANAGER.

VRL/EN

LUSAKA, ZAMBIA   INTER-CONTINENTAL HOTELS   CABLE: INHOTELCOR

TELEX No: 2214 BD
CABLES: "BUSHMEN"

TEL: FRANCISTOWN 247 AND 216

BOTSWANA GAME INDUSTRIES (Pty.) Limited

Game Skin Tanners, Taxidermists and Ivory Traders

REGISTERED

WITH DEPOTS AT –
MAUN - KASANE - NATA - GHANZI - SEHITWA

OUR REF.

YOUR REF

12th November, 1980.

To whom it may Concern

This is to introduce Mr. Michael Walsh of Game Skin Curios who I have personally known for the last twenty years and who we have commissioned to undertake a feasability study of sales of our products in the Middle East.

He has similar appointment in Zambia and in Far East with great success and we are sure that the exhibition and sales that he will hold in your area will also prove of great interest.

Any assistance that can be given to Mr. Walsh will be much appreciated.

PETER BECKER
<u>MANAGING DIRECTOR</u>

Part Four

South Africa: 1970–1983

Chapter One

Back to Civilisation

We were in no hurry to reach our new home in Umkomaas, on Natal's beautiful south coast, and made the most of visiting friends in Rhodesia and South Africa on our way. I still remember how lush and green everything seemed when we finally reached the south coast. After we had left Bulawayo the countryside had become arid and the climate very hot and dry. Few places can be as unpleasant as Beit Bridge – and Messina (just over the border in Northern Transvaal) wasn't much better. So the contrast as we approached the coast was very noticeable.

It was a much more interesting trip down to Natal before the new double-lane freeways were completed in the 1980s. The old road passed through numerous small towns and we enjoyed seeing the well laid-out gardens and attractive houses. The Zulus we passed on the road in Natal were very different to the Zambians, and noticeably more cheerful. The women, especially, all seemed to be on the large side and it wasn't long before we found out why: our children's nanny, Isabel, soon let us know that she expected at least a pound of sugar every day and my wife, Eve, had to fill a one-pound jar with sugar for her daily – otherwise she told us very firmly that she hadn't the strength to work.

Living in Umkomaas reminded me of rural England before World War II. Within a day or so of our arrival, just about everybody in the street had brought us cakes and other goodies to keep us going until we had got ourselves organised. What a contrast to living in London or any other city in the West!

Although I was glad to be out of Zambia, I did miss the free and easy lifestyle I had enjoyed for most of my twenty-two years in East and central Africa. I knew, from speaking to others who had come to South Africa after a lifetime up north, how difficult it was going to be to get used to the different way of life.

South Africa was, of course, well run and safe, but I must admit I found most South Africans very smug and insular (very much the same as their counterparts in the West), and without the slightest interest in what was happening in the rest of Africa. There was also a firm and widely held belief, which I did not share even then, that the troubles elsewhere would never spread to South Africa. Why should they worry? Thanks mainly to their generals, Botha and Smuts, South Africa had enjoyed almost uninterrupted peace and prosperity for about seventy years – since the Anglo-Boer War ended in 1902.

None of us had any inkling then of how the communists would bring about the sudden collapse of the Portuguese colonial empire in 1974. In 1975 Machel's Frelimo gained independence in Mozambique, as did Neto's MPLA in Angola in the same year. This changed the whole situation in central and Southern Africa, and led to Mugabe taking over Rhodesia in 1980. Thus the communists had succeeded in virtually surrounding South Africa with hostile Marxist states and in 1989 they took over Namibia, thus completing the job.

In the early 1970s I made business trips to Rhodesia, once my curio and skin shops were operating satisfactorily in South Africa, and when I visited Victoria Falls I sometimes bitterly regretted having moved, instead of following my inclination to stay in the area I had loved most since leaving my farm in Tanganyika. The odd trip to Wankie Game Reserve was all I could manage to remind me of the old days in unspoilt Africa.

The children's education was one reason I agreed to move to South Africa, but there was another. In my last few years in Zambia I had found it increasingly difficult to undertake the long Land Rover trips to Barotseland that I had always enjoyed so much: the back problems I had suffered ever since the war, due to the lack of proper medical attention in India, had been getting progressively worse. Previously I had always found a day or two in bed sufficient to cure the worst of the pain but, during those last few years in Zambia, I found I was lucky if I spent only a week in bed or resting at home after each trip

While I was in South Africa it became so bad that, eventually, I had to give up my almost daily drive to Durban from Umkomaas, although it was only a matter of a sixty-mile round trip. I found it almost impossible to get into my car and, when I managed to do so, the agony of getting out was even worse. So I decided that I would drive only when I had to combine a visit to Durban with a visit to our other curio shop – at Umhlanga Rocks.

I disliked the train journey, as it took far longer, but it turned out to be the only solution. The train was seldom crowded, so it was possible for me to walk about when I felt the first twinges in my back, and this always seemed to ease the pain. It was not always possible to go by train, however, as I often had to deliver stocks to my shops. Not having to drive on a daily basis certainly seemed to help because, now that my driving days were infrequent, I managed without too much trouble – provided I took breaks in the journey.

I never made the mistake of thinking it would be safe for me to visit Livingstone again, much as I would have liked to do so. My British passport now carried a special stamp which granted me permanent residence in South Africa, and I knew that things had changed for the worse since we had left Livingstone and that the Zambian immigration officials had become almost paranoiac about South African spies. I had heard about a number of innocent British passport holders who had been gullible enough to believe that their passports guaranteed them safety (as they had done in colonial days) and who had been held for months in very primitive Zambian jails, without trial, merely because they were suspected of being either Rhodesian or South African spies.

*

Unfortunately, far too many people have been taken in by the Western media's reports on conditions in independent, black-ruled, former colonial countries in Africa and they have no idea of the very real risks they run of being arrested and imprisoned purely on suspicion or through spite. Even in 'safe' African countries like Kenya there are considerable risks, especially for women travelling alone, as the tragic case of Julie Ward shows only too clearly.

There is absolutely no doubt in my mind that, but for the efforts of her father, her brutal murder would have gone unpunished. Few people have Mr Ward's financial resources, or the time and tenacity to travel backwards and forwards to Kenya, as he did over the course of several years following his daughter's murder in September 1988. Due to the lack of help from official channels, Mr Ward had to spend over £250,000 in order to bring his daughter's murderers to trial.

The last thing the Kenyan government wanted was any kind of investigation into Julie Ward's death and, from newspaper reports, it appears that British consular officials weren't exactly over-helpful during Mr Ward's enquiries. It appears almost miraculous that, against all the odds, enough evidence was found for Scotland Yard detectives to be brought in. Their investigations culminated in Kenya's Attorney-General ordering his commissioner of police to arrest two African game wardens at the Masai Mara Game Reserve, where Julie Ward's burnt body had been found. The local police had claimed, originally, that she had been killed by wild animals after her Land Rover had broken down in the Masai Mara Game Reserve, but the experts brought in by Mr Ward were able to prove that the wounds which had been responsible for her death were from a panga (a long knife used for cutting sisal), not from wild animals.

★

The horrifying death of Julie Ward, an innocent tourist, serves to pose the question of just how many other murders in Africa (and elsewhere) have been covered up without any kind of official inquiry taking place. Few British families have the financial resources to see that a proper police investigation is carried out, and don't realise just how anxious local officials are to cover up the truth, so that their tourist trade is not affected. Many local officials are both lax and venal – and efficient inquests are rare, since there is seldom the safeguard, which we have in Britain, which requires a proper coroner's certificate to be obtained.

With ever-increasing numbers of Britons, and other Western nationals, visiting remote places in all corners of the world, one would suppose that some of the British newspapers would investigate the subject of British tourists' safety, but they don't seem to be interested in doing this.

It should not have been Mr Ward's responsibility to track down killers and I think a national campaign should be started with the object of ensuring that he is reimbursed for all the money he had to spend to get some justice.

A government emergency fund should be started, so that British embassies or consulates anywhere in the world could draw on it as necessary for money to carry out their own full investigation into any death or disappearance of a British national in their country. Where there are suspicious circumstances and the local authorities seem to be dragging their heels, the embassy or consulate should insist that they be allowed to bring in Scotland Yard and, when necessary, they should pay the fare for a close relative to visit the country and finalise matters to the family's satisfaction.

Few in Britain seem to understand the very real risks of travel in today's Africa, where there are civil wars going on and bribery and corruption is an accepted way of life.

★

Ironically, Neil Kinnock and his wife, who both agonise so eloquently in public on the evils of apartheid, were given a very salutary lesson in the realities of Africa during their 1988 trip to Zimbabwe.

One evening there was some kind of mix-up over where their plane was meant to land and the Kinnocks' party ended up at the wrong Zimbabwean airport. To those who know Africa, there is nothing particularly unusual in this sort of fiasco, nor in the fact that the Zimbabwean troops guarding the airport were all drunk. The corporal in charge was also drunk and refused to believe that they had accidentally landed at the wrong airport. He suspected they were spies – probably South Africans as they were all white. It was part of Mugabe's propaganda to get all Zimbabweans to believe that just about every white was spying for South Africa.

This general paranoia created by Mugabe could have backfired tragically when the Zimbabwean corporal started menacing the party with his Russian AK-47 automatic rifle and prodding and pushing them towards a small tin hut, where they were all to be locked up for some hours. It was very fortunate that, on this occasion, Neil Kinnock had the sense to keep a rein on his notoriously short Welsh temper. He contented himself with a vigorous protest and then led his imprisoned party in singing Welsh songs, to keep up their spirits and to help while away the hours they had to spend in the very hot and badly ventilated hut.

It must have seemed almost unbelievable to the Kinnocks that they should be treated in this very undignified manner, especially in a country run by their friend Mugabe.

This is, of course, what made the incident so amusing for those of us who have lived in Africa. There is no doubt in my mind that it was extremely lucky for Kinnock that he did not provoke the drunken Zimbabwean corporal any further than he did: there might well have been a very different, tragic, end to this farce.

As it is, the Kinnocks received a very unpleasant lesson about the realities of life in Africa, and I hope they realise that they were very fortunate to have come out of it so lightly – with nothing but their dignity impaired!

*

That there has to be some form of power-sharing is obvious, but it is a great mistake to rush it through. The communists, and socialists like the Kinnocks and many churchmen in the West, ignore the harm they will cause to the lives of all South Africans, not only the five million whites, if the changes are made too hastily.

It was for this reason that, when I returned to Britain after thirty-five years in Africa, I decided that we ex-servicemen simply cannot stand by and allow the Western politicians to create even more destruction in Africa. Even at this late stage, all ex-servicemen must do more to ensure that South Africa, with its two million South Africans of British descent, is not handed over to the ANC and the SACP. Elsewhere in Africa, urgent action has to be taken to stop the civil wars that have brought ruin and starvation to so many countries.

Colonel Slovo always kept a low profile in public, and it was a sign of the confidence of the South African Communist Party and the African National Congress that in his later years he appeared regularly on television with Nelson Mandela. Few in the West have any idea of his role as Moscow's man in the ANC, or the fact that he founded and masterminded the ANC's military and terrorist wing, Umkhonto we Sizwe, which carries out numerous murderous attacks on 'soft targets' in South Africa.

Like most people living there, I was always too busy earning a living to bother with politics and so, when I returned to Britain in 1983, I knew little, if anything, about the very dangerous conspirators who were plotting against South Africa and had succeeded in creating widespread chaos and starvation in the name of progress and communism.

As the communists and socialists get more confident that there is no longer any need to worry about public opinion in the West, it is becoming easier to investigate below the surface, to discover the extent of the conspiracy against South Africa. Helping to start TAAL in early 1986, after recovering from my heart problems, was obviously only the start of what had to be done and a letter from TAAL to Lord Wyatt in February 1991 (regarding media bias in the West) highlights the need for further ex-service action.

It is for these reasons that TAAL's letter to Lord Wyatt, who has been campaigning against media bias, is reproduced (see Appendix), together with six pages of information that is rarely included in Western media reports about South Africa. While the Mandelas get almost daily coverage, for instance, it is seldom mentioned that their ANC has less support than Dr Buthelezi's Inkatha movement or that, whether the Western media like it or not, the seven million Zulus (who mainly support Dr Buthelezi) are a vital factor in the negotiations to find a peaceful solution for South Africa's political future.

The communist and socialist influence has never been more clearly shown than it has since Nelson Mandela's release from prison, with the Western media portraying him and his Marxist ANC as the only solution to South Africa's political future.

★

After our first few weeks at Umkomaas, which we spent relaxing and getting the garden into shape (our neighbours had very kindly seen to it that the hedges and grass were cut before our arrival), I was keen to start visiting the rest of the south coast. When we had come down on holiday from Livingstone we had spent most of our time on the beach at Amanzimtoti, with visits to Durban, and had rarely gone further down the south coast than Scottburgh, five miles from Umkomaas. So it was quite a revelation when we went as far as Port Edward, near the Transkei border, and visited booming coastal holiday resorts like Margate and Ramsgate (having been at school in Kent, I became quite nostalgic!) and saw how the curio and game skin businesses were progressing.

Trips to the north coast followed as, while we had been based in Livingstone, we had only once travelled in that direction: when we visited the St Lucia Game Reserve and stayed at Charter's Creek to see the flamingos landing in their hundreds. I wanted to see the rhinos at Umfolozi and Hluhluwe and I liked the area so much that I always felt that, if it hadn't been for the children's education, I would have settled there, somewhere between the St Lucia and the Ndumu Game Reserves, as it resembled so much the Barotse-Livingstone area – with the added bonus of the Indian Ocean.

We also visited the Eastern Transvaal and, again, were surprised by the extent of the curio and game skin businesses in these areas.

It took us quite some time to get acclimatised, as Natal's weather, especially on the south coast at Umkomaas, was much more variable than we had been used to at Livingstone. Not long after we arrived, and had had a few warm days swimming, a sudden cold and wet spell set in and, believe it or not, we were very glad of the fireplace in the lounge, a room which we seldom used except when it was cold, as there was a magnificent closed-in porch with delightful views, not only of the golf course but of the sea as well. The porch ran the whole length of the house, passing in front of the bedroom, the dining room and the lounge. The front door opened on to the porch as well, with steps leading up to it as it was in an elevated position.

There was a local Indian contractor who delivered cut logs, so we ordered five tons and sat by the fire for the next two weeks. It reminded me of my early days in East Africa, when I had been recovering from malaria in the

Highlands of Kenya and we had needed a log fire there every evening. What was so incredible to me was that it was only a week or two away from the Christmas school holidays when it became really hot again.

Although we did not know it then, we were shortly to witness the annual Christmas holiday exodus of Transvaalers and Orange Free Staters, who filled every available sort of seaside accommodation in Natal over this holiday period – some of them even slept on the beaches.

In the southern hemisphere the seasons are reversed, so December is summer and the South African schools have a long break over Christmas, beginning in the first few days of December and lasting until the middle of January. I knew, after seeing the exodus for the first time, that if we could set up a shop by the main south coast road, which (in the days before the new double-lane freeways were built) passed close to Umkomaas, that would be the ideal place to start our skin and curio business on Natal's south coast. Once again, more by luck than good judgement, everything was to turn out just as I hoped.

The last thing I wanted to do was to buy an existing business before I had had a chance to see the ins and outs of the area. I had heard plenty of stories about people coming down from the north to settle in South Africa and being taken in by some of the local wide boys, who sold them businesses that turned out to be far less profitable than expected.

So when I met Pat and Doreen Schlanders, who used to farm in Northern Rhodesia and were now the owners of the Woodhill Garage, Widenham, on the main south coast road and only about a mile from where we lived in Umkomaas, I had a feeling I was going to be lucky once again – and so it turned out. They owned some empty land next to their garage and were happy to let me have it for a shop, provided I put up my own buildings – and got permission to do so from the Natal provincial authorities in Pietermaritzburg (who controlled all the businesses that operated near the main south coast road).

They let me have the land for a nominal rent of ten rand per month (in 1970, this was about £5). Very many thanks, Pat and Doreen. I only hope that they are both still alive as, just before I left South Africa, Pat had a serious heart attack that left him paralysed down one side. Pat died four or five years after I left Umkomaas.

It was only after returning to Britain that I began to understand there weren't many people like them left in this money-grabbing world. It was that kind of help that made it possible for us to afford to send both children to Durban University.

After my experiences in dealing with black government officials in East Africa and Northern Rhodesia, I was a bit apprehensive about the kind of treatment I would get from the Natal provincial authorities in Pietermaritzburg. But I needn't have worried – their efficiency and helpfulness is something I remember to this day. The contrast with the inefficiency and delays of Zambia, only a month or two in the past, was incredible.

Although the communists, socialists and Western media rarely deal with facts where Africa is concerned, it has to be mentioned that the efficiency of provincial authorities goes a long way towards explaining South Africa's prosperity – especially when compared with the indescribable mess in all the newly independent African states to the north.

While I was in Pietermaritzburg, I also explained that Pat's Woodhill garage opened seven days a week, to cater mainly for tourists, and how much it would help our business, which was also mainly for tourists, if we could be given permission to open over weekends.

In view of the Afrikaners' religious background, I knew it was not easy to get the special weekend licences, which were restricted to tourist businesses only, and it was a great relief when the permission eventually came through in time for the Christmas holidays of 1970. We found we took more over these holidays (about six weeks) than in six months of normal trading. Our building plans had to go to Pietermaritzburg for approval, and it is a remarkable tribute to the help we received that we were able to open our shop at the Woodhill Garage within eight months of our arrival in South Africa.

With the Natal provincial authorities' approval, work on building the shop was able to go ahead. I had already decided the best, quickest and cheapest way to build was to adapt a very attractive prefabricated type of building made locally by a firm called Timbrik. Two large display windows were put into the side of the building that faced the main south coast road. The wall panels looked like strips of wood and were painted white. The entrance, facing the car park that was used by customers going to the garage café and the takeaway, as well as to the curio shop, had double glass doors with display windows and shelves, and inside there was a coloured tile floor.

With the hedges and lawns around the curio shop, it all looked very attractive and certainly drew crowds of tourists in those early years of the 1970s. In fact, the only mistake I made was not having doubled the size of the buildings: we found we could barely cope with the Christmas rush of Transvaalers and Orange Free Staters. Later we had to add a large painted aluminium roof extension on the side, that was closed in to take the extra stocks we found we had to carry at Christmas and Easter.

Most of the locals in Umkomaas thought we were mad and predicted our curio business would not last a year. In fact, it exceeded all my expectations in those early years and, when one of Durban's best-known curio shops came on the market a few years later, the Umkomaas shop was able to pay for the purchase.

Aussie Frolich (who owned Aussie's Taxis in Durban) had originally opened a curio shop called African Curios and Carvings on Durban's Esplanade for his daughter but, when she went to Europe and stayed there, he had eventually decided to sell – and we were lucky enough to be able to buy on easy terms.

*

Another great advantage we had in those early days in South Africa was the fact that, during my last few years in Livingstone, I had been stockpiling as many skins as possible: getting them tanned in Botswana but not returning them to Zambia. I looked on these skins as part of my personal assets from Zambia that I could not bring out in cash. In those first few months before we opened our shop at Umkomaas, therefore, I was able to wholesale enough of these skins to cover most of our living expenses. In reality it was a few years before we eventually finished selling all our Zambian skins.

Fortunately, there were two storerooms at our Umkomaas house where we were able to keep the skins. It would have caused problems to keep them in the store at the shop, as they were fairly bulky and we could only sell two or three a month, but they certainly helped with our personal expenses in those early years in South Africa.

It was difficult in those days (the 1970s) to resist the urge to open further curio shops, and travelling to our Durban shop daily made it easy to drop off stocks to the new shops we opened in Amanzimtoti and Umhlanga Rocks.

In quiet periods I liked going up the north coast to relax from business, as I found the area around St Lucia and up to Ndumu still unspoilt enough to remind me of my halcyon years in East Africa and the Rhodesias. So, although I knew it would never be very profitable, I arranged to open a curio shop in the Hluhluwe Holiday Inn – to give myself an excuse to visit the area (with my expenses paid) more often and, while I was there, to go to the game reserves at Umfolozi and Hluhluwe.

The Holiday Inn shop arrangement had been worked out with the manager's wife and worked very well until, quite a time later, there was a change in management and the new manager wanted to take over my shop there It had served its purpose as far as I was concerned, and we had not provided the shop fittings, so there were no complications. I just packed up all the stock and distributed it around my other curio shops on my way back to Umkomaas.

*

My present wife, Joyce, is an Indian from Natal and, when we returned to Britain in 1983, both of us were absolutely amazed at the media attitude to South Africa. We became aware that there never seemed to be any interest in providing balanced coverage and most media reports were so biased that we found it difficult to accept that they were talking about the country we had just left.

Led by Channel 4, with communist producers like Tariq Ali, everything bad about South Africa is represented sensationally, while the impression is deliberately given that everything is completely satisfactory in the newly independent African countries. The starvation, chaos and corruption are rarely reported.

What we also found completely astonishing was the blatant effrontery of Commonwealth countries like India criticising South Africa's treatment of her million Indians. Those who, like myself, served in India during World War II, are only too well aware of the iniquities of Hinduism. Much as the Indian government tries to pretend otherwise, the lives of the Indian untouchables have worsened, not improved, since the end of the days of the British Raj in 1947.

In fact, with the exception of the old dominions, there are poverty and appalling living conditions (of which the average Briton is completely unaware) in most of the rest of the Commonwealth. Yet the Commonwealth hypocrites, backed by the communists and socialists in the UN have managed to waste millions of Western taxpayers' money on anti-apartheid activities.

The reality of South Africa, just like the rest of Africa, is totally different to the impression given by the Western media.

Just as I am writing from personal experience, more of the people who have real knowledge of Africa must be encouraged to write about it, in order to counter the erroneous flood of left-wing books trying to justify the damage that the communists and socialists have caused there.

There is nothing so infuriating to those of us who have spent many years in Africa as the so-called experts from Britain (and elsewhere in the West) who seem to think that, after only a few weeks in Africa, they are qualified to appear on television, write in the national newspapers and publish books.

Take even the BBC's expert on Africa, Michael Buerk. Admittedly he did spend a few years as a BBC reporter in South Africa, but I get the impression that he has no deep knowledge of the realities of Africa. Most of the televised violence I have seen him reporting was laid on by the ANC, on the orders of KGB Colonel Slovo, head of the South African Communist Party.

★

Although the Afrikaner now realises that apartheid has to go, it would be very unwise for the West to try and push reforms too quickly, just as it would be madness to allow the usual UN chaos and mayhem to engulf prosperous South Africa.

Too few people in the West realise that the African does not understand democracy. To him, as to the people of most Third World countries, to allow an opposition party is a sign of weakness – Iraq is a good example in the Middle East. It is no coincidence that the most stable countries in Africa tend to have a strong-willed dictator as president for life.

The tradition of strong leaders is well established in Africa and it was only when the British broke the power of autocratic African rulers like Shaka, Dingane and Lobengula that the system started to change. African tribal life had always been based on apartheid (separate development), and the different tribes rarely mixed. No Masai would dream of mixing with his traditional enemy, the Kikuyu (or vice versa), and just over the border from Kakonko there was the classic case in Ruanda-Urundi (now Rwanda and Burundi) of the very impressive Tutsi, like Masai in Kenya of mixed Hamitic stock, who for centuries had dominated and enslaved the local Bantu tribe, the Hutu.

Apparently, and how ironic, the ex-Nazi Kurt Waldheim saw nothing wrong if apartheid was practised by black on black, but he waxed most eloquently all over Africa when it was practised by white on black, as in South Africa.

Although I was brought up and educated in a very liberal public school (The King's School, Canterbury), with the 'Red Dean', Dr Hewlett Johnson (who distributed the *Daily Worker*), next door, having seen the ghastly mess in independent Africa during the past thirty years, I sympathised with the reluctance of most South Africans to hand over power to the South African Communist Party and the ANC.

I quite understand how difficult it is for the large majority of nice, well-fed and democratically secure citizens of Britain to understand the realities of life in most of Africa, especially as the Western media seem to be determined that the appalling truth about independent black-ruled Africa over the past thirty years should be concealed from their readers. I quote the last three paragraphs of Peter Worthington's Foreword:

> When one looks at the evidence that unfolds daily, for all to see who want to see, there is a war going on, not against apartheid, but against South Africa itself.
>
> I'm afraid I am convinced that the Western media, Western politicians, academics and all too many church figures are not so much interested in a peaceful solution to South Africa's problems, but want bloodshed and an overthrow of the system at any price, and the installation of another form of government, even if it ends up being a Marxist regime.
>
> I mostly blame the media for what can only be described as disinformation about South Africa. Instead of going where the story takes them, that is, of honestly reporting events as they see them, too many media people are reflecting what they think their audiences or editors want to see, hear, read, or what they personally believe should be the case.

*

In much-maligned South Africa, it was obvious (from as early as my first trip to Natal in the early 1960s) that progress towards power-sharing was taking place all over the country. The University of Zululand, on Natal's north coast not far from Empangeni, was for black students, and an indication that more higher educational facilities were being provided for black South Africans. At that time there were only eighteen black academics with suitable qualifications to teach at university but by 1985 this figure had risen dramatically and there were 333 black academics teaching at the five black universities in South Africa.

Natal's biggest development scheme during this period was the new port and town at Richards Bay, which was completed in the mid-1970s. It provided a great economic boost for Kwazulu, which came into existence shortly afterwards. By 1984 the port of Richards Bay was handling forty-five million tons of cargo annually, more than double the turnover of Durban (twenty-one million tons). This made Richards Bay South Africa's premier commercial port – quite an achievement.

Nearer to home, on Natal's south coast, the development was on a much smaller scale, but it was just as noticeable. When we first arrived at Umkomaas (at the end of 1969), most of the African housing near the main south coast road consisted of the traditional thatched, round mud huts. These gradually gave way to small cement-block houses with standard doors and windows – not, perhaps, such an aesthetic sight for tourists, but much more comfortable to live in. With the views of the Indian Ocean and Natal's balmy climate, it always seemed to me a much better way to live than in some depressing inner city in Europe – even if there was no television.

Another amenity for Africans on Natal's south coast started shortly after we had moved there from Livingstone. At Umgababa, only a few miles from Umkomaas on the old south coast main road to Amanzimtoti, several large commercial buildings with plenty of surrounding grounds had been taken over and converted into a large holiday complex for black South Africans. Chalets were built for the more prosperous African businessmen and holidaymakers and the whole holiday complex occupied one of the most attractive sites on the south coast. It was on the sea side of the main coast road, so the families had no roads to cross on the way to the beach and sea. The local African businessmen who ran the beer halls, bars and liquor stores soon became rand millionaires.

Not far from Umgababa there were lots of roadside curio kiosks, licensed and organised by the local Zulu chief. Before opening my first game skin and curio shop at Widenham (which is almost a suburb of Umkomaas), I visited these kiosks several times, to see what they sold and the prices they charged. What surprised me was the amount of Far East junk that was mixed up with the genuine Zulu and Swazi beadwork, and I later found out that most of it was supplied by Indian curio wholesalers from Durban.

The Natal provincial road authorities had provided a convenient drive off from the main road to the Woodhill Garage, so there was a steady stream of Transvaalers and Orange Free Staters coming in for petrol, and getting drinks and snacks at the café, as I checked up during that first Christmas period (1969). Many of them took advantage of the break in driving to stretch their legs and I was pretty confident that they would wander into any shop that was there – and we would get in more than our share of these potential buyers, as no skin products were sold at Widenham, nor by the African roadside curio dealers, before I opened in 1970.

Later I was able to buy quite a lot of Zulu beadwork from some of their suppliers for my curio shops in Durban, Amanzimtoti and Umhlanga Rocks – on the understanding that I did not sell it at my Widenham shop. I was quite happy to give this undertaking, if only because I could never hope to sell their beadwork at the ridiculously low prices they were able to charge. Their overheads were very, very low and it was accepted business practice in the curio retail business in Durban to mark up at least one hundred per cent on most items. I rarely dropped prices at Widenham, although the overheads there were very low when compared to my shop in central Durban.

During the 1970s there was considerable building development all along the south and north coasts, but none was as dramatic as the change that came to Umhlanga Rocks which, even in the 1960s, was still a small, sleepy village near Durban. Then the developers took over and it lost most of its early charm. It all looked very impressive but, by local standards, it was expensive – and I thought it very overrated.

In Umkomaas we were very lucky as, in all the years we were there, there was very little change. The hotels filled up at Christmas and Easter, but that made very little difference to our lives, except that it was very hectic for our business and it was never possible for us to take a break over these holiday periods.

The development I saw taking place was restricted mainly to Natal, but it was the same story over most of the RSA. When I returned to Britain after thirteen years in Natal, therefore, it was very difficult for me to understand the continual ravings of the communists, the left-wing weirdoes and the pinkish prelates like Archbishop Huddleston who were continually harping on about the oppressed Africans in South Africa.

Archbishop Huddleston left South Africa over thirty years ago, and surely he must know that it has changed since then. I find it impossible to believe that, while he was there as a bishop, he did not see the misery in Tanzania caused by his Marxist friend, President Nyerere. Yet he had the unmitigated gall to go on television and blame the West for Tanzania's economic woes!

While I don't condone apartheid, there is no doubt in my mind that prelates like Huddleston and organisations like the Anti-Apartheid Movement deliberately ignore all that is good in South Africa in order to spread communist propaganda. They seem to be unmoved by the bloodshed they have helped to cause and most of the Western media seem to be quite happy to help them.

This imbalance in the media was one of the main reasons for starting TAAL. I believe it is ex-servicemen who must bring more pressure to bear, as they know from personal experience just how bad conditions are in India and most Third World countries. Those who are in a position make comparisons know that conditions in South African townships like Soweto are much better than in the slum areas of many other African countries.

The first people I came across who have spoken out about the lies being spread, not only about South Africa but the rest of Africa as well, were the authors of *The Destruction of a Continent*. Now, just as importantly, the experienced Canadian journalist and author Peter Worthington has condemned the Western media for their policy of disinformation about South Africa.

None of us living in Africa had the slightest idea of the extent or the success of the communist propaganda campaign. It was about two years after our return to Britain, in fact, before my wife and I began to have any inkling of the extent of this campaign.

★

Certainly we had no idea how successful the Russians had been since we left Zambia at the end of 1969. Had I been asked then, I would have said that Rhodesia could last out indefinitely, with South Africa's help over sanctions. The first alarming cracks began to appear in 1974, with the collapse of the Portuguese in Angola and Mozambique, but it was felt that Rhodesia would still be able to contain the floodgates that were opening for Russian arms and equipment – even though these two African countries now had Marxist regimes.

Worse news followed in 1975 with South Africa's 'Suez' when, succumbing to American pressure, the RSA withdrew all its forces from Rhodesia. There was a further blow in 1976, when South Africa withdrew more than half of the forty helicopters on loan to Rhodesia, and fifty pilots and technicians were also recalled. The helicopters had played a vital role in enabling the Rhodesian security forces to respond quickly to any terrorist incursions into the country.

To coordinate the communist gains, Moscow's linkman with the ANC and head of Umkhonto we Sizwe, Colonel Slovo, at ANC headquarters in Lusaka, instructed agitators in Soweto to increase their subversive activities. In June 1976, Soweto exploded into violence, which quickly spread to other African townships on the Rand, then to the Cape and also, to a lesser extent, to Natal. It was another triumph for communist propaganda, as the Western media poured into South Africa, eager to report every violent incident that occurred in the townships.

Worse was to follow at the end of 1977, with the tragic death of Steve Biko. The Marxist Mugabe, who had shot and beaten to death thousands of unarmed Matabele in Zimbabwe, wasn't slow to realise the propaganda value of Biko's death. Although Zimbabwe was bankrupt and receiving millions of pounds annually in aid from Britain and America, he was still able to finance *Cry Freedom* to the tune of five million dollars and to provide film-making facilities for it to be produced in Zimbabwe.

The communists very successfully concealed most of the mayhem and the mass murders that were being committed all over Africa during the 1980s, just as it had done for the past twenty years or so (most African countries became independent in the 1960s and 1970s – there were a total of over forty African countries becoming independent during this period, while in the 1950s there had been only six). Most of the newly independent states were ready tools of the Communist bloc at the UN. The UN Secretary-General over this crucial period was Kurt Waldheim, who never missed an opportunity to criticise both South Africa and the colonial powers as he continued to further the aims of the Communist bloc.

When, in August 1978, Waldheim submitted the Namibian settlement plan to the UN Security Council and it was approved (Resolution 435 of 1978), he had completed most of his work for the Communist bloc and the OAU, although Namibia only received its independence some years later, when the Marxist Swapo took over.

Before Waldheim's suspected war crimes were exposed, he had high hopes of receiving the Nobel Peace Prize – just about the final irony in how he managed to hoodwink the West! It is a very sobering thought that, if Waldheim had been content to retire after his ten years as UN Secretary-General (1972–1982), instead of becoming president of Austria, it is unlikely that any of his unsavoury past would have emerged: it was only during his campaign for the presidency that his political opponents started revealing details of his Nazi past.

Being now of a distrustful nature, I wonder whether the Russians awarded Waldheim, like Slovo (privately, of course), the Order of Lenin. He certainly deserved it, or an even higher award, for the damage he did on their behalf in Africa while he was the UN Secretary-General.

It has to be stressed that a great deal of Waldheim's deliberate damage to the West still continues. Readers will have noticed that Western politicians still talk of a New International Economic Order (NIEO), or a New International Order or, now, just a New Order. We are never told who instigated NIEO – it was, of course, Waldheim, with discreet Russian backing – or that it still operates today. In fact, as conditions continue to worsen in Africa, so it expands. It takes huge sums of money and large amounts of goods and food, as well as other Western resources, from the Western taxpayer. These are 'redistributed' to the Third World without payment. The Russians see this as the easiest way to overburden the free enterprise Western system.

Chapter Two

The Waldheim Conspiracy and the OAU

During the course of this book, I have made several references to the harm done by Kurt Waldheim during his ten-year term as Secretary-General of the UN (1972 to 1982), during which time he worked closely with OAU – the Organisation of African Unity – and the communists to support and finance African terrorist movements as, in the name of liberation, they attempted to destroy the last two prosperous countries in East, central and South Africa: Rhodesia and the Republic of South Africa.

A typical example of how Waldheim abused his influential position, and gave a very slanted account of everything, was at Addis Ababa in 1973, when he addressed the OAU meeting there and spoke not a single word of praise for what the white man had achieved in Africa over the past three hundred years.

★

I think it is worth listing some of the more important communist coups in which Waldheim played an important part during his tenure of office.

1. 1974 – At a special session of the UN General Assembly, Waldheim inaugurated the New International Economic Order (NIEO), whose basic aim is to increase steadily the huge sums of aid money already being given by the West, via the UN, to Third World (mainly African) countries. The eventual aim of NIEO is to make aid compulsory, automatic and permanent, so that the West will forever continue to transfer ever-increasing amounts of aid money, goods and other resources to the Third World without any compensation. A concerted propaganda campaign was mounted by Waldheim's UN, the communists, the socialists, trade unions and radical intellectuals, via the Western media, to get

across the new message of anti-colonialism and the redistribution of wealth.

2. 1974 – Waldheim helped further communist plans to destabilise South Africa and Swapo, by orchestrating the UN General Assembly to arbitrarily (and illegally) deprive South Africa of its right to participate in UN activities.
3. 1975 – The Soviet-backed minority party, MPLA, usurped power in Angola. The other parties (UNITA and FNLA), who represented the majority, were excluded from the Angolan government. There were no protests from Waldheim's UN about Marxist minority rule.
4. 1976 – To support the minority rule, thirty thousand Cuban troops poured into Angola, as well as thousands of East Germans and Russians. Again, there was no UN protest.
5. 1977 – To further communist plans for the conquest of Southern Africa, Waldheim and his communist friends in the UN pushed through a Security Council's mandatory arms embargo against South Africa. It had been anticipated that this would facilitate a Russian-Cuban victory in Angola, which would then lead to military victory in South West Africa and Namibia, but Waldheim had misread the situation. The arms embargo helped Armscor (The Armaments Corporation of South Africa) to expand dramatically, so that it was able to supply all of the South African forces' requirements in Angola, and also to establish a thriving export market.
6. 1978 – Waldheim submitted his detailed plan for a South West Africa and Namibia settlement, knowing it would eventually lead to Marxist control of Namibia. His report and settlement plan were approved by UN Security Council Resolution 435. Although South Africa originally refused to accept Resolution 435, mounting world pressure meant that it eventually had to accept Waldheim's proposals. Its later delaying tactics managed to postpone the handover for only eleven years.
7. 1979 – Waldheim and his communist allies continued their propaganda campaign against South Africa in the UN and, at the January session, the General Assembly reaffirmed: 'The legitimacy of the struggle of the oppressed people of South Africa and their national liberation movement... [should continue] ...by all available and appropriate means, including armed struggle...' This, of course, constituted completely un-

warranted interference in South Africa's internal affairs, and encouraged the terrorist activities of the ANC. Having succeeded in Namibia, the communists were determined to succeed in South Africa as well.

8. 1980 – Further triumphs for the communists as the Marxists took over in Zimbabwe. Both the so-called liberation movements (Zanu and Zapu) had been heavily dependent on communist aid and arms. Since then President Mugabe has consolidated his position and now rules Zimbabwe as a one-party state – no opposition is allowed.
9. 1984 – South African forces decisively defeated Cuban-Angolan forces at Cuvelai in southern Angola: over twenty Russian tanks were destroyed and hundreds killed. Russians were found to be in command of the Cuban troops.
10. 1989 – As the Cuban troops withdrew from Angola, Namibia gained its independence as another Marxist-ruled country.

In late 1989, we began to see the collapse of the communist empire in East Europe and this, together with the withdrawal of the Cuban troops from Angola, should signal the end of the communist military threat to South Africa. However, the era of Mandela may prove just as dangerous for South Africa and extreme caution has to be adopted. The ultimate aim of Mandela's ANC and their SACP allies, formerly under KGB Colonel Slovo, now deceased, remains the same.

*

Few in South Africa, or the West, know the full extent of the UN communist-inspired conspiracy against South Africa and the importance of the role played by ex-Abwehr officer Waldheim in those ten crucial years as Secretary-General, during which he was able to direct the communist plans for the takeover of Southern Africa.

Waldheim used apartheid as an extremely useful propaganda weapon against South Africa. He was fully aware that there was more democracy in South Africa, even with apartheid, than in all the Marxist and military regimes. When he sang the praises of black-ruled Africa in the UN and the OAU, he was under no illusions about the ghastly misrule, mayhem and mess in most of independent Africa, including oil-rich Nigeria, and he knew the faults of apartheid were trivial in comparison.

Why was Waldheim also so willing to ignore the murderous excesses going on in countries like Argentina, Chile and Peru, where literally tens of thousands were being brutally murdered every year? Because, above all else, his friends in Russia wanted the big prize: South Africa.

Including the six self-governing black national states, South Africa accounts for only 4.3% of Africa's population and 3.7% of its surface area.

Yet it produces about twenty per cent of the continent's total gross national produce, forty per cent of the industrial output, forty-five per cent of the mining production, forty per cent of the maize and fifty-two per cent of the wool clip.

It uses two-thirds of all the steel in Africa, two thirds of all the electricity generated there, has forty-three per cent of all the motor vehicles and thirty-seven per cent of all the telephones.

In Southern Africa there are twelve countries which, combined, are roughly the size of Western Europe, and have a population of about a hundred million. South Africa accounts for more than seventy-five per cent of this region's economy.

This is the prize that Russia wanted, and nearly got with Waldheim's help at the UN. Ironically, since the West and Japan supply about seventy-five per cent of the annual UN budget, they have been financing the communist onslaught in Africa. It is worth noting that over US $100,000,000 was wasted annually on the anti-South Africa propaganda campaign, by over two hundred full-time UN staff, whose work permeated into almost every sphere of international relations.

The scope of the anti-South Africa propaganda campaign, which reached its height during Waldheim's ten years as Secretary-General (1972–1982), was truly mind-boggling, as the General Assembly, the Security Council, the Secretariat and the Economic and Social Council all had their own anti-South Africa projects and programmes. In addition, they established fifteen subsidiary bodies which are exclusively, or primarily, concerned with Southern Africa.

Waldheim's anti-South Africa propaganda activities at the UN are self-evident. He was able to manipulate the UN to suit the communist plans for Africa. From the seventh point in the list, it is clear that he encouraged and legitimised the ANC's terrorist activities in South Africa, including the use of the barbaric necklace against anyone who did not agree with the ANC's aims.

That the General Assembly should approve the violent pursuit of political ends gives some indication of the depths to which the world peace organisation has fallen since that great South African soldier and world statesman,

Field Marshal Jan Smuts, played a leading role in drafting the preamble to the UN Charter, and in its foundation in 1945.

Even in the early days, however, some Indian members of the South African Communist Party had started their scheming, in conjunction with India and the communists. In 1946, at the first session of the UN General Assembly in London, the question of the position of Indians in South Africa was placed on the UN agenda. Thus started the illegal interference in the domestic affairs of member states which Secretary-General Waldheim used to further communist aims in Rhodesia and South West Africa, when he masterminded Resolution 435 through the UN Security Council in 1978.

*

The original principles of the UN were being eroded continually, with ever-growing interference in the internal affairs of South Africa and South West Africa. This inexcusable behaviour culminated in the majority of UN members, predominantly made up of the Communist and African blocs, refusing to accept the 1966 judgement on South West Africa that was handed down by the International Court of Justice in South Africa's favour. They proceeded arbitrarily to terminate South Africa's League of Nations mandate, which they had no right to do.

In 1972, with the start of Waldheim's ten-year tenure as Secretary-General at the UN, the final stages of the communist conspiracy were put in hand, masterminded by him. They culminated in the 1978 report and settlement plan for a Marxist takeover in South West Africa – now renamed Namibia – and the report was approved by Resolution 435.

No doubt Waldheim's experience as an intelligence officer came in useful as he skilfully expanded the most important anti-South Africa organisation at the UN – the Special Committee Against Apartheid. This collaborated very closely with anti-apartheid movements around the world, as well as with Africa's terrorist movements, like Swapo (South West African People's Organisation), ANC and PAC (Pan-Africanist Congress).

Under Waldheim, the Special Committee's scope for disinformation against South Africa was gradually being expanded to cover all the international conferences and anti-apartheid initiatives taking place in the West. Most people in the West believed these meetings and demonstrations were spontaneous – nothing could be further from the truth. The AAM in Britain, as elsewhere, was very efficiently organised by a few radical Marxists, with financial help from Waldheim's Special Committee Against Apartheid.

Waldheim had learnt the value of propaganda from his Nazi masters during the war, for they were experts at spreading disinformation. He made sure the UN spy tentacles reached into every sphere of life in South Africa.

His Special Committee Against Apartheid maintained a detailed surveillance of South Africa's trade, economic and business links all over the world, as well as checking on its military, diplomatic, sporting and cultural ties with other countries, especially those, like Britain, who have any family links with it. It applied considerable pressure on the countries, companies and individuals concerned to end those relationships.

It was in the field of sport that sanctions hurt the ordinary South African most. Any naive hope that the overseas restrictions would be lifted after genuine efforts were made to make South African sport multiracial were soon dispelled by anti-South Africa organisations like SANROC (South African Non-Racial Olympic Committee), who only increased their efforts, backed and financed by Waldheim's UN, to isolate all South African sport overseas.

Many people were nauseated by the way SANROC and the very unsavoury Anti-Apartheid Movement (also financed by Waldheim's UN) persecuted that very talented South African athlete Zola Budd. With a British father and grandfather, she had the automatic right to a British passport – just like over a million South Africans of British descent in South Africa, many of whom are ex-servicemen who have fought for Britain in the world wars.

Like so many of South Africa's Indians, many of whom have never been to India, SANROC's spokesman in London has to be reminded about some of the harsh realities of life in the Indian subcontinent. Both India and Pakistan have absolutely appalling human rights records since independence, shortly after the end of World War II. South Africa's apartheid faults pale into insignificance by comparison.

Apartheid is now changing, while the problems of India's untouchables have been part of the Hindu religion for centuries and recent laws to try and change the system haven't had the slightest effect. The same can be said of the Hindu custom of suttee, whereby a widow casts herself on her husband's pyre. It has been officially banned, but it is still practised – and has actually become more frequent since the end of the British Raj as, nowadays, there are few attempts to enforce the ban.

Pakistan's military dictatorships are very similar to those in Africa. The Pakistani leaders are, however, much better educated, and some of the traditions from the British days still linger. Quite a few of the senior officers were Sandhurst trained.

Unfortunately, the British public tends to judge Commonwealth countries by their sportsmen who play in Britain, such as Imran Khan and Kapil Dev. What they do not understand is that these men have little in common with the ninety-nine per cent of their countrymen who live in dire poverty.

★

Some of the major UN projects included documentation and assistance for the Special Committee Against Apartheid, and providing financial support and other forms of assistance to countries running special anti-apartheid campaigns on specific issues: such as the release of political prisoners. A good example of this was the worldwide campaign to free Nelson Mandela: very considerable financial contributions were made directly by the World Council of Churches, and other such bodies, which included giving direct aid to some terrorist organisations in Africa.

It is worth noting that the Nordic countries always headed the list in the percentage of their GNP (Gross National Product) given in aid to Africa. It is, of course, no coincidence that the socialist Nordic countries were enthusiastic supporters of Waldheim and his scheme to destabilise the West through NIEO, which started in 1974.

The Soviet Union, with typical duplicity, liked to condemn NIEO in public while supporting it behind the scenes as a model for world socialism, which the Nordic countries see as the start of a world socialist welfare state.

In Africa and Asia it is seen as a very useful weapon to blackmail the industrialised countries of the West, as the puppet Marxist African states take over from the former colonial powers. In late 1989, Namibia was added to the list of African Marxist States and Russia's influence stretched over about forty per cent of Africa.

★

The tragedy behind the madness of the last thirty to forty years is that the real problems of Africa are being almost completely ignored. The most serious problem is undoubtedly the population explosion. Europe's population growth rate is less than 0.5%, while Africa's is over three per cent. This means that, by the year 2000) most of the already-starving African countries will have doubled their 1980 populations.

★

Population in millions		
Year	1980	2000
Kenya	16	34
Mozambique	10	20
Tanzania	19	35
Uganda	13	24
Zambia	6	11
Zimbabwe	7	15

This means that aid will have to double – and continue to double every twenty years – obviously an impossible situation. So a completely new approach to this problem has to be found, before it is too late.

★

With the start of the disintegration of the Soviet empire in the late 1980s, the whole African scene changed and a great deal of pressure was taken off South Africa. Nelson Mandela's release from prison has also given the West a great opportunity to right some of the wrongs perpetrated in Africa by the UN over the past four decades.

Most of those who have spent their adult lives in Africa, and who care deeply about the continent, concur with the view that everything has deteriorated to an alarming degree and the West is probably being given its last chance to avoid the final catastrophe: unmanageable famine due to overpopulation.

There is, however, still a frightening lack of understanding in the West about the urgency of Africa's problems, and a great deal of the blame for this must be placed at the door of Waldheim's NIEO. Their propaganda managed to conceal the seriousness of the situation in Africa for far too long and we must now act quickly, before the situation becomes irreversible.

There are already, fortunately, some people and organisations who are trying to publicise the realities of life in Africa. Some in Britain who come to mind are the honorary president of the Rhodesia Christian Group (the Reverend Father Lewis, who spent forty years in East and central Africa as a missionary), and its director (Mr W. Denis Walker), the president of the Scottish/South African Society (Mr Harvey Ward) and the founder international president of the Weaving International Friendship Foundation (Mr Stuart Weaving).

These are just a few of those who know the truth and they, as well as ex-service members of TAAL (Truth About Africa League), share the opinion that Africa must be left alone to decide her own future, while wanting a fresh approach to solving Africa's most urgent problems: civil wars, overpopulation and starvation.

Old prejudices have to be forgotten and advice has to be sought from the *White Tribe of Africa* (this was the title of a BBC TV series in the early 1980s, about the history of the Afrikaner, but I include all whites in South Africa), as well as from any European who has lived in Africa for a long time (I would say a minimum of twenty years) and can speak at least one African language.

Few in the West realise the damage that has been caused in Africa by the mania for urbanisation, which has been encouraged by some of the UN madmen in the NIEO. They have very little appreciation of the fact that Africa's tribal system, which was based on a rural lifestyle, worked very well for hundreds of years. In the colonial era there was very little interference with the tribal system.

All that changed after the end of World War II and the granting of independence; most African governments did their best to break up the tribal system, as they saw it as a threat to their own regimes. The socialist, Marxist and military governments had little concern for the welfare of the tribal Africans – with disastrous results in East, West and central Africa.

★

Two African countries, Tanzania and Nigeria, illustrate the folly of unwise government decisions. Julius Nyerere of Tanzania has received more international aid than any other leader in Africa, yet he still refuses to admit that his socialist-Marxist agricultural policy has been a complete and disastrous flop, with less and less food being produced each year.

Nigeria's problem is not money; it is an oil-rich country which has squandered its wealth: an example of capitalism gone mad. Democracy never had a chance to work, as it is just as alien to Africa's way of life as Marxism.

For most of the time since independence (in 1960), Nigeria has suffered under brutal military regimes that were too stupid to understand the need to foster the excellent self-supporting agricultural base they were given as a legacy by the colonial service. So, in about three decades of self-rule, Nigeria has deteriorated so much that, instead of being able to export its surplus of commodities such as groundnuts, it has become an importer of food to the tune of a billion US dollars a year.

This decline in agricultural produce has been caused largely by the drift of small farmers and farm labourers to the cities in unprecedented numbers, lured by the tales of good money to be earned. Most end up unemployed and are among the several million people who produce nothing and depend on charity to survive. By 1990 Nigeria was having to import over forty per cent of its food requirements. If this is the situation in Africa's richest country, the outlook for the other, less fortunate, countries is bleak.

Yet the madmen at the UN do little except hold expensive conferences all over the world that do absolutely nothing to solve Africa's problems. Those problems are worse now than they were when we started pouring billions of dollars into the continent over thirty years ago.

*

Somewhere, and soon, a campaign has to be started by ex-servicemen in Britain and elsewhere to force our politicians to face up to the true facts of the disaster in Africa, and to see that extensive reforms are carried out at the UN. A more practical approach must be made to Africa's problems by using people who have actually lived in Africa for most of their working lives and have personal experience of the problems there.

The real curse of Africa (and, indeed, of many Third World countries) is corruption on a scale so vast that it has crippled any hopes of real development. In Nigeria, for instance, 'dash' reigns supreme. It is so widespread that it is almost official and no business is ever done, nor any contract awarded, without everyone concerned receiving some dash. It permeates every level of society and any visitor to the country who is not prepared to accept the system will be lucky to get beyond the airport – or the harbour.

With the departure of the incorruptible British colonial civil servants, today's Nigerian civil servant expects, and gets, his dash before any contract can go ahead. This means that foreign companies have to cover their extra expenses by loading their multimillion dollar contracts by around thirty to thirty-five per cent – to the detriment of the ordinary Nigerian, who faces vastly inflated prices for everything he needs: including food, rent and other basics. None of this is ever mentioned at the UN, even though it must be obvious that aid money is not immune, as dash operates everywhere.

In the shake-up that is so long overdue at the UN, all the ridiculously expensive and wasteful anti-apartheid organisations have to be disbanded with the minimum amount of delay. At the same time there must be a drastic scaling down in the numbers of bureaucratic staff employed at the UN. There has to be an end to the plague of bureaucrats who have achieved nothing but harm in Africa.

Experts from Africa, with a lifetime of practical experience there, are required, especially retired people and ex-colonial civil servants who cannot be bribed.

★

But even corruption pales into insignificance when compared to Africa's most pressing problem, which, to date, the UN has almost completely ignored: the population explosion.

By the year 2000, unless a change is made now, Africa's population will have doubled from the 1980 figure of 450 million to a massive 900 million. Possibly the most serious aspect of this huge increase is that most of it will be in urban areas, which means there will be no compensatory increase in the production of food crops.

Not even prosperous South Africa can sustain its present population growth indefinitely, especially as most of the increases are in the section of its population which is moving in ever-increasing numbers to the major towns. South Africa's population was 16 million in 1960 and 37 million in 1988. By the year 2000, it is expected to be 52 million! So it will be seen that South Africa's population will have almost doubled twice in forty years. If the old tribal system were intact, many of the new people would work on the land and produce food; as it is, most will produce nothing and will just be extra mouths to feed. This madness has to be stopped – and quickly!

★

Another fallacy beloved by international bureaucrats is that bigger is better. Nothing, of course, could be further from the truth. It is the individual who counts, but the bureaucrats are well aware that it is the independent individual who initiates criticism of their methods.

The same is true of politicians and, unless action is taken soon, we are going to see the EC bureaucratic madness develop into as expensive and unnecessary a monster as the UN. In fact the unnecessary expense has already started.

Who wants hundreds of MEPs and other European bureaucrats to batten on to the taxpayer? MEPs should have been seconded from the Houses of Parliament (and the similar institutions in Europe), so that the taxpayer would have to pay no more. The same should apply to Brussels: as one bureaucrat takes up a position in Brussels, one bureaucratic position in the country he or she came from should be cut. In this way the bureaucratic monster emerging in Europe could be controlled.

There is, however, a more immediate task to be tackled. It is imperative that the bureaucrats should get the message that the days of wasting billions of dollars of Western taxpayers' money are over. Never again should bureaucrats like Waldheim of Austria and Ahtisoari of Finland (UN special representative for Namibia) be allowed to interfere in African affairs.

To avoid interference by ignorant outsiders, each continent should have a senior UN representative on the spot and he must have lived there for at least twenty years before he could be considered eligible for the job. Bureaucratic experience would be unimportant: what would matter would be knowledge of his area. As Africa's problems are so urgent, it might be necessary for the continent to have two regional headquarters: one concerned with Southern and central Africa and the other with North, East and West Africa.

It would be clearly understood that the headquarters in each continent was there only to collate and coordinate all the UN work in the area. The expensive junketing around the world to participate in completely unnecessary UN conferences (currently seen as a perk of the job) has to stop. Close financial control on all UN projects could be carried out by voluntary aid workers, from organisations like Britain's VSO (Voluntary Service Overseas). One of their (unpaid) workers could see that proper financial books were kept and sent, at regular intervals, to the local UN headquarters, together with progress reports on each project.

But overriding everything else, except curbing the population explosion, is the need to get rid of the mess created by Waldheim during his ten years as Secretary-General – starting with the immediate abandonment of the NIEO. It is a dangerous body, created by Waldheim as a subversive communist front that drew together just about every radical working against the West, in the guise of a new socialist and economic order. The irony of the situation is that, through NIEO, the West has been paying for its own destruction!

The tentacles of Waldheim's NIEO stretched far and wide. One reached out to Ramphal, at the Commonwealth Secretariat in London – another organisation funded by British taxpayers, and which has set up yet another clique within the UN: the Commonwealth Experts Group.

Nobody illustrates better the type of bureaucrat attracted to the UN than Australia's Malcolm Fraser. While on a trip to the USA, he turned up at his hotel one morning very much the worse for wear and minus his trousers. He was unable to give any explanation of what had happened and, given his reputation, there was some very colourful speculation. Yet this man was quite prepared to stand for the post of Commonwealth Secretary-General, and he was the chairman of the Eminent Persons Group (an offshoot of the Commonwealth Experts Group) that went to South Africa in 1986 and had the impertinence to lecture the government there about how they should run their country.

A description of this typical UN bureaucratic scrounger's attitude to his work appeared in a small Australian magazine, published in London in November 1989, as a report from Canberra:

> Canberra: Former Prime Minister Malcolm Fraser's tastes for high living are creating problems for the Australian Government and the UN. The Nareen millionaire grazier has been having trouble making ends meet on the allowance given to him as the Chairman of the African Commodities Study set up by the UN Committee for Trade and Development. And he's also worried about Aids. Because his job takes him all over Africa, he has requested special 'high quality Aids free, medical treatment' if he is injured in an accident.
>
> Details of Mr Fraser's straitened circumstances are contained in a letter from the former Australian Ambassador to the General Agreement on Tariffs and Trade, Mr Alan Oxley, to the Deputy Secretary of the Department of Foreign Affairs, Mr Peter Field. According to the letter, Mr Fraser's demands on both the UN and the Australian Government have been many and varied.
>
> As well as the request for the 'Aids free' medical treatment, the Australian Government has also been asked for:
>
> An officer to assist him while he was working in Geneva.
>
> An allowance to help him with entertainment costs and to possibly upgrade his accommodation.
>
> The letter from Mr Oxley, who has now left Foreign Affairs, makes it clear that the people at UNCTAD, UN Conference on Trade and Development are somewhat 'exasperated' by Mr Fraser, it appears that Mr Fraser was regularly presenting the UNCTAD Secretariat with accounts over and above the daily allowance rate and for such things as dry cleaning and hair dressing.

Mr Fraser has very little knowledge of Africa, but he has found it extremely profitable to join the motley socialist-Marxist crowd at the UN and in the

Commonwealth, and he seems to think he has a job for life, paid for by the gullible Western taxpayer. Let us prove him wrong.

Another well-known Australian critic of South Africa, when he is not on television tearfully giving the Australian public details of his marital infidelities, is another of their prime ministers – Bob Hawke. What a pair he and Fraser make!

★

The deeply ingrained bureaucratic scrounging, at the expense of the Western taxpayer, permeates the UN at all levels, and one of the most urgent priorities is to use retired businessmen, instead of bureaucrats, to stop the waste of money.

It cannot be stated often enough that Waldheim used NIEO and the so-called ICIDI (Independent Commission on International Development Issues) to spread anti-Western propaganda on behalf of the communists and their Third World allies. Thanks to his very efficient training as an officer in the Nazi Abwehr, he soon realised the value of the continually expanding UN development organisations to get his anti-South Africa message across.

An absolute priority is to get rid of the numerous unnecessary and expensive UN organisations.

Some are mentioned here, and there are plenty of others that need investigation, and possibly closure: Unesco (UN Educational Scientific and Cultural Organisation), Unep (UN Environmental Programme), Habitat (UN Centre for Human Settlement), WFC (World Food Council) and ridiculous ones like Uncod (UN Conference on Desertification), Unctad (UN Committee for Trade and Development), UNCSTD, Unido, UNDP – the list is almost endless.

Even some of those, like Unicef, which are worth retaining (after cutting down on unnecessary staff and expenditure) need continual checking.

An executive from an efficient organisation, such as the Save the Children Fund (of which Princess Anne is patroness) should be sent regularly to UN headquarters in New York to check on expenditure. Unnecessary junketing around the world should cease and the hundreds of thousands of pounds spent on delegates' luxury hotels, airfares and their expenses should be diverted to the causes for which they were intended – in the case of Unicef, to the children.

Part of the Waldheim conspiracy was to create such a monstrous bureaucratic maze at the UN that it would be impossible to check on the multitudinous organisations and their activities. Josef Goebbels, Hitler's minister of propaganda, would be proud of the achievements of his pupil Abwehr Leutnant Kurt Waldheim, and of the mayhem he achieved in Africa during his ten years as UN Secretary-General.

★

What Western ex-servicemen, and other members of the public, have to ask their governments is why, now that the Russian threat has been removed, at least temporarily, from the world scene, nothing has yet been done to stop the incredible waste of taxpayers' money.

Since the October Revolution in 1917, the Soviet authorities have been responsible for the deaths of more than 110 million of their own citizens. No other nation, not even Nazi Germany, has ever come near to matching the USSR's endless flow of propaganda. The Russians weren't slow to realise the potential of the UN to help spread their message of hate against the West and enable them to use the West's generosity to heir own advantage. In public they condemned international Western aid as an 'instrument of capitalist imperialism' but behind the scenes, at the UN and elsewhere, they encouraged every tinpot country to demand ever-increasing amounts of aid money as a right – and on a permanent basis. The USSR preferred to spend its own money financing Cuban troops for Angola and sending arms to communist guerrillas in the Congo, Rhodesia, Angola, Namibia, Mozambique and South Africa.

The monstrous anti-West and anti-South Africa propaganda machine built up by Waldheim during his ten years as UN Secretary-General must be destroyed with as much publicity as possible, and as quickly as possible. The public in the West must be fully informed about the most gigantic, expensive apparatus for propaganda and indoctrination the world has ever seen. It must be explained to them that they, as taxpayers, are funding many departments of the UN, including the vast international bureaucracy that is dealing with aid to Africa and simultaneously spreading anti-Western propaganda.

The following points should be taken into account by those who genuinely wish Africa well:

1. The builders of the British Empire were right to allow the Africans to continue in a way of life that suited their tribal traditions, which had developed slowly over the centuries. The pioneers brought law and order and progress with the least possible amount of interference in tribal affairs.

2. Most of the UN work in Africa has been a complete waste of time and money. The USSR and Western socialists, with UN compliance under Secretary-General Waldheim, destroyed a great deal of Africa's tribal life for cheap political reasons. It is time that the UN dispensed with handouts and started using its funds to encourage the Africans to help themselves.

3. Unless something is done, Africa's population will have doubled by the turn of the century. In colonial times its mainly rural population was controlled by its ability to produce its own food. Misguided UN aid and subversive communist propaganda have helped to break the African's ability to survive using his own resources, but the free food (and other forms of UN aid, including medical care) have helped to create the disastrous population explosion. Something must be done, and quickly, to reverse the trend.

4. UN handouts have encouraged millions of Africans to leave their rural homes and drift into the towns and cities, where they soon forget their tribal traditions and cannot produce their own food. There must be a massive 'return to the land' programme – and Nigeria's oil wealth and South Africa's agricultural expertise should be used in conjunction with any UN programme.

5. Africa has solved her own political problems in the past, and must do so again. The Africans themselves must get rid of their Marxist and socialist leaders and return to a system compatible with their tribal way of life

6. The UN madness in Africa has to stop. The continent is in a bad enough mess without having to add South Africa to the list of disaster areas. Black Africa needs the help of a prosperous, well-run South Africa and the ANC, a communist-dominated organisation, is not the answer. Like the other countries, South Africa must solve its own problems, without UN interference.

7. UN aid has to be scaled down, not up, every year, and must be made dependent on the recipients doing their best to become self-supporting. Any country requiring aid should have to give the UN representative in its continent regular progress reports and details of every project funded by the UN. The Western taxpayers who ultimately foot the bills should be kept informed, through the media, of how their money is being spent – and aid should stop, pending an investigation, immediately any wastage came to light.

8. For humanitarian reasons, a UN emergency fund could be set up to cover genuinely unexpected natural disasters, such as earthquakes, floods or swarms of locusts.

9. However, it should be made clear to countries which regularly suffer from some form of natural disaster (for example, floods in Bangladesh and droughts in Ethiopia), that they must do everything possible to prepare for the next disaster, and thus limit the damage when it does occur. It should be clearly understood by such countries that UN help of all kinds will be much more readily available for prevention than for cure.

★

Too few people in the West are aware of the full extent of the waste of public money by the various UN bureaucratic organisations. Furthermore, the UN bureaucrats increase the waste every year – mostly at the expense of the long-suffering Western taxpayer.

The madness of the whole situation was shown very clearly by a report in the 'Business Day' section of the *Evening Standard* on 15th October, 1991:

> There are a phenomenal 78 German delegates at the International Monetary Fund meeting, taking up one enormous section at the Bangkok conference centre, writes Peter Osborne.
>
> During the day they wander around looking important and wondering what to do. By night they descend in beery swathes on Pat Pong, Bangkok's famous red light district.
>
> Then there are the Japanese – 56 of them and many like lost souls.
>
> At night they, too, are welcome visitors – the madames say they like the Japanese most because they all have 6.30 breakfast meetings and leave early next morning.
>
> The third largest contingent is the 51 Saudis. They are barely to be seen at the conference centre at all.
>
> Needless to say, there are plenty of French – 37 in all.
>
> There are 28 Nigerians and 27 Argentinians, leading one official here to suggest that the more poverty-stricken and indebted a country, the more delegates it sends.
>
> The British and the United States come out of this analysis as sleek, streamlined operations. The British delegation contains just 24, including three from Hong Kong who are not really British at all, and there are 23 Americans.

As a whole, the Brits appear sober, hard-working and impervious to the more exotic local attractions.

It should be noted that there are countless international UN conferences and meetings held every year which achieve absolutely nothing, at huge expense, except to turn out mountains of reports that no one outside the UN ever reads.

Three examples are given below, to give some idea of the numbers of highly paid bureaucrats involved in the abortive, but extremely costly, meetings:

1. 1,500 delegates met in Nairobi in 1977 for a UN Conference on Desertification. Imagine the huge amounts spent on their expenses: air fares, hotels, entertainment allowances, and so on.
   Achievements? *Nil.*
2. In 1981, 3,000 delegates from 125 countries met, again in Nairobi. As I know from personal experience, Kenya has some magnificent game parks, and I am sure the majority of the delegates would have managed to visit some of them – I imagine a good few would have rounded off their stay with visits to Malindi or Mombasa (on Kenya's beautiful Indian Ocean coast). The ostensible reason for the meeting, however, was to discuss the world's energy problems.
   Achievements? *Nil.*
3. 3,500 delegates from 142 countries met in Paris (also in 1981) to discuss the problems of the least-developed countries. This conference was a follow-up to one held in Manila in 1979 and, like most UN conferences, the outcome was to call for more aid money from the Western taxpayer.
   Achievements? *Nil.*

★

To understand how UN Secretary-General Waldheim was able to continually increase the pressure on the West for more and more aid money and other resources, it is necessary to understand the important role played by Europe's socialists. These included such prominent politicians as West Germany's ex-chancellor, Willy Brandt, and Sweden's ex-prime ministers, Palme and Fälldin – and similar men in the other Scandinavian countries.

Waldheim's great breakthrough came on 28th September, 1977, about three years after he and the communists had masterminded the start of NIEO at a special session of the UN General Assembly in 1974 – two years after he had taken over as UN Secretary-General and fourteen years before his suspected war crimes began to surface.

The international breakthrough that Waldheim needed to make NIEO respectable came when Willy Brandt announced, at a special press conference in New York, that he would launch and chair the Independent Commission on International Development Issues. To listen to Chairman Willy Brandt, one would have thought that he and ICIDI were full of high ideals, as the Commission's first task, to quote him, was:

> To study the grave global issues arising from the economic and social disparities of the world community, and to suggest ways of promoting adequate solutions to problems involved in development and in attacking absolute poverty.

In fact the ICIDI, which became known as the 'Willy Brandt Commission', was only plugging the same line as the UN's NIEO, in wanting to spend huge amounts of the Western taxpayers' money to solve problems in Africa that were insoluble unless Africa's population explosion was tackled first.

So all the eighteen members of the Willy Brandt Commission were really doing was to publicise Waldheim's NIEO aims, which were identical, if unexpressed:

> The rich in the West must indefinitely give to the poor in the Third World.

If Josef Goebbels had still been around, I am sure he would have been very proud of his devious pupil in the German Abwehr, Leutnant Kurt Waldheim.

*

Corruption and communism often go together, but many in the West find it difficult to believe the extent of the problem in countries like Nigeria, where bribes are an accepted way of life: nothing works, and no business can be done, unless you pay dash to everyone involved. In India, it is called baksheesh and, again, virtually nothing gets done unless you pay it. The system stretches right to the top and was one of the reasons Rajiv Gandhi's Congress Party lost the last general election in India that was held before his death.

One of the great strengths of the British Empire was the incorruptibility of the vast majority of its colonial civil servants, and their impartiality in judging any dispute that came before them in the course of their work was unimpaired by financial or religious considerations. I am proud that my father was part of this fine body of men in HM's colonial administration in Nigeria.

When the colonial era drew to a close after the war, Russia wasn't slow to capitalise on the situation in Africa. It soon realised that the UN could be used to further the Soviet aims and, by using their socialist allies in Europe to preach the doctrines of Marx and Lenin (and to stir up hatred against capitalist ideas and whites), the Russians managed to destroy almost completely the progress made in colonial days. Their plans really reached fruition with the appointment of Kurt Waldheim as Secretary-General of the UN in 1972.

During the ten years of Waldheim's tenure at the UN, many in the West were puzzled by his obvious zeal in destroying colonial Africa, and his avid support for every pro-Marxist organisation there – even when it was a group dedicated to murdering whites, and any black moderates who supported them.

With Waldheim's formation of the NIEO in 1974, the world (especially Africa) was treated to an unprecedented communist propaganda campaign against the capitalist West. The slaughter that followed all over Africa was approved both by the communists and the UN, provided it helped the cause of Marxist socialism in Africa. Allied to the senseless destruction was the irrevocable damage done by NIEO's UN aid programme, which tried to force change on Africans far too quickly and in the process, helped to destroy Africa's old tribal system of agriculture. It also succeeded in displacing millions of rural people, so they were forced into the already overcrowded towns where, as they were unemployed, they had to rely on UN aid organisations.

The UN bureaucrats have never been interested in listening to local advice. Success or failure means little to them, as they are not accountable to anybody. It is not their money that they are wasting, and they have been encouraged to believe that plenty more would be available from the Western taxpayer whenever it was required.

No business in the West would be successful if it operated in such an irresponsible and wasteful manner, without any well-defined goals or proper time limits. It was the aim of both Waldheim and the communists to create so much confusion that it would be almost impossible to check on expenditure or results.

To sum up what has happened at the UN, I am sure that Winston Churchill would not mind me misquoting his famous Battle of Britain speech: 'Never have so few wasted so much without any complaints from so many.'

*

Waldheim is already a proven liar and there is little doubt, from the facts already available, that he is also a war criminal, although the full details of his wartime activities have not yet been revealed. Yet there is a definite feeling among many observers that the UN and Western politicians do not want any more revelations about his suspected war crimes, as further disclosures are likely to reflect badly on them, by showing how easily they were fooled by him.

He concealed his wartime activities so well (by omission in his official biographies as well as in his own memoirs) that the truth started to emerge only at the time of his election to the presidency of Austria – in 1986.

It is a sobering thought that, had Waldheim been content to retire gracefully in 1983 (when he formally retired from the Austrian Foreign Ministry at the age of sixty-five), instead of staying on the public scene to fulfil his ambition of becoming the president of Austria, it is probable that he would have taken his guilty secrets with him to the grave.

Fortunately for those of us who want justice to be done, his ambition caused him to miscalculate the risks involved. Becoming Secretary-General of the UN, under communist protection, was rather different to fighting a democratic election and, as it happened, a member of the opposing socialist party a historian called Georg Tidl, had already uncovered parts of Waldheim's hidden military file, so extracts were soon published in the Austrian magazine *Profil*.

Sensational as these were in revealing facts about Waldheim's hitherto unknown Nazi past, they weren't enough to convince the world, or the Austrian voters, of his guilt – and he won the presidential election of 8th June, 1986!

But the events in Austria did attract the attention of the World Jewish Council in New York, and they asked the distinguished historian Robert Herzstein to investigate Waldheim's background, with particular attention to his wartime service in the Balkans.

In 1945 the Allies had taken possession of huge amounts of German military and political documents. Among them were quite a number that either mentioned Leutnant Kurt Waldheim or bore his signature. Eventually these were stored in Washington, DC. The Russians would have had access to the papers, via their Yugoslav allies, and it is certain that they were well informed about the suspected war crimes of Leutnant Waldheim even before they helped him to be elected to the very influential position of Secretary-General of the UN in 1972. Since they are experts in the use of blackmail, the situation would have suited the Soviets' devious purposes.

In 1988, the British media covered the story of the result of Herzstein's delving into the archives. Even in the preliminary stages of his examination of the German documents, he had found enough evidence against Waldheim to force him into an admission that the impression he had been giving, in other words, that he had spent only a few months in the Balkans on active service, was completely false and that, in actual fact, he had served through most of the Balkans campaign. More damaging still, he was forced to confess that he had been present at the Kozara massacre in Yugoslavia – a massacre which he had previously claimed had never even happened! This revelation of his duplicity enraged the Yugoslavs and a Serbian newspaper, *Politika*, began an investigation that produced more damning evidence against Waldheim, and the active role he had played in the Abwehr.

As further details of Waldheim's murky wartime activities came to light, after his election to the presidency, it seemed to most people that it could only be a matter of time before he was forced to resign but, incredibly, no action was taken against him.

In July 1990, the results of the *Politika* investigation were featured prominently in the British national newspapers, to coincide with their coverage of the Salzburg Festival in Austria.

Once proof began to appear that he had been a Nazi, and rumours about his war crimes began to seem well founded, Waldheim – despite the fact that he was now the president of Austria – found himself being ostracised by most world leaders. He tried to improve his image by inviting Western leaders to the Salzburg Festival, but his scheme backfired. Only two Western dignitaries accepted his invitation: the West German President von Weizsäcker and the Czech President Havel. In what had been expected to be the usual bland speech of thanks for hospitality, Havel attacked Waldheim's attempt to cover up his dubious wartime past and warned him that the truth cannot be concealed for ever. Significantly, Havel was given a standing ovation.

Politika had spent three years researching into Waldheim's wartime activities in the Balkans and had found still more documents which proved that Waldheim had played an active role in Hitler's military intelligence service, the Abwehr. It was becoming increasingly obvious that he had not been an ordinary infantry battalion officer, despite the fact that he was still trying to give that impression. Although he had now had to concede that he had been at Kozara, he was still maintaining that his presence had been innocent – that he was there simply as a matter of routine because he was a supply officer on General Stahl's staff. But it was becoming ever clearer that his role could not have been as innocuous as he claimed.

Infantry battalion intelligence officers in the British Army had no special training, and their role was strictly military. But the same was not true of intelligence officers in Hitler's Abwehr. To hold a commissioned rank, as Waldheim did, one had to be a staunch member of the Nazi party and to have links with the Gestapo. Abwehr officers were given special training, as they were involved in the political, as well as the military, aspects of the war. No ex-Abwehr officer can, therefore, plead ignorance of the atrocities that were taking place in Germany and German-occupied territories although, naturally, some were more personally involved with the horrendous happenings than others.

*

The story of the OAU is much the same as that of the UN: the same communist and socialist policies, encouraged by Waldheim, ensured that none of Africa's real problems were tackled.

The OAU came into being in Addis Ababa, Ethiopia. After two days of speeches, the leaders of thirty-two independent African countries signed the OAU Charter on 25th May, 1963. Less than twenty years later, only two of the original thirty-two leaders still ruled their countries – King Hussein of Morocco and President Houphouët-Boigny of the Ivory Coast.

Among those leaders who were predominant in founding the OAU, but who later fell victim to military takeovers, were Emperor Haile Selassie of Ethiopia and President Kwame Nkrumah of Ghana. In 1980 President Tolbert of Liberia, then chairman of the OAU, was killed in a military coup in Liberia, which necessitated President Senghor of Senegal taking over as chairman of the OAU.

These facts are indicative of the political instability of most of newly independent Africa and help explain why South Africa's whites had good reason to believe, after reading reports about the barbaric atrocities of the Mau Mau in Kenya and the Simbas in the Belgian Congo, that apartheid was their best chance of survival. The present spate of brutal tribal killings in South Africa between Buthelezi's Zulus (Inkatha) and Mandela's Xhosa (ANC) only strengthens this belief in most whites. A great many of the one million Indians and three million Coloureds in South Africa also share this belief, but they are now far too scared to admit it.

★

Once again the West played right into Russian hands. Whilst the West (via the UN) was pouring in aid for mainly peaceful purposes in Africa, there were no protests when the Russians poured in their military hardware, from Kalashnikovs to MiG fighter aircraft.

It was not long after Waldheim had taken over as Secretary-General at the UN that he began carrying the communist message of hate against colonialism and South Africa to Addis Ababa, where he addressed the assembled heads of state and government at the OAU's annual meeting in May 1973. In his disgraceful speech, he mentioned neither the progress and achievements of the white colonial era in Africa, nor the colonial stability that had made progress possible. Instead, he gave assurance that the UN would continually increase its efforts to decolonise Africa.

To assist the OAU in its efforts to 'liberate' all those countries still ruled by white minorities, he pledged UN support for every pro-Marxist organisation in Africa with, of course, special reference to the communist interest in Swapo and Namibia. In 1978 he was able to boast that he had played a crucial role for the communists in helping to surround South Africa with hostile Marxist states by manipulating the Security Council into accepting his whole South West Africa-Namibia report by Resolution 435. Eleven years later, when Namibia became independent, the Marxist Swapo took over.

While UN money poured into every so-called liberation movement in Africa, the OAU formed a special Liberation Committee. This would receive generous support from Waldheim's UN but, in all the false euphoria of African independence, no one was prepared to listen to warnings about the economic dangers of the African population explosion, or the dangers of doing nothing about the steadily deteriorating economic position all over independent Africa. No one would, of course, admit that the main reasons for the problems were misrule, corruption and political instability following the end of colonial rule. All the newly independent African countries were affected, from the richest (Nigeria) to the poorest (for example Mali or Chad).

For twenty years nothing was done by the OAU until, in 1980, they held an Extraordinary Assembly on Economic Affairs, in Lagos. What Nigeria should have done with its oil wealth, instead of wantonly squandering most of it and neglecting its prosperous colonial legacy, was to have expanded its own agricultural economy and used its influence to help the farming economies of the rest of the OAU countries. It should have helped to form and finance an international agricultural selling organisation, to protect the prices paid for all the African export products like groundnuts, cocoa, coffee and cotton.

It has long been one of Africa's main complaints that a fair price is not always paid by the international companies that dominate the overseas markets in agricultural products. With Nigeria's oil wealth, Africa could have been, for the first time in its history, in a position to hold up sales until a satisfactory price was agreed.

The tragedy for Africa was that few, if any, of its politicians realised that it suited Russian plans to keep it as impoverished as possible, and that their 'friend' at the UN, Secretary-General Waldheim, was interested only in Russia's ultimate goal: control of the mineral resources of Southern Africa. In late 1989 half of that final objective was achieved when the Marxist Swapo took over in South West Africa (now Namibia). Through supplying most of the money to run the UN, the West has been furthering Russia's ambitions.

*

In 1980 Nigeria's first civilian ruler for many years, President Shagari, made a speech at the UN in New York. In typical fashion, he blamed the West for all Nigeria's (and Africa's) economic woes and, prompted by Waldheim, demanded that the UN should launch a decade of reparation and restitution for Africa.

He conveniently forgot, like all African politicians, that his predecessors had taken over a prosperous colonial economy, and that most of Nigeria's economic problems were self-inflicted since independence. None of its leaders would admit that Nigeria's economic situation was getting worse the whole time.

No questions were ever asked in the UN as to why Nigeria, as Africa's richest country, had done nothing to help the OAU start an urgently needed economic section to improve prices for Africa's agricultural produce and why, for twenty years, nothing had been done to tackle Africa's ever-worsening population explosion. In 1975 it was estimated that Nigeria's population, then about 68.5 million, would have increased to a staggering 198 million by the year 2000.

Waldheim ignored this problem, and encouraged the UN to waste most of its time and money on committee meetings and liberation movements which helped to create yet more millions of starving Africans for the UN to feed.

Almost as ridiculous was the OAU-UN blacklist for sportsmen who played in South Africa. It would have been much more to the point for President Shagari to demand that the UN started a blacklist of all the overseas firms who won contracts in Nigeria by bribery.

Shagari represents a small African elite in Nigeria, and he is just as dishonest and hypocritical as all the others. He knows full well that dash is so widespread that honest business is impossible in his country and, as long as that is the case, prices for everything (including basic necessities) will remain artificially high.

★

The final link in the chain of communist conspiracy against South Africa was provided by the Commonwealth connection in Africa, made up of the seventeen ex-British colonies in the OAU, which were dominated by socialist and Marxist regimes with close connections to the Marxists in Angola, Mozambique and Namibia.

Even though the OAU had, in 1980, increased its membership to fifty member states (Zimbabwe joined that year), the seventeen ex-British colonies still wielded a great deal of influence when dealing with South Africa, and it was only moderate leaders like President Houphouët-Boigny (of the Ivory Coast) who were in favour of dialogue as the means to try and solve South Africa's problems.

Ramphal, the Commonwealth Secretary-General for fifteen years, was closely connected to Waldheim's UN and the NIEO, and, through the Commonwealth Experts Group, was ready to support NIEO policies with all the other UN organisations that Waldheim was continually building up – under people like M'Bow at Unesco, Haquani at Unclad, Menon at the UN headquarters in New York and Mahbub ul Haq at the World Bank.

These UN organisations were continually pressing for more sanctions against South Africa and it appeared that far worse violence and oppression in South America, and elsewhere in the world, were completely ignored as they helped to further Russian plans to take over South Africa's mineral wealth. There was seemingly no limit to Ramphal's interference in Britain's Commonwealth affairs, even to the extent of trying to cause trouble between the Queen, as Head of the Commonwealth, and Mrs Thatcher, as Britain's prime minister.

Ramphal, from Britain's only colony in South America, tiny Guyana – where democracy, as we know it, is an alien concept – personifies all the worst faults of well-paid Third World bureaucrats, and he also has an apparently insatiable desire for personal publicity. And who paid for most of his junketing around the world? The British taxpayer! Britain also paid a large proportion of his salary (£62,000 per annum) while he continually criticised British policy on South Africa.

It costs Britain several million pounds every year to keep the Commonwealth going and the Commonwealth Secretariat occupies huge premises in the West End of London to accommodate its staff of over four hundred. I am quite sure that it would not be too difficult to get rid of about three-quarters of these bureaucrats – a hundred or so should be sufficient to do the necessary work.

Why cut our armed forces by over thirty per cent but allow Commonwealth scroungers to continue to waste millions of pounds? Ex-servicemen must ensure that politicians get their priorities right. At the CHOGH in Harare in October 1991, PM Major agreed to cancel £500,000,000 of Commonwealth debts!

Farther down the road, in Kensington, there is the vast Commonwealth Institute. Similar drastic staff cuts among the bureaucrats could be made there and then the remaining members of the Commonwealth Secretariat could be moved into the Institute. A similar organisation, which costs the British taxpayer over ten million pounds a year, is the Commission for Racial Equality. That would benefit from cuts, too, and the much-reduced staff could also be fitted easily into the Commonwealth Institute. Then we would have the whole bunch of bureaucrats in the same building.

More and more people in Britain are realising that you cannot successfully legislate against racial prejudice – it is largely a matter of educating the young properly. For far too long in Britain, and elsewhere, fanatics have managed to turn racial injustice into a very profitable business. Our politicians seem to have forgotten the old adage that charity begins at home, and the millions saved by cutting the superfluous Commonwealth staff and other expenses could be spent on providing homes for our own citizens sleeping rough on the streets of London and other British cities.

The time is long overdue for Britain to face up to the painful realities of the Commonwealth, and to accept the fact that most of it is now in a far worse state than it was in the colonial era. This is especially true of the African member states. Things are never going to improve if we leave the present bureaucratic system to continue wasting the taxpayers' money.

The Commonwealth Institute itself, and the lavish displays there about every Commonwealth country, provide a very good example of how the public relations people try (very successfully) to disguise the truth about how terrible conditions really are in many Commonwealth countries. There is a lot of good in the Commonwealth, too, but it is very foolish never to mention that the bad exceeds the good. The British public, and other visitors, get a completely false impression.

★

During the course of TAAL's investigations into the ANC, we came across a very informative booklet entitled *The ANC Method – Violence* by a Canadian journalist, Peter Worthington. He first went to Africa in 1960, to cover the chaos of independence in the Belgian Congo for a Canadian newspaper. He then went on to stable South Africa where, he reckoned, eighty-five per cent of whites supported apartheid and only fifteen per cent were prepared to let the blacks have a real say in government.

When he returned to South Africa twenty-seven years later, he reckoned the percentages had been reversed and about eighty-five per cent of the whites were now against apartheid. But it is what he says about the Western media in the Foreword to his booklet that I find so interesting – and true (for the full Foreword, see Appendix):

> But what offends me now as an individual and as a Canadian, but most particularly as a journalist, is the lack of recognition and understanding in the West of what exactly is going on in the whole of Southern Africa today, not just South Africa.
>
> When one looks at the evidence that unfolds daily, for all to see who want to see, there is a war going on, not against apartheid, but against South Africa itself.
>
> I'm afraid I am convinced that the Western media, Western politicians, academics and all too many church figures are not so much interested in a peaceful solution to South Africa's problems, but want bloodshed and an overthrow of the system at any price, and the installation of another form of government, even if it ends up being a Marxist regime.
>
> I mostly blame the media for what can only be described as disinformation honestly reporting events as they see them, too many media people are about South Africa. Instead of going where the story takes them, that is, of honestly reporting events as they see them, too many media people are reflecting what they think their audiences and or edi-

tors want to see, hear, read, or what they personally believe should be the case.

With the welcome departure of Sir Shridath Ramphal, there are encouraging signs that the new Commonwealth Secretary-General, the Nigerian Chief Emeka Anyaoka, will take a more pragmatic and balanced attitude towards South Africa. Since taking over (in July 1990), he has gone on record as saying that South Africa should now rejoin the Commonwealth. Hopefully it will also join the OAU and bring its much-needed economic expertise to that organisation.

It should never be forgotten just how close the Russians came to gaining their final goal in Africa – South Africa's mineral wealth. Years of anti-apartheid propaganda by the UN, and the socialists in Europe, had softened up Western opinion to accept a communist takeover in South Africa. The Cubans in Angola were only the start. If the Russian empire had not collapsed in 1989, a second front would undoubtedly have been opened up in Mozambique, and a third front would probably have followed in Zimbabwe, before the final communist onslaught on South Africa began.

Chapter Three

The Anglo-Boer War

My mother was South African. Not long after the end of the Anglo-Boer War the family moved home and business from Kimberley to Port Elizabeth when she was seven years old. She was brought up on the family farm there (called 'Aloe Park') and educated in Port Elizabeth. My father was in HM's colonial service in the Nigerian administration, so we saw our parents only when they were home on leave (for six months every eighteen months). We went to preparatory and public schools in Kent and were brought up by our paternal grandparents, in Felixstowe.

My first experience of South Africa, when the troopship called at Durban en route to Octu, at Mhow in India, is something I've always treasured and, shortly afterwards, I was able to compare it with India – what an appalling scene Bombay presented by contrast!

This sort of experience was shared by hundreds of thousands of other servicemen during the war and afterwards, which is why, nowadays, so many are sceptical about most of the anti-South Africa propaganda from Commonwealth countries like India. 'Lagos Chaos', an account of a black Briton's visit to his father's country, Nigeria, sums up the reality much better than the propaganda of places like London's Commonwealth Institute.

Like most people in Britain, I had little knowledge of the real causes of the Anglo-Boer War (1899–1902). I was therefore very surprised when, in the 1960s and 1970s, I visited the Orange Free State and Transvaal with my second wife, Eve (who had relatives there), at the open hatred of everything British in the predominantly Afrikaner small towns – 'dorps' as they are called locally. On more than one occasion, when I went into local shops and spoke in English I was refused service, and it was only when my wife explained, in Afrikaans, that I was from Rhodesia that we got served. The same applied in the small country pubs, and I soon learnt to order my beer in Afrikaans – otherwise they wouldn't serve me.

It was these experiences that made me curious about the events that had led to the Boer War.

*

I discovered that the Boer War was, in fact, the second Anglo-Boer conflict. The first (short) one took place in 1880, shortly after the discovery of diamonds. It was a disaster for Britain – and came only a year after the British Army had suffered one of the worst defeats in the annals of its colonial history: when the Zulus had wiped out a large British military force at Isandhlwana in Northern Natal.

In 1877 Whitehall had formally tried to annex the Transvaal, but the senior British administrator in the Transvaal hadn't the forces to control the Boers and, after the British military defeat at Isandhlwana, war between the two sides was inevitable.

On 16th December, 1880, the Boers raised the four-colour flag of the Transvaal Republic, the Vierkleur, and within four days had annihilated the British military force marching on Pretoria. Three more British military defeats occurred in quick succession and the last, at Majuba Hill, was so conclusive that Gladstone's new Liberal government ended the war and the Transvaal Republic was given back its independence.

The Boers returned to their farms convinced that, with God's help, they had defeated British imperial designs to expand their influence in South Africa.

*

A few years later, however, fate was to pay a cruel trick on the Boers when (in 1886) gold was found in almost unbelievable quantities on the Witwatersrand in the Transvaal Republic. This effectively destroyed the Boer's agricultural way of life for ever, as the greed of international mining companies now backed the imperial designs of the British Empire, which was at the very pinnacle of its power.

In the British High Commissioner for South Africa, Sir Alfred Milner, the Boers had an implacable enemy. His openly avowed aim was to destroy the Transvaal Republic, using the grievances (some real, but most imaginary) of the Uitlanders (foreigners) as an excuse to put pressure on Transvaal's President Kruger.

With Whitehall's tacit approval, Cecil Rhodes's friend Dr Jameson planned the infamous Jameson Raid into the Transvaal Republic. It was a miserable failure, badly planned and executed, and Dr Jameson and his men were captured almost without a fight, but the raid did achieve one of its objectives, which was to raise tension in the Transvaal.

Even though President Kruger made various concessions to meet some of the Uitlanders' demands, Britain continued her policy of gradually encircling the Transvaal with hostile troops. Kruger's only possible counter was a defensive alliance with the other Boer Republic, the Orange Free State, in 1899.

The policy of continual harassment paid off for Britain when the Volksraad, Transvaal's parliament, backed President Kruger's ultimatum for British troops to withdraw from Transvaal's borders or war would be declared. Britain, of course, rejected the ultimatum and tried, with machiavellian hypocrisy, to convince the world that the two tiny Boer republics were really the aggressors.

*

So started the second Anglo-Boer War (in October 1899). It was to have tragic consequences for the tiny Boer nation, who had fully expected to repeat the resounding defeats that they had inflicted on the British forces nearly ten years earlier, which had culminated in the victory at Majuba Hill.

Three Afrikaner columns invaded Natal in the first few weeks of the war and drove the British forces back to Ladysmith, where the Boers were quite content to besiege the town, as they were doing at Mafeking and Kimberley in the Cape. Thus the Afrikaners failed to capitalise on their early military advantages, not realising that huge British reinforcements were on their way to South Africa. By not bypassing Mafeking, Kimberley and Ladysmith, and driving deep into Natal and the Cape while they had the chance, the Boers lost their only hope of getting the British to negotiate.

What the Boer High Command had failed to realise was that Britain had not been all that interested when only diamonds were at stake, and its efforts to win the first Anglo-Boer War had been fairly superficial. Now, because of the recently discovered gold, the potential wealth was enormous and the British were prepared to mobilise the full might of their empire, if necessary, to gain control of Transvaal's minerals.

*

It was exactly the same motivation that caused the Russians to send thirty thousand mercenary Cuban troops, together with thousands of East German technicians, into Angola in the 1970s and 1980s. It is worth quoting again President Brezhnev's words (in 1973):

> Our aim is to gain control of the two great treasure houses on which the West depends: the energy treasure house of the Persian Gulf and the minerals treasure house of central and South Africa. [My note: you should include Namibia here.]

Events in Eastern Europe since 1989 have foiled this communist aim, but it should be remembered that we now have a Marxist regime in Namibia and the only reason the ANC of Nelson Mandela is now prepared to negotiate is that it has lost its main paymaster and arms supplier: Russia.

★

What must be admitted is that nothing can excuse some of the methods used by the British forces to defeat the Boers. One wonders how many people in Britain knew, at the time, of the concentration camps in which 26,000 Afrikaner women and children died, or how many would have approved of the ruthless scorched earth policy that destroyed just about every farm building in the two Boer republics, as well as killing all the cattle and burning all the crops, to deny food to the Boer forces.

When it is remembered that the Boer forces never, at any one time, exceeded 35,000 men, it is extremely difficult to justify such extreme measures, especially as Britain had built up her forces in South Africa to about 500,000 men.

When the details began to leak out, there was a public outcry in both Europe and America against Britain's military actions in South Africa, but nothing concrete was ever done – except that some European countries, notably Germany and Holland, sent money and supplies to the Boers, to try and halt the overwhelming British onslaught against the two tiny republics.

It took an Englishwoman, Emily Hobhouse, who refused to be silenced by the British authorities in South Africa, to bring home to the public in Europe just how horrific conditions really were in the concentration camps. Her reports and speeches after she returned to Britain finally started to rouse the national conscience and, although conditions in the concentration camps were then improved, it was too late to prevent the deaths of 26,000 Boer women and children. Appropriately, Emily Hobhouse is buried just outside Bloemfontein, where there is a memorial, the Vrouemonument, to those who died in the concentration camps as victims of imperial greed.

It is interesting to reflect that although, at The King's School, we were given a pretty good grounding in the history of our imperial glory, and I knew about Cecil Rhodes, the Jameson Raid and our eventual victory in the Boer War, I knew nothing about the concentration camps, the scorched earth policy or the Boer victory at Majuba Hill. I learnt about these for the first time when I went to South Africa on holiday from the Rhodesias in the 1960s. Before then I had always believed that it was Hitler's Germany that had originated concentration camps in the 1930s, and that it was also Germany that had used the scorched earth policy for the first time – in the campaign against the Russians in World War II.

What must be remembered is that Britain had not fought a major war in Europe since the Battle of Waterloo in 1815 – apart from sending an expeditionary force to the Crimea to fight the Russians in the mid-1850s, together with France and Turkey.

So recent military experience had been restricted to colonial wars in various parts of the British Empire – places like India and the Sudan – and good generals were not exactly plentiful. This had been demonstrated in the 1870s and early 1880s, when both Zulus and Boers had inflicted heavy defeats on badly led British forces.

So Field Marshal Roberts, who was nearly seventy, had to be brought in to command the British troops in South Africa in 1899. Field Marshal Roberts was the hero of Kandahar: he had defeated the Afghans and was used to fighting a brutal and ruthless enemy who never took prisoners. No wounded soldier could ever be left, as the Afghans tortured prisoners to death and normally, as a final insult, cut off the sexual organs and put them in the dead man's mouth.

Earl Kitchener of Khartoum, who took over from Roberts, had recently arrived from the Sudan, where he had been sent to avenge General Gordon's death in Khartoum. He therefore had no qualms about carrying out Sir Alfred Milner's scorched earth policy in the Transvaal and the Orange Free State.

This brought about the inevitable collapse and defeat of the Boer forces, on 31st May, 1902, but they had kept at bay for nearly three years a British force that outnumbered them over twenty times. At no one time were there more than 35,000 Boers in the field, although the number who fought during the course of the war was far greater, since there was no shortage of volunteers to replace those who were killed or captured. The 21,000 Boers who rode in to surrender had lost 6,000 comrades killed in battle, and 30,000 Boer prisoners had already been shipped out to India and Ceylon. When they returned eventually, it was to find a desolation of burnt-out buildings and land.

With Whitehall and Sir Alfred (now Lord) Milner, the British High Commissioner in South Africa, having achieved their objective in defeating the two tiny Boer republics, the policy of suppressing as much Afrikaner culture as possible was rigorously enforced and, to stop the Afrikaners ever gaining political power in South Africa, Lord Milner recommended that increased numbers of English settlers should be encouraged to migrate there.

No one would have given any odds on an Afrikaner political recovery after the end of the war, yet within a few years there was another extraordinary change in the fortunes of the two Boer republics, due mainly to the vagaries of the British political system, and the gathering storm in Europe.

★

In the British general election of 1905, the Liberals were returned to power. Lord Milner was forced to resign. Smuts went to London on the most important mission of his long political career: to meet the new Liberal PM, Campbell-Bannerman, and convince him to change British policies towards South Africa.

Within a year, the two Boer republics were self-governing again. Within another four years (in 1910), came the Union of South Africa and the amazing sight of three Boer generals in the South African government: Prime Minister Louis Botha, Jan Smuts (Minister of the Interior, Defence and Mines) and Barry Hertzog (Minister of Justice).

World War I was only four years away and, with the Germans now in South West Africa and Tanganyika, the right decision had been made, as it would have been disastrous for Britain if the Boers had thrown in their lot with the Germans, as many of them wanted to – and who could blame them?

So, within eight years of the end of the Anglo-Boer War, the South African political stage was set for Afrikaner independence. It came fifty-one years later, in 1961.

★

No account of this fascinating period of South African history would be complete without a tribute to two of the greatest men of this century, who dominated events in their respective countries: Winston Churchill and Jan Smuts.

Winston Churchill saved Britain in World War II, and Jan Smuts changed the course of South African history in 1905. Without their inspired leadership, it is probable that neither Britain nor South Africa would have survived the threats to their very existence.

Winston Churchill, unlike the Whitehall Warriors, had previous personal experience of the realities of war, in both India and the Sudan, before he went to South Africa to report on the Anglo-Boer War of 1899–1902. His capture and escape from the Boers, via Mozambique, made world headlines and captured the imagination of the British public in the early stages of the war, when things were not going well for Britain.

This enabled him to start an illustrious political career that culminated in his role as the British premier in Britain's darkest hour, after Dunkirk, when no one would have given any odds for British survival against the victorious Nazi forces. They, with their blitzkrieg tactics, had conquered most of Western Europe, sweeping the British forces into the sea at Dunkirk (where only the miracle of the small boats saved about 340,000 troops to fight another day) and forcing the surrender of France.

It is impossible for those who know British and South African history not to draw a parallel between Britain's situation in 1940 and the one that faced the Afrikaners in 1902, at the end of the Boer War. Yet, only three years later (in 1905), their whole situation changed when Smuts met the new Liberal Prime Minister Campbell-Bannerman, and persuaded him to change British policy in South Africa. Jan Smuts had been the Attorney-General in Transvaal before he became one of the outstanding Boer commando generals. In 1910, after the Union of South Africa came into being, he became the first Minister of the Interior, Defence and Mines under another Boer general, Prime Minister Louis Botha. A third Boer general, Barry Hertzog, had been a judge in the Orange Free State and became the Minister of Justice.

Smuts knew that, for South Africa to survive, the Afrikaners had to forget their past bitterness at British imperialism, as nearly half the white population was made up of settlers of British descent and loyal to Britain. It would have been more, but Lord Milner had not been able to achieve his aim of greatly increased British settlement before he was forced to resign in 1905.

★

In only four years the loyalty of both Smuts and Botha was to be tested to the full, with the start of the World War I. Hertzog had left the government, to form the Afrikaner National Party, and pro-German Boers were in open rebellion – led by Boer generals de la Rey, de Wet, Beyers and Kemp. Within three months the rebellion had been put down. De la Rey and Beyers were dead, Kemp and de Wet were jailed for treason. Only then could Smuts and Botha carry out the British request to send South African troops to conquer German South West Africa.

In January 1915 General Botha started assembling an invasion force that he would take by sea to Walvis Bay, a South African enclave on the west coast of the territory and, after a build-up of troops there, General Botha moved out (on 13th May, 1915) to take Windhoek, the capital, while General Smuts carried out a three-pronged attack from the south and, within two weeks, had mopped up all German resistance in the vast area south of Windhoek. In the meantime, General Botha had continued his advance north, in pursuit of the retreating German troops, and on 9th July the Governor of South West Africa surrendered the remnants of the German forces at Khorab, south of Tsumeb.

As well as sending South African troops to France, Britain needed more South African troops in Kenya, where the German forces in Tanganyika were proving much more elusive and difficult to defeat, under the very able command of General von Lettow.

In February 1916 General Smuts was sent to take command of the Allied forces in Kenya. His South African troops pushed south into Tanganyika, while other South African troops (under Brigadier General van Deventer, who later commanded all the Allied troops in East Africa) joined the British forces under General Northey, who was trying to cut off the German retreat near Lake Nyasa. But, even though the German forces were heavily depleted and harassed, they still carried on guerrilla attacks until the end of the war.

In 1917 Smuts left for London, where he was needed by the Imperial War Cabinet of Prime Minister Lloyd-George. In 1918, when Churchill returned from France to become Secretary of State for War, there began a political association between two of the most famous and experienced politicians of their generation. It continued, with great benefit to both Britain and South Africa, until the death of Field Marshal Jan Smuts in 1950. He was sorely missed in the years that followed.

Although South Africa's role in World War I is better known for the South West African, East African and Middle East campaigns, the sacrifices of the South African Brigade in France (then attached to the famous Scottish 9th Division) cannot be overstated. On 5th July, 1916, 132 officers and 3,530 men went into the line near Delville Wood – about ten days later the remnants were withdrawn: there were only 29 officers and 751 men left! Other South African troops were sent to safeguard the Suez Canal and others, under General Allenby, distinguished themselves fighting the Turks in the Middle East.

Like those from Australia, Canada and New Zealand, the 254,666 South African troops who fought so valiantly for Britain in World War I were all volunteers.

★

In 1919, on the death of General Louis Botha, Jan Smuts returned from London and took over as Prime Minister of South Africa. He was well aware of the ill feeling of the National Party, under General Hertzog, who had supported Germany and bitterly resented Botha and Smuts bringing South Africa into the war on the side of the Allies.

One of the reasons for the Boer rebellion in 1914 was the Afrikaners anger and disgust at Botha and Smuts agreeing to undertake the conquest of German South West Africa and Tanganyika, when Germany was one of the few countries in Europe which had actively supported the Boers in 1899, by sending them money and supplies to help in their fight against the British.

Memories of the Anglo-Boer War of 1899–1902 were still too fresh for most Afrikaners to understand the wisdom of Smuts's policy towards Britain. He knew he needed not only its financial backing, but also the business skills and goodwill of English-speaking South Africans who, at that stage of South Africa's development, controlled most of the industrial and commercial wealth of the country.

Although Smuts won the 1920 election, the 1922 general strike (in which martial law was proclaimed) did not help him and, in 1924, the National and Labour parties combined to win the election – and General Hertzog replaced Smuts as prime minister.

★

During this period (in 1921), the British Empire Service League was founded, at the instigation of Field Marshal Earl Haig and General Smuts. The inaugural conference was held in Cape Town in that year, and was attended by the seven founder members from ex-service associations of the old Commonwealth countries, in other words, Australia, Canada, New Zealand and South

Africa. In 1958 the name was changed to the British Commonwealth Ex-Service League, to accommodate the hordes of small, now independent, countries in the Commonwealth.

In 1983 these totalled fifty-two. Although South Africa was forced out of the Commonwealth by a bunch of newly independent countries who didn't understand the meaning of democracy, let alone practise it in their countries, it still remains a member of the BCEL. Most of the credit for this must go to the far-sighted policies of Jan Smuts.

★

In 1933, as the Great Depression continued and South Africa's economic position worsened, General Hertzog, to his great credit, agreed to form a coalition between his National Party and General Smuts's United Party, with Hertzog as PM and Smuts as his Minister of Justice.

In 1939 this coalition was to play a vital role in South Africa's history as – after the outbreak of World War II – a crucial vote was held in Cape Town about whether South Africa should enter the war. Hertzog and his supporters favoured neutrality, while Smuts and his pro-British supporters wanted to declare war on Germany. The vote was close but Hertzog's neutrality motion was defeated by thirteen votes: sixty-seven for, eighty against. Hertzog resigned and Smuts became premier again. South Africa declared war on Germany the same day, 6th September, 1939, and Smuts continued as prime minister until 1949.

Most ex-servicemen are aware of the debt we owe to Smuts and the South African volunteers, but it appears that the continual communist-socialist propaganda campaign against South Africa, aided and abetted by the media in the West (especially television), has warped the minds of a great many of the younger people in Britain, to the extent that they are incapable of making any balanced judgement of South Africa.

What has further aggravated the whole situation is an almost complete lack of knowledge in the West about the real conditions in newly independent black-ruled countries, whose leaders are largely responsible for the appalling conditions and starvation that are now considered normal in most parts of Africa. The situation has not been helped by both the communists and the West being prepared to flood Africa with arms and ammunition. None of those involved will ever admit that conditions in colonial days were very much better for the ordinary Africans than they are now. Starvation in those days was almost unknown.

With Field Marshal Jan Smuts once again leading South Africa's war effort, there were soon over 330,000 South African volunteers (over one third of whom were Afrikaners). Fighting for Britain in Ethiopia, they drove the Italians out in 1941, then went on to North Africa – where battles included Sidi Rezegh, Bardia and El Alamein. Moving on to Italy, the 6th South African Armoured Division, together with other South African units, fought in most of the battles in the Italian campaign. South African casualties were heavy: about 30,000 in all, with over 12,000 killed. South African troops were awarded with a total of 6,389 decorations, including three VCs.

Also of vital importance to the Allies were the South African ports and their facilities: 7,500 merchant vessels and 2,600 fighting ships were repaired there during the course of the war. Large quantities of munitions were also manufactured for the Allied war effort, and mention should be made of the many pilots and other aircrew who were trained in South Africa under the Empire Air Training Scheme.

Memories of the South African war efforts and sacrifices may conveniently be forgotten in today's materialistic society in Britain, but the time has surely come when the 16 million ex-servicemen and women and their families should make it clear that they have had more than enough of the constant anti-South Africa propaganda.

★

Although a great many people, especially ex-servicemen and women, will be aware of South Africa's role in both world wars, far fewer will be aware of the part it played in helping to form the UN.

South Africa was one of twenty-six nations which signed the UN Declaration in 1942 and Field Marshal Smuts played a prominent role in drafting the preamble to the UN Charter when the UN came into being officially in 1945, with South Africa as one of the original fifty members.

Although the UN Charter specifically states that there should be no interference in the domestic affairs of any member state, this rule was ignored at the very first session of the UN General Assembly in London (in 1946), when the position of South Africa's Indian population was placed on the agenda.

The media in the West, especially television, have been heavily penetrated by left-wing crypto-communists. The Russians learnt about propaganda from their German allies at the beginning of World War II, and they were great admirers of the skills of Goebbels, the Nazi minister of propaganda. They have managed to manipulate the Western media very successfully, and it is no coincidence that the numerous mass murders in Africa since the end of World War II are very rarely reported, although the smallest incident that can be blamed on apartheid gets full coverage. Recently we have seen a massive media build-up supporting Nelson Mandela, the Marxist leader of a terrorist organisation: the ANC.

The wholesale slaughter of black Christians by black Muslims in the Sudan and the brutal civil war in Marxist Ethiopia are almost completely ignored – except when they affect charity work. The fact that the communists supplied most of the military hardware used in these conflicts is, of course, ignored by the media.

Yet television in the West regularly reports on conditions in the so-called 'front-line states' and South Africa is blamed for all the carnage there.

★

Once again it is greed (the desire for gold, diamonds and the rest of South Africa's mineral wealth) that motivates the UN, the Communist bloc and the Third World countries, just as it was the cause of the Anglo-Boer Wars. It is largely due to the courage and foresight of the two Boer commando generals, Smuts and Botha, that the communists have not succeeded (at least, not yet) in their plan to take over South Africa.

It would be very foolish to underestimate the communist success in Africa, as a whole, since the end of World War II. In 1966 the Russians successfully manipulated the UN General Assembly into arbitrarily overturning a judgement by the International Court of Justice with which they did not agree. This terminated South Africa's 1918 mandate in SWA, thus leaving South West Africa exposed to malevolent outside forces, culminating in a Marxist Swapo takeover in 1989.

★

After World War II, the ungrateful British public decided they wanted a change and the most famous Englishman of the century, Winston Churchill, lost the 1946 election.

Jan Smuts was then in his mid-seventies and, next to Churchill, he was the best known and most respected leader in the British Empire. Both of them knew that Britain's finest hour had come with victory over the Nazis in 1945 and that the days of the British Empire were rapidly drawing to a close.

Only the British Empire could have created someone like Field Marshal Smuts. A distinguished Boer commando general who fought against Britain, he saw his country laid waste by Kitchener's scorched earth policy and knew that 26,000 Boer women and children had died in British concentration camps in South Africa. But he was also a far-sighted patriot who, in the best interests of South Africa, was able to put the past behind him and pledge his friendship to Campbell-Bannerman, the new British Prime Minister, when they met in London in 1905.

As a friend as well as a valued colleague of Winston Churchill, Smuts had, virtually single-handedly, brought South Africa into two world wars on Britain's side. Without his firm leadership, South Africa could easily have disintegrated into civil war between the Boers and British settlers: a pattern familiar in the rest of Africa since the end of the war.

As a valued counsellor to two British war cabinets, and respected adviser to the Allied High Command in both world wars, Smuts's knowledge of British Empire affairs was only rivalled by Winston Churchill. No one knew better than Smuts that Britain's days of imperial glory were drawing to an end and that the time was due for South Africa to stand on its own feet. With a Labour government in Britain, the time was coming for South Africa, under Afrikaner leadership, to break its ties with the new British Commonwealth, as Third World countries began to dominate the Commonwealth and its meetings.

What happened at the first meeting of the UN (in October 1946) must have confirmed Smuts's views on South Africa's future. He presented South Africa's application to incorporate SWA into the Union of South Africa, only to see it turned down. But the basic UN principle of non-interference in the domestic affairs of member states was violated when the question of South Africa's Indian population was placed on the agenda.

What happened in the South African election of May 1948 is now history: the result was an unprecedented swing to the Afrikaner National Party, which had needed a swing of twenty-eight seats for victory. They got it, because the mainly rural Afrikaner voters won seventy-nine seats while Smuts's United Party won only sixty-five.

Smuts was to die less than two years later, in 1950, having completed his work for South Africa. He had also kept his promise of loyalty to Britain in a truly magnificent manner over a period of forty-five years and through two world wars.

Events in the Commonwealth since Smuts's death in 1950 have shown how right he was about South Africa needing a nationalist Afrikaner government that was capable of withstanding the communist onslaught, even if that meant leaving the Commonwealth, now dominated by Third World countries. On 31st May, 1961, South Africa became a republic outside the Commonwealth.

★

What Smuts could not have foreseen was the trouble that would be caused by Dr Verwoerd's lack of international experience when he institutionalised apartheid laws at the very time the USA was dismantling the most discriminatory laws in its southern states. Although having the appalling human rights records themselves, Russia's Communist bloc and the Third World countries were able to dominate the voting in the UN General Assembly and to mount a massive propaganda campaign, as part of their strategy to take over South Africa and its mineral wealth.

Through their leftist socialist allies in the Western media, the Soviets were able to carry their anti-South Africa propaganda even further, by ensuring very little was ever reported about the truly horrific conditions they had helped to create in most of Africa, while news about apartheid was reported almost daily.

It should be remembered in the UK that there are about two million English-speaking South Africans, our kith and kin, and over a million of these still have the right to a British passport.

★

It was only after I started to write this book that I established contact with my mother's relatives in Port Elizabeth, South Africa, and it is due to the kindness of Mary and Jack Cordingley White (DFC) of Port Elizabeth that I am able to include (see Appendix One) pictures of my grandfather, Greenwood White, as captain in command of K Company at the time of the siege of Kimberley in the Anglo-Boer War (1899–1902).

A more recent picture (which appeared in the business section of the *Johannesburg Sunday Times* on 28th January, 1990) shows their son, John White, and the covering article (see Appendix One) gives the date my mother's father came to Cape Town from England in 1878, and how he trekked to Kimberley and founded the firm of Greenwood White there in 1889. In 1905, Greenwood White moved his head office to Port Elizabeth, so my mother spent most of her school years there.

It must be mentioned, here, that I owe a great deal to the Lowns, Dorothy and Dennis, of Summerstrand, Port Elizabeth. I met them at the Victory

Services Club (over three thousand ex-servicemen from South Africa are members) and, in June 1988, I invited them to a party there for Gurkha and South African ex-servicemen.

About a year later, when I had started writing this book, I wrote to the Lowns, asking for their help in finding my mother's South African relatives in Port Elizabeth. Just about all I could send them were pictures of my parents, taken in Port Elizabeth when they visited my mother's brother, Albert Percy White, in 1947 – and some pictures taken at Albert's funeral (in 1951) that had been sent to my mother.

From the details on Albert's grave, they were able to trace the firm of monumental masons who had made the tombstone and, through them, they were able to send me Mary and Jack Cordingley White's address. Truly quite an achievement, and I am very grateful for all the trouble they took on my behalf.

★

There is a lesson here for ex-servicemen, and others with relatives or friends in South Africa and other old Commonwealth countries. It shows how easy it is, over the years, to lose contact with them.

After what I saw during my thirty-five years in East, central and South Africa, I am convinced we must all do more to encourage links with our African (and other old Commonwealth) kith and kin. The world must see that we will no longer allow our relatives, however distant, to be dispossessed.

One suggestion that has been made is that a club (perhaps 'Dominion Club' would be a good name) should be opened in London, with branches to follow in South Africa, Australia, New Zealand and Canada. The main aim of the club would be to help those with blood ties to Britain (wherever they may now be in the Commonwealth) to re-establish and foster their family relationships and all ex-service links – so that the role played in two world wars by the four dominions (Australia, Canada, New Zealand and South Africa) is never forgotten.

There is an increasing need for all of us to see that the traditional links that were built up in the bloody battles of two world wars are not forgotten by the politicians in Europe and America – so many of whom seem to be interested only in their own political achievements and advancement.

Chapter Four

The Final Years in Africa

Nothing can ever change my view that the British Empire, with all its faults and mistakes, was still the greatest force for good since the Roman Empire. There is also no doubt in my mind that the Anglo-Boer War of 1899–1902 was a tragic mistake that Britain was to pay for very dearly later, in World War I.

Kaiser Wilhelm II and his advisers were not fools, however they were portrayed in the British press at the time. The Germans had inflicted a most humiliating defeat on the French at Sedan in 1870, when Emperor Napoleon III was captured by the Germans (he was deposed three years later).

Germany, for reasons of its own, had been one of the few nations in Europe to actively support the Boers during the Anglo-Boer War, and the Kaiser would have received regular reports on the early reverses suffered by the badly led British forces in the early stages of that war. The Kaiser would not have been very impressed by the fact that it took a force of about 500,000 British troops to defeat the Boer forces – which rarely exceeded 20,000 men on the battlefield. Those reports from the Anglo-Boer War must have influenced the Kaiser and his advisers in 1914, when they decided that Germany could defeat the armed forces of Britain and France – the result of that belief was World War I.

Britain never recovered fully from the appalling losses it suffered, and the same applied to France, when most of the best of a generation were wiped out in the mud of the Flanders trenches. I believe that these losses played a decisive role in the defeat of France at the beginning of World War II and the decline of the British Empire that followed the end of that war.

★

The fact that South Africa has enjoyed almost ninety years of comparative peace and prosperity since the end of the Boer War in 1902 owes very little to the British, but just about everything to two Boer generals – Botha and Smuts – who were patriotic and sensible enough to put aside their personal feelings about the Anglo-Boer wars as they realised that, if South Africa were to survive and prosper, Britons and Boers had to live peaceably together in South Africa.

It can't have been pleasant to have had to put down a small pro-German uprising among some of their own followers, but there can be very little doubt that their courageous decision to do this, and to enter the war on Britain's side, saved South Africa from a bloody civil war that would have torn the whole country apart.

What the West, and especially Britain, have to face up to is the fact that it was very lucky that it was two of the white tribes of Africa who were in charge. It doesn't take much imagination to realise what would have happened if the decision had rested with the two dominant black tribes of South Africa, Mandela's Xhosa (about seven million) and Buthelezi's Zulu (also about seven million).

Elsewhere in Africa between 1963 and 1987 there was an incredible total of sixty-eight successful coups – no one has ever troubled to count the unsuccessful ones.

In any African country other than South Africa, Archbishop Tutu would have been the first to go, as no black ruler would have tolerated his interference, while Mandela and his fellow ANC leaders would have had a quick bullet in the back of the head long before now. Even clergymen are not safe if they dare to disagree with their leaders. Idi Amin of Uganda, for instance, not only killed and cut the head off one of Uganda's archbishops who had annoyed him, but actually kept the head in his refrigerator as a powerful witch doctor's medicine!

Those of us who are familiar with the way things work in Africa know that there will never be any real kind of democracy in the black-ruled states. Yet Western politicians persist in calling for one man, one vote in South Africa – the Marxist ANC would be quite happy to come to power in this democratic fashion (using intimidation to achieve the desired result is the norm in Africa), but if they won it would be the last free election in South Africa.

Dr Buthelezi, the leader of Inkatha and seven million Zulus, showed a grasp of the realities of the South African situation better than any Western politician when he said it was 'a live, do or die country' for many of South Africa's whites. Western politicians would do well to remember this.

★

The communists and their Western socialist allies have always tried to confuse the issue, but there is no other country with which to compare South Africa. The nearest in numbers, although most of the circumstances are completely different, is Algeria.

France occupied Algeria only in 1830 but in 1871 it actually became part of France in political terms: it was divided into three departments, each of which elected deputies to the French parliament in Paris.

Algeria had had French settlers for only 130 years when independence was granted (in 1962), whereas South Africa's first white settlers arrived about 350 years ago.

In 1956, shortly before the start of the Algerian war, a last population count of European settlers was taken: the total was about one and a half million. In South Africa there are five million – plus, of course, three million Coloureds and one million Indians.

In 1962, at Evian, a ceasefire agreement was reached between de Gaulle and the Algerians. Part of the treaty concerned minority rights for the colonists yet, less than a year later, the number of Europeans left in Algeria was only one hundred thousand!

★

Ever since Britain's humiliation over Suez in 1956, the Communist bloc has been able to manipulate the West at the UN and the founding of the OAU, in 1963, gave it the opportunity to carry out an unprecedented propaganda campaign against South Africa.

The recent collapse of the Communist bloc gives the West what might well be the last opportunity to rectify the mistakes that have been made in Africa by the UN during the past thirty-five years, and to start to tackle Africa's most serious problem – the population explosion – before it is too late.

★

That great Prime Minister Margaret Thatcher stood firm over the Falklands and the question of British sovereignty within the EC and, in doing so, helped restore Britain's pride and purpose in world affairs. Combine this with her solitary stand opposing sanctions against South Africa and there must be some hope that other Western politicians will copy her courage and act more positively over Africa's problems and the need for reform at the UN.

The present situation at the UN is absolute madness, and Russia has exploited it to further the aims of communism, and not only in Africa.

The fifty African states that make up the OAU have fifty votes at the UN, but the 1984–85 budget revealed that they paid only one per cent of UN expenditure. Similarly, the Asian countries had thirty-five votes and paid three per cent, and the Latin American countries had thirty-three votes and paid four per cent. The Communist bloc (which includes the USSR, China, Eastern Europe and Asian communist satellites) contributed only eighteen per cent of the total expenditure, but that didn't stop such countries dictating UN policy. The West, with Japan, paid a massive seventy-four per cent, and they should have been the people who were laying down UN policy.

The time is long overdue for the taxpayers to insist that the UN is run in a way that is satisfactory to the people paying for it, in other words, the ordinary citizens of the Western democracies and Japan. The necessary reforms include running all the UN agencies on a proper businesslike basis, with proper accounts and targets. Many, such as Waldheim's NIEO, should be terminated forthwith, and most of the remainder need to be rigorously reformed, with conferences and travel cut to an absolute minimum.

While the Western and Japanese taxpayers are being asked to pour money into Africa annually, Africa's vote should be restructured so that its voting power corresponds to the percentage it pays of the total UN budget. At the present one per cent, the OAU should have only one vote at the UN – it would be increased if and when its annual UN contributions increased.

★

A great many of Africa's misfortunes are self-inflicted, and the continual coups and long-running civil wars are an indication of the appalling conditions that now prevail.

The communists (and the West, to a lesser extent) have to bear the responsibility for the present disastrous mess at the UN. When South Africa, together with twenty-five other allied nations, signed the UN Declaration in 1942 (and after South Africa's distinguished international statesman and Prime Minister Field Marshal Smuts later played a leading role in drafting the preamble to the UN Charter), none of those involved could have foreseen how the Communist bloc would manipulate Third World countries, including the fifty member states of the OAU, to dominate the voting at the UN.

The communists then backed the appointment of ex-Nazi Kurt Waldheim as UN Secretary-General and in 1974, with Waldheim's connivance, they were able to deprive South Africa of UN membership. This was followed (in 1977) by a mandatory arms embargo against South Africa. In 1978 Waldheim submitted his communist-backed settlement plan for Namibia, which was approved by UN Resolution 435.

This Resolution separated South Africa from South West Africa (now Namibia), although South Africa managed to delay the Resolution's implementation for another eleven years. Eventually, in 1989, the unrelenting pressure succeeded and Swapo took over in Namibia. During his time at the UN, Waldheim also masterminded the introduction of NIEO, the New International Economic Order, at a special session of the UN General Assembly in 1974.

Little or nothing was known then of Waldheim's Nazi past and suspected war crimes, but his importance to the communists over this crucial period of Africa's history (from 1972 to 1982) cannot be overstated. The communist vendetta against South Africa was legitimised by his influence as the UN Secretary-General.

During his period of power, nothing received greater attention at the UN than the campaign against South Africa – except, perhaps, for the New International Economic Order, which was being discreetly pushed by the Communist bloc, as being the best way of weakening the Western economy. The Western socialist countries played their part in helping, none more so than the Nordic countries, who continually supported the aims of the NIEO and hosted UN conferences on the subject.

At the UN the Communist bloc was always assured of the votes of the 119 Third World countries (there were fifty African votes from the OAU), who were the main recipients of billions of dollars of Western aid. It is only the economic collapse of Russia and the Eastern bloc, coupled with the Gulf War, that has started to bring about some change, especially as a great deal of UN aid money is now going to be wanted in East European countries.

★

This does not change the fact that there is still a great need to face up to the realities of Africa. Aid money will run out sometime, and there is an urgent need to control the population explosion, which is not just restricted to Africa, but affects most of the Third World countries.

It may be that the UN is, very belatedly, waking up to the fact that there is a worldwide problem as, just before Easter 1991, there was an item on TV regarding India's population census. Over the ten-year period between one census and the next, the Indian population increased by 160 million! For the first time, there was a UN acknowledgement that the whole earth's environment is threatened by these huge increases in the population.

It must be obvious to most people that the present voting system at the UN has to be changed and, whatever reforms are eventually decided upon, the communists and the Third World must be stopped from blackmailing and dictating policy to the West. Perhaps very small countries with relatively small populations, like Cape Verde and São Tomé, should have spectator status only – except, of course, on the rare occasions when their particular problems are being discussed at the UN. Maybe the OAU could represent such tiny nations. The larger ones, like Nigeria and Libya, would have to run their countries in such a way that their potential wealth is realised and they can afford to pay their fair share of the UN expenses.

Africa's civil wars have to be stopped, so there will be no repetition of what happened in Liberia, which was virtually destroyed before Nigerian peace forces were sent in – a year too late. I suggest that there should be a permanent UN peace force of Gurkhas (of about brigade strength) to stop these civil wars and the destruction that results from them – it is the Western taxpayer who has to pay to replace what has been destroyed. No more Western-communist armaments should be allowed: such as the MiG fighters and the tanks that are currently being used in countries like Ethiopia. The excesses and corruption of African dictators have to be curbed.

President Mobutu of Zaire is just one example of a leader who is known to have become one of the world's richest men at the expense of his people. Even by African standards, Mobutu is brutal and corrupt, yet Western paratroopers were sent in, on two separate occasions, to save his regime. His army and police forces were often not paid, so they terrorised the people and stole whatever they wanted from the oppressed city dwellers and exploited farmers. In consequence, the wretched people, far worse off than they were in the colonial era, revolted almost annually – but they were brutally repressed by Mobutu's troops, using helicopters and other modern arms and equipment from the West. Zaire is potentially one of Africa's wealthiest countries, but it has been so misgoverned that huge amounts of food have to be imported and there is a staggeringly high foreign debt.

At the time of writing, the disturbances have been worse than usual and the Europeans (mostly French and Belgian) have been evacuated from Zaire. Mobutu has lost an election and it is to be hoped that, this time, he will be unable to regain power – and that his successor will prove less tyrannical and avaricious.

What has been happening in Zaire is, to a greater or lesser extent, the story of what is happening all over black-ruled Africa.

★

When I travelled to Usumbura in the 1950s and 1960s, in what was then Ruanda-Urundi, the Tutsi aristocracy, who were of mixed Hamitic stock, controlled and ruled the local Hutu (of Bantu origin) as they had done for centuries. This was black apartheid, but it seemed to work very well. At least, then, there were no massacres and no political refugees.

But the mania for change which was part of the communist campaign meant that not even such small peaceful corners of Africa as Ruanda-Urundi were allowed to escape the chaos and carnage sweeping over the continent in the name of African socialism.

Now the world is seeing the collapse of communism and it is clear that Africa, more than most, has paid a very heavy price for being taken in by communist propaganda. There are plenty of faults in the Western capitalist system, of course, but at least there is a basic belief in democracy and what is needed in Africa is peaceful democratic reform, not the destructive methods preached and practised by the communists.

All that independence brought to Ruanda-Urundi was UN interference and bloodshed, as the two small independent states, Rwanda and Burundi, came into being in 1962. Since then, there have been uprisings and massacres in both states, and over one hundred thousand people (both Tutsi and Hutu) have become exiles in neighbouring African countries.

Nothing shows the ineffectiveness of the UN more than the population figures of these two tiny African countries. In 1956, when I was there, the total population of Ruanda-Urundi was 4.4 million. By 1975 this figure had just about doubled to 8.5 million and I'm sure that, by now, the figure is far greater. This population explosion is happening all over Africa, and the need for urgent action is very obvious.

It is madness that the thousands of Britons who know Africa well, having lived and worked there, have not already been consulted.

A small cutting from *The Times* was sent to me (by a TAAL supporter), which mentioned that the British government had given Ethiopia, a Marxist country that is busy murdering its own people, forty-six million pounds in aid over the past two years. This aid is in addition to millions given by the UN and such charities as Oxfam.

★

In the November/December 1989 issue of the *Legion*, a journal of the Royal British Legion, there was an indication of what the sixteen million ex-servicemen and women, with their families, could do to influence the government and get some action, not only in Europe, but at the UN as well.

There is an indication that some kind of similar action could come from Britain's eleven million or so pensioners, who are also beginning to organise themselves. In the East, the wisdom of age is respected and the West would do well to adopt the same attitude. Pension party power, combined with the influence of ex-service people, seems to me to be the answer in the Britain of today.

I believe most ex-servicemen will share my views about the incredible double standards typified by the British condemning violence in South Africa while they were retraining Mugabe's notoriously brutal 5th Brigade (which murdered tens of thousands of unarmed Matabele), and running training courses in Zimbabwe's Eastern Highlands for Marxist Frelimo officers from Mozambique.

It should be remembered that, at the very time this was happening, some senior RAF officers serving with the Zimbabwe Air Force had been thrown into jail and were being tortured, because a number of aircraft had been sabotaged and Mugabe, quite unjustly, suspected the British officers were the saboteurs.

Real knowledge of any country must include having first-hand experience and being able to converse, at least to some extent, in the local language. It is also necessary to meet the ordinary, non-political people in an informal, unofficial way. However well meaning British Foreign and Commonwealth Office staff are, they represent a foreign power and get to see and hear only what their African (or other) hosts think is suitable.

The only way to get to know the Africans is to spend some time alone with them out in the bush. As you listen and talk about everyday matters, watch them going about their routine activities and share their lifestyle, you begin to understand their values and they begin to trust you. Only then will they relax in your company and begin to let you know what they really feel and think about political matters and their rulers. Only then can you claim to have meaningful first-hand knowledge and experience of Africa.

Certainly sitting in an embassy or consulate achieves very little – it can only, at best, give a very superficial knowledge of the country.

★

The Russians have now given us another chance to help correct the terrible failures that have occurred in Africa over the past thirty-five years, and we must draw on our past experiences to find a way of helping those in Africa who really need our help – the rural Africans.

As I said in a recent letter to Bishop Paul Ruzoka of Kigoma diocese, the son of Chief Mzee Ruzoka, who was so helpful to me when I was farming at Kakonko:

> It was only after I returned to the UK in 1983, after 35 years in Africa, that I began to understand how privileged I had been in having the opportunity to get to know the rural African really well & that something had to be done about the appalling ignorance in the West about what really went on in Africa. After heart troubles in '84 & '85 I therefore helped start TAAL in early 1986 with others who had spent most of their lives in Africa.

It is, of course, one of the tragedies of Africa, including South Africa, that so few Europeans ever get to know the African in his proper rural surroundings where crime, and all the other imported urban problems, are virtually unknown.

I think I speak for most TAAL supporters with years of African experience when I say that one of the most infuriating aspects of the Western media's African coverage is the plethora of so-called experts who rarely say anything sensible or contribute anything of substance about the continent's real problems. How true then, and how appropriate, was a remark by Prime Minister John Major about common sense counting for more than university degrees. The resulting uproar was an indication of how many people in the West have been indoctrinated to believe the opposite.

In our public libraries there has been a flood of books with a definite leftish tinge that try to blame either the colonial era or South Africa for every mistake that the UN and the Africans themselves have made over the past thirty-five years. It did not greatly surprise me that, conversely, one of the few unbiased books on Africa, *The Destruction of a Continent*, was unavailable in any of Westminster's public libraries, and had to be ordered especially for me.

★

It is impossible to live in today's Britain and not notice how the issue of race has been used by black politicians like Paul Boetang and Bernie Grant, and the Salman Rushdie affair should be a warning for the future. It should have been obvious that organisations like the Commission for Racial Equality (which costs the long-suffering British taxpayer well in excess of ten million pounds annually), only help to create ill will between the races.

Education on racial issues should have been started long before legislation was brought in, forcing multiracialism on the British public, by a Labour Party so interested in gaining votes that it didn't pause to consider the problems that its hasty actions would bring. In consequence, by the time we returned to Britain in 1983 (at least I returned, Joyce came here for the first time, from the Indian suburb of Chatsworth, in Durban), my wife had to suffer racialist insults on London's streets – something which she never had to endure on the streets of Durban.

It is the hypocritical attitude so prevalent among British politicians and bureaucrats that is so repugnant to those of us who have spent our lives in Africa – or elsewhere overseas. It is simple for people who live in privileged surroundings to strike high moral attitudes, but it is less easy for the millions who live in overcrowded slum houses or ghastly high-rise concrete apartment blocks all over the country and who have to compete with the immigrants for too few jobs. It's hardly surprising that so many of them blame all their woes on the ethnic minorities.

The Labour Party is still not satisfied with the damage it has done and, at the 1991 party conference, Roy Hattersley, then Labour's deputy leader, promised to increase substantially the number of immigrants allowed into Britain.

The drug-related problems so prevalent in today's inner city areas all over the Western world are only one indication of the moral decay that has affected the traditional values and Christian beliefs on which the great Western civilisations were based.

After centuries of the internecine struggles in Ireland, everybody in the British Isles must be aware of the problems created by religious differences, yet British politicians have seen fit to ignore the obvious dangers of allowing into the country millions of non-Christian immigrants, mainly Muslims and Hindus. Several recent events, most notably the Salman Rushdie affair, have demonstrated very clearly that a considerable number of the Muslim immigrants consider that Islamic law should take precedence over British law.

What will happen to the British way of life if the militants eventually outnumber the moderates?

★

The UN must lose no time in funding an agricultural programme in Africa, to be run by a voluntary organisation such as the British VSO (Voluntary Service Overseas). Small pilot plots in famine regions must be planted with cassava, certain types of desert melons, and other desert plants that provide food for the Bushmen in the Kalahari Desert – what will grow there will grow anywhere! Although there are few Bushmen left who follow their traditional nomadic way of life, there are still a few who could be consulted.

It is a common fallacy in the West, carefully fostered by the socialists and their left-wing allies, that nothing can be done to stop famine and starvation in Africa, so every year a multitude of Western charities appeal for money for the starving millions. But in the colonial era there were no famines in Tanganyika and similar countries, and no basic food imports were required, so the current large-scale importing of food is necessary only because of disastrous agricultural policies – and there is no reason why these should not be reversed.

The NIEO, started by Waldheim in 1974, has been indoctrinating the Western taxpayer into believing that it is his duty to provide the huge sums of money needed for the starving millions in the Third World (the Russians, discreetly in the background behind Waldheim, saw NIEO as an excellent way to weaken the Western economy). Carefully not mentioned was the fact that, with efficient agricultural planning, most African countries could produce sufficient subsistence crops for their own needs and thereby minimise the amount that would be needed in the form of aid from outside sources.

The rains in Africa do not fall every year but in the colonial era the authorities were far-sighted enough to plan for droughts and to enforce the planting of such anti-famine crops as cassava which could be stored indefinitely until wanted for grinding into flour. It was never a popular crop, as it does not taste as nice as maize flour, but it does sustain life – which is obviously a better alternative than starving.

But the UN has nothing practical to encourage self-help. Apparently it prefers to spend millions of pounds on the anti-apartheid organisations which have helped to further Russia's communist aims in Africa. Surely even the most ignorant UN employees in Africa, and at the UN headquarters in New York, must have been aware that an anti-famine campaign and an equally important tree-planting campaign (to replace the millions of bush trees cut down annually for firewood for cooking purposes) would have done more to help the African people than just doling out ever-increasing amounts of aid. But nothing useful was implemented.

Now, instead of pandering to the ridiculous political prejudices that were nurtured by Waldheim, the UN should seek expert advice from South Africa's Forestry and Agricultural Departments, who are experienced in dealing with the problems of dryland farming in areas like the Karoo, and could apply South African methods to similar infertile regions in the other African countries.

It must be understood that the wasteful madness of the Waldheim era at the UN still continues and reforms must be implemented without further delay.

★

The virulent anti-South Africa campaign by the UN and the communists had begun to affect the number of tourists visiting the country and a gradual decline was obvious as early as 1972.

Then, on 16th June, 1976, Soweto erupted into violence, which spread to other African townships in the Transvaal. Fortunately Natal was not involved, so we weren't affected personally. When, in 1977, the township riots were followed by the much publicised death of Steve Biko while in police custody, it was obvious that the troubled state of the country would lead to far fewer overseas tourists visiting South Africa.

We began to notice the difference almost immediately, as did all the local tourist-dependent businesses. The cruise ships and the organised overseas air tours were obviously avoiding South Africa and when the Japanese fishing fleets also stopped calling at Durban we really began to feel the pinch.

I began to think nostalgically about the Saturday morning when I had sold three zebra skins backed on black felt to one family, visitors from one of the large tourist ships visiting Durban. I recalled, wistfully, the time I had had to stay open until about nine in the evening to deal with a crowd of Japanese from the fishing boats. I had sold them five or six boxes of ostrich eggs (twenty-four eggs to a box), as well as my entire stock of ostrich handbags, purses, wallets and lamp stands. Most of them wanted a pair of springbok horns, or something larger, and copper fire screens were also in great demand, as well as a variety of smaller game skins.

By 1977–78 most of the gilt had gone from the curio and skin business and I knew the time had come to sell out, before it got worse.

By the mid-1970s I had already done a trip to Hong Kong, for a game skin display and sale, and I felt sure, from the results there, that I could do even better in the Middle East.

Before I tried that, however, I wanted to make one last trip to Rhodesia, where the terrorist war had already started to escalate. Eve and I did the round trip: up to the Victoria Falls, then via Bulawayo and Salisbury to Umtali and the Eastern Highlands, before going via Fort Victoria to Beit Bridge, and thence back to South Africa. It was shortly after our trip that ZIPRA terrorists, using Russian missiles, shot down an Air Rhodesia Viscount. They slaughtered ten of the survivors in and around the wrecked aircraft, but a further eight fled into the bush and managed to survive. We had friends among the dead.

During the rather protracted arrangements for the sale of my curio shops, I started a small wholesale game skin business in central Durban, which dealt with quite a lot of Natal's retail shops. As the profit margins were far lower, it obviously wasn't as profitable as the retail side of the business, but it did have the great advantage of allowing me freedom of movement, because it was easy to close when I wanted to: when, for instance, I travelled to Botswana to make arrangements for the supplies of game skins that I would need for the displays and sales I intended to hold in the Middle East.

Fortunately both kids had got their degrees from Durban University by now, so the quite considerable expenses involved in their education had come to an end and I felt free to spend money going off to the Gulf.

*

'Going off to the Gulf' makes it sound very easy, but it wasn't and there were a number of hiccups.

I had no option but to arrange my advance publicity through a firm in the Gulf, and I wasn't best pleased, when I eventually reached the various hotels, to find that most of the advertising pamphlets had just been dumped in the hotel foyers, instead of being distributed to potential customers.

The hotel bookings had to be arranged – for display rooms as well as accommodation – and (the hardest thing of all, since I could only guess at quantities) I had to make a selection from the game skins on offer from BGI (Botswana Game Industries). Apart from the skins I got from BGI, most of the things I was intending to take came from South Africa, but this was not something that I wanted to advertise although I wasn't prepared to lie about it and later, when my Arab customers asked me where I was from, I told them South Africa. Fortunately it didn't put them off – they just thought it was a big joke!

Everything had to go by air via Nairobi, and the cost of organising everything was pretty fantastic. I still had my sales figures from the displays I'd held in Zambia and Hong Kong, and I decided to triple these as I was going to three places in the Gulf: Dubai first, then Abu Dhabi and then Bahrain.

This estimate turned out to be very inadequate. For instance, I took thirty zebra skins with me, most of them backed on felt, and I had to have more flown to Abu Dhabi or I would have had none for Bahrain. Stocks of other items of which I ran short could not be topped up so easily. The lion skin rugs with mounted heads proved very popular, as did the elephant feet, and by the time we were halfway through at Abu Dhabi I was having to keep back one each of several items, as samples, and promise that I would send customers their orders later, as soon as I returned to South Africa.

Despite the problems, I must admit that I enjoyed all the planning that went into organising these overseas displays and sales, but I still missed the old days in Tanzania and Zambia, and the free and easy ways of the colonial era, now vanished for ever. I still count myself very lucky to have had twenty-one glorious years of that lifestyle before it came to an end.

South Africa was, in many ways, too much like Europe for my taste, but at least it had glorious weather.

I was glad to be finished with the curio shops. I was much happier working hard on the displays and sales for a month or so and then taking it easy, just doing a bit of wholesaling for the next six months.

The hours were very tough when I was working on the displays, however, and I usually kept going from ten in the morning to ten or eleven in the evening. On most days I didn't bother to eat lunch, but I did drink fairly steadily most of the time. Then I would have a meal in my room at about midnight; sometimes later.

All this, together with fairly heavy smoking, must have contributed to my later heart troubles. I found it difficult to cut down on my smoking at all. This was especially true during the period around my divorce from Eve (in 1982), at which time I left Umkomaas and moved to Durban.

⋆

The response in the Gulf to my first displays was far better than I had expected. The hotel staff at the Hyatt Regency in Dubai couldn't have been more helpful and they readily displayed my posters and pamphlets in the hotel foyer. The daily expenses were high: at least US $300 a day (including the cost of the display room), but I found I was taking ten times this during the course of a day, so I never had any cause to complain – especially as I did even better in the evenings. A newspaper cutting with the headline 'Botswana fair takes Dubai by storm' (see Appendix) gives a good idea of the impact I made. The irony is that, knowing money was not short in the Gulf, I had upped my prices by 200–300%, but they were still considered reasonable by the Arabs.

Everything went so well at the Hyatt Regency in Dubai, in fact, and my display impressed the locals so much, that I was asked to take a display stand at the nearby Sharjah's Trade Fair. The daughter of one of the local expatriates whom I had met at the hotel agreed to run the Sharjah stand for me so, while a friend helped out at the Hyatt Regency, I took some sample skins, including a lion rug with a mounted head and two or three zebra skins, to hang at the back of her stand – and it all looked very impressive. The exhibition at Sharjah also brought in a lot of extra business: pamphlets advertising the display at the Hyatt Regency were handed out to everybody who passed by and, again, the response was even better than I had hoped. So the extra work and expense involved in the Sharjah stand paid off very handsomely.

By the time we had finished at the Inter-Continental Hotel in Abu Dhabi a week later, my Gulf trip was already a great success, and my only commercial worry was whether I would have sufficient stock to see me through the last display and sale – at the Regency Inter-Continental Hotel in Bahrain.

But I did also have a personal worry: and that was that my back might not be able to stand up to all the bending and stretching involved in packing and unpacking all the exhibits – a job which I preferred to do I myself. Sure enough, on the last day in Abu Dhabi my worst fears were realised, very painfully, when my back seized up completely just as I was finishing the packing for Bahrain. But, in agony or not, I had to go to Bahrain. With the aid of plenty of painkillers and whisky, I got through the flight and made it into my room at the Regency Inter-Continental in Bahrain.

The hotel staff must have thought I was mad, but I couldn't sleep on their mattress, which was too soft for my back. The management helpfully provided several changes of mattresses, but it was no good – I found them all too soft. Eventually someone suggested putting boards under the mattress, and that did help a great deal.

Fortunately I had allowed two days in Bahrain before I opened and, with a lot of help from the hotel staff, I recovered sufficiently to open on time. But I really missed the special therapeutic mattress I used at home, as well as the electric chair which heated my back whenever I was in pain. I always travelled with a hot-water bottle and, although this did help my back pains a lot, it was nowhere near as effective as my special chair.

Apart from my back, everything had been going far too smoothly to last and I was not too surprised, when I opened the local Bahrain newspaper on the first day of my display there, to find an article by some British expatriates who were animal rights activists and wanted my display closed.

But their protest backfired because, as a result of their article, a local reporter turned up at the hotel to interview me, shortly after I had finished reading it. I had with me a copy of the favourable article that had been published about me in Dubai and gave it to him, adding a few remarks about Europeans interfering in Arab (or African) affairs. He went on his way and, when his article appeared in the local newspaper the next day, business improved immensely.

I had been dismayed, on arrival, to find that my display room was on the first floor. I had expected the same arrangement as in Dubai and Abu Dhabi, where I had been on the ground floor – just off the hotel foyer and near the bars and restaurants. But the publicity created by the journalist's favourable article outweighed the unfavourable site and more and more Arab customers came in. Most of them made a special point of complimenting me on the excellence of the game skins and all of them, without exception, told me to ignore the nonsense in the newspaper from a bunch of foreigners. They said they liked the display and sale and it was their country. I agreed wholeheartedly with their sentiments and thanked them for their support.

So you could say I owed much of my success in Bahrain to that bunch of misguided Britons, who appeared to know little about Africa and how the Africans, especially in Botswana, needed the money from game skins to survive. Both the Botswana government and Botswana Game Industries did, and do, ensure that strict game conservation controls are adhered to and BGI is an important earner of foreign currency for Botswana.

*

The firm to whom I had entrusted my advance publicity was based in Bahrain and I had to settle up with them before the end of my display and sale there. I hadn't been at all satisfied with the way they had just dumped my pamphlets in the various hotels and I had no intention of paying their full account which amounted to several thousand US dollars.

I discovered that, although it was Europeans who did most of the advertising work, the purse strings were held by an Arab. I told him I wasn't going to pay his bill in full because I expected him to give me a reduction due to the lack of proper distribution of my promotional material.

He turned quite nasty and I think he believed that, because I came from South Africa, I couldn't afford any trouble and would pay the full amount. I let him know, in no uncertain way, that I was not a South African national but had a British passport and I had no intention of paying in full as he had failed to do his job in full. At that he threatened to have me locked up and I left, telling him that I would be consulting the local agent of Thomas Cook, as they had organised my whole trip from Durban.

Looking back now, I think I might have handled matters more tactfully, but I was irritated at having to hang around in Bahrain while I sorted the problem out, instead of being on my way to a hard-earned holiday: I was intending to visit the Seychelles and Mauritius on my way back to South Africa.

I had no desire to be locked up in the Bahrain jail, however, so I went straight to Thomas Cook. The manager couldn't have been more helpful, but he did warn me that if I were not careful I could well end up in jail. He then phoned the Arab who, by this time, had calmed down a bit, and said that I had agreed to pay (via their Durban office) any figure that Thomas Cook agreed with him was reasonable.

I must say that I was very glad to get on the plane to the Seychelles the next day, as the Middle East countries are notoriously unpredictable and anything can happen there.

A few months after I had returned to South Africa, a settlement figure was agreed between the Arab and Thomas Cook – and I was happy to pay the (considerably reduced) account.

*

The mess that was created in Africa by the UN covers just about every aspect of life there. Nothing illustrates this better than the recent furore over the plight of the African elephant. Very laudable, but, as usual dealing with Africa, the media's reports are very one-sided and ignore the facts.

In the area of Tanganyika where I farmed, the Kakonko-Kibondo district, elephants were a menace, as they regularly destroyed the local Africans' maize and other food crops. They were such a problem that the Tanganyikan Game Department had to cull them annually to stop some of the destruction.

Additionally, some elephants were killed for sport, but the numbers were small, as this could be done only with a licence and the number of licences issued was very limited.

Neither the culling nor the hunting for pleasure was responsible for the subsequent tragic decimation of the African elephant, rhino and other species.

What caused this was primarily the later indiscriminate distribution of the Russian Kalashnikov AK-47s and less efficient firearms from the Western countries. Naturally the undisciplined and ill-trained men who suddenly found themselves in possession of powerful weapons could not resist using them on the animals, and they killed anything that moved – with devastating results for most species.

But it is unrealistic to blame the Africans for the wholesale slaughter of the wildlife. You don't blame a small child for starting a fire: you blame the person who gave it the matches. Similarly, it is time for Western countries to stop blaming the poachers and to admit that they themselves are to blame for supplying their share of the arms.

*

At Easter 1991, there was another spate of publicity about the fate of the African elephant in the British national newspapers, set off by Wilbur Smith's latest book, *Elephant Song*. The *Sunday Express* published a two-page extract from the book under the heading 'Is this the brutal truth about how to save the elephants?' Then the paper said readers would be able to judge for themselves the following week, after reading an article by Virginia McKenna: 'Why Wilbur Smith is wrong'. Virginia McKenna and her husband, Bill Travers, became interested in the subject of African wildlife while they were filming *Born Free* and their son, Will Travers, is a director of Elefriends.

Pressure from Elefriends succeeded in stopping a publicity stunt for *Elephant Song*. Wilbur Smith had agreed to sign copies of his book at Harrods and the store had arranged for Flora, a baby elephant from the Longleat Safari Park, to parade at Harrods while the signing was in progress. To quote from the *Daily Express*:

> Publishers MacMillan and Harrods backed down after the *Daily Express* relayed the horrified reaction of campaign groups like Elefriends.

I find this whole episode amusing, but its ridiculousness highlights more serious issues. I'm sure that Flora was quite happy to remain peacefully with her family at Longleat, but I think it's unlikely that she would have been particularly disturbed by travelling up to London and walking around for a while.

It did make me wonder just how much people like Elefriends actually know about African wildlife. Certainly 'conservation' and 'preservation' are words that are constantly bandied around in the media, but it is seldom that one hears about such realities as the necessity of culling some species in some areas.

So, in an attempt to set the record straight, I wrote to the *Sunday Express*, enclosing copies of two pages about Botswana Game Industries and my correspondence with Bishop Paul Ruzoka in Tanzania. I asked them to use these as the basis of a serious article about conservation and to include the real reasons for the tragic decimation of Africa's wildlife (including elephant and rhino), which had less to do with hunting and poaching than with the indiscriminate use of the Kalashnikov AK-47s and other firearms since the 1960s. Britain played a part in this tragic slaughter – even if its hardware was less efficient than that supplied by the Russians.

I received a very garbled and nonsensical reply about my reunion notice being considered for publication, but I was not to be disappointed if it failed to appear. Needless, perhaps, to say that nothing I sent was published. The media do not like the truth about Africa!

★

After I had sold all the South African curio shops, I could not have managed without the help of a very good friend, John Coelen.

We formed a company, Game Skin Exporters International, to handle wholesale exports of skins to the Middle East. Unfortunately the wholesale business did not develop as profitably as the retail business, which was boosted by my displays and sales in the Gulf. The main difficulty lay in finding reliable firms or individuals to handle the wholesale side of the business in the Gulf. Another difficulty was the fact that the Arab Emirates were tightening up on imports from South Africa. But the setbacks never affected the help John continued to give me, right up to the time I left in 1983.

John Coelen was related to Penny Coelen (one of the last girls to become Miss World when the competition was held in London). He was a great character who, like myself, had spent most of his life in Africa before finally settling in Durban. He always wore a French-type beret and stood out in any crowd, being impressively tall. He was an office manager for one of Durban's largest firms of lawyers and worked in the Volkskas Bank Buildings in Gardiner Street, almost opposite my premises in Syfret House.

John and his wife also ran a very successful business selling Zulu tribal dolls. His wife had trained all their Zulu staff and the dolls were in great demand, not only with the local curio shops, but overseas as well. We had sold the dolls in all our curio shops and I also took several boxes of them when I had my displays in Hong Kong and the Middle East. They sold well everywhere. After his wife died (in the 1970s), John continued the business very successfully: a tribute to how well his wife had trained the Zulu staff.

In early 1981 Syfret House was due for refurbishment, with large increases of rent to follow, so I had to find other premises for my wholesale business, Game Skin & Curios (Pty) Ltd. Again it was John who helped me out. His Zulu doll-making business was in the next street (in the Barclays Bank Building, on the corner of Smith and Field Streets), and he agreed to rent out one of his storerooms. It was next to an empty office, which I also rented, and, although the unit was much smaller than my previous premises in Syfret House, it was also very much cheaper than the increased rent there. There was another great advantage: John and his staff took messages for me when I was away in the Middle East or travelling elsewhere in Africa.

I had met the Coelens in 1970, shortly after we had moved to Natal but it was only in 1981, after I had separated from Eve and moved to Durban, that I really got to know John well.

I was drinking fairly heavily during this period and John, an old Africa hand, was one of the few people I felt at ease with, as we had both travelled extensively all over Africa and had a great many experiences in common. We killed many a bottle of whisky as we talked of the old days in Africa, and how tragic it was that the Cold War had brought nothing but misery and starvation to millions of rural Africans. In fact, John played a big part in making my life in Durban tolerable as I waited for my divorce from Eve to come through, which it did in 1982.

After John's wife died he would quite often work late on his Zulu doll business in the Barclays Bank Buildings and, as he often had boxes of dolls to dispatch, he was given a key to the back door. That opened on to a badly lit backstreet which led down to Durban's Esplanade, where he had a large flat overlooking the yacht harbour. I had warned him about carrying a briefcase when he walked alone down the backstreet at night, but he wouldn't believe there was any danger. Tragically I was proved right because, one evening, he was mugged and badly beaten up by two or three Africans, then left lying unconscious in the car park behind my curio shop on the Esplanade – this was shortly before the shop was sold.

When I left this curio shop, African Curios and Carvings, late at night, I always stuffed the takings (usually several thousand rand) into my bush jacket and trouser pockets – and I always carried a swordstick, too. Only once did I have to draw the sword out, and the mere sight of the cold steel was enough to send the two Africans running for their lives as I chased them right out of the car park!

Poor John was in hospital for quite a while, and he never really recovered completely. I was very sorry when I heard that he had died not long after we left Durban (in 1983).

There just wasn't room in my one-bedroom flat to spread things out and pack properly so, just before we left South Africa, John had very kindly given us the use of one of his spare bedrooms, thus we had plenty of space to pack our tin trunks with those of our belongings that were going by sea. Both of us were bringing things in to pack right up to the last minute, and there were quite a few things that we just couldn't fit in and eventually had to leave behind. We made quite a mess in John's spare room, and how we would have managed without him I do not know. He even got the African staff from the flats to take our tin boxes down in the lifts for loading on to the truck that would take them to the docks.

I have lost touch with John's daughter (who married someone in British Airways), but I hope that, some day, she will read this as a tribute to her father.

*

I had never intended to leave Africa and doing so after thirty years there was a great wrench. But there was no choice. Joyce and I wished to marry and, because she is an Indian, we could not legally do so in South Africa at that time. The law against mixed-race marriages has since been repealed, so now we could return.

In Europe's pale sun I never feel more than half alive, and I still miss Africa's hot weather. After forty years, I had got used to colour and I found Europe rather pale and insipid, and the British people obsessed with racial problems.

When I left Britain in 1948 there were about thirty thousand non-whites, who were no threat to the British way of life. Over forty years later, there are about five million non-whites, including a fair number of illegal immigrants, who have taken over considerable areas of Britain's largest cities. London is the worst and, in quite a few parts, you rarely hear English spoken and it no longer feels English. This is increasingly resented by many of the native British inhabitants, who were given no say in the changes that have affected them.

The days when we could rely on our politicians to guard our national interests are long gone, as events over the past forty years have shown very clearly. What is puzzling is why so few have been prepared to lodge even a mild protest about the constant erosion of our traditions and way of life.

Before South Africa became a republic (on 31st May, 1961), a referendum was held. Why was no referendum ever held in Britain over a matter that has completely changed the British way of life?

★

We left Durban at the beginning of March 1983, but I didn't want to fly straight to Britain during the winter, as I knew we would both want plenty of time to get acclimatised. Athens, being so far south, was obviously one of the best places to start and we found it reasonably sunny and warm by day, even if the nights were still pretty cold.

We stayed in Greece for a couple of weeks, then started across Europe by boat and Eurail – apart from its cheapness, this form of travel gives a good view of the countryside without the hassles of driving. From Athens we had an overnight trip by sea to Brindisi in southern Italy, then we boarded our first train for an overnight journey to Rome. Another slightly longer train journey (taking both a night and a day) took us to Paris, where we stayed until the end of March.

As things turned out, it was lucky that we did take our holiday while we had the chance because our daughter, Jenny, was born in London in November 1983.

★

I had had some vague chest pains in 1983, but I had put them down to a bit too much drinking – I found alcohol helped to keep out the cold of Europe. Less than six months after my daughter's birth, however, I awoke one morning with agonising heart pains, which steadily got worse.

It was fortunate that I was in central London rather than somewhere remote in Africa as, within hours, I was on a heart-regulating machine in St Charles Hospital. I wasn't allowed to move for the first few days: indeed I couldn't, being wired up to the heart machine, but I had a deep fear that I might be partially paralysed, or worse, like my Umkomaas friend Pat Schlanders. So, every now and again, I would try to wiggle my toes and move my legs a little. The relief I felt when I found they still seemed to be working is indescribable!

For the first few days I was in a closed-off part of the ward, and had round-the-clock nursing care, which I found ominous, so it was a great relief when, later, I was moved into the main part of the ward. The hospital was very well run but, after my wartime experiences with the Indian Medical Services, I disliked being in any hospital and after about ten days, when I was allowed up for a shower (baths were not allowed), I decided to discharge myself.

This was frowned upon, of course, and I had to sign a form saying that I was leaving at my own risk and request. I felt a bit weak in the taxi on my way home, but it was only when I arrived at our first floor flat in Bayswater that I began to realise that I might have been a bit foolish in going home so early – I must admit that I found it very difficult and exhausting getting up the stairs. There were only twenty of them, but I doubt if I could have made it without my wife's help.

St Charles Hospital was my first experience of the National Health Service and I must say that I found everything very impressive – except for the food, which was adequate enough, but far too stodgy for my liking. I now needed my habitual health food to keep me regular, so I was suffering by the end of my stay in hospital – I do not like enemas!

Fortunately, a day or two at home was all I needed to get back to normal once I was back on my usual diet and getting lots of roughage. However, it took me about two weeks to get some of my strength back and to attempt to climb the stairs after collecting the mail.

The doctors at the hospital had warned me that I must stop smoking and cut down on my drinking, but I found it extremely difficult to give up smoking and if Joyce had not helped me by giving it up, too, I doubt whether I could have succeeded – certainly not so quickly.

An added incentive to give up was provided by my daughter, Jenny, who played with me for hours while I was in bed for most of my first fortnight at home. The temptation to reach for a cigarette is greatly reduced when your hands are full with a constantly moving baby!

Convalescence is a slow business that cannot be rushed, and it was only after two ECG tests that I began to believe that I would eventually make a full recovery. That was a crossroads in my life and, for the first time in years, I had plenty of time (too much in fact) to think back over my forty years in India and Africa.

★

I had never had the slightest interest in politics and I was now sixty-two and had never voted in my life. It had never bothered me that I was not eligible to vote during the twenty-two years I lived in colonial East Africa and the Rhodesias, and was then officially a foreigner in South Africa for thirteen years. If it did not bother me, you can imagine the lack of interest in politics among the uneducated rural Africans. Like most British ex-servicemen in Africa, I despised most politicians, in particular the ones who were responsible for gradually destroying the Africa I loved, but that was as far as my interest went and I had never given much thought to wider political issues.

During my convalescence I was forced to be idle and, for the first time in my life, I watched a great deal of television. Gradually I began to understand how some unsavoury people were creating a profitable industry by stirring up racial discord – usually under the guise of encouraging good race relations through organisations like the Commission for Racial Equality, the GLC (Greater London Council) under 'Red Ken' Livingstone, far-left Labour councils, the World Peace Council and CND (Campaign for Nuclear Disarmament).

I discovered that it is the gullible British taxpayer who has to foot most of the Commonwealth bills, which includes supporting such freeloading specimens as Ramphal and Ramsamy. These gentlemen were to be seen regularly on television, smirking and spewing out anti-South Africa propaganda – and biting the hand that fed them as they criticised Britain for being racialist. In the meantime, in Africa, millions continued to starve.

Listening to the annual Labour and TUC conferences, Joyce and began to see just how widespread the communist and socialist conspiracy was and we were both amazed and horrified by the continual stream of anti-South Africa propaganda programmes that were being broadcast, by Channel 4 in particular.

I was virtually immobilised for some months: my daily exercise after a few weeks was restricted to trying to walk up and down the twenty steps on our stairway, and it took me quite some time to do this without discomfort. During this period I began to believe that God had had a purpose in saving my life and that even sinners like myself could play an active part in His plans. As my health continued to improve, I started going to church regularly and I began to see what had to be done. The outcome was that I helped to get TAAL started in 1986 and, in May 1989, I started writing this book.

In mid-1985, with my wife's approval (she was just as sickened by the blatant anti-South Africa propaganda as I was), I arranged a meeting with Bill Van Gass, the war veterans' representative at the South African embassy in

London. Over a bottle of South African wine we discussed our World War II experiences, and he happened to mention that his brother was killed in action in Italy, and is buried there.

Imagine my fury when I later emerged from the South African embassy to be confronted by an unwashed bunch of AAM supporters flying the red revolutionary flag. On questioning them, I found that not one of them had ever been to Africa.

It was on that day that TAAL was born in my mind.

★

It was at about this time, also, that I began to question the current British government's attitude to South Africa. Without Mrs Thatcher's brave stand, the situation would have been even more serious and, from books I read later, I gathered that British attitudes have changed very little since the Anglo-Boer War of 1899–1902, except that, with the greed for gold and diamonds being acknowledged as the real cause of that war, guilt has now been added. This guilt, together with the ignorance about Africa that is constantly exploited by the communists, makes for a very dangerous situation.

Most of my anger is directed towards the Commonwealth and the UN, but there is little doubt that Labour Party support for action against South Africa helped make the situation much worse. There are encouraging signs that this kind of attitude may be changing, but there has to be much more ex-service pressure, both in Britain and in the old Commonwealth, to stop the present slide into anarchy and the black internecine killings which are the direct result of UN and Western policies towards South Africa.

The time is now long overdue for the sixteen million British ex-servicemen, women and their families, and the hundreds of thousands in Australia, Canada, New Zealand and South Africa, to stand up and say 'Enough is enough' to their politicians and the UN. There are over two million South Africans of British descent and we do not intend to allow them, or the Afrikaners, to be dispossessed in their own country. If some of them want a separate white state, they should have it. But I am sure the large majority will adjust to a multiracial South Africa run on Western democratic lines – but with allowances made for the fact that the country combines a First World economy with a mainly Third World population.

There are some encouraging signs that the British media are, at last, beginning to accept certain facts about South Africa that have been consistently ignored in the past. I quote from author Bruce Anderson's article in the *Daily Express* on Tuesday, 16th April, 1991, 'Leftist bias lurking behind the cameras':

> ...But even when apartheid was at its height, South Africa's human rights record was one of the best in Africa, Asia and Latin America.
>
> ...For years the white South African government has been trying to reform and then abolish apartheid – while British television has been trying to ignore its efforts.
>
> ...For most of the time, television is only interested in two African stories: the evils of South Africa and famine.
>
> ...The evils of South Africa are always blamed on the whites, plus their conservative allies in the West. Famine is also always blamed on the West. [My note: blaming the West for everything possible is a favourite communist ploy.]
>
> ...There is never any attempt at a deeper, more complex study which would link the South African question and famine.
>
> ...One of the reasons why South Africans are so nervous about power-sharing with blacks is because of the way black governments have turned much of the African continent into a shambles – in which there are regular famines.
>
> ...It is the West who pay annually millions to keep these Africans alive. Not the communists.
>
> ...Anyway, when it comes to human dignity and human rights why does our television concentrate on South Africa? How much fair voting takes place in the corrupt one-party regimes of black Africa? Their concept of democracy is one man, one vote – once.

The following Monday, 22nd April, 1991, in the *Daily Express* opinion page, Kilroy-Silk (an ex-Labour MP) actually dared to question the 'Price of our Aid':

> We are being asked to help Ethiopia again. And the Sudan. And Somali. And East Timor. And every other part of the globe where people are dying of starvation. We should help them, of course. But before we do we ought insist on a few conditions.
>
> Like: that they stop fighting each other, and that their governments get their sticky fingers out of the tills and start helping their own people first.

Let us hope that this is the start of a much-needed reassessment of South Africa's very complex problems and of the crippling problems facing the rest of Africa, which also need a fresh approach. To name just a few of them: population explosion, famine, starvation, corruption, misrule and economic disaster.

The recent economic collapse of the Soviet Union, including the satellite countries, gives the West what may be the last chance to put right at least some of Africa's ills, but this process of reform must begin with the UN, or nothing lasting will be achieved.

*

A step in the right direction is the recent resumption of diplomatic visits to South Africa. This is the start of what most ex-servicemen expect to be done in the rapid normalisation of South Africa's international relations in politics, sport and other matters which we see as its right because of the contributions it made to British victories in both world wars.

This is, therefore, an appeal to the sixteen million British ex-servicemen, women and their families, to put more pressure on organisations like the Royal British Legion, and also to lobby their local politicians, to see that action is taken. After Britain's unstinting support for its American allies during and after the Gulf War, it should be able to expect full American support, both in Africa and for extensive reforms at the UN.

We have all been silent for far too long and, since noisy protests in London seem to be the only language politicians understand, let us make sure our voices are loud and clear. We must ensure they get the message that we expect some kind of accountability from them, both at home and overseas.

That there are over sixty Labour MPs with known communist connections is disturbing enough, but it is the 'sleepers' in our society, who seem to have penetrated into every sphere of life in Britain, who should worry us most, as we can never be sure where they are or what they are doing. Recent events in Russia and Eastern Europe should not blind us to the dangers of such subversive elements, as part of their job is to remain dormant until they are needed by their masters: for decades, if necessary.

It is obvious that there is a limit to the stresses and strains that can be put on even the excellent British system of democracy. A great many of the present ills of British society, including drugs, violent crimes, racial tension and generally lower standards of behaviour, are the result of foolish policies over the past forty years, including the mass immigration of people from alien non-Christian cultures, and it is a matter of some urgency to correct these policies.

★

I have been into hospital twice more since my heart troubles – nothing serious, only the inevitable ageing process. Once was to have an operation for a cataract and, with ex-service grants, I received treatment at one of London's best, the King Edward VII Hospital for Officers. As I sat in the library-cum-waiting room, waiting for a taxi to take me home, I noticed it was in this same room that, due to his ill health, Prime Minister Harold Macmillan had handed in his resignation to Queen Elizabeth. I reflected then that the hospital epitomised all that was good in the British way of life and, as soon as I had recovered from my cataract operation, I started on this book, in mid-1989.

Now I am finishing my book in the hope that it will open some people's eyes to the realities of Africa and the need for a new, common sense, approach to her problems. I confidently expect that, having read the facts which expose the complete ineptitude (and worse) of the UN, most people will consider my indictment completely justified.

I believe that a great many more ex-service people will agree that the time has come for them to play a more active role in seeing that matters are put right in Africa. I hope that they will also accept the fact that South Africa must be asked to play a part in helping to solve the problem of famine in Africa as a whole and will want action taken.

★

Nowadays I quite often sit alone, enjoying the peace among the trees in Kensington Gardens. It's a favourite spot of mine, away from London's petrol fumes and noise and not far from a monument to a great Victorian explorer in Africa, which reads:

In Memory of
Speke
Victoria Nyanza
and the Nile
1864

(Victoria Nyanza is the Swahili for Lake Victoria.)

I remember the great achievements of our Victorian ancestors, and ponder why everything was allowed to go so very wrong.

Postscript

More ex-servicemen should think back to the dark days of 1940, after Dunkirk and the fall of France, as Hitler's Nazi forces overran Western Europe.

Britain stood alone, with her only additional effective fighting forces (all volunteers) coming from the four self-governing dominions: Australia, Canada, New Zealand and South Africa.

The debt we owe to Field Marshal Jan Smuts has never been acknowledged fully. If General Hertzog, South Africa's Prime Minister, had won the crucial vote on 4th September, 1940 and South Africa had remained neutral, it would have created very serious difficulties for Britain.

Loyalty to her dominion allies has never been one of Britain's strong points. As Britain's ties to Europe become closer in 1992, ex-servicemen will have to see that the debt we owe to our gallant allies in the dominions is never forgotten.

There are over eleven thousand ex-Gurkhas, veterans of World War II, who do not qualify for a service pension (the minimum requirement is fifteen years of service), and there is no welfare or medical help in Nepal. So anything readers can do to help would be much appreciated. The address is:

The Gurkha Welfare Trust
88 Baker Street
London W1M 2AX

Appendix Five

TRUTH ABOUT AFRICA LEAGUE

TAAL TAAL

A British & Commonwealth Ex-servicemen's Organisation Working for peaceful Change in R.S.A.

The Rt. Hon. Mrs M. Thatcher, Prime Minister,
10 Downing Street,
London SW1A 2AA

10 October 1989.

Re: Commonwealth Heads of Government Meeting/Mad Hatter's Tea-Party.

Dear Mrs Thatcher,

As you will see from the above heading most of our ex-service members with years of experience in Africa find the Commonwealth Heads of Government Meetings amusing in their absurdity, however there is now an ever growing feeling among ex-servicemen that the consequences for Africa are growing too tragic to be ignored for much longer.

It is also our opinion that you represent just about the only sane view on Africa by standing so resolutely against sanctions against South Africa & in wanting to tackle Africa's real & ever increasing problems of over-population & bad farming methods that have reduced millions of Africans to semi-starvation and worse, rather than wasting time continually critizing apartheid in South Africa.

Our ex-service Committee on the United Nations & Commonwealth has asked me to stress that they feel not enough has been done to expose further the WWII war-crimes of Kurt Waldheim, for ten years the Secretary-General at the United Nations. Our Committee members are aware of how the Russians operate & want an investigation to concentrate on how the Russians would have used their dossier on Kurt Waldheim to influence his actions during those ten vital years, 1972 to 1982 , when he was Secretary-General at the United Nations. You have only to read some of Waldheim's speeches in Africa during this period to see how useful he must have been to the Russians in furthering their Communist aims in Africa.

It is of course no coincidence that it was only after Waldheim had left the UN & was therefore of little further use to the Russians that some details of his WWII war-crimes were so conveniently leaked to the West. In their excellent book on the UN & Africa, " The Destruction of a Continent " the authors who both worked in Africa for over 25 years frequently mention Waldheim & their book exposing the UN should be required reading for all those attending the CHOGM

In view of these facts we feel strongly that there must be far stricter checks on those being considered for the post of Commonwealth Secretary-General & that those with any dubious incidents in their past, like Malcolm Fraser on his US trip, must automatically be removed from consideration for the post. Especially as we have seen in Britain recently 'Glasnost'does not stop Russian spying etc.

Finally we think it appropiate to end with a reminder of South Africa's contribution to Britain's victories in two World Wars & we attach page 5 " The Ex-Service Issue " from our 1987 report on South Africa sent to your Foreign & Commonwealth Office in London.

Yours sincerely,

M.Walsh

M.Walsh. General Secretary.

NATAL PARKS, GAME AND FISH PRESERVATION BOARD

P.O. Box 662,
PIETERMARITZBURG. 3200

SGP/ 46 /1983

REF. : J.G/2/ g

PERMIT TO SELL OR DISPOSE OF GAME TROPHIES

In pursuance of the provisions of the Nature Conservation Ordinance, Chapter 3, and the Regulations framed thereunder, authority is hereby granted to:-

(Name) Messrs Game Skin and Curios (Pty) Ltd (Mr M. Walsh, Director)... ...

(Address) 810/811 Barclays Bank Buildings, Corner Smith and Field Streets, ...
DURBAN, 4001... ...

to sell or dispose of the following game trophies:-

ANY GAME TROPHY EXCLUDING THOSE LISTED IN APPENDIX 1 (iv) AND (v) BELOW:

....

....

....

TERMS AND CONDITIONS UNDER WHICH THIS PERMIT IS ISSUED:

1. It is:

(i) valid from ..1 JANUARY 1983........ to .31 DECEMBER 1983;....... ..
(ii) valid in the original only;
(iii) personal to the holder named above and is not transferable;
(iv) this permit shall exclude the import into and sale in Natal of all animals as listed in Appendix 1 of the International Convention on Endangered species of Wild Fauna and Flora;
(v) No Import/Export/Sale of rhino products of any sort is permitted;
(vi) the holder must advise customers that a Veterinary Health Certificate must be obtained before any Warthog products are exported from the Province of Natal;
(vii) this permit is renewable annually.

Dated at PIETERMARITZBURG, Natal, this ..10th.. day of ..DECEMBER..... 1982.

NATAL PARKS BOARD
PIETERMARITZBURG
10 DEC 1982
NATAL
NATALSE PARKERAAD

J Brooks
for: DIRECTOR

TRUTH ABOUT AFRICA LEAGUE

TAAL TAAL

A British & Commonwealth Ex-servicemen's Organisation Working for peaceful Change in R.S.A.

Lord Wyatt,
House of Lords,
London SW1A OPW.

18 February 1991.

Dear Lord Wyatt,

Our members have noted your efforts against Media bias, Television in particular, & they hope you will extend your efforts to include Africa, especially South Africa. TAAL was formed a few years ago to try & bring some sanity to the way the Media & indeed Parliament approach the problems facing Africa.

We believe that once the war in the Gulf is over the harsh realities of Africa in 1991 have to be faced . The United Nations role in Africa over the past thirty years has been absolutely disastrous with billions of dollars of Western taxpayers money completely wasted. The enclosed book review on " The Destruction of a Continent " refers.

The West just cannot afford to let the same United Nations madness & chaos engulf prosperous South Africa, where since the end of the Anglo-Boer War in 1902 comparative peace & prosperity has lasted for nearly ninety years. Every encouragement has to be given to President de Klerk as he brings apartheid to en end & Law & Order has to be maintained during this very dangerous period of reform. Parliament must always remember that there are about two million South Africans of British descent , many are ex-servicemen who fought for Britain in WWI & WWII.

Over the past year TAAL members have become increasingly perturbed at the Media's obsession with the almost daily doings of the Mandelas & the almost total exclusion of other events in Africa. There are continuing civil wars in at least five African countries of long duration & two more African countries are being destroyed Liberia & Somalia, both Monrovia & Mogadishu have been looted & destroyed. To bring some reality to the situation we enclose Canadian journalist, Peter Worthington 's Fore-word & his page on Moscow's Man in the ANC, KGB Colonel J.Slovo, also Signposts three pages, " Mandela's Big American Shock ". Page 3 shows what happens to African moderates ! Finally Inkatha's pragmatic leader, Dr. Buthelezi shows in his last para: a real understanding of the South African situation.

Yours sincerely,

M. Walsh. General Secretary.

All communications to be addressed to: The General Secretary
TAAL 377 Edgware Road, London W2 1BT

Foreword by Peter Worthington

The first time I came to South Africa was in 1960. I was a journalist for the old Toronto Telegram – fresh from covering the Congo, which had just got independence from Belgium.

The Congo was in chaos and dangerous – South Africa orderly and safe. At the time the Canadian Prime Minister John Diefenbaker had just made moves that resulted in South Africa quiting the Commonwealth and becoming a Republic and the Afrikaans and English population were at odds over what the future held. And yet at the time as a Canadian with no experience with, or exposure towards the policy of apartheid I was appalled and offended at the attitudes and policies of South Africa.

I even preferred the chaos of the Congo to the discrimination of South Africa and I wrote as much in my newspaper. At the time although Afrikaner and English South Africans disagreed with each other they all seemed to favour apartheid as a policy. I would estimate that 85% of South Africans generally supported the policy of apartheid.

When I returned to Canada I even made speeches opposing apartheid and on occasion appeared on the same platform as Harry Belafonte, deploring the policy.

Now some 27 years later, I found the country still the richest and most civilised in Africa yet with one dramatic difference. This time instead of ordinary South Africans generally favouring apartheid, most white South Africans seemed opposed to it.

In fact, I would say the percentages of 25 years earlier had been reversed. Now 85% of the white population disapproved of apartheid, recognising it as obsolete, unworkable and to be dismantled.

The only question is how?

Comparatively speaking, as fast as attitudes and policies are concerned, South Africa of the '80s bears little resemblance to South Africa of the '60s.

But what offends me now as an individual and as a Canadian, but most particularly as a journalist, is the lack of recognition and understanding in the West of what exactly is going on in the whole of Southern Africa today, not just South Africa.

When one looks at the evidence that unfolds daily, for all to see who want to see, there is a war going on, not against apartheid, but against South Africa itself.

I'm afraid I am convinced that the Western media, Western politicians, academics and all too many church figures are not so much interested in a peaceful solution to South Africa's problems, but want bloodshed and an overthrow of the system at any price, and the installation of another form of Government, even if it ends up being a Marxist regime.

I mostly blame the media for what can only be described as disinformation about South Africa. Instead of going where the story takes them, that is, of honestly reporting events as they see them, too many media people are reflecting what they think their audiences or editors want to see, hear, read, or what they personally believe should be the case.

The film *"The A.N.C. Method – Violence"* is therefore an attempt to place the problems of South Africa in a new perspective. Nothing can justify the inhumanities of apartheid, as it existed, before the process of dismantling it began, or in fact justify the remaining semblances of it in South African society today. But attitudes die hard and one of our most important aims should be to see to it that as the old order passes on to a new one, it should be done in an attitude of peace and acceptance by all, so that when the dust settles, it does not then take decades to heal the scars.

PETER WORTHINGTON
Writer and Presenter of
"The A.N.C. Method – Violence"

"My methods are non violent methods, if we escalate violence there can only be destruction, not only of our people, but of the whole country, and nothing frightens me more than facing a country with no infrastructure."

Chief Mangosutho Buthelezi
Leader of the Zulu nation.

MOSCOW'S MAN IN THE ANC

THE SLOVO DOSSIER

- Born in Lithuania (Soviet Russia) in 1926.
- Arrived in South Africa with his parants in 1935.
- Joined the local branch of the SACP when studying at the University of the Witwatersrand in Johannesburg during the late 1940's
- Co-authored the Freedom Charter, the official policy document of the ANC in 1953.
- Became a member of the Central Committee of the SACP in 1954.
- Was a member of the ANC when he left South Africa in 1963.
- Founder member of the ANC's military wing, Umkhonto we Sizwe.
- Was made a member of the ANC's now defunct Revolutionary Council in 1964 and is currently a member of the Politico-Military Council which replaced the Revolutionary Council in 1985.
- Was chief of staff of Umkhonto we Sizwe but stood down in April 1987.
- Made member of the ANC's National Executive Committee in 1985.
- May 22, 1986, was awarded The Order of the Friendship of Lenin on his 60th birthday, for his appreciable services rendered to the Soviet Union.
- Elected chairman of the SACP in July 1986.

Joe Slovo (General Secretary of the S.A. Communist Party and ANC National Executive Committee Member) with YASSER ARAFAT (Chairman P.L.O.) at Samora Machel's funeral in Maputo.

***"The Communist bogey is being exploited in an attempt to weaken the major force of our liberation, the ANC* – J. Slovo**

(African Communist, No. 107, Fourth Quarter 1986, P.19)

Perhaps the most interesting figure in the ANC hierarchy is Joe Slovo, who is the only white sitting on the ANC Executive Committee. He is the Kremlin's point man in the ANC who co-ordinates the flow of strategy decisions between the ANC, SACP and the Soviet Union.

Two independent sources have identified Slovo as a colonel in the KGB. The first was made by Soviet KGB agent Major Alexei Kozlov, who was captured by South African Intelligence Services in 1980. The second source comes from Jorge da Costa former **Head of Mozambique's Intelligence Service – SNASP** who **defected** to South Africa in 1982. He stated that "Slovo outranked the local KGB resident in Maputo who carried the rank of Major". Western Intelligence experts believe that he may have been elevated to the rank of General, and the French Counter Intelligence Service, DST, stated in 1984 that Slovo may have replaced the late Henri Curiel to head the KGB's international terrorist network in Paris.

He is also a ruthless man, a ruthlessness exemplified by his control over the activities of the Special Operations Groups, the elite members of the ANC military wing Umkhonto we Sizwe; who have been primarily responsible for the numerous attacks on civilian targets through the placing of landmines, limpet mines and carbombs in the rural and urban areas of South Africa. Joe Slovo is the real power behind Oliver Tambo in the ANC.

From: VIP's of Violence
By Nicolas Partridge

MAT. 16:3

VOL 9 NO 4 1990

SIGNPOSTS

A DIGEST OF RESEARCHED INFORMATION FOR CONCERNED CHRISTIANS

MANDELA'S BIG AMERICAN SHOCK

A Black South African telling Americans that the African National Congress did not represent all South African Blacks was the last thing that Nelson Mandela, the ANC's deputy president, expected to encounter on his recent visit to the United States!

Tamsanqa Linda threw a big spanner into Mandela's heavily financed, high profile tour with his outspoken criticism. "The ANC is nothing more than a front for the Communist Party in South Africa," he said. "Nelson Mandela is as much a hardline Communist as Fidel Castro. And if the United States gives the ANC money, it will be promoting violence in South Africa."

Moreover, Mr Linda is not a Zulu, so he could not be dismissed as a puppet of Chief Minister Mangosuthu Buthelezi. He is a Xhosa, just like Mandela! It is also not possible to label him as a government stooge.

"It is beyond belief," the former mayor of Ibhayi told his American audiences in 10 cities, "that the criminal, Mandela, could be viewed in America as some sort of hero. He is not a hero in my country. He is a militant Communist who pours gasoline on the embers of apartheid. We are frankly astonished to see Mandela, who calls for violence, terrorism and sanctions, being treated like a legitimate foreign dignitary. He is a criminal and should have been kept in jail. It was a mistake for State President De Klerk to release him."

Mr Linda, who works for the United Conciliation Party promoting negotiations with the De Klerk government and the free enterprise system, is committed to reform. But he insists changes should take place within the framework of the law. "It is not apartheid that ravages our country. Continued trade sanctions have destroyed the jobs of millions of Blacks. For change to come in South Africa, it must be based on a strong economy. We must be able to provide jobs."

"Mandela is not a friend of African Blacks, but has terrorised them to silence their opposition to his violence," he told a Philadelphia radio talk show, "The ANC and UDF are against everyone in the local authorities in South Africa and they oppose me because I've always been an outspoken critic of violence." The ANC has used violence and intimidation to prevent rival Black political groups from negotiating with the government. He charged that Mandela would simply replace the apartheid system with a repressive Communist one.

Tamsanqa Linda addressing Washington's National Press Club

Hailed by the *Washington Times* as Mandela's "negative advance man", Mr Linda not only had harsh words for Mandela. He accused American President George Bush of "glorifying an unrepentant terrorist and his wife, Winnie, who calls for violence." He urged Mr Bush to warn the American people of the true character of the ANC and of its association with the SA Communist Party.

A SUCCESSFUL TOUR

"Congratulations on having completed a successful media tour in the United States in the sole interest of freedom and truth," said Mr Linda's sponsor, Don Fotheringham of the American Opinion Speakers Bureau. "You have done everything we have asked and you have conducted yourself well before the American people. **You have laboured tirelessly, many long hours, while maintaining high spirits and a pleasant disposition.** All our coordinators have found it a pleasure to work with you. When representatives of the media treated you with rudeness, you returned kindness. In facing ignorance, you have been very patient. Confronted with error, you have sharply reproved and corrected your detractors.

"Your mission has been very effective. Your radio and television audiences consisted of millions of Americans who now have a far clearer view of the peril facing our friends in South Africa. Many now see through the blanket of obfuscation and realise that they have been deceived by our own government, with the aid of an accommodating mass media...

"The war for your country,

we are convinced, is in the United States. Policies of our government, if not corrected, will fuel the very fires and foment the anarchy desired in SA by our mortal enemies. Those US policies can only be corrected by an alert US electorate. This is the key to world freedom and our enemies know it. **That is why your sudden appearance in the US so terrified them. You have the capacity to shatter their fragile but gigantic fraud.** That is also why we are hated and derided. We know, however, that God honours truth and that it penetrates all things and that we will ultimately succeed if we remain steadfast and true to it."

WELCOME CANCELLED

In Miami, Florida, Mr Linda used Mandela's praise for the Cuban Marxist, Fidel Castro, to rally the thousands of Cuban exiles, who hate Communism, against Mandela. As a result, Miami's mayor, Xavier Suarez, a Cuban American, **cancelled a planned welcome resolution from the Miami City Commission.** The proclamation would have welcomed Mandela and praised his struggle. Mayor Suarez said that Mandela's praise for Castro "pained many, many members of the Miami community. There was an unwillingness to analyse other struggles for freedom. It was sort of 'He's my ally and my ally can do no wrong'." The Spanish language Radio Mambi talk show, which hosted Mr Linda (he spoke through interpretation), was bombarded with telephone calls condemning Mandela. "We Cubans should protest," a Spanish-speaking caller said, "Out with Mandela - we have enough of Communism."

On June 22, two days before Mandela arrived in the city, Mr Linda addressed hundreds of journalists at Washington's prestigious National Press Club under the glare of TV lights. His appearance was sponsored by The John Birch Society, Accuracy in Media, Conservative Caucus, Council for the Defence of Freedom, Conservative Network and the International Freedom Foundation. From seven in the morning to seven in the evening, he gave interviews on radio and television and answered reporters' questions.

Everywhere he went, he gave TV interviews and appeared on radio talk shows. The talk shows lasted for up to three hours with the switchboards jammed by callers wanting to put their questions to him. While some callers were hostile, the majority were appreciative of the views he put across. A lady missionary who had worked in Zululand for many years expressed her grateful relief that finally the American public was getting the true picture of what was happening in South Africa.

An appearance in one city resulted in requests from other stations for interviews. Often he had already left for the next venue. This resulted in frantic phone calls to locate him and frequently he went on the air from an airport telephone while waiting for his plane. Caught off guard, **ANC representatives repeatedly refused to debate Mr Linda live on the air.**

"MANDELA A HERO?"

In each city, Mr Linda's visit was preceded by a newspaper advertisement headed **"MANDELA A HERO? Hold on a minute! It is wrong to grant a hero's welcome to a man who wants to destroy his country with Communist-style socialism.** It is wrong to tout as a 'prisoner of conscience' a man who planned sabotage. Consider the record." The ad went on to examine Mandela under the heading of Treason, Terror and Tyranny. It appeared in ten major city newspapers and in more than twenty others.

Most Americans believed their media when told that there was no longer any violence in South Africa. It came as a surprise to learn that Black policemen, councillors and moderates were still being murdered at the rate of two or three a day. Mandela was repeatedly embarrassed by journalists' questions about the ANC's continued commitment to the armed struggle.

After Winnie Mandela, with a raised clenched fist, told a cheering Black crowd in Harlem at the first big rally in America, that if talks broke down **"We know you will be there if we go back to the bush to fight the White man"** (*Sunday Telegraph* 17/90), she was banned from making further public statements. However, during their interviews with Mr Linda, most TV stations showed Winnie's famous statement **"Together, hand in hand, with our boxes of matches, with our necklaces, we shall liberate this country. We have no guns - we have only stones, boxes of matches and petrol"** (*Chicago Tribune* 14/4/86). The impact was so great that Winnie was forced to give an interview to explain that this quote was "taken out of context". She failed to explain what the correct context was, however!

THE SUCCESSFUL ENTREPRENEUR

Tamsanqa Linda is a successful businessman. Despite the limited opportunities available to Blacks, he built up a flourishing business within a few years. In other words, he epitomises the type of person that South Africa so desperately needs - a go-getter who creates job opportunities for others, a leading member of the emerging Black middle class.

For these very reasons he is the type of person most feared by the ANC - a Black who thinks and acts independently and who is capable of building a strong economic base for himself. In other words, a man who will not easily submit to ANC party dictates. This is why the ANC is determined to destroy what it terms the Black petty bourgeoisie. Its ideology teaches that there are only two groups in South Africa - the wealthy White oppressors and the poor, exploited and oppressed Blacks. There is no place in their ideology for successful, wealthy Black businessmen. Rather than adjust their ideology to fit reality, they must reshape reality to conform to the ideological mould. Successful businessmen must be destroyed!

Thus in 1986, Mr Linda's R400 000 shop, consisting of separate sections for groceries, fresh vegetables and a butchery, was burned to the ground. The previous year his R200 000 double storey home was gutted by fire. He and his family were lucky to escape death and injury, but they were unable to save any of their possessions. His mother's house was petrol-bombed eight times before it too was destroyed by fire.

Although a prosperous businessman, Mr Linda was not selfish. He was concerned to improve the lot of his people. So when the government opened the way for Black involvement in local government, he was elected and held the post of mayor of Ibhayi, with a population of over 400 000, from 1982 to 1985. In addition to being responsible for the towns of New Brighton, KwaZakeli,

Zwide and Walmer, which make up Ibhayi, Mr Linda was President of the Eastern Province Councils Association which consisted of 74 town councils. In that position, he controlled a budget of R35 million and had 220 primary and 105 secondary schools under his jurisdiction.

The local town councils were the prime target of the ANC-inspired revolutionary violence which swept through South Africa from 1984 to 1986. Between September 1984 and May 1985, 197 councillors, including 22 mayors, were forced to resign. The homes or businesses of 124 councillors were burnt or destroyed. The Eastern Cape was particularly hard hit. A number of the councillors were murdered, some in the most horrific fashion.

Mr Tamsanqa Kinikini, a colleague and friend of Mr Linda and also a successful businessman, refused to resign on March 15, 1985 with the other 15 KwaNobuhle councillors. On March 23, he **was dragged from his burning funeral parlour by a revolutionary mob and hacked to death. Shortly before his 16-year-old son, Selunko, and two nephews tried to escape. They were caught by the crazed mob, brutally murdered, their bodies burned and parts of their flesh eaten. Mr Kinikini's last act was to shoot his 12-year-old son, Kwala, to save him from a similar fate!**

Mr Linda's wife, Pamela, a nurse at the Livingston Hospital, Port Elizabeth, was told by other nurses not to use the lift because some people wanted to see her dead. She had to resign. Their sons were intimidated and threatened with death at school.

Despite his tremendous financial losses and the great physical danger he and his family constantly face, Mr Linda continues to speak out courageously against the ANC and its determination to impose itself on the people through violence. After being forced out as mayor, he co-founded the United Conciliation Party. He is also an elder in the Presbyterian Church of Africa.

His present position is not an easy one. Because he is known as an outspoken critic of the ANC, trade unions sympathetic to the ANC ensure that no-one will employ him. Nor is there any possibility of re-starting his own business. Radicals would wait until it is well stocked and would burn it down again.

But he has a steady stream of secret visitors who seek his advice. They share his dislike of the ANC, its policies and its methods, but lack his courage and boldness. From his contacts with people he knows that the ANC has the support of only about 20 percent of the Black population. Moreover their main support is found among the youth who are easily influenced and have no experience of life. The older people reject them, but they fear them too much to speak out against them.

MANDELA'S BLUNDERS

Despite great euphoria on his 6-week tour of Europe and North America, Nelson Mandela, the deputy president of the ANC, made a number of blunders which counted heavily against him.

During his visit to Libya, Mandela embraced Colonel Muammar Gaddafi, America's pet hate figure, and said, "In our situation, as in other countries, an armed struggle is one of the most effective ways of fighting for political change in our country. Your readiness to provide us with the facilities for forming an army of liberation indicated **your commitment to the fight for peace and human rights in the world. We consider ourself comrades in arms**" (*Los Angeles Times* 19/5/90).

Mandela also described Yasser Arafat as "a comrade in arms", and said it would be "a grave mistake" to change his view of Arafat "on the basis of the interests of the Jewish community" (*Washington Post* 2[illegible]/6/90).

"We identify with the PLO because, just like ourselves, they are fighting for the right of self-determination... To think that, because Arafat is conducting a struggle against Israel that we must therefore condemn him, we can't do that. It is just not possible" (*Los Angeles Times* 23/6/90).

Speaking about Castro's Cuba, he said, "There's one thing where that country stands out head and shoulders above the rest ... that is in **its love for human rights and liberty**" (*Daily Telegraph* 3/7/90).

(For anyone interested in learning about "human rights and liberty" in Cuba, SIGNPOSTS recommends Armando Valladares' book *Against All Hope*, the account of his 22 years in Castro's prisons!)

"One of the **mistakes the Western world makes**", Mandela said during an American television interview, "**is to think that their enemies should be our enemies.** Yasser Arafat, Colonel Gaddafi and Fidel Castro support our struggle to the hilt. There is no reason whatsoever why we should have any hesitation **hailing their commitment to human rights. We identify with the PLO** because, just like ourselves, they are fighting for the right of self-determination" (*The Times* 23/6/90).

"The progress we have made in our struggle is owed largely to Angola, and **we hope that one day we will be as free as you,**" he said in Luanda on May 10, 1990.

Mandela was asked about three Puerto Ricans who were seated in the VIP row

THE HEAVY HAND OF CENSORSHIP!

Winnie Mandela silences her husband at a press conference in London on July 4.

Dr MG Buthelezi at theAnnual General Co■ ference.

12 Reasons to back Inkatha

1. It is the biggest black political movement in South Africa.

2. It is lead by the much-respected President Buthelezi.

3. It led the opposition to apartheid from inside South Africa.

4. It lead the fight against 'homelands'.

5. It fought successfully for the release of political prisoners.

6. It is against violence, and pro-peaceful negotiation.

7. It is liked and respected by moderates of all kinds in South Africa.

8. It believes in an enterprise-led growth economy.

9. It believes in establ■shing a multi-party democracy and it is actively building from its strength a fully effective, well organised, democratic political party to fight elections in the new South Africa.

10. It is dedicated to harnessing the great resources of the country to fight the real enemies of the people, namely: poverty hunger, unemployment, disease, ignorance, insecurity, loneliness, and moral decay.

11. It has opened its membership to all South Africans.

12. It is seeking alliances and partnerships with like-minded moderates and democratic parties.

"The outside world must be careful in likening South Africa to pre-independence countries like Zimbabwe or Mozambique . . . A great many people regard South Africa as some kind of blown-up version of these countries. They see revolutionaries in exile returning home to become a Government returned from exile and they make the analytically fatal error of judgment of looking at white society in South Africa as they looked at white society, say, in Zimbabwe. White South Africa is not dominated by expatriates who can be repatriated or who have somewhere to go when the going gets tough. South Africa is, for whites in the country, an end-of-the-line country. It is a live, do or die country . . ."

Epilogue

An Indictment

The only thing necessary for the triumph of evil is for good men to do nothing.

Edmund Burke

The Background to Africa's Starving Millions: 1991 – 27 million Africans

Once again we are witnessing the now almost annual plea for aid from the starving millions in Africa. In April 1991 British television reported that Oxfam, Save the Children, and other informed sources, gave the incredible and horrifying figure of 27 million starving Africans in seven African countries – Sudan, Ethiopia, Eritrea, Mozambique, Angola, Liberia and Somalia. What is hardly ever mentioned is that there are civil wars in all these countries, most of long duration. The Western priority has to be to stop the civil wars, which are the main factor in the famines.

On 23rd April, 1991, television's BBC2 broadcast an excellent *Assignment* programme on the famine in the Sudan, and the tragic delays in providing relief that were brought about by the intransigent attitude of the brutal ruling military junta. The hour and a half programme was hosted by Jonathan Dimbleby. Also taking part were the minister of overseas development, the Right Honourable Mrs Chalker, and the Sudan's finance minister, together with representatives of the aid agencies and the UN.

To the few of us who know Africa well the programme unintentionally showed just why the UN and all the aid agencies, and other interested parties, have failed so miserably to solve the tragedy of the ever-increasing millions of starving Africans. Mr Dimbleby proudly mentioned the UN satellite pictures which had shown two years ago, when the rains were reasonable, no shortage of food; last year, when the rains were not so good, there had been a manageable shortfall of food, but this year's pictures had shown little rain and the complete failure of the crops in Sudan.

But what he, the UN and the multitude of aid agencies do not understand is that the UN helped to create these famines, by destroying the colonial system in Africa after the end of World War II, and then taking no action in the good years to prevent famine in the bad years.

What must also be stressed is that famine in Africa is nothing new. In the Old Testament (Genesis 37–50), we are told that the Pharaoh had a dream about seven fat cows coming out of the Nile. Then came seven thin cows and the thin cows ate up the fat ones. Joseph, the son of Jacob, was shown by God what the dream meant, and was able to tell the Pharaoh that there would be seven good years of food harvests, which would be followed by seven hungry years. He also advised the Pharaoh to store food in the good years, so people would not starve in the bad years, and Joseph was appointed to do just that.

What few in the West now realise is that in colonial times the Africans were forced to plan and to plant for the inevitable bad years in Africa, and that the current famines cannot be blamed solely on the droughts that occur all over Africa, including large parts of South Africa. The UN has to bear a great deal of the responsibility for the tragedy. The colonial agricultural legacy meant Africa was self-sufficient in food annually until the early 1960s. Independence brought famine, starvation, corruption, misrule and economic disaster.

What the UN should have done was to build on the advances in agriculture made in the colonial era, not destroyed the system in order to placate the Communist bloc and Third World countries in the UN. The West is continuing to pay a very heavy price for the mistakes in Africa, which seem to get worse every year, regardless of billions of aid money from the West.

The UN has had over thirty years of failure in Africa. The Western taxpayer must insist that those who have spent their lives in Africa, like the writer (from 1948 to 1983), must now be listened to.

The Early Days of the UN and the Groundnuts Scheme in Tanganyika

The story starts with the first Labour government in Britain after the end of World War II and the fiasco of the Groundnuts Scheme in Tanganyika in my early days there. The scheme failed mainly because the so-called experts were unable to comprehend that, in Africa, good rainfall years are invariably followed by bad years. During these, their modern machinery just could not get the groundnuts out of the sun-baked earth, in fact it was so hard it smashed up their machinery.

Few in Africa had the opportunity to compare the above farce in Tanganyika with a small, well-run Portuguese agricultural scheme in Luso, Angola. Portuguese peasant farmers had been brought from Europe to live in the same primitive conditions as the locals: grass huts with no modern amenities and only hand tools. Their task was to show the local Africans what could be done with hard work and a bit of ingenuity. The results were amazing.

It is a common misconception that most of Africa lacks water. This is just not true. But few Africans understand or use simple irrigation methods like those at Luso, which transformed the area. These are especially effective if they result from a combined village effort, as at Luso. The yield of maize, vegetables and other agricultural produce must have amazed visiting Africans, just as it did me.

Back in Tanganyika, we were starting to get the first UN missions, made up of freeloading specimens from (mainly) Asia and South America, who, with no knowledge of Africa, came to criticise what was being done in Tanganyika.

In colonial times it was compulsory for every rural African to grow a certain amount of cassava as a safeguard against famine. The UN Mission wanted this stopped, as well as the month of compulsory work on the district roads, for which the Africans were paid in salt. This method of payment was preferred by the Africans, but the UN said it was slavery! In the next forty years the stupidity and greed of many UN personnel was only matched by their arrogance and ignorance. The result of allowing this madness to continue for over forty years is: *27 million starving Africans*.

Apart from the immediate need for a complete overhaul of every function of the UN, and a close scrutiny of all its financial affairs, there is now a very real danger that the violence and mayhem of the rest of Africa could spread to prosperous South Africa where, since the end of the Anglo-Boer War in 1902, there has been comparative peace for nearly ninety years.

It cannot be emphasised too strongly that the communists and the Third World have a great deal to answer for in the UN and whatever South Africa's faults they pale into insignificance compared to the excesses of her African neighbours to the north. The same applies to the communists. It is up to the West to see things are put right at the UN.

What Has to Be Done to Put Things Right at the UN and in Africa

1. Complete reform of the UN.

2. A strong Western Secretary-General for the UN. My personal choice would be someone like Mrs Thatcher.
3. A UN headquarters for Africa based in Nairobi and headed by someone who has had at least twenty years experience of living in Africa.
4. Civil wars in Africa to be stopped immediately (as in the Gulf).
5. Permanent brigade of Gurkhas, as special UN force based in Nairobi, to stop any future civil wars.
6. New UN agricultural policy for Africa, with experimental training HQ and farm in South Africa, making use of RSA's knowledge of dryland farming in the Karoo and Kalahari areas. British VSO (Voluntary Service Overseas) and South African agricultural experts to be trained to start similar experimental dryland farms in the seven African drought countries. Corruption has to be treated as a way of life in these African countries, so the distribution of cassava, seeds and other basics has to be handled by them.
7. Aid agencies and UN agricultural staff also to be trained in these experimental farms, so that other demonstration dryland farms can open in centres elsewhere.
8. Retired Gurkha officers and SA agricultural officers, after a dryland agricultural course, to be used to make annual progress checks and report back to UN headquarters in Nairobi.
9. Few in Europe, and even less of the mindless morons at the UN, have any idea that South Africa lies in the drought belt, with large areas of the country frequently suffering from long periods of drought, with even more disastrous flooding often following in many areas of Natal and the Cape.
10. Yet, with judicious use of over half a million boreholes, large areas of the drought-stricken parts of the country have been utilised to produce food. There is no reason, except ineptitude, why this can't be done in other parts of Africa, provided competent agricultural staff are sent to show the Africans how it should be done.
11. It should be obvious to all, except those at the UN trying to protect their jobs at the Western taxpayers' expense, that it would be very much cheaper and better for all concerned if the Africans were, once again, to produce their own food requirements, as they did so successfully in the

past, and especially during the colonial era. So this is an appeal to common sense and a return to the rural ways that suited the African and his tribal way of life much better than the Marxist-socialist nonsense from Europe that has caused untold misery and hardship and brought unnecessary starvation to millions of rural Africans.

12. It is also imperative that Africa's population explosion be curbed as quickly as possible. The UN must link aid to birth control, not only in Africa but in the rest of the Third World. In fact it should have done this forty years ago. It is no use Europe and the rest of the West limiting their populations if they have to continue paying for the huge increases in Third World populations who cannot support themselves.

13. Another madness that has to cease is the present policy of allowing political refugees from war-torn African countries to come to Britain, and other European countries, when it is openly admitted that about eighty-five to ninety per cent are unemployable in Europe due to their lack of education and language problems. Yet they are still coming here.

14. This is another area where the West has to get tough with the UN, and to insist that proper refugee camps are set up in both East and West Africa, situated in some of the relatively stable African countries, like Kenya and the Ivory Coast. The UN must provide proper educational facilities and the refugees must be encouraged to grow their own food while at the camps. So much could be done with just a bit of interest and imagination. Their lives as refugees would be much easier if they could stay in the familiar environment of Africa and it would be easier for them to go home when their particular civil war ended.

15. Exactly the same applies elsewhere in the world. It is madness for Tamil refugees from Sri Lanka to head for Britain when a UN refugee camp could have been started in India's Tamil Nadu province. Another example is the 250,000 Chinese from Hong Kong who, with their families, may come to Britain in 1997. Surely it would be better for everyone concerned if they could go to the Nationalist Chinese, in nearby Taiwan?

★

It is my hope that this indictment will finally explode the myth that we can all sit back and allow the politicians and bureaucrats at the UN and elsewhere, including the European Parliament, to solve the problems of Africa, while in reality this is a case of the blind leading the blind.

Finally, it is impossible to exaggerate the importance of the book by the academics, Karl Borgin and Kathleen Corbett, who have both worked in Africa for over twenty-five years, at both black and white universities. In their book, *The Destruction of a Continent*, their analysis of the Nigerian situation is truly devastating and applies, to a lesser or greater extent, to the rest of Africa. The authors repeatedly warn that time is running out for Africa, and the West must listen to these warnings before it is too late.

London, 1991

Index

D

E

F

G

H

N

O

P

R

S

T

U

V

W